To Ed,

With grateful thanks

love and support you have given St. Ann's in the last two years.

You can work anywhere now!

Love & best wishes

from all the Staff

THE PILGRIM'S PROGRESS DEVOTIONAL

THE PILGRIM'S PROGRESS DEVOTIONAL

A DAILY JOURNEY THROUGH
THE CHRISTIAN LIFE

CHERYL V. FORD

The Bible Reading Fellowship
OPENING THE BIBLE

Published by
The Bible Reading Fellowship
Peter's Way, Sandy Lane West
Oxford OX4 5HG
ISBN 1 84101 090 1

US edition published 1998
This edition published 1999
10 9 8 7 6 5 4 3 2 1 0

Acknowledgments
Unless otherwise stated, scripture quotations are taken from the *Holy Bible, New International Version*, copyright © 1973, 1978, 1984 by International Bible Society. Used by permission of Hodder & Stoughton Ltd. All rights reserved. 'NIV' is a registered trademark of International Bible Society. UK trademark 1448790.

Scripture quotations taken from the Revised Standard Version of the Bible, copyright © 1946, 1952, 1971 by the Division of Christian Education of the National Council of the Churches of Christ in the United States of America, are used by permission. All rights reserved.

Extracts from the Authorized Version of the Bible (The King James Bible), the rights in which are vested in the Crown, are reproduced by permission of the Crown's Patentee, Cambridge University Press.

Scripture quotations taken from the New Revised Standard Version of the Bible, copyright © 1989, 1995 by the Division of Christian Education of the National Council of the Churches of Christ in the United States of America, are used by permission. All rights reserved.

Portions of this book were taken from *The Pilgrim's Progress, Faithfully Retold in Modern English*, by Cheryl V. Ford, published by Tyndale House in 1991

A catalogue record for this book is available from the British Library

Printed and bound by RR Donnelley

TO THE MEMORY

of John Bunyan,

who suffered many years

in prison for his faithfulness

to the Gospel,

and to the multitudes

of persecuted Christians

throughout the world today

who are suffering, often severely,

for their faith in Jesus Christ.

❧

A portion of the royalties from this

book will be donated to:

The Voice of the Martyrs, Inc.

Open Doors with Brother Andrew, Inc.

World Evangelical Fellowship's Religious Liberty Commission

to help suffering Christians around the world.

❧

Blessed are those whose strength is in you,

who have set their hearts on pilgrimage. . . .

They go from strength to strength,

till each appears before God in Zion.

—Psalm 84:5, 7

CONTENTS

ACKNOWLEDGMENTS

Thanks to my husband, Dr. Clayton Ford, for his verification of theological concepts presented and for his help in writing and rewriting this volume. Thanks also to those who have prayed with me for this project: Billy and Denise, Hannah, Bill and Virginia Ford; the brothers and sisters of Arcata First Baptist Church, especially John Sullivan, Marlene Mattison, the various prayer groups, Jim and Linda Atchley's home fellowship group; my "Green Lake" Conference friends—Pat Schmitz, Judy Chiles, Helen Mooradkanian, Edna Den Hartog, Denise Van Zile, and Norelle Lutke. Thank you to Ida Crotty for her generous contribution to my computer need. Thanks to my mother, Dorothy Verkler, for her contribution and to my dad, Robert Verkler, for first introducing me to computers.

I am grateful to God for the privilege of working with Crossway Books. I wish to express my utmost appreciation to the Crossway staff, especially to Lila Bishop and Chris Glidden, whose dedication to excellence made their contributions invaluable.

Besides John Bunyan himself, I also acknowledge my other dear friends of yesteryear whose writings so inspired me during my research—Rev. George B. Cheever (*Lectures on the Pilgrim's Progress*, 1847), Dr. Thomas Scott (*The Pilgrim's Progress with Illustrative Notes*, 1852), and Dr. John Kelman (*The Road: A Study of John Bunyan's Pilgrim's Progress*, 1912). I look forward to meeting these great saints one day in the Celestial City.

It is my prayer that you will continue to be "one who looks intently at the perfect law, the law of liberty, and abides by it, not having become a forgetful hearer but an effectual doer" (James 1:25). May this devotional be a wonderful encouragement in that pursuit!

PREFACE

Welcome to an exciting devotional journey through John Bunyan's brilliant classic, *The Pilgrim's Progress.* Every Christian has much to gain from becoming acquainted with Bunyan's "pilgrims" and their pilgrimage to the Celestial City. Yet because we are often in a habit of doing a quick read for pleasure, we can easily miss much of this story's profound truth. Bunyan clearly intended for his readers to dig deeply as they search for its hidden nuggets of truth. As he says at the story's end, "Ponder my metaphors. . . . What if my gold is wrapped up in ore?"

Because we want you to find the hidden gold, we have provided 365 selections, each like a chunk of ore with the promise of gold inside. In the devotional commentary, Scripture verses, and prayer, you will easily find a rich gold nugget to extract and claim for your own life's pilgrimage. You can move through the selections at your own pace, using the book as a daily devotional or reading straight through if so desired.

This book is for sincere and earnest pilgrims. Often as I pondered the truths presented and applied them to my own life, I found myself deeply challenged. It is my earnest prayer that you, too, will find this book a wonderfully enriching source of inspiration. May your pilgrimage be exceedingly blessed!

INTRODUCTION

THE AUTHOR

John Bunyan was born in 1628 in Elstow, a little village near Bedford, England. His family was of low social standing, and he had only a limited education. His early history provides no clues that this poor and confused lad would go on to become one of the leading preachers and writers of his century, authoring one of the most widely read books in history.

When he was sixteen, Bunyan's world came crashing down. Within a three-month period, both his mother and sister died, and his father remarried. John joined the army and became, by his own admission, a godless, profane, and profligate youth. Upon returning to civilian life, he entered his father's trade, becoming a tinker—a traveling mender of broken pots and tools.

At the age of nineteen, he married an orphan girl who was so poor that her entire dowry consisted of only two Christian devotional books. Reading these books caused Bunyan to reflect seriously on his earlier moral failure, and he decided to change his ways. He became a dedicated churchman and enthusiastic Bible reader. His attempts to reform his life, however, kept him on a perpetual emotional roller coaster, vacillating between light and darkness, hope and despair.

In God's sovereignty one day he overheard two women talking about their new birth in Christ and sharing their testimonies with one another. Bunyan was keenly interested, so they introduced him to their Baptist pastor who in turn gave him a copy of Martin Luther's *Commentary on Galatians*. Deeply moved as he read, he became a born-again Christian and a devoted member of the little Bedford Baptist congregation. Christ's love so transformed Bunyan that he became a powerful witness for Christ, first as a young deacon and then as an ordained preacher. Ultimately, he became so influential that people risked arrest to hear his impassioned and anointed preaching.

During that period of England's history, Christians who held beliefs not endorsed by the state-sponsored Church of England were called "irregulars" and were often persecuted for their faith. As one who believed in such controversial doctrines as salvation by grace through faith alone, Bunyan was dubbed an irregular. Persecution became a way of life for him.

He wrote, "I have determined, the Almighty God being my help and shield, yet to suffer . . . even till the moss shall grow on mine eyebrows rather than thus to violate my Father and principles." Because of his refusal to give up his "illegal" preaching, he spent more than twelve years in prison. Obviously, he did not allow any moss to grow on his person; while in prison, he penned no less than sixty literary works that were in turn read by thousands.

THE STORY

Bunyan's grandest contribution, *The Pilgrim's Progress*, was written during his final six months of imprisonment. The story's original title—*The Pilgrim's Progress from This World to That Which Is to Come*—clarifies its theme. This is the story of Christian pilgrims going *from* one place *to* another. Far from being mere travelers, however, they are on a sacred quest—a pilgrimage. While coming to Christ is certainly an event, it is also and even more so a journey. As "strangers and aliens" sojourning through this present world, Christ's pilgrims have the exalted purpose of pilgrimaging to their final destination—the Celestial City, God's home and their own home.

Some may wish to simply purchase a ticket, climb on board, and cruise to heaven as they would to some romantic getaway. A pilgrimage to the heavenly country, however, is no vacation. It is rather a long, challenging, and sometimes arduous journey up the King's narrow highway of eternal life. Many obstacles as well as a full gallery of devils and impostors can be found along the way. Still, despite the hardships, it is a wonderfully blessed and even exciting adventure.

The Pilgrim's Progress was an instant runaway bestseller when first published. Within the first year of its publication, three editions were issued. In no time 100,000 copies were sold—a phenomenon in seventeenth-century England. It was destined to become one of England's greatest literary works. This book is one of the world's greatest and most endearing literary classics. Amazingly, it has been translated into more languages than any other book except the Bible—nearly 200—and is second only to the Bible in all-time distribution. A copy was present in nearly every home in England and in early America.

For more than 300 years the timeless appeal of *The Pilgrim's Progress* has inspired millions of believers in their own spiritual pilgrimages and has placed John Bunyan among literary immortals. Through the years sermons have been preached from it, commentaries written about it, and artistic portrayals made of it.

C. S. Lewis once said, "One of the reasons why it needs no special education to be a Christian is that Christianity is an education in itself. That is why an uneducated believer like Bunyan was able to write a book that has astonished the whole world."

D·A·Y
1

As I walked through the wilderness of this world, I came to a place where there was a den. Inside, I lay down to sleep, and as I slept, I had a dream.

It is appropriate to begin with a reference to John Bunyan, the author of *The Pilgrim's Progress*. The "den" represents none other than Bunyan's own jail cell. Confined there for preaching the Gospel, he "dreams"—that is, he receives the inspiration for this story.

Jesus specifically said in the Gospels that we must expect to carry a cross during our life's pilgrimage. Bunyan's cross was the loneliness and distress of separation from his loved ones while enduring imprisonment.

Did Bunyan's imprisonment turn him bitter? In no way! Trusting in Christ's sustaining and transforming power, he refused to consider his misfortunes anything less than a sacred duty. No one could ever say that he sat "rotting" in prison. On the contrary, by the Lord's grace, he turned his personal tragedy into astonishing victory.

Life in this world is not easy. Chronic complainers will find no lack of troubles to whine and lament over. Trials are similarly no stranger to the victorious Christian. Yet what a difference in perspective! While the first is focused on his circumstances, the second is focused on the Savior. While one remains in a bitter state of paralysis, the other soars on eagles' wings.

If we can keep our eyes on Jesus—remembering his suffering and death on the cross to deliver us from certain disaster—we can surely find abundant cause for renewed strength, courage, and gratitude.

Jesus said, "A servant is not greater than his master. If they persecuted me, they will persecute you . . ." (John 15:20 RSV). It should come as no surprise then when we encounter resistance, opposition, and even hostility toward our faith. Let us determine to remain courageous and faithful, trusting in Christ's power to transform our difficult circumstances into launching pads for fruitful service.

What is *your* "den"? Will you allow Christ to join you there? He may either grant you immediate release from it or grace to triumph through it. Whatever your case, will you trust him completely? He intends to guide you victoriously in your life's pilgrimage.

Scripture: Hebrews 11:36-38; 12:1-2; Acts 5:41-42

Prayer: Lord Jesus, I think of the great Christian pilgrims who have preceded me in carrying the gospel torch. Help me likewise to bravely bear my hardships and trust you in every circumstance. I want a faithful, victorious pilgrimage. Amen.

D·A·Y 2

In my dream I looked up and saw a man clothed in rags standing in a certain place with his face turned away from his home. He carried a Book in his hand and a great Burden on his back. As I watched, I saw him open the Book and begin to read. And as he read, he wept and trembled. Then, not being able to contain himself any longer, he cried out in anguish asking, "What shall I do?"

While still in this condition, he returned to his home. Not wanting his wife and children to perceive his distress, he restrained himself for as long as he could. He couldn't hide it for long, however, because his anguish only increased. Finally, he bared his soul to his wife and children and began to talk to them.

"Oh, my dear wife, and my children, the fruit of my own body, I, your beloved friend, have lost all peace because of a great Burden weighing heavily upon me. What's more, I have been informed that our City is most certainly going to be burned with fire from Heaven. And unless some way of escape can be found by which we can be rescued, all of us—you, my wife and sweet children, as well as I—will come to a dreadful end in this destruction."

To the ragged burdened man, it may seem that his troubles began when he came upon "the Book." Actually, he had been in deep trouble all along, living where fire from heaven was slated to fall. Oblivious to this, he went happily his own way—that is, until the Book came with its truth piercing to the core of his being.

We can assume that the man is now aware that his usual attire, which had previously seemed perfectly functional, is just filthy rags. Even more distressing is the burden he received while reading the Book. It is too late simply to discard the Book in favor of lighter reading, for, despite his misery, its authority captivates him. He no longer possesses the Book; it possesses him.

God's Word, like a scalpel, can cut painfully deep. It denounces our self-congratulating virtues as radically impaired, convincing us that we are sinners and that our own righteousness is woefully inadequate to justify us before God. Such realization can weigh on our souls as a crushing burden, but God uses it to bring us to his saving grace.

Have you ever felt the weight of your sins? Is it time for you to renew your devotion to God's Word?

Scripture: Hebrews 4:12; Isaiah 64:6; Psalm 38:4

Prayer: Lord, I admit that any perceived righteousness on my part falls far short of your standard. I am determined to take your Word to heart, welcoming its convicting power. Have your way in me that I might in every way be made whole. Thank you, Jesus. Amen.

D·A·Y 3

At this his family was greatly perplexed—not that they believed there was any truth in what he was saying, but they feared he was losing his sanity. Since nightfall was approaching, they quickly helped him to bed, hoping that some sleep might settle his troubled mind. But the night was as disturbing to him as the day, and instead of sleeping, he groaned and cried all night.

When morning came, his family asked him how he felt. "Worse and worse," he answered. Once again he began to tell them about his fears, but they were not receptive, and their hearts began to harden.

They also thought that perhaps they could drive the mental illness away by treating him harshly and rudely. Sometimes they ridiculed him, sometimes they rebuked him, and sometimes they totally ignored him. Consequently, he began staying in his own room, pitying and praying for his family and also grieving over his own misery. At times, however, he walked alone in the fields, sometimes reading and sometimes praying. He spent several days this way.

❦

The poor man's family is no help at all. They have not read the Book, nor do they care to. Like so many others who reject Christ, they think their loved one is suffering some delusional flight from reality. He has gone over the edge emotionally while they are at peace and in harmony with both themselves and their world. They refuse to consider his claims, choosing instead to try bringing him back to normal. As these attempts fail, their hearts harden.

Families can be like that. Saint Francis of Assisi's conversion completely estranged him from his father. After the conversion of the Indian missionary Sadhu Sundar Singh, his Sikh family nearly poisoned him. Even Christ's family said of him, "He is out of his mind"(Mark 3:21).

When the man in our story turned his face from home, his new orientation virtually assured him of family turmoil. When we begin to come to Christ, it is a turning point. Those who are most familiar with us, who have loved us and always been there for us, may suddenly seem to turn from us. This hurts, but we are really the ones who have turned. They have not changed; *we* have changed. We beg them to understand, but they cannot unless they, too, should turn with us. Unlike the man in our story, many give up at this difficult time. Reading God's Word along with earnest praying provides the needed strength to keep on. Have you ever come to such a turning point when, despite what others thought, you heeded God's call?

❦

Scripture: Matthew 10:35-37; Luke 21:16; Hebrews 3:15

Prayer: Jesus, I gratefully turn my face away from this world to head into your will for my life. By your grace, I will allow nothing to interfere with my decision. I pray that my friends and family will also turn to you. Amen.

DAY 4

Now I saw that one day when he was walking in the fields, he was reading in his Book, as was his habit, and his mind was greatly distressed. As he read, he burst out crying, as he had done before, "What shall I do to be saved?" I also saw him looking this way and then that, as if he would run, yet he stood motionless. I perceived that he must not have known which way to go. Then I looked and saw a man named Evangelist coming toward him. Upon reaching him, he asked, "Why are you crying?"

It seems that the man's family has all but abandoned him. He is left alone to meditate upon the words of the Book. Though he understands enough to recognize his guilt and danger, he is confused. He wants salvation but doesn't understand how to find it. He feels compelled to run but doesn't know which way to go.

God is aware of our need for help at such times. Because he is the one who brings us to a place of awareness of our need, he won't abandon us there. For this reason he has given various gifts to his people, one of which is evangelism. While Christ calls all Christians to be "fishers of men," he specially commissions some as evangelists. The faithful evangelist will respond by proclaiming the gospel message anywhere God sends him or her. Evangelist in our story is found faithfully traversing the countryside looking for some soul who is receptive to the Gospel. He comes upon the lonely and distressed man at just the right time.

The word *evangelist* comes from two Greek words: *eu*, meaning "good," and *angelos*, meaning "messenger." While an angel is a spiritual messenger sent from God, an evangelist is a human one. Both have vital functions in the advancement of God's kingdom in the earth. Unfortunately, we can never find enough evangelists. Multitudes in our world today sit confused, struggling with spiritual issues. They wonder what direction to go, having neither the benefit of a Bible nor an evangelist to point the way.

We all have Jesus' words of life and can share them. Have you accepted the call to do so? Are you willing to become more "evangelistic" in your prayers, attitudes, and lifestyle?

Scripture: John 4:35; Luke 10:2; 2 Timothy 4:5

Prayer: Savior of the world, I yield my heart to your message to me. I open it to receive part of the burden you carry for the lost and confused souls of this world. I ask you, Lord of the harvest, to send out many more laborers into your harvest fields. Show me what you would have me do. Amen.

"Sir," he answered, "I can see by the Book in my hand that I am condemned to die, and after that I will be brought to judgment. I find that I am not willing to do the first, and not able to bear the latter."

Then Evangelist asked, "Why aren't you willing to die, since this life is so filled with evil?"

The man answered, "Because I fear that this Burden on my back will drive me lower than the grave and into Hell itself. And, sir, if I am not even able to face prison, then surely I cannot bear the judgment and its subsequent execution. Thinking about these things makes me cry."

❧

Now we see that the man desperately wishes salvation. The Book has awakened within him the overpowering guilt and dread of his sinful state. He fears death and, even more, judgment. He is convinced that he will stand convicted of a serious enough crime to land him in hell.

Have you ever heard someone respond to the question, "Do you want to be saved?" by saying, "No thanks; I don't need it"? This is not a surprising reaction considering that most people lack any real idea of what they need saving from.

Luke records John the Baptist's words about judgment and hell. He goes on to say, "So, with many other exhortations, he proclaimed the good news to the people" (Luke 3:18 NRSV). Wait! How can talk of judgment and hell be identified with *good* news? Simply put, no one appreciates "good news" until he comes to terms with the "bad news" that makes the good news so wonderfully good!

Not many years ago, if someone had excitedly announced, "I have a cure for AIDS!" no one would have lifted an eyebrow, unless to ask, "What is AIDS?" Today a cure for the dreaded international killer would be received with worldwide cheers. And *no one* appreciates a cure more than the one who knows he has the deadly disease.

All of us, the Bible says, are sinners, falling short of God's glory (Romans 3:23). The consequence of our sin, unless we accept the cure, is eternal separation from God in hell. Unfortunately, many today contend that sin bears no consequence. They see no need for good news.

The man in our story read the Book and took its words at face value. Because he took its message to heart, he was ripe for good news. Have you accepted God's good news of salvation through Christ Jesus?

❧

Scripture: Hebrews 9:27; Ephesians 2:12; Romans 5:12

Prayer: Lord, you are Master of all, and your Word is true. I accept what it says about eternal matters. Protect me from those who attempt to diminish the authority of your Word. I admit that my only hope is in you and your good news. Amen.

DAY 6

Evangelist then asked, "If this is your condition, why are you standing still?"

He answered, "Because I don't know where to go."

Then Evangelist gave him a Parchment Scroll inscribed with these words: "Flee from the wrath to come."

The man read it and, looking at Evangelist very carefully, asked, "To where do I flee?"

Then, pointing his finger to a very wide field, Evangelist replied, "Can you see the Wicket-gate in the distance?"

The distressed man is particularly vulnerable. He knows he needs salvation but has not yet received sufficient illumination to find the way himself. False friends attempt to soothe such people with false mercy and cheap grace. In their desire to make the Gospel more palatable, they deem the call to flee the guilty city as unnecessary, too radical. They say, "Now calm down; you shouldn't feel such guilt. God accepts you just the way you are. You aren't in any real danger. You just need a good hug and some self-esteem."

Such messages ignore the seriousness of sin and always lead back to, not away from, the doomed city. The world abounds with false peace, false security, and false hope. Yet Evangelist's message is different. His instructions are not watered down or confusing. They are explicit, urgent, and unashamedly simple: "Flee from the wrath to come." Don't walk; don't dilly-dally—*flee!*

The Spirit of God has already been preparing the man for this moment of decision. An able witness will never encourage such a person to wait longer than necessary. His task is to stir souls to make their move decisively. If people wait, their waiting may turn to procrastination, which often results in the fatal decision to disregard the Spirit's prompting. Evangelist faithfully points the way to the Wicket-gate. Though the man cannot yet make it out, he does think he can see the shining light in the distance. Evangelist instructs him to keep his focus on the distant light and to move directly toward it.

Distressed souls are wonderfully encouraged when someone shows them that a genuine way out exists. This is not false hope. It is real! It is good news; it is great news! Did someone point out the way of salvation to you? Are you pointing the way for others?

Scripture: Matthew 3:7; Romans 10:14-15; 2 Peter 1:19

Prayer: Lord Jesus, please keep me from listening to messages that will direct me back to the world's solutions to my needs. I open my heart to your instruction. Grant me a responsive heart to the guidance you want to give me through your faithful servants. Amen.

D·A·Y 7

So I saw in my dream that the man began to run. He had not run far from his own house when his wife and children saw what was happening. They cried after him to return, but the man put his fingers in his ears and ran on, crying, "Life! Life! Eternal life!" He would not look behind him but fled toward the middle of the plain.

The neighbors also came out to see him run, and as he ran, some mocked and others threatened. Some of them, however, cried out for him to return. Among these neighbors, two resolved to go after him and force him to come back. The name of one was Obstinate and the other, Pliable.

By this time the man had traveled a good distance from them, but they still resolved to pursue him, and in a short time they overtook him.

"Neighbors," the man asked them, "why have you come after me?"

"To persuade you to come back with us."

"No way!" he replied.

❦

Before Evangelist's arrival, the man felt there were no options, but now he knows a way out exists. Because Evangelist has faithfully proclaimed the way of salvation, no matter how the man responds, Evangelist has successfully fulfilled his mission. The man must now choose his course.

We, too, are left with a choice of loyalties. Many opt for middle ground like someone straddling a rowboat and a dock. That is no problem until the rowboat pulls away from the dock. Emergency! God is in the boat, and he is heading out to sea. Momentarily you will end up over your head in water. What will you do?

The man wastes no time in choosing to flee the city. However, his friends and family immediately notice he has gone and done it—he has forsaken the world—*their* world. They spring to action. Some ridicule, some implore, all oppose. Though most of them give up quickly, the man cannot so easily shake off two of their number.

The world's response to us who choose to seek God can be shocking. Some believers say their families and friends would have much preferred them becoming prostitutes, drug pushers, or even dying, to becoming Christians. But our man has made his choice, and no one will turn him away from it.

Whose voices are you listening to—Jesus' call to forsake all and follow him or the voices of friends and the world?

❦

Scripture: Matthew 19:29; Luke 14:26; John 12:25

Prayer: Father in heaven, please forgive any double-mindedness within me. I resolve to turn my back on this world's values and move out in your direction. Thank you for providing the way of escape. Amen.

D·A·Y 8

"You live in the City of Destruction where I also was born. If you stay there, however, sooner or later you will sink lower than the grave into a place that burns with fire and brimstone. Find peace, dear neighbors, and come along with me."

"What!" Obstinate objected. "And leave our friends and our comforts behind?"

"Yes," said Christian (for that was his name), "because what you will leave is not worthy to be compared with even a little of what I am seeking to enjoy. If you will come along with me and not turn back, you will find blessing as I will, for where I am going there is enough for all and plenty to spare. Come away with me and see if I'm telling you the truth."

"But what things are you seeking, for which you would leave all the world to find?" Obstinate asked.

"I seek an inheritance that is not subject to decay, that cannot tarnish, and that will never fade away. It is kept safely in Heaven to be given at the appointed time to all who diligently seek it."

Christian shows concern not only for himself but for his neighbors. He invites them to come along with him. To Obstinate the cost seems unbelievably high. Some at this point would attempt to soothe Obstinate into pseudo compliance: "You don't really have to give up everything; it just looks that way." Obstinate, however, recognizes reality. Leaving the city means abandoning friends, possessions, way of life—"all the world." For those like Obstinate, nothing could be worth this price. For those like Christian, however, who have already weighed the cost of remaining in the city, the cost seems a small price to pay.

Until now Christian's escape seemed to be his preoccupation. Now we see that the hope of a heavenly inheritance has not eluded him. He tries to convey this hope to Obstinate.

Christian has told his friends about both heaven and hell. Today many believers are so ashamed of the judgment that they never mention it. Talking about knowing Jesus and "the blessed hope" seems enough. This approach, however, lacks the whole counsel of God's Word. Shouldn't we trust that God can work with the truth? He draws people to himself by varied means. Some need love and comfort, some want eternal hope, some fear judgment. Second-guessing God in this matter might prevent someone from seeking salvation. Ask God to give you a loving yet straightforward approach as you share his truth with others.

Scripture: Romans 1:16; Acts 2:40; 10:42; 20:26-27

Prayer: Dear Lord, I want to encourage my friends and loved ones to come to you. I ask for help in explaining the truth faithfully to them. Please enable them to perceive the importance of this decision and to join me on my pilgrimage. Amen.

"If you will, you can read about it right here in my Book."

"Ridiculous! Get your Book out of here!" responded Obstinate. "Are you going to come back with us or not?"

"No, I'm not," said Christian adamantly, "because I have already put my hand to the plow."

Then Obstinate turned and addressed Pliable. "Come on then, neighbor Pliable; let's turn back and go home without him. A lot of these crazy-headed fools get an idea in their head and think themselves wiser than seven reasonable men."

"Don't insult him," Pliable answered. "If what Christian says is true, the things he is searching for are better than ours. I am inclined to go with him."

"What?" demanded Obstinate. "Another fool! Listen to me and go back. Who knows where this sick-headed man will lead you? Go back! Go back if you have any sense at all!"

"Come with me, neighbor Pliable," Christian pleaded. "Besides the things I told you about, there are many other glorious things to be gained. If you don't take my word for it, read it here in this Book. And if you want to be sure of the truth expressed within it, look closely, for all is confirmed by the blood of Him who wrote it."

At that Pliable said, "Well, Obstinate, my friend, I am making a decision. I intend to go along with this sincere man and to cast my lot in with him."

Obstinate and Pliable are of opposite dispositions. Obstinate, a forceful man, attempts to sway Christian to return to the sinful city. When Christian suggests he read the Book, Obstinate reveals his true nature. Stubbornly proud and unyielding, he feels personally insulted. No misunderstanding exists here. Obstinate will have no one interfere with his worldly ways. Representative of self-sufficient, self-directed people, he has no use for God's Word. He scornfully reacts by hurling contempt at Christian.

Then there is Pliable. He is a much more agreeable sort. Like his name, he is naturally pliant and adaptable. Christian easily persuades Pliable.

As pilgrims along life's way, we will meet people with various ideas, opinions, and responses. It is essential that we know who we are and where we are headed. Christian is unmoved by Obstinate's abuse. How do you fare when suffering similar abuse? If you are prepared to face scorn and are firm and decided in your conviction, you won't succumb to the hampering pressures and persuasions of those around you.

Scripture: Matthew 5:10-11; Malachi 4:1-3; Isaiah 55:7

Prayer: Lord, enable me to be fixed in my purpose to be your pilgrim. I pray that you will keep me from giving in to those who would sway me from your plan for my life. When I am abused, help me to respond with grace. May I never return insult for insult. Amen.

D·A·Y 10

"But, Christian, my good companion, do you know the way to this desirable place?"

"A man named Evangelist directed me to travel quickly to a little Gate up ahead where we will receive instructions about the Way."

"Then come on, neighbor, let's go!" Pliable said excitedly. And they left together.

Obstinate called out after them, "And I will go back home. I refuse to be a companion to such crazed fanatics!"

Now I saw in my dream that when Obstinate had gone, Christian and Pliable went walking on over the plain, talking as they went.

"So, Pliable, my neighbor," Christian said, "let me get to know you. I am glad you decided to come along with me. If Obstinate had been able to feel what I have felt of the powers and terrors of what is yet unseen, he wouldn't have so easily rejected us."

Pliable was brimming with questions. "Come on, Christian, since we're the only people here, tell me more! What things are we seeking? How will we enjoy them? Where are we going?"

"I can better imagine them with my mind than speak of them with my tongue," said Christian, "but since you want to know, I will answer from my Book."

"Do you believe the words in your Book are really true?"

"Absolutely. For it was written by Him who cannot lie."

Pliable is full of questions. Christian goes straight to his Book for the answers. The man, who only a short time ago was weeping in distress, has now found hope and confidence through its pages. Someone has said that the Word of God comforts the afflicted and afflicts the comfortable. So it is with Christian. Whereas before it sorely chastised him, it has now become his life's comforting anchor.

Christian begins his pilgrimage with absolute confidence in this Book. It is pure truth from cover to cover. His assurance is born of the fact that the Author cannot lie. He emphatically testifies of his unswerving belief in its authority. Pliable will do well to follow Christian's example and begin to study the words of this Book.

With friendly companionship and bright promises, it is a happy day. Caught up in the romance of the pilgrimage, the young pilgrim is not anticipating storms and snares ahead. Nevertheless, these are not far off. When stormy times crash in upon us, we quickly discover the importance of having the anchor of God's Word fixed securely within our hearts.

Are you a student of God's Word? If not, it is time to begin. We find the answers to all of life's ultimate questions within its pages.

Scripture: John 17:17; Titus 1:1-3; 2 Timothy 3:16-17

Prayer: Dear Lord, give me diligence to devote myself to the study of your Word. I pray for a heart that delights in your truth. Amen.

D·A·Y 11

"This sounds good. What are the things we are seeking?"

"There is an endless Kingdom to be inhabited and everlasting life to be given us so that we will live in that Kingdom forever."

"Wonderful! What else?"

"There are crowns of glory to be given us and garments that will make us shine like the sun in the heavens above."

"Excellent! What else?"

"There will be no more sorrow and crying, for He who owns the place will wipe all tears from our eyes."

The Book convinced Christian to cast off the transitory life of the City of Destruction. In so doing, he will not only escape perishing in the wicked city but will find unspeakable treasures, even everlasting life. He will enjoy this life in a marvelous eternal kingdom. Pliable feels a growing excitement about these things, too. Just as thoughts of eternity have always fascinated humankind, discussing these wonders inspires both men as they walk along.

Eternal life speaks not only of the duration of the life to come but of its essential quality. Life in the eternal kingdom will include crowns of glory, garments that shine like the sun, an absence of sorrow and tears. Christian has pondered these things well, but the mortal soul can hardly fathom the joys and mysteries of the kingdom. Life there is far beyond our ability to understand or even imagine.

Despite the mysteries, one thing is clear to Christian. It is in his heart to find this heavenly country. This desire is now his passion. Forsaking all else for this pursuit, he no longer lives according to worldly norms. He has joined the ranks of those who are "aliens and strangers."

Those who forsake the world for lives as pilgrims have heaven in their hearts. "But as it is, they desire a better country, that is, a heavenly one." Is heaven in your heart? Or have the values of this present world dulled your passion? Cast off the world, and let us with joyous anticipation look "forward to the city that has foundations, whose architect and builder is God" (Hebrews 11:10 NRSV).

Scripture: 1 Corinthians 2:9; Hebrews 11:14-16; 1 John 2:25

Prayer: Heavenly Father, I look forward to life in your eternal kingdom. Give me a fresh glimpse of heaven. As I live out the remainder of my days on this earth, let my heart burn ardently with heavenly hope. Amen.

DAY 12

"And who will be there with us?"

Christian's face shone as he went on. "There we will be with seraphim and cherubim—beings who will dazzle our eyes when we see them. We will also meet with the thousands and ten thousands who have gone on before us to that place. None of them will cause harm; all will be loving and holy. Everyone there will walk before God and stand approved in His grace and presence forever. Furthermore, we will see the elders with their golden crowns and the holy virgins with their golden harps; and we will see men who by the world were cut to pieces, burned in flames, eaten by beasts, and drowned in seas, all because of the love they had for the Lord of the place. Everyone there will be completely well, made whole, and clothed with immortality as with a garment."

Christian continues to describe what he expects to experience in the eternal kingdom. So many wonderful things await him, but one is best. Not only will there be eternal life in a glorious place, but there will be the delight of eternal fellowship. The loving relationships there will measure the richness of heaven's life.

First and primary, of course, is our relationship with God. We will see him face to face and will enjoy unending and harmonious companionship with him. We will meet members of his kingdom whom we have never before seen—dazzling angels and multitudes of saints including elders, martyrs, heroes. We will also see beloved friends and family members who have gone before us to their eternal reward. No one can begin to imagine the indescribable joy and awe we will feel as they invite us to join the everlasting throng. Together we will exult as we are clothed with immortality to live ever and always in the light of God's glory and grace. We will never again feel unloved, lonely, forgotten, or afraid.

This is the pilgrim's destiny. His true homeland is where God lives. As children who have never seen our homeland, we are on our way there. Oh, how our hearts should rejoice in the hope of seeing our God face to face. How we should thrill to think of one day joining our heavenly family. How we should cherish those around us who are likewise on their journey to that place. What personal comfort do you take from thoughts of heaven's fellowship?

Scripture: Matthew 13:43;
Revelation 7:9; 21:3-4; Psalm 16:11

Prayer: Eternal Father, let my heart be enraptured with thoughts of seeing you in your glorious kingdom. Let me regard your home as my own home. Because I will live with you and with your family forever, help me make these relationships a top priority. Amen.

D·A·Y 13

Pliable could hardly contain himself. "My heart is seized with ecstasy at hearing all this. But are these things really for us to enjoy? How can we come to share in them?"

"The Lord, the Ruler of that Country, has given the answer in this Book. It says that if we are truly willing to receive it, He will freely give it to us."

"Well, my good friend, I'm glad to hear all these things. Come on, let's quicken our pace."

Christian sighed. "I can't go as fast as I would like to because of this Burden on my back."

❧

Christian has won a convert. Pliable can hardly contain himself as he hears about life in the City to which he and Christian are journeying. It sounds fabulous. There is no doubt in his mind that much will be gained in making this pilgrimage. Trading the City of Destruction for the vastly superior country described in the Book makes great sense. He is now as excited as Christian at the glorious promises extended to them.

In an obvious burst of zeal, Pliable even tries to get Christian to pick up his pace. Yet poor Christian is already giving his best effort. If he could go faster, he would, but his burden is simply too heavy. Now the question arises, "Why doesn't Pliable bear a similar burden?" To this we may reply that, though Pliable wants to escape one city for a better City, he is not yet conscious of his own sinfulness. While Christian languishes under an oppressive sense of guilt that he is unable to shake off, Pliable doesn't feel the slightest twinge of conviction.

So which man is better off? Who is healthier? Many would choose Pliable. After all, who wants to feel guilty and unhappy? Many in our modern culture would tell us that any feeling of guilt is self-destructive. Nevertheless, let us not forget that it is precisely Christian's distress over his guilty condition that has driven him to begin his pilgrimage.

Do you listen to your conscience and the Spirit of God warning of your need to confess and change some behavior? When you feel you have offended God, what do you do with your feelings of guilt?

❧

Scripture: Jeremiah 31:19; Ezekiel 18:27-28;
Isaiah 66:2

Prayer: Dear Lord, thank you for the times you bring me under a burden of conviction for my sin. Without this burden, I would so often fail to recognize the things that displease you. When I sin, help me to discern the difference between godly grief and condemnation. Amen

D·A·Y 14

Now I saw in my dream that, just as they had ended their conversation, they approached a miry Slough [a muddy swamp] in the plain. Neither of them paid attention to it, and both suddenly fell into the bog. The Slough's name was Despond. Covered with mud, they wallowed in it for some time. And Christian, because of the Burden on his back, began to sink in the mire.

"Oh, Christian, my neighbor!" Pliable cried out. "Where are you now?"

"To tell you the truth, I don't know," Christian answered.

Hearing this, Pliable became offended and angrily scolded his companion. "Is this the happiness you have told me about all this time? If we have such terrible misfortune here at the beginning, what are we to expect between here and the end of our journey? If I can possibly get out of here with my life, you can possess that wonderful Country for you and me both!"

❧

The pilgrimage has come to a dead stop. Neither man anticipated this type of trouble. The mud that covers them perplexes them. Christian, who seemingly had all the answers, is at a loss to explain this predicament.

Pliable becomes irate. His heart is a good example of the rocky soil in the Parable of the Sower. Trouble arises, but he has no roots. This one who joyfully embraced the good news is found abruptly denouncing it.

Yet wasn't it just a short time ago that Pliable, with surging emotions, was ready to lead the charge to the heavenly country? What an impressive beginning! Any uninformed observer could envision Pliable easily striding past Christian and think that, of the two, he was the most well suited and zealously committed to the pilgrimage. Nevertheless, his outward zeal is deceptive, and we find within him significant character weaknesses. Being pliable has not made him humble. His shallow, untested faith so lacks inward strength and conviction that he fails his first test as a pilgrim. The same flexible disposition that allowed him to embark on a pilgrimage has just as quickly permitted him to abandon it.

Some of us are more compliant by nature, and some more strong willed. What strengths and weaknesses in your life can your spiritual adversary exploit? How can God use these same characteristics? Think of some steps you can take to give God a better advantage.

❧

Scripture: Matthew 13:1-9, 18-23;
Psalm 106:12-14

Prayer: Dear Lord, please keep my life in good balance. Help me to be flexible and adaptable as I respond to Your will for my life, but help me also to be firm and resolute when facing trials and temptations that discourage me from following you. Amen.

DAY 15

With that, Pliable gave a desperate struggle or two and was able to get out of the mire on the side of the Slough that faced his home. So away he went, and Christian never saw him again. Thus, Christian was left to roll around in the Slough of Despond by himself. Even then, however, he tried to struggle to the side of the Slough that was farthest from his own home and closest to the Wicket-gate. He continued to struggle but couldn't get out because of the Burden on his back.

❦

Pliable had enough determination to get himself out of the slough to return home but not enough to stay, face the problem, and go on with his pilgrimage. Christian, in the meantime, is left to fend for himself. Both the slough and his burden seem allied against him. Still, while he desperately wants out of his trouble, he doesn't want it so badly that he will turn back toward the City of Destruction. He dreads its doom far more than he does the slough. The hope of deliverance from God's wrath and the blessings of salvation are so desirable to him that he refuses to give in to this present dreadful circumstance. If he must perish, he much prefers to do so here than in the City of Destruction.

Christian manages to struggle on over to the far side of the slough, the side closest to his destination. Despite his confusion and fear, he is proving with this first terrible test that he has no intention of setting his face to the plow and looking back (Luke 9:62).

Sometimes on the pathway of life unexpected trials seem to come out of nowhere. It is in those times that we must persevere and refuse to abandon our purpose. The enemy of our souls would love to seduce our hearts into joining Pliable in forsaking the way. But what attraction can the City of Destruction hold for one who has already smelled the smoke of its doom? Those with a true passion for the pilgrimage will keep looking for deliverance to come from somewhere up ahead. They will never forfeit their quest for eternal life. A way out must surely come.

How resolved are you to keep hoping in God when unforeseen trials discourage you? Will you climb out on the side nearest God's will?

❦

Scripture: Joel 2:13; Isaiah 42:3;
Matthew 11:28-30

Prayer: Father, even when my circumstances take a terrible turn for the worse, please help me by your grace to stay faithful to my pilgrimage. I prefer perishing on my pilgrimage to giving up and returning to the City of Destruction. Help me when I am wrestling in my own slough to keep looking in your direction. Amen.

D·A·Y
16

Then I saw in my dream that a man named Help came to him, and he asked Christian what he was doing there.

"Sir," explained Christian, "a man named Evangelist instructed me to go this way. He gave me directions to that Gate up ahead where I might escape the coming wrath. As I was going toward the Gate, I fell in here."

"But why didn't you look for the steps?" asked Help.

"Fear pursued me so hard that I fled this way and fell in."

"Give me your hand."

So Christian reached out his hand, and Help pulled him to solid ground and told him to continue on his way.

❧

Here we find both Fear and Help personified. Fear is the one who drove Christian and Pliable into the Slough of Despond. It seems that fears of God's wrath suddenly caught up with the men. Perhaps the trouble arose as they compared themselves with one another, each thinking the other would be accepted at the Gate while he would be rejected. Unlike Christian, Pliable bore no burden. He may have suddenly realized this reflected very poorly on him. Christian, on the other hand, may have feared that his burden and subsequent slow pace proved him a much worse sinner than Pliable. Whatever the case, the men's fears were so unnerving that they failed to look for the steps, and both landed in the slough. Taking our eyes off our own pilgrimage by judging ourselves according to someone else's apparent condition can be a dangerous mistake.

While Pliable angrily makes his escape and stomps off, Christian tries hard but remains powerless to find a way out. Nevertheless, the Lord of the Heavenly Country will never forsake this struggling pilgrim. He sends Help to lend a hand. Why did Help wait so long before coming? Would not both men have fared better if he had arrived sooner? After all, Pliable deserted the pilgrimage, and Christian is suffering great trauma.

It is a mystery of God's sovereignty that he allows many pilgrims to become discouraged so he can expose their hearts. Once these two men reveal the intentions of their hearts, the sincere one receives ample encouragement. The next time you feel desperate, perhaps God is searching your heart. Make sure you are bent on remaining faithful to him and his path for your life. Trust him; he will surely send his help.

❧

Scripture: Proverbs 21:2; Psalm 33:20; 40:1-2

Prayer: Father, you are faithful. Thank you for providing help in my times of need. When I am troubled, grant me faith to wait patiently and not cave in to fear. I know that in your time you will restore me to solid ground. Amen.

D·A·Y
17

Then I stepped up to the one who had pulled Christian out and asked, "Sir, since this is the way from the City of Destruction to the Gate, why isn't this place fenced off so that poor travelers may go by more safely?"

And he answered me, "This miry Slough is the type that cannot be fenced. It is the lower ground where the scum and filth that accompany conviction of sin continually accumulate. Therefore it was named the Slough of Despond because, as the sinner is awakened to his lost condition, many fears, doubts, and discouraging anxieties arise in his soul. All of them come together and settle here in this place, and that is the reason this ground is no good.

"It is not the King's desire that this place should remain so bad. By the direction of His surveyors, His laborers have been working for almost two thousand years to fence off this patch of ground. Yes, and to my knowledge at least 20,000 cartloads of profitable instructions—yes, millions of them—have been swallowed up here. In all seasons they have been brought from all places in the King's domain, and those who are knowledgeable say that these materials have the best potential for making the ground good. Nevertheless, it remains the Slough of Despond, and so will it be even when all has been tried and failed."

❧

The Slough of Despond represents discouraging fears that often harass those converting to Christ. We can distinguish this type of anxiety from the beneficial fear that caused Christian to "flee from the wrath to come." The fear of God comes by the reading of God's Word, but discouraging fears are ungrounded and deter the pilgrim's progress.

While a seasoned Christian may fall prey to doubts and discouragement because of yielding to temptation or complacency, this despondency is peculiar to those who are just coming to God, unfortunately when they are the most conscientious. While diligently seeking God, they begin to understand his perfect holiness and, in contrast, their abhorrent wretchedness. Doubting they can ever span the gulf, they are overwhelmed with feelings of unworthiness, self-contempt, and rejection.

Just as Christian sank deeper as he struggled, those striving to deliver themselves soon discover even more evil lurking in their hearts. As fears of judgment increase, no amount of godly instruction can quell these panicky feelings.

In becoming aware of your sins, have you ever similarly found yourself caught in a depressing slough-like dilemma? What did you learn from your experience?

❧

Scripture: Psalm 27:14; 31:24; Lamentations 3:25-26

Prayer: Lord, "'twas grace that taught my heart to fear, and grace my fears relieved." Help me to understand the difference between fear that motivates and fear that suffocates. Also I am willing to extend my hand to those caught in quandaries who need your peace. Amen.

D·A·Y 18

"It is true that some good and substantial steps have been placed evenly throughout this Slough by the command of the Lawgiver. Even then, however, this place spews out so much filth that when the weather gets bad, the steps can hardly be seen. And even if people do see them, because of confusion they step the wrong way and fall into the slime. In any case, the steps are there, and the ground is good once they go through the Gate."

When Help asked Christian why he had not looked for the steps out of the slough, Christian explained that he was fleeing from Fear and fell in. These trustworthy steps (or stepping-stones) are found in Scripture. They represent the promises of forgiveness and acceptance that come through faith in Christ. Many steps are available to those who seek the Lord's salvation and follow his prescribed way of attaining it. Those who take these steps will be spared the very unhappy slough experience.

The slough lies en route between destruction and life. Therefore, those who travel this way will at one time or another either wallow in the slough or pass over it by way of the steps. In his haste Christian never noticed the steps. But even if he had seen them and had begun to walk across them, he may not have avoided falling in. A lot depends upon the "weather" at the time of one's crossing. When we are particularly tempted or confused, it is very easy to lose sight of the promises, miss a step, and land in the slough.

This points out the importance of helping young pilgrims to guard their emotions and to look for the promises God has carefully provided them. While millions of man's instructions—albeit godly ones—have been lost in this bedeviling despondency, we can be assured that God's promises are absolutely immovable and immutable. Also encouraging is the fact that even if we should stumble into some mucky pit, God in his great compassion will mercifully send us help to deliver us and restore us to good ground.

Perhaps you have experienced the joy of being delivered by God's merciful "help." And perhaps you have experienced the joy of walking above a distressing situation on the stepping-stones of God's promises. Isn't it wonderful that our loving God sees our need and provides for our safety? Take a moment to praise him for his help.

Scripture: Psalms 37:23-24; 43:5; 116:1-9; Job 33:26-28

Prayer: Father, thank you for the many promises you give to help me on my way. I want to keep focused on you in times of trouble. Please help me to memorize, believe in, and apply your promises to my walk. Thank you, too, that when I am weak and forgetful, you will send other help to rescue me. Amen.

D·A·Y 19

Now I saw in my dream that by this time Pliable had arrived back home, and his neighbors came to visit him. Some of them called him a wise man for coming back, and some called him a fool for endangering himself with Christian. Still others mocked his cowardice, saying, "Surely, if I had begun such a venture, I would not have been so cowardly as to have given up because of a few troubles." So Pliable sat cowering among them until he finally gained enough confidence to raise an objection. At this, they immediately left him alone and began to insult poor Christian behind his back because of what had happened to Pliable.

Inasmuch as nonbelievers tend to disdain those who make decisions for Christ, they often have even less respect for ones who fail to remain true to their convictions. Such is the case with Pliable's neighbors. If any favorable testimony to them had previously existed, it is now gone. Surely Pliable hoped to simply sneak back into town unnoticed. But an old saying warns, "Watch your step because everyone else does." His neighbors come to hear about his misadventures, and all have opinions, most of them unfavorable.

This is not unlike a story Jesus told. A foolish builder began a construction project but ran out of money before its completion because he hadn't bothered counting its cost. Jesus explained that everyone who sees it ridicules the man (Luke 14:29-30). A wise person, unlike Pliable and the foolish builder, undertakes a rational self-examination before beginning a pilgrimage.

Consider Ruth the Moabitess. Counting the cost—changing her religion, becoming a foreigner in a strange land, even possibly dying—she firmly decided to move with Naomi to Israel. Never turning back, she structured her life on hard work and good character. Earning herself a sterling reputation, she was highly praised. God so honored her that she, while not Jewish, is in the Messianic lineage, great-grandmother to King David.

Grace is free, but carrying the cross that grace demands is no casual matter. You should decide to answer the following essential questions: "Am I expecting an easy, trouble-free Christian life? Will I abandon my pilgrimage because I didn't count the cost of commitment to it?" "Am I prepared to live my life as a godly example?" If we carefully count the cost of becoming Christ's pilgrims before we begin, we won't be as likely to succumb to temptations to turn back in difficulty.

Scripture: Luke 14:25-33; Proverbs 24:3, 27;
Ruth 1:15-17; 2:11-12; 4:13-16

Prayer: Dear Lord, the world is ungracious to quitters. I want my life to be a faithful testimony. Give me the grace to build my life wisely. Amen.

D·A·Y 20

Now as Christian was walking on alone, he saw someone in the distance coming across the field toward him, and they met just as their ways crossed. The gentleman's name was Mr. Worldly-wiseman, and he lived in a very influential town called Carnal-policy. This town was near to the one from which Christian had come. The man, upon meeting Christian, had some idea of whom he might be, for the news of Christian's leaving the City of Destruction had become the talk of the town there. It was even becoming much bandied about in other areas as well. Thus, Worldly-wiseman, seeing Christian's intense effort to travel and listening to all his sighs and groans, guessed who he was.

The reports of Christian's decision to become a pilgrim have been well circulated, not only in his own hometown but throughout the region as well. A decision to forsake the worldly system to follow Christ will not likely be ignored. If not producing outright persecution, this decision is at least good fodder for gossip, especially in a town like Carnal-policy.

Deriving from the Greek word, *sarx,* meaning "flesh," the word *sarkikos* means "carnal." It speaks of having the nature of flesh, i.e., governed by the lower nature, the sensual animal appetites, instead of by the Spirit of God.

Genuine godliness is as rare as hen's teeth in the worldly town of Carnal-policy. With carnality as its guiding principle, the town charter boasts its carnal appetites. Smaller than the City of Destruction, it is evidently an influential town of the elite, an ancestral home to the worldly wise. No doubt, Worldly-wiseman is proud of his citizenship in this town.

It is best for a young pilgrim to avoid those who make carnality their policy. Nevertheless, Christian would likely have found it difficult to avoid meeting this man, since he probably kept an eye out for Christian, hoping for an opportunity to set him straight. Don't the wise of this world seem to watch and wait for opportunities to dispense their worldly wisdom? If allowed, they will certainly poison our faith.

Ask the Holy Spirit to help you to detect ways in which the worldly wise are influencing you with their carnal reasoning. How do you think you can better keep a cautious guard up against their influence?

Scriptures: Romans 1:22; 8:5-8;
Ephesians 4:22-24

Prayer: Dear Lord, may my attitudes and values reflect a godly disposition, not a carnal one. Let me, by your grace, avoid those who would corrupt my intention to live purely for you. Amen.

D·A·Y 21

So he decided to start a conversation with Christian. "How are you, sir? Where are you going in such a burdened state?"

"Yes, in as burdened a state as I can imagine a poor creature could be," answered Christian. "And since you asked where I am going, I will tell you. I am going to that Wicket-gate that lies ahead because I have been informed that I will find a way to get rid of my heavy Burden."

"Do you have a wife and children?"

"Yes, but this Burden so weighs me down that I cannot enjoy them as I once did. I feel as if I had none."

Worldly-wiseman looked deeply concerned. "Will you listen to me if I give you some advice?"

"If it is good, I will," answered Christian, "because I definitely need some good advice."

❦

Just as God sends help, so the enemy of our souls sends hindrances. Worldly-wiseman from Carnal-Policy is on a different route but sees Christian struggling with his burden. He is more than ready to offer his misguiding hand.

Who is this Mr. Worldly-wiseman? He represents those who have rejected the true wisdom of God in favor of temporal wisdom. Driven by worldly values, this person looks upon Christian with patronizing compassion, believing his own wisdom of inestimably higher value. Just as the devil tries to "rescue" young pilgrims before their new convictions become established, Mr. Worldly-wiseman hopes to advise Christian before his situation turns desperate.

The struggling pilgrim could use supportive concern at this point, and Worldly-wiseman speaks with an air of authority and self-confidence that pulls Christian in. Christian quickly takes the man into his confidence. In this, he has made a terrible mistake. He says he is open to "good" advice but doesn't yet have knowledge and discernment to decide between good and bad advice, godly and worldly wisdom. He will withstand every persuasion to return home; yet he is unprepared to resist the proposals of this carnal counselor.

When vulnerable to worldly influences, we must hold on to the godly advice we have already received. How careful are you about the advice you listen to?

❦

Scripture: 1 Corinthians 1:18-25; 3:19-20; Proverbs 26:12

Prayer: Lord, I'm tempted daily by those wanting to influence me with their worldly values. I don't want their opinions to lead me astray. Grant me discernment as I meet both true and counterfeit friends and tune in to the media. Amen.

D·A·Y 22

"I would advise you to get rid of your Burden quickly. You will never have peace of mind until you do, and you will never enjoy the blessings God has given you until then either."

"That's what I am looking for, to get rid of this heavy Burden. But I can't get it off by myself, and nobody in our country can take it off my shoulders. So I'm going this way, as I told you, to get rid of my Burden."

"And who told you to go this way to get rid of your Burden?"

"A man who appeared to me to be a very admirable and trustworthy person. His name, as I recall, is Evangelist."

Ah, peace of mind. How desperately humankind craves this cherished but rare quality. Worldly-wiseman has touched a raw nerve when he appeals to Christian's obvious desire for some peace of mind. He has come at a time of great vulnerability. Christian's burden weighs on him like a millstone. His shoulders are drooping. His gait is slow and unsteady. Worldly-wiseman seems to understand Christian's predicament completely. He knows what he is talking about when he says no peace will be found until the burden is gone.

What Worldly-wiseman fails to convey, however, is that a world of difference exists between the genuine peace of God and counterfeit peace. He advocates treating the symptom—"Get rid of your burden quickly"—without dealing with the sin that brought on the burden. One of our enemy's best tools is the dangled carrot of fabricated peace.

This carnal friend would see Christian's burden removed and peace restored, but at what cost? Christian will lose far more than his burden if he opts to compromise with this man's worldly ways. As God's people, we don't take our cues from the voices of the fallen culture around us. Our paths inevitably intersect, but we must not linger at the intersection. The true peace of God is a peace of heart and soul that comes from knowing and walking with the Lord.

If you are in turmoil, God has peace for you. Commit yourself to finding his peace alone, and accept no worldly substitutes.

Scripture: James 3:15-18;
Philippians 4:6-7; Psalm 119:165

Prayer: Lord, I want your true, heavenly peace. It is your peace alone that is wonderful. By your grace, I won't be lured by the false sense of peace that the world offers. Help me to seek your peace always, even in my most difficult circumstances. I know it's there for me, and I thank you for it. Amen.

D·A·Y 23

Now Worldly-wiseman became indignant. "I curse him for his counsel! No way in the world is more dangerous and troublesome than the one he has steered you toward. And that is what you will find if you allow yourself to be led by his counsel. I can tell that you have already had some trouble, for I can see the dirt of the Slough of Despond on you. That Slough is only the beginning of the sorrows that come to those who take this Way. Listen to me, for I am older than you. If you take this Way, you will likely meet with fatigue, pain, hunger, dangers, nakedness, swords, lions, dragons, darkness, and, in a word, death. This is the truth, and many testimonies have confirmed it. Should a man be so careless as to throw his life away by giving heed to a stranger?"

"Listen," Christian groaned, "this Burden on my back is more terrible than all these things you have mentioned. No, I don't care what I encounter on the way, as long as I can also find deliverance from my Burden."

Worldly-wiseman wastes no time in declaring his hostility for Evangelist and his message. Having never actually walked the pilgrim's Way himself, it should occur to him that he may be less than informed. To his way of thinking, however, he is the one with street smarts, and Christian should listen to him. He asserts that unending woes lie ahead for Christian, and as supporting evidence, he points to the residues of the slough on Christian's person. In essence he says, "I see you've been through a lot, but, trust me, you haven't seen anything yet!"

Comparing himself with the evangelistic "stranger," Worldly-wiseman claims to be the reliable and truthful one. What makes the man most dangerous, however, is that he really is, in part, telling the truth. Many testimonies *have* confirmed what he is saying. The apostle Paul said he suffered countless beatings, imprisonments, and exposure to all kinds of hardships. What Worldly-wiseman neglects to add, however, is that Paul also said, "For his sake I have suffered the loss of all things, and count them as refuse" and "I can do all things in him who strengthens me" (Philippians 3:8, 4:13 RSV).

The worldly wise find it easy to undermine God's truth. To successfully refute their ideas and logic, we must become well acquainted with God's wisdom as revealed in his Word. Are you experiencing any areas of confusion in your life? If so, will you seek God's wisdom? He certainly wants to share it with you.

Scripture: 2 Corinthians 5:16;
James 1:5; Proverbs 2:6

Prayer: Dear Father, I don't want to give heed to the enemies of your truth no matter how convincing they may sound. They think I am walking the way of fools, but they are the fools. My heart is fixed upon you, and I dedicate myself to seeking your wisdom. Amen.

DAY 24

Worldly-wiseman resumed his interrogation. "How did you first receive your Burden?"

"By reading this Book in my hand."

"I thought so. And it has happened to you just as with other weak people who, meddling with things beyond their understanding, fall into the same mental confusion and obsessive behavior as you have. This can only break a man down, and I can perceive this is the case with you. These people take off on desperate ventures seeking to receive something they know nothing about."

Christian, straining under the weight of his Burden, immediately replied, "I know what I am seeking—freedom from my heavy Burden!"

Worldly-wiseman, so confident in his own speculations and assumptions, is hostile to the Word of God, contemptuous toward godly advice, and wise in his own conceits. We easily detect his smug condescension by his "I thought so." He has already censured Evangelist's advice, and now he shows his contempt for every pilgrim's competence. He confidently assumes that this pilgrimage has arisen from some diminished capacity—either inferior intellect or emotional instability. Christian is obviously "weak" and should not be poking around in things he cannot understand. These things are best left to the experts. How many times in history has the Word of God been held captive to ecclesiastical "experts"?

To Worldly-wiseman, the young man's running off on this harebrained pilgrimage proves he has fallen prey to some unreasonable anxiety or delusion. Making a radical decision for a pilgrimage is, in his view, tantamount to acquiring an obsession. It is clear to this worldly mind that too much concern about sin and eternal things draws one away from the stability that comes from remaining entrenched in secular interests and pursuits.

Christian's intention to obey Evangelist has been broadsided. In a weak and befuddled state, he takes in this confident man's assessment of his condition. We see here no mere philosophical difference in perspectives. Rather, this is a very dangerous and intense spiritual assault. If only the world were rid of devils and deceivers, we would never suffer confusion—God's ways would always make perfect sense. As it is, a great spiritual battle for people's minds rages on today. It is imperative that we set our minds on God's truth and resolve to stay true to the pilgrimage. Do this, and you will be a victor. You don't need to let unbelievers undermine your victory.

Scripture: 2 Corinthians 11:3-4, 13-15;
Psalms 73:3-5; 119:29-31

Prayer: Dear Lord, my confidence is in you, not in me nor anyone else. When I am weak and assaulted, help me to hold more tightly to your truth. I am not ashamed of being a pilgrim on your pathway. Amen.

D·A·Y 25

"But why do you seek for freedom in this way, seeing that it's so dangerous? If you had the patience to listen, I could direct you to what you are looking for without the dangers that you'll encounter by going this way. Yes, the remedy is here. Besides, I might add, instead of those dangers, you'll find abundant safety, friendship, and contentment."

This sounded wonderful to Christian. "Sir, I beg you, please reveal this secret to me."

"Well, a short distance from here there is a Village named Morality. In this Village lives a man named Legality. This man has sound judgment and a very good reputation. He has skill in helping people like yourself get such Burdens off their shoulders. Yes, to my knowledge, he has done a great deal of good this way. Why, he even has skill in curing those who are being driven to distraction because of their Burdens. Like I say, you can go to him and be helped right away."

❧

While the fatal nature of his sin burdens Christian, he is unaware of the fatal nature of Worldly-wiseman's advice. In his earnest desire for relief, he has exposed himself to the danger of searching for it in wrong venues. Although no legitimate detours exist on the pilgrims' path, Worldly-wiseman's specious arguments are attractive. He smoothly takes Christian the next step away from true salvation.

Karl Barth said, "The devil may also make use of morality."[1] So the city of Morality, home to man-centered, works-based religion, has recruited multitudes of devoted citizens. This religious yet worldly city uses Scriptures to legitimate its doctrine while mutilating the true gospel message. Because the heart of Morality's religion is an idolatrous self-love that leaves no opening for an authentic devotion for God, external duties are kept the focus. The "good" folk of Morality outwardly obey God's law by doing virtuous deeds and abstaining from scandalous vices. They glory in themselves without any inward sincere reverence for God.

Legality, the sage of the worldly-minded folk of Morality, is not unlike the scribes and Pharisees who promoted a defective obedience to a small portion of God's law. With the reputation for relieving guilt-stricken consciences, he is Morality's most notable resident.

Let us beware. Those who seek justification by their own good deeds will never be true worshipers of God. The most dangerous worldly temptations don't come as things immoral or illegal but from prevailing attitudes of what the world considers "good." As you look out over the religious landscape, can you see how "all that glitters is not gold"? How can you avoid glittery seductions?

❧

Scripture: Romans 3:20; Galatians 2:15-16; Acts 13:38-39

Prayer: Lord Jesus, may I never succumb to the temptation to enthrone self by substituting good works for a walk of faith. I trust in your grace alone to give my heart rest. Amen.

DAY 26

"His house is less than a mile from here. If he is not at home himself, he has a son, an impressive young man named Civility. He can help you just as well as the old man. You will be able to find relief from your Burden there. If you don't want to go back to your former home, and I wouldn't blame you, you can send for your wife and children to come to this town. There are houses vacant at this time, and you can purchase one of them at a reasonable price. You can also buy good provisions there at low prices. All you need to make your life happy is there, and you will live by honest neighbors who are successful and of a good reputation."

❦

Worldly-wiseman speaks of honest neighbors. Are they as honest as he? This deceiver has skillfully diverted Christian away from the Gospel back to man's solution to his sin problem. To his way of thinking, it doesn't matter what kinds of sin have a person bound—the remedy is reformation in Morality, not the way of the pilgrims. In Morality troubled consciences are relieved in a way much more preferable.

Civility, the son of Legality, is one who persuades those afflicted that decent, benevolent behavior will bring relief from conviction. How does it work? As a person embraces a self-righteous spirit, he takes on a distorted view of himself as one who has become upright. The burdens of guilt and pain is effectively masked. It seems like a wonderful solution. After all, none of the self-assured citizens in this refined community are aware of any clumsy burdens on their backs. Ah, but in the words of Elizabeth Barrett Browning, "The devil's most devilish when respectable."[2]

Remember Christian's excitement as he recited to Pliable the delightful things the Book promised to pilgrims who persevere to the end? Worldly-wiseman has so duped Christian that his former convictions are all but forgotten. Common sense now tells him that by settling in Morality, he can't go wrong. This way he can escape the doom of the City of Destruction while avoiding the difficulties and dangers of the pilgrimage. And all this at an affordable price!

The Morality alternative presents a counterfeit way of salvation. From the worldly point of view, those choosing it will be "successful" and have a "good reputation." Along the pilgrim's pathway, however, success and good reputation are measured far differently. Have you renounced the worldly definitions of success and good reputation in favor of God's definitions?

❦

Scripture: 1 Corinthians 1:26-29; 2 Peter 2:18-19; 1 John 1:8

Prayer: Father, I don't want deceptive worldly-wise solutions to dazzle me. They are diversions, and I refuse them in favor of walking in your wisdom. Please keep me in your Way; it alone provides genuine life and peace. Amen.

DAY 27

Now Christian had come to a standstill, not sure what to do. Before long, however, he concluded that if what the man was saying was true, his wisest course of action would be to take his advice. With that, he questioned the man further.

"Sir, how do I get to this honest man's house?"

"Do you see that high Hill over there?"

"Yes, very well."

"You have to go by that Hill, and then the first house you come to will be his."

So Christian turned out of his way to go to Mr. Legality's house for help. But when he drew near to the Hill, it seemed very high, and the path he was following passed under such an ominous looking overhang that he was afraid to continue on for fear that it might fall on him. So he stood still, wondering what to do next. To make matters worse, his Burden now seemed even heavier than when he was on the Way. Suddenly, flashes of fire came out of the Hill and made Christian afraid that he would be burned. So he continued to stand there, sweating and shaking with fear. Now he was sorry he had ever taken Worldly-wiseman's advice.

Christian's progress is halted. Not only does he reject Evangelist's wisdom, but he never thinks to consult his Book. Instead, he relies on his own fleshly reasoning, concluding that *if* Worldly-wiseman is telling the truth, his way must surely be the best way. Yet how does he determine whether this man's way is correct? He takes *his* word for it. How we must guard against gullibility!

Since the only way to Morality goes past Mt. Sinai, Christian soon encounters a terrible predicament. Mount Sinai, representing the weight of the Law of Moses, might crush him! While those who feel little conviction of sin realize little danger and pass by quickly, Christian finds this supposedly safer and happier way to be a nightmare. Profoundly aware of the gravity of his sinful condition, he realizes he may never move quickly enough to get by Mt. Sinai. Christian is sorry; worldly wisdom is exposed for what it is. To make matters worse, the already heavy burden is now overwhelmingly oppressive. Why? The Law indicts us as sinners but is unable to remove our guilt.

We must remember that our best efforts will never establish our own righteousness. Measured against God's holy standard, our righteousness is like filthy rags (Isaiah 64:6). Be sure to flee every thought of finding a better way than God's Way to eternal life. Christ's Gospel is the only legitimate way of salvation. Resolve to commit your life to him.

Scripture: Romans 9:31-32; Hosea 4:6; Philippians 3:4-9

Prayer: Father, I acknowledge my vulnerability to worldly wisdom and ask that you keep me from the mistake of following fleshly instinct and wandering from your Way. Amen.

D·A·Y
28

All of a sudden, he saw Evangelist coming to meet him. The sight of him caused Christian to blush because he was ashamed. Evangelist came nearer and nearer, and Christian could see that he had a very stern and almost frightening look on his face.

"What are you doing here, Christian?" asked Evangelist.

Christian didn't know how to answer, so he stood speechless in front of him.

"Aren't you the man I found crying outside the City of Destruction?"

"Yes, dear sir, I am the man," Christian replied faintly.

"Didn't I instruct you to go to the little Wicket-gate?"

"Yes, sir."

"Well, how can you be so quickly led astray? For now you are completely out of the Way."

"I met a man soon after I had gotten past the Slough of Despond who convinced me that in the Village up ahead I could find a man who could remove my Burden."

"What was he like?"

"He looked like a gentleman and talked with me for quite some time, finally persuading me to come this way. When I got here, I saw this Hill and how it hangs over the way, so I stopped because I was afraid it might fall on me."

❧

God in His grace sends Evangelist to find the wayward pilgrim. The look on Evangelist's face as he approaches reflects God's view of Christian's choice of paths. The sin committed is very serious, a choice of spiritual death.

Due to our current culturally fashionable belief that many paths exist for reaching God, truth, and enlightenment, few are offended by those who choose alternate paths to one's own. But Evangelist would be offended. He is a straightforward person with a clear and narrowly defined message. And rightly so; for to be counted a faithful gospel minister, one must preach that there is only one true path—God's, as revealed through Christ and the Scriptures.

The "gentleman" promised a quick and easy way of salvation. While Christian found this tantalizing, he soon discovered that there is no "quick fix." The Puritans referred to a process they called "heart work"—a deep work of God in the sinful human heart to bring it to Christ's light. Short-circuiting this process has led Christian "completely out of the Way." How quickly we can move away from God's design for our lives! If we aren't careful, easier options can lead us astray. Is there anything in your heart that you haven't given him? Allow him to do a deep "heart work" in you.

❧

Scripture: Acts 4:12; 10:43; John 3:36

Prayer: Dear Lord, I choose to obey your Gospel. I do not want to take even one step away from it. I acknowledge that it is the only way to life. Please keep my heart faithful. Amen.

D·A·Y 29

"And what did this man say to you?"

"Why, he asked me where I was going, and I told him."

"And then what did he say?"

"He asked me if I had a family. I told him I did, but that I was so weighed down by the Burden on my back that I could not even enjoy them anymore."

"And what did he say then?"

"He encouraged me to get rid of my Burden right away. I told him that relief was what I was looking for, therefore I was going to the Gate up ahead to receive further direction in how I might get to the place of deliverance. At that, he said he wished to show me a better way—shorter and not so full of difficulties as the Way that you offered me, sir. He told me his way would take me to the house of a gentleman who had skill in taking off these kinds of Burdens. So I believed him and turned from that Way into this so that I might soon be free of my Burden. But when I arrived here and saw how things are, I stopped, like I said, because of the danger I feared. And now I don't know what to do."

Being in the Lord's service is an exciting challenge. While sometimes exhilarating, it can also be quite frustrating. This is one of those frustrating instances. Evangelist faithfully proclaimed the Gospel and thought he had won a convert, only to find his convert quickly diverted to another path. Paul lamented over the Galatian believers' quick departure from the true Gospel.

Sometimes it is tempting to walk away from someone who has blatantly rejected our counsel. Because of our disappointment and pain, we want to avoid dealing with it further. Evangelist, however, doesn't give up on the wayward pilgrim. Rather than taking Christian's rejection personally or angrily condemning him, he patiently asks questions and listens to Christian's answers with genuine concern.

Christian confesses the whole incident. His faith had shifted from the truth to a worldly-wise sham religion. Now he admits he is afraid and confused, not knowing what to do next. While seeing Evangelist frightened Christian, he must have also felt some comfort. This is a man who helped him before, so perhaps he has come to help him again.

Have you had "evangelists" in your life who shared the Gospel with you and never gave up on you? If so, thank God for them. Ask God to raise up more faithful witnesses to lead stumbling souls into the truth. Be one of those witnesses yourself.

Scripture: Galatians 1:6-12; 2 Corinthians 11:27-28; Acts 20:20-21

Prayer: Lord, thank you for your faithful servants. Please raise up many who have a passion for bringing your truth to lost and confused souls. Grant me your power to be your witness. Amen.

DAY 30

Evangelist said firmly, "Stand still and listen while I show you the words of God" [1 Samuel 9:27]. So Christian stood trembling, waiting for Evangelist to speak.

Then Evangelist said, "See to it that you do not refuse him who speaks. If they did not escape when they refused him who warned them on earth, how much less will we, if we turn away from Him who warns us from Heaven?" [Hebrews 12:25]. He also said, "But my righteous one will live by faith. And if he shrinks back, I will not be pleased with him" [Hebrews 10:38].

Evangelist then explained and applied the words: "You are the man who is running into this misery. You have begun to reject the counsel of the Most High and to shrink back from the Way of peace, even risking utter destruction."

Then Christian fell down at his feet like a dying man, crying, "Woe is me, for I am ruined!" [Isaiah 6:5].

When Evangelist saw this, he took him by the right hand, saying, "Every sin and blasphemy will be forgiven men. Don't be faithless any longer. Believe!" [Matthew 12:31]. Then Christian began to feel some relief, so he stood up, once again trembling before Evangelist.

❧

After listening carefully to Christian's tale of woe, Evangelist's first priority is not to relieve his stricken conscience but to get him back on solid footing. If in his desire to comfort Christian, Evangelist treats the sin too lightly, Christian might easily stray again. So Evangelist straightforwardly confronts Christian with the serious nature of his sin. He prefaces his words by saying that these are not his own words at all but the very words of God. He then quotes appropriate Scriptures.

Christian was guilty of directing his belief toward another gospel of salvation. Therefore, Evangelist's warning is sobering. Let there be no mistake about it: Turning aside from the Gospel is an affront to Christ, and those who sin against him will come to ruin. Christian's humble response to this rebuke is a fitting one. Subsequently, Evangelist once again extends God's grace to him.

We live today in a rebellious and independent society. This infection has profoundly influenced even God's people. We bristle at godly correction, thinking no one but God has a right to confront us. But God often uses others to do his correcting. When you are out of line, how ready are you to receive godly correction? If you will humble yourself, believe the "words of God," and receive correction as a gift, you will quickly find your pilgrimage renewed.

❧

Scripture: 1 Peter 4:11; 5:5; Hebrews 3:12-15

Prayer: Lord God, you know my heart. I acknowledge I have many blind spots that need your correction. When I am confronted with sin, help me to receive your Word and your messenger humbly and respectfully. Amen.

D·A·Y 31

"You must take more seriously what I tell you," Evangelist continued. "I will now show you who it was that deceived you and also to whom he was sending you. The man who met you is called Worldly-wiseman. His name is appropriate, partly because he respects only the values and wisdom of this world and therefore always goes to church in the town of Morality. Also, he loves the wisdom of the world best because it spares him from facing the Cross. Also, because he is of a carnal disposition, he seeks to pervert my ways even though they are right.

"Now there are three things in this man's counsel that you must utterly abhor. First, his turning you out of the Way. Second, his effort to make the Cross repulsive to you. And third, his setting your feet in the path that leads to death."

Early editions of the story insert this poem here:

When Christians to carnal men lend their ear,
They go out of their Way and pay for it dear;
For Mr. Worldly-wiseman can only show
A saint the way to bondage and to woe.

Evangelist now begins to explain the real issues to Christian. What differentiates his counsel from Worldly-wiseman's is the cross of Jesus Christ. People who go to church in "Morality" have a shallow form of godliness. They don't experience the transforming power of God's grace that only comes by way of the cross. The cross is an embarrassment to them, and they avoid it. They want a way much more palatable to their egos, one that bypasses their need to humble themselves and receive God's grace and mercy at the foot of the cross.

Finding a preacher who panders to self-righteous pride isn't difficult. The godly preacher, however, will have none of this. The apostle Paul became distressed with the Galatians when they gave heed to false teachers who promoted an alternate way to right standing with God. Like Paul, Evangelist holds the narrow view that only the way of the cross leads to salvation. He tells Christian that he must "utterly abhor" the doctrine of the worldly wise. In our society, a host of preachers and teachers employ various means of securing a following. Let us beware of any who offer a way that sidesteps the cross of Christ. Are you avoiding the cross in any area of your own life?

Scripture: Luke 11:39; Galatians 6:12-16; 1 Corinthians 1:22-24

Prayer: Lord Jesus, I thank you for the way of salvation you have secured for me through your death on the cross for my sins. Keep me strong in true faith, and please reveal your truth to those caught in the deception and false comfort of "Morality." Amen.

DAY 32

"First, you must abhor his turning you out of the Way—yes, and your own consenting to it, since it was rejecting the counsel of God for the sake of the counsel of a Worldly-wiseman. The Lord says, 'Work hard to get in through the narrow Gate'—the Gate to which I sent you. 'The Gateway to Life is small, and the road is narrow, and only a few ever find it.' This wicked man turned you aside from this little Wicket-gate and from the Way that leads to it and nearly brought you destruction. Therefore, you must hate how he turned you out of the Way and despise yourself for responding to him."

The gateway to eternal life is narrow. Contrary to worldly-wise opinions, we can neither save ourselves nor work ourselves into God's favor. Salvation isn't earned; it is a free gift granted to those who respond in faith to God's grace in Christ.

At the same time, finding true salvation takes a willingness to resist every voice and force that stands in the way of saving grace. This requires some effort and battling on our part. We cannot simply go with the flow but must take a course that rubs against the grain of popular culture and much of popular religion. As Jacob wrestled the angel for God's blessing, we must wrestle against the sins of our own hearts such as pride and unbelief, against those who would sidetrack us with worldly arguments, and against Satan himself. Far from being easy, the way to life can be intensely difficult. No wonder we tend to become passive or fearful or look for other low-cost solutions. Yet there is just no getting around it: Salvation takes an earnest desire to know Jesus Christ and a diligent commitment to follow him, no matter the cost.

It should not surprise us that the route to the narrow gate is an unpopular one. Since few ever find it, it is clear that few really decide to follow Christ. Many choose from a smorgasbord of spiritual options. Or they reserve the right to trade in what they have should something more alluring come along. Evangelist exhorts Christian to "despise" all such tendencies within himself. When it comes to eternal life, the narrow gate is the only true option. No one finds salvation apart from this gate.

"Despise" and repent of any offense you might feel toward the "narrowness" of Christ's way. First, acknowledge that he, as God, has a right to make his way narrow. Then acknowledge that since he didn't have to provide for your salvation at all, he is worthy of your utmost gratitude for providing a way.

Scripture: Matthew 7:13-14; Hebrews 2:1-3; Proverbs 3:7

Prayer: Dear Jesus, I dedicate myself to fight every hindrance to my faith. You said that few find life, and I intend to be in that number. I praise you for providing salvation through the narrow gate of the cross. Amen.

D·A·Y 33

"Second, you must abhor his effort to make the Cross seem repulsive to you—for you are to desire the Cross more than the treasures of Egypt. Besides, the King of glory has told you that 'If you insist on saving your life, you will lose it' [Matthew 10:39]. And 'Anyone who wants to be my follower must love me far more than he does his own father, mother, wife, children, brothers, or sisters—yes, more than his own life—otherwise he cannot be my disciple' [Luke 14:26]. I tell you, then, it is despicable for a man to try and persuade you that the truth shall lead to death, when, in fact, without it you cannot hope to find eternal life. This teaching you must completely renounce."

❦

Christian must desire the cross more than Egypt's treasures. Why? Simply because the cross of Christ is the heart of our faith. It holds eternal and cosmic significance as God's supreme manifestation of love toward sinful humanity. It wields a deathblow to the guilt and sin that so offends His holiness and severs our relationship with him. Through the cross, all people have access to redemption. When Christ announced, "And I, when I am lifted up from the earth, will draw all people to myself" (John 12:32 NRSV), he was claiming that people from all time and all places would be drawn to him by the power of his cross.

Philosophies and theologies that devalue the cross have abounded since Christ died on it. The apostle Paul saw the danger. He explained to the Corinthians how God had commissioned him to preach the Gospel "not with words of human wisdom, lest the cross of Christ be emptied of its power" (1 Corinthians 1:17). Worldly wisdom always attempts to empty the cross of its power. Representing the prevailing view of today's worldly-wise, one modern theologian said, "I don't think we need a theory of atonement at all. . . . I don't think we need folks hanging on crosses and blood dripping and weird stuff."[3]

Christian must abhor such views. While the worldly-wise despise the cross of Christ, God's pilgrims must despise worldly doctrines concerning it. The cross is the supporting structure of our faith. It is at the core of God's plan. Those who remove the cross embrace a powerless dead religion. Those, on the other hand, who honor the cross find abundant life and peace with God.

Will you say "Amen" to the words of "The Old Rugged Cross"—"O, the old rugged cross, so despised by the world, / has a wondrous attraction to me" and "To the old rugged cross I will ever be true, / its shame and reproach gladly bear"?

❦

Scripture: 1 Corinthians 2:2-5; 2 Corinthians 5:19-21; Job 5:13

Prayer: Dear Jesus, thank you for dying on the cross for me. I refuse to accept views that try to strip it of its power. I will keep it central to my faith. Amen.

D·A·Y 34

"Third, you must hate the way in which he set your feet in the path that will surely deliver you to death. And because of this, you must consider the one to whom he sent you, and how unable that person was to deliver you from your Burden.

"The one named Legality, to whom you were sent for relief, is the son of a Slave-woman who is now in bondage along with her children. It is a mystery, but she is Mount Sinai, this high Hill which you feared would fall on your head. Now if she and her children are in bondage, how can you expect them to set you free? This man Legality, therefore, is unable to set you free from your Burden. No one has ever been set free from a Burden by him—no, and never will be. You cannot be justified by the works of the Law, for by the deeds of the Law no person alive will be able to find relief from his Burden. For these reasons, Mr. Worldly-wiseman is an alien, and Mr. Legality is a cheat. As for his son Civility, in spite of his alluring appearance, he is no more than a hypocrite and cannot help you. Believe me, there is nothing in all this noise that you have heard from these stupid and foolish men but a design to deceive you away from your salvation by turning you from the Way that I had set before you."

Legality is a "cheat." Seeking to be justified by works of the Law "cheats" us out of the true freedom God intends for us in Christ. As Evangelist said, "By the deeds of the Law no person alive will be able to find relief from his Burden."

When Abraham lost patience with waiting for God's promise to give him a son, he became the father of Ishmael by his wife's maid, Hagar. Hagar and Ishmael were cast out for the sake of Sarah's son Isaac, the rightful heir. Paul teaches in Galatians that Hagar represents the Mosaic Law, and Ishmael represents the effort to be justified by religious effort; Sarah represents God's grace and Isaac the believer born by God's promise. Because Ishmael was born of a slave, he was a slave; because Isaac's mother was free, Isaac was free.

When Christ nailed to the cross the legal demands of Mt. Sinai, a new way of salvation replaced the old. Those who choose a works-based religion sever themselves from God's grace in Christ and are left in sinful bondage. All who profess Christ while still depending on religious practices to justify themselves are guilty of the same fatal error. You cannot be both a slave-child and a child of promise. You must choose either Ishmael or Isaac, bondage or freedom. What is your firm choice?

Scripture: Colossians 2:14; Galatians 4:21-31; Isaiah 29:14

Prayer: Lord, I gratefully choose freedom by the New Covenant in your blood. Please help me to speak your truth to those who are enslaved in legalism. Amen.

D·A·Y
35

After this Evangelist called aloud to the Heavens for confirmation of what he had said. With that, words and fire came out of the Mountain under which poor Christian stood, making the hair on his skin stand up. The words could be heard clearly: "All who rely on observing the law are under a curse, for it is written: 'Cursed is everyone who does not continue to do everything written in the Book of the Law'" [Galatians 3:10].

Now Christian expected nothing but death, and he began to cry out miserably, even cursing the moment he had met Mr. Worldly-wiseman. He kept calling himself a thousand fools for listening to his advice. He was also very ashamed to think that this man's arguments, proceeding from the flesh alone, could have prevailed in his thinking so as to actually cause him to forsake the right way.

Worldly-wiseman's alternate route to life is, in fact, a way to spiritual death. Evangelist has fully enlightened Christian to the facts of his condition. Christian stands beneath Mt. Sinai as the children of Israel had stood before it in the wilderness. Then, it quaked violently before them, spewing out thick smoke as lightning flashed round about. Unearthly trumpets blared from the mountain. Moses perceived God's voice saying that he would break out in wrath against these sinful people if they dared so much as to touch his holy mountain. This was a terrifying approach to God, and Christian is experiencing the same terror.

No grace but only curses exist on Mt. Sinai. Those who choose to reject grace and rely upon the Law have no hope but to stick to all of God's Law perfectly. This Law is inflexible, intolerant, unyielding. It shows no mercy and takes no prisoners. C. S. Lewis said, "Law can only kill till gospel comes to transcend it."[4]

Off the pilgrim's path, under the shadow of Mt. Sinai, Christian fears no hope remains for him. He full well sees his guilty condition and the lack of provision for it. He is under a miserable curse of death, and he curses himself for it.

If you are seeking God's approval, don't forget that Mt. Sinai is a most unfriendly place to look. If you are on its ground, you are in sin. Remove yourself from it, and humbly flee to Christ. You will never find redemption at Mt. Sinai. Stay as far away from it as you possibly can.

Scripture: Exodus 19:10-22; Galatians 3:10-11; James 4:7-10

Prayer: Dear Lord, I will not trust in my own efforts to keep your laws. I trust in your righteousness alone. As your pilgrim, I intend to walk your pathway of grace. Amen.

D·A·Y 36

Once again he turned to Evangelist. "Sir, what do you think? Is there any hope? Can I return and resume my journey to the Wicket-gate? Will I now be abandoned and sent back in shame? I am sorry I gave heed to this man's advice, but can I be forgiven?"

Evangelist replied, "Your sin is very serious. By your action you committed two evils; first, you abandoned the good way, and then you walked in forbidden paths. The man at the Gate, however, will receive you, because he wants the best for everyone. Do not turn aside again, or you might be 'destroyed in your way, for his wrath can flare up in a moment'" [Psalm 2:12].

Although no grace can be found at Mt. Sinai, the one who repents does not need to stay there. Christian is a repentant and broken soul, now desperate to be restored to the "good way," if only Evangelist permits. To the one who has seen the seriousness of his sin and experienced the harsh realities of legalism, hearing that there is forgiveness is extremely comforting. Evangelist offers comfort and hope along with stern warnings. He further convinces Christian that his sin is, indeed, very serious, perhaps even greater than he realizes.

The encouraging news for Christian is that, even though his sin is great, it isn't so great as to keep him from finding forgiveness. The Man at the Gate is amazingly gracious. He wants to see all people saved. He desires the best for every person and rejects no one who comes to him. It is clearly not his will that any should miss eternal life.

We see here two facets of God's nature that we must seek to understand and regard with appropriate appreciation and reverence. God is both holy and merciful. We can err either by overemphasizing his holiness and wrath upon sin, thus devaluing his mercy toward humble and repentant sinners, or by overemphasizing his mercy to the point where our "chumminess" with God erodes a proper reverent fear for his holiness and wrath upon sin.

In offering hope and comfort, Evangelist maintained his emphasis on the seriousness of sin and the peril awaiting those who forsake him. Let us never presume upon God's kindness or take his grace for granted. How seriously are you taking the demands of following Christ and his way?

Scripture: Colossians 2:8;
Romans 2:4; 1 Timothy 2:4-6

Prayer: Lord, may I never abandon your way to walk in forbidden paths. I don't want to forget what a serious sin that would be. I am ever grateful for the rich grace that keeps my heart faithful to my pilgrimage. Amen.

D·A·Y

37

Christian determined to go back, and Evangelist embraced him, smiled, and wished him a blessed and successful journey. So he hurried along, refusing to speak to anyone on the way, even if someone asked him a question. The entire time he walked like one treading on forbidden ground. He wouldn't believe he was safe until he was back on the Way which he had left to follow Mr. Worldly-wiseman's counsel. So eventually Christian arrived at the Gate. Now above the Gate was written: "Knock and the door will be opened to you" [Luke 11:9]. Therefore, he knocked more than once or twice.

He who would enter must first stand without
Knocking at the gate, but with no need to doubt.
For he who is a knocker will surely enter in
For God will love him and forgive all his sin.

Christian renews his pilgrimage with cautious determination. With the last experience etched deeply on his soul, he intends to avoid any additional painful departures. Without further incident, he gets to the Wicket-gate and sees the Lord's instruction to knock. He knocks, but he must knock again, and still again. Why isn't the Gate more inviting? Shouldn't someone be right there waiting to swing it open and welcome pilgrims in? Why is it shut at all, for that matter? A sinner standing outside God's grace, knocking and pleading for admittance, seems so contrary to our conception of Christ knocking and pleading at our heart's door. The fact is that sin has shut and barred the door to life, and God alone must open it.

Yet why must Christian keep knocking, and why doesn't the Gate immediately open at the first knock? Perhaps for Christian's own sake, God is testing his heart. A student once asked a wise sage, "How can I know God?" The sage pushed the student's head into a basin of water until he began flailing his arms in desperation. The sage, after letting him resurface, said, "When you want God as much as your lungs wanted air, you will find him."

As we continue knocking at his Gate, we discover for ourselves the depth of desire for God in our hearts. Do we really want him, his love, his kingdom? Are we earnest enough to go through with our commitment? As we realize the Gate is too small for our sinful affections, our worldly friends and idols, our fleshly pride and ambition, will we become halfhearted about our desire to enter? We find the answers to these questions within our hearts as we keep knocking. Have you been knocking? Don't give up.

Scripture: Matthew 7:7-8; Isaiah 55:6; Jeremiah 29:13

Prayer: Dear Jesus, it is the cry of my heart to follow you wholeheartedly. Where I must knock, let me knock until I see the way open before me. Amen.

D·A·Y 38

Christian cried,

"May I now enter? Will he within
Open to me though I have been
An unworthy rebel? Then will I
Not fail to sing His praise on high."

At last a solemn-looking person whose name was Good-will came to the Gate. He asked Christian who he was, where he came from, and what he wanted. Christian answered, "Here is a poor, burdened sinner. I come from the City of Destruction but am going to Mt. Zion so that I might be delivered from the wrath to come. Sir, since I have been informed that through this Gate is the way to get there, I would like to know if you are willing to let me in."

"I am willing with all my heart," Good-will quickly responded.

❧

Christian stands crying at the Gate, afraid he will be rejected. But Good-will rejects no one. Christian's past and present sins, various mistakes, problems, habits, and temptations don't matter so long as he doesn't turn from the Way. Good-will's reply to the plaintive cry says it all: "I am willing with all my heart."

Good-will seems to represent God's compassionate love for sinners through Jesus Christ. God waits to be gracious. Many, like Obstinate, have no interest in salvation; others like Pliable begin the journey only to turn back. Then there are those, like Worldly-wiseman, who hold some external form of godliness that ultimately denies the Gospel. Yet the Lord patiently waits for anyone who seeks him in earnest. Indeed, the Father actually seeks for those who will worship him in spirit and truth.

What a contrast we see between Christian's welcome here and the terrifying specter that greeted him at Mt. Sinai. He is going to Mt. Zion, representing the church, God's New Covenant holy dwelling, the City of God. Darkness covered Mt. Sinai, and God's revelation was shrouded in dark types and shadows; Mt. Zion shines with clarity and brightness. Mt. Sinai was approached with fear; joy resounds at Mt. Zion. Mt. Sinai was a dangerous place where a thundering distant God hid from all but Moses and Aaron. At Mt. Zion he is a welcoming and affirming Father who lovingly invites all to personally know him and commune with him in his kingdom of love, joy, and peace.

What an incomparable treasure! Have you accepted the invitation to Mt. Zion?

❧

Scripture: Isaiah 30:18-19; Hebrews 12:18-24; John 4:21-24

Prayer: Dear Lord, I am no longer shut out from your presence; you have opened the door of mercy and grace to me. Thank you for inviting me to walk with you in Mt. Zion with a joy-filled heart. Amen.

DAY 39

With that he opened the Gate. When Christian was stepping in, the man gave him a pull. "Why did you do that?" asked Christian.

The man replied, "Not far from this Gate stands a strong castle, of which Beelzebub is the captain. From there both he and his allies shoot at those who approach this Gate, thus hoping to kill them before they can enter."

Then Christian said, "I rejoice and tremble." So when he was in, the man guarding the Gate asked him who had directed him there. "Evangelist encouraged me to come here and knock, and I did. He told me that you, sir, would tell me what I have to do."

Good-will said, "See, I have placed before you an open door that no one can shut" [Revelation 3:8].

"Now I begin to reap the benefits of the risks I took," Christian replied.

Beelzebub is one of several biblical names for Satan. He has been rebellious toward God's plan for humanity since sin eternally entered his heart. This archenemy of God covets divinity and God's throne. He is no idle spirit; ruining pilgrimages is his most passionate cause. He looks for those considering salvation so he can attack them with daunting and disconcerting temptations. It is when one begins to seek Christ that the devil becomes militant in his opposition. That is why his fortress lies so close to the Gate to salvation. Even the place of grace cannot escape the grand conflict of the ages.

At the same time, most people are blind to this conflict and to the fact that Satan is alive and very involved in human affairs. As Thomas à Kempis explains, "The devil does not tempt unbelievers and sinners who are already his own."

Despite the devil's determination to undermine God's purposes, he is still only a created being with certain limitations. Beelzebub fails to attack Christian at the Wicket-gate. In his faithfulness, God has evidently shielded the pilgrim from notice. Those who cry to him for grace and mercy can rest assured that he is only too happy to oblige. When Christ opens the way to us, nothing in Satan's arsenal can shut it again.

Place yourself under God's protection for this day's journey and be watchful for the ways your enemy will try to trip you up through temptations that appeal to your old carnal nature.

Scripture: Psalm 118:19-20; Revelation 2:13; 1 Peter 5:8-11

Prayer: Lord God, you are the great and almighty one. Thank you that no weapon forged against me can prevail. No matter what the satanic scheme employed against me, you are greater still. I trust in your all-sufficient grace to pull me to safety. Amen.

DAY 40

"But why did you come by yourself?" asked Good-will.

"Because none of my neighbors could see their danger as I had seen mine."

"Did any of them know that you were coming here?"

"Yes, my wife and children saw me first and called after me to turn back. Then some of my neighbors stood crying and calling after me to return. But I put my fingers in my ears so I could continue on my way."

"But did not any of them follow you and try to persuade you to turn back?"

"Yes, both Obstinate and Pliable; however, when they saw that they could not succeed, Obstinate went away scoffing, but Pliable came with me a little way."

"Why didn't he continue?"

"We did come together until we came to the Slough of Despond, into which we accidentally fell. Then my neighbor Pliable became discouraged and refused to venture farther. He got out of the Slough on the side facing his own home and told me I should go on alone and possess the blessed Country for him. So he went his way and I came mine, he following Obstinate, and I on to this Gate."

None of Christian's family, friends, or neighbors related to what God was doing in Christian's heart. Although Pliable came closest to sharing Christian's dream of reaching the heavenly country described in the Book, he failed his first test. Ultimately, Christian arrived at the Gate intact but by himself.

A spiritual continental divide exists from which differing destinies flow. We may walk awhile together but, depending on what decision we make with regard to Christ, we may ultimately end up in opposite directions, a great distance apart. Christian says of his short walk with Pliable, "He went his way and I came mine."

Christian's pilgrimage thus far has largely been a lonely and frustrating one. He has experienced scorn, rejection, failure, despondency, deception, fear, and an enormously heavy burden. How heartening it is to be inside the Gate actually experiencing Good-will's genuine concern and compassion. When we feel abandoned and alone in our Christian pilgrimage, let us remember that God is on our side and that his untiring love and mercy will never fail us. Thank him right now for being your best Friend.

Scripture: Psalms 27:10; 46:1; Deuteronomy 31:8

Prayer: Dear Lord Jesus, help me to remember that you are with me in all my life's experiences. Others may misunderstand and reject me, but you don't forsake me. When I feel lonely and distressed, you are there with your loving consolation. Thank you, Lord, for your faithfulness. Amen.

D·A·Y
41

"Oh, the poor man!" exclaimed Good-will. "Is the celestial glory of so little value to him that he didn't count it worth the risk of hazarding a few difficulties in order to obtain it?"

"Honestly, I have told you the truth about Pliable, and if I should reveal all the truth about myself, it would appear that I am no better. It is true, he went back to his own house, but I also turned aside to go into the way of death, having been persuaded by the carnal argument of a Mr. Worldly-wiseman."

Good-will looked somewhat surprised. "Oh! Did he happen to find you? How remarkable! He would have you searching for ease at the hands of Mr. Legality! Both of them are cheats. Did you take his advice?"

"Yes, as far as I dared. I went to find Mr. Legality until it seemed to me that the Mountain that stands by his house would fall on my head. So I was forced to stop there."

"That Mountain has been the death of many and will be the death of many more," said Goodwill. "It is good that you escaped being dashed to pieces by it."

❧

Good-will reflects God's heart as he wonders aloud why people so easily trade in the celestial glory to escape a few temporal difficulties. The apostle Paul had the divine perspective when he proclaimed that his many trials were but a "slight momentary affliction" weighed against the glory that was coming to him.

Christian finds no basis for self-glorying. He feels his performance thus far has been disgraceful. His failures have humbled him greatly. He easily recognizes that grace alone has brought him to stand before Good-will. He accurately perceives, however, that he cannot accuse Pliable without indicting himself. Instead, he acknowledges his own guilt in being deceived.

What a difference the grace of God makes. Although both Pliable and Christian sinned, Pliable turned away from the pathway to life, while Christian humbly repented and resolved to follow it again. Christian's sin has been forgiven while Pliable's has not. Christian has fallen upon the grace of God while Pliable has abandoned it. *Grace* is the difference. Jonathan Edwards said, "Grace is but glory begun, and glory is but grace perfected." Christian is no longer a resident of the City of Destruction, doomed and facing God's judgment. He is a pilgrim on the pathway to life. He is on the road to the Celestial City of God!

Are trials pressing you hard today? Lift your eyes from your circumstances and look into the face of God. He is waiting for you to come to him for help. Think upon the glorious inheritance he is keeping for you in heaven if you persevere to the end.

❧

Scripture: 2 Corinthians 4:17-18; John 1:14, 17; Galatians 6:14

Prayer: Dear Lord, by your grace I will never under any circumstance trade the glory of living with you in heaven for an easier way now. I humbly thank you for your grace. Amen.

D·A·Y
42

"Well," said Christian, "I surely do not know what would have become of me there if Evangelist had not come along again. I was standing there, depressed and confused, wondering what to do. But it was God's mercy that he came to me, for if he hadn't come, I wouldn't have made it here. But here I am now, such as I am, indeed more worthy of death by that Mountain than to be standing here talking with you, sir. Oh! What a blessing this is for me, that I am still allowed to enter here."

Good-will smiled and said, "We do not reject anyone from entering here, in spite of all they may have done before entering. The King says, 'Whoever comes to me I will never drive away'" [John 6:37].

❦

Christian fully realizes there is nothing of merit inherent within him and that he is worthy only of death. However, he is learning more about his merciful and gracious God, and his heart overflows with gratitude. Christian had been lost and without hope in the City of Destruction and was helpless to do anything about it. It was God's mercy that drew him out and placed his feet on the way to the Celestial City. When he went astray from the Way of saving grace, it was God's mercy that drew him back again.

Grace and mercy can be variously explained. Grace is undeserved blessing freely bestowed on guilty humanity. Mercy is undeserved compassion freely bestowed on helpless humanity. Grace is God's attitude toward the lawbreaker and rebel; mercy is his attitude toward those in distress. Grace is God's way of giving us what we do not deserve—eternal life. Mercy is his way of not giving us what we do deserve—eternal destruction.

Throughout Scripture we see the inexpressible greatness and inexhaustible richness of God's grace and mercy. It was grace that moved him to send his Son to die for us, even while we were still sinners rebelling against him. It is mercy that welcomes us and all people into his arms when we come to him.

How much credit do you give to God's grace and mercy? Christian attributes his being brought to the Gate to God's mercy alone. His heart of humble thankfulness serves as an example to us. We are all completely dependent upon God's grace and mercy, and our hearts should overflow with thanksgiving for our wonderful Father in heaven.

❦

Scripture: Psalm 103:8-14; Ephesians 2:4-5; Hebrews 4:16

Prayer: Dear Father, I admit that if it weren't for your grace and mercy, I would have no hope. I bless you, Lord, for being rich in mercy and grace. Thank you for reaching my heart. It now belongs to you. Amen.

D·A·Y 43

"Therefore, good Christian, come with me awhile, and I will show you the way you must go. Look ahead of you—do you see this narrow way? It was constructed by the patriarchs and prophets and by Christ and His apostles, and it is as straight as a ruler can make it. This is the way you must go."

"But are there no bends or turns so a stranger might lose his way?" Christian asked.

"Yes, there are many ways adjoining this, and they are crooked and wide. But you can distinguish the right from the wrong, since only the right way is straight and narrow."

Christian came through the small, narrow Wicket-gate. Now he sees that the way he must travel is also narrow. Those who walk the broad and crooked ways have chosen paths most agreeable to their tastes. They can easily switch paths when their current one no longer suits them. However, God's pilgrims all walk the same narrow path. No one gets a special dispensation to avoid this way. On it we all face similar trials, temptations, and enemies; we are all compelled to walk in repentance, self-sacrifice, faith, and love.

Not only is this way narrow, but it's also as straight "as a ruler can make it." The broad ways of the wicked, on the other hand, have many bends and curves. The multitudes, often lost in a sea of religious and moral relativism, believe themselves free to chart their own course, to create their own "truths," thus avoiding accountability to God while deceiving themselves and others with them. The straight way doesn't allow this "freedom." It requires accountability to God and uniformity of purpose. All true pilgrims are in search of the heavenly city; all want their lives made suitable for that place; all want to be found faithful at the journey's end. Their goal precludes leaving this narrow way.

Christian asks whether there are any bends or turns that could cause one to get lost. Good-will's answer implies that those who are careless and self-willed are, indeed, easily led astray. The solution is very simple: Don't deviate from the straight and narrow way.

These are dangerous times today. Myriads of broad, twisting paths, offering a host of "salvations," crisscross our culture's spiritual landscape. These paths all attempt in some way to replace Christ. Many use his name; they borrow from His teachings. They are, nevertheless, false. Jesus is "the way, the truth, and the life"—the only way to God. He alone is the determiner of what is true and right. The straight and narrow way is God's way. Are you unreservedly committed to it?

Scripture: Ephesians 5:15-17; John 14:4-6; 1 John 2:18, 22

Prayer: Father God, thank you for giving us a way that is not confusing if we keep our eyes straight ahead. I purpose to walk this straight and narrow path. Please help me to stay true to it. Amen.

DAY 44

Then I saw in my dream that Christian asked Good-will if he could help him get the Burden off his back. For he still had not gotten rid of it and could not find any way to get it off without help.

Good-will told him, "As for your Burden, be content to bear it until you come to the place of deliverance. There it will fall from your back by itself."

Then Christian tightened his belt and began to prepare for his journey. So Good-will told him that, after walking some distance from the Gate, he would come to the House of the Interpreter, at whose door he should knock. There he would be shown excellent things. Christian then said good-bye to his friend, and Good-will wished him success on his journey.

Christian wants to be freed from his burden, and why should he wait? Shouldn't Good-will, who so earnestly pulled him through the Gate, also willingly unstrap the burden from Christian's back? The answer is no. One place and one place only exists where burdens such as Christian's come off. Christian is not yet there.

Today we tend to use the terms *guilt* and *guilt feelings* interchangeably. A vast difference exists between them, however. If Christian's condition were a simple matter of guilt feelings, Good-will would simply give Christian a hug and unfasten the burden. But Christian's problem goes much deeper than mere feelings; it is one of actual guilt. The verdict is in on sinful Christian. Not only has his sin damaged his own life, but it has offended and brought pain to the heart of God. His legal status is "guilty" as charged, and God requires that guilt be met with justice. The just reward for Christian should be a swift and full punishment.

Again, however, we see God's wonderful grace and mercy expressed in Good-will's assurances. He gently explains to Christian that he must wait until his arrival at the place of deliverance. Once he gets to that place, his burden will, indeed, fall off by itself.

The place of deliverance, of course, is at the cross where Jesus Christ offered himself as a guilt offering for sinful humanity. Whether or not we *feel* guilty before God is irrelevant to our need. Our guilt is an established reality, and we desperately need to come to God's authorized place of deliverance. Do you have unresolved guilt in your heart? Take it to the cross now and leave it there.

Scripture: Isaiah 53:4-6;
Psalm 53:2-3; Colossians 1:19-20

Prayer: Lord, I acknowledge that, whether or not I feel guilty, I have in many ways sinned against you. I thank you that you have provided a place of deliverance through Jesus Christ. I go to that place by faith to have my guilt removed. Amen.

DAY 45

Christian traveled on until he came to the House of the Interpreter, where he knocked repeatedly. At last someone came to the door and asked who was there. "Sir," said Christian, "I am a traveler who was told by an acquaintance of the owner of this House that for my own benefit I should call here. Therefore, I would like to speak to the master of the House."

So he called for the master of the House, who, after a short time, came to Christian and asked him what he wanted. "Sir, I am a man who has come from the City of Destruction, and I am on my way to Mount Zion. I was told by the man who stands at the Gate where this way begins that if I called here, you would show me excellent things that would be of help to me on my journey."

The man, who was called Interpreter, said, "Come in; I will show you what will be profitable to you." So he had his servant turn on some lights and beckoned Christian to follow him.

❦

Jesus said, "Blessed are the pure in heart, for they will *see* God" (Matthew 5:8). Through the Holy Spirit God reveals his truths to those who seek him. Paul writes, "We have not received the spirit of the world but the Spirit who is from God, that we may understand what God has freely given us" (1 Corinthians 2:12). The Interpreter symbolizes the Holy Spirit who interprets the things of God to honest seekers.

Christian is earnestly desirous of divine guidance. The first time he pounded on a door, he knocked to enter; this time he knocks to understand. With a scanty knowledge of eternal truth, he needs further guidance, and Good-will promised excellent instruction here. Interpreter, who is happy to instruct pilgrims so they can more fully understand the truth, gladly welcomes him.

Jesus described the Holy Spirit in two ways—first, in his ministry to the heart, and second, in his ministry to the mind. He is the Counselor (or Comforter) who helps, encourages, and strengthens; and he is the Spirit of Truth, who teaches and illuminates the truth.

When we are no longer satisfied with mere human instruction, like Christian, we can come to the Holy Spirit for guidance. He reveals, bestows, testifies of, and defends God and his truth. As we meditate on the Scriptures and learn to listen in prayer, he enlightens our hearts and minds. What a wonderful blessing to have the Holy Spirit as Friend and Guide. Have you in any way shut your heart to the Holy Spirit? Open it now, and ask him for his blessings.

❦

Scripture: John 14:16-17; 15:26; 16:12-15

Prayer: Come Holy Spirit, I need your presence; I need your truth. I earnestly desire to seek your instruction and heed your advice. Let me learn life's lessons from you. Amen.

DAY 46

He led him into a private room and told his servant to open a door. When he had done so, Christian could see hanging on the wall a picture of a very intense-looking man whose eyes were looking toward Heaven. He had the best of books in his hand, the law of truth written on his lips, and the world behind his back. He stood there as if pleading with men, and a golden crown rested upon his head.

"What does this mean?" asked Christian.

Interpreter explained, "The man in this picture is one in a thousand. He can bring children into being, suffer birth pains with them, and nurse them himself after they are born. And since you see him with his eyes looking toward Heaven, the best of books in his hand, and the law of truth written on his lips, you may be assured that his work is to know and reveal hidden things to sinners. That is why you see him standing there as if pleading with men."

Interpreter begins his tour with a picture of a faithful minister. In learning to discern counterfeits, it is best to study the authentic. Numerous carnal hirelings, blind guides, and false teachers dress in ministerial garb and speak from lofty church pulpits but are far from the Gospel. How can they be trusted to safely lead anyone? It is of utmost importance, therefore, for unseasoned pilgrims to learn as soon as possible to distinguish between true and false pastors.

Oh, but stare awhile at this picture! All who look for a guide, and all who aspire to be one, study it well. Observe a serious-minded man, not frivolous about his duty of leading souls to God. He could easily stumble, thereby damaging many souls, so he looks upward, utterly dependent upon God. His resource material consists of the Bible. It is at his fingertips, on his lips, in his heart. He lives for God's kingdom. This man expresses no duplicity in either word or deed. He has left the world's values and pursuits behind him and will never look back.

Observe an unashamed preacher of the Gospel. His heart pounds with God's compassion. Yet he is much more than a preacher; he is a dedicated shepherd. Presenting people with the truth, he doesn't leave them alone there. He births, teaches, prays for, leads, loves, and does anything else he can to nurture them. So focused is he in ministry that he is likely unaware of the crown he wears. Many would call this man a fanatic; God calls him "one in a thousand." By your prayers, help your own pastor to become a more dedicated shepherd—like this one.

Scripture: 1 Corinthians 4:15; 2 Corinthians 2:17;
1 Thessalonians 2:7-12

Prayer: Dear Lord, thank you for your faithful ministers. I pray that you will raise up more who are like the man in the picture. Please strengthen my own pastor where he is weak and in the places where he struggles with temptation. Amen.

D·A·Y
47

"And you see that the world is cast behind him and that a crown rests upon his head. That is to show you that by disregarding and despising the things of this present world because of the love he has for his Master's service, he will surely have glory for his reward in the world to come.

"Now," continued Interpreter, "I have shown you this picture first because the man in the picture has authority to be your guide in all the difficult places you may come to on your way. He alone has been authorized by the Lord of the place where you are going. Therefore pay careful attention to what I have shown you, and always keep in mind what you have seen. For you may encounter someone on your journey who will pretend to lead you the right way; in reality, however, his path will lead to death."

❧

Authority. Here is something we don't much care for—that is, unless we have it! We especially don't like to have it used to correct us. Christ has set us free after all! But are there no limits? We see the cultural breakdown of authority as increasingly people are their own authority, making their own rules and answering to no one. Cultural icons shake their fists at God and at anyone else who crosses them. But the fruit is bitter. Plunging headlong into a new type of bondage—one of abysmal decadence—many cry out, "Can't someone do something?"

Authority is important. The New Testament word for it, *exousia,* means the rightful and unimpeded power to act, possess, control, use, or dispose of. Clearly, such authority is God's alone. Ultimately, all authority is his. Jesus Christ, God's Son, has authority over everything in heaven and earth. All human authority derives from his. He delegates a measure of his authority to the church, and those who use it are accountable to him for how they use it. The man in the picture has been authorized to guide pilgrims. Still this leader, as all others, merely receives authority as he walks in humble obedience to the expressed will of God in the Scriptures.

Unrestrained freedom is a danger to the church, but so is unrestrained authority. Inordinate authority snares leaders and quenches legitimate Christian liberty. Abuses of authority seriously corrupt the Gospel and cause tremendous bondage. The proper use of authority, however, has a vital function. We need it for guidance, encouragement, and correction. Listening to godly authority can sometimes mean the difference between spiritual life and death. How bad a word is *authority* to you? Are you willing to submit to godly authority?

❧

Scripture: Hebrews 13:17; Titus 2:15; 2 Corinthians 4:5

Prayer: Dear Lord, please forgive my rebellious tendencies. I can't say I'm submissive to you when I resist godly leadership. Help my heart to invite guidance. Amen.

DAY 48

Then Interpreter took him by the hand and led him into a very large room that, because it was never swept, was full of dust. Upon inspecting it for a while, Interpreter called his servant to sweep it. When he began to sweep, such a cloud of dust arose that Christian almost choked. Then Interpreter told a young woman who stood watching, "Bring some water in here and sprinkle the room." After she had done so, the room was easily swept and cleaned.

"What does this mean?" Christian asked.

"This room is the heart of a man who was never sanctified by the sweet grace of the Gospel," answered Interpreter. "The dust is his original sin and inward corruptions that have defiled his entire person. The one who first began to sweep is the Law, but she who brought water and sprinkled it is the Gospel. Now remember you saw that no sooner had the first begun sweeping than the dust made such a cloud that the room could not be cleaned by him—and you were almost choked by it. This is to show you that the Law, instead of cleansing the heart from sin by its works, revives and adds strength to sin. Even as that soul sees and tries to get rid of the sin, it has been granted no power to overthrow it.

"Again, you observed the young woman sprinkle the room with water so that it could easily be cleaned. This is to show you that when the Gospel comes into the heart with all its sweet and precious influences—even as you saw the young woman still the dust by sprinkling the floor with water—sin is vanquished and subdued. The soul is cleansed through faith and is consequently fit for the King of Glory to inhabit."

❦

Here Christian hears about the important work of God's grace called sanctification. The Law, unable to sweep souls clean, only "raises the dust" and exposes sin. Yet the Gospel, like water that keeps the dust down, enables a cleansing or sanctifying work in the heart.

The Hebrew word for sanctification is *hagiasmos* (to purify). It involves being set apart for God's exclusive use and separated from evil worldly ways. Beginning at conversion, it includes both the putting to death of our old sinful nature and the imparting of our new nature in Christ. As we progressively die to selfishness and sin and increasingly live for Christ and his righteousness, we are being sanctified. This process of spiritual growth and purification continues till the end of our earthly pilgrimage when we will be completely sanctified as we see Christ face to face. How are you cooperating with God's attempts to make your heart "fit for the King of Glory to inhabit"?

❦

Scripture: John 17:17-19; 1 Corinthians 1:2; 1 Thessalonians 5:23

Prayer: Thank you, Lord, for setting me apart for your holy purposes. I'll do my part by putting to death my old sinful habits. Sanctify my heart and life until I'm exclusively yours. Amen.

D·A·Y

49

I next saw in my dream that Interpreter took him by the hand and led him into a small room where two little children sat, each one in his own chair. The name of the older one was Passion, and the younger, Patience. Passion seemed to be quite discontented, but Patience was very quiet.

Then Christian asked, "Why is Passion so unhappy?"

Interpreter answered, "Their guardian wants them to wait for the best things until the beginning of next year, but Passion wants everything now. Patience, however, is willing to wait."

Then I saw someone come to Passion, offering him a bag of treasure and pouring it out at his feet. Passion quickly picked it up, rejoiced over it, and began to laugh scornfully at Patience. I noticed, however, that before long Passion had wasted all of his treasure and had only rags left for clothing.

Christian turned again to Interpreter. "Explain this matter to me more fully."

"These two boys are symbols," answered Interpreter. "Passion represents the people of this world, and Patience represents those of the world to come. As you can see, Passion wants his treasures now, this year, that is to say, in this world. This is how the people of this world are; they must have everything they want right now. They can't wait until next year, that is, until the next world, for their good inheritance. That proverb, 'A bird in the hand is worth two in the bush,' carries more weight with them than all the divine promises of the blessings of the world to come. But as you observed, he quickly spent it all and was left with nothing but rags. And that is how it will be with all such people at the end of this world."

Now Christian observes Passion and Patience. Passion, addicted to self-gratification, represents those driven by insatiable carnal appetites. Whatever he wants, he wants now, and pouts miserably when told to wait for his heart's desire. He has no use for some heavenly hope of an eternal inheritance. Offered something that satisfies his craving, he idolatrously grasps it. Those like Passion judge the righteous as fools.

But what happens next? Wasting his treasure, he is left with only ragged garments. This is how it will be with the Passions of this world in the end. Oh, how deceitful are this world's treasures! God's people desire much better things.

How much passion and how much patience can you see in your life? Decide now to surrender your lustful cravings to God. Ungodly passions will increasingly govern your perspective and your actions until you do.

Scripture: Luke 16:25; Matthew 6:19-20; James 5:1-3

Prayer: Dear Lord, please forgive me when I begin craving the things of this present world. Help me to keep my eyes on your purposes for my life. Help me to successfully conduct my pilgrimage for your glory. Amen.

DAY 50

Christian said, "I can now see that for many reasons Patience has the best wisdom. First, because he waits for the best things, and second, because he will have glory, while the other has nothing but rags."

"Not only this," said Interpreter, "but you can add another. Know for certain that the glory of the next world will never wear out, but these present glories are suddenly gone. Therefore Passion did not have good reason to laugh at Patience simply because he had his treasures first. Patience will, in the end, laugh at Passion because he received his best things last. First must give way to last, because last is still to come, and last gives way to nothing, for there is nothing to follow. . . . It is said of a certain Rich Man, 'Son, remember that in your lifetime you received your good things, while Lazarus received bad things, but now he is comforted here and you are in agony.'"

"Then I can see," said Christian, "that it is best not to covet the things of this world but to wait for things that are to come."

Interpreter nodded. "You are speaking the truth. For the things that are seen are temporal, while the things that are not seen are eternal. But though this is true, since the present things and our own fleshly appetites are so compatible with each other, and since the things to come and our carnal senses are such strangers to each other, the first of these easily become friends while the latter are kept distant from one another."

Virtuous Patience has made the best choice. First, he waits for "the best things." Second, his waiting will bring him glory—eternal glory. In this light Passion's mocking is misguided and ridiculous.

Ours is a hedonistic, materialistic, status-seeking, self-indulgent society. To the church's dishonor, believers often mirror these same values. The Lord intends to greatly bless His people. He will give us everything our hearts could ever hope for, more than all the blessings the world has to offer, and still more—but most of these blessings await us in heaven, not here. The things that now glitter are fleeting, while the faintly perceptible eternal things are vastly superior and well worth waiting for.

You will experience a true triumph of faith if you, like Patience, cheerfully say no to worldly cravings in order to embrace true wisdom. As the Passions of this world see you denying yourself, rejecting worldly trifles, and waiting for eternal glory, they will laugh. Theirs won't be the last laugh, though, will it?

Scripture: Revelation 2:9; Luke 12:32-34; Malachi 3:17-18

Prayer: Dear Lord, help me to be content with waiting for the rich blessings of your eternal kingdom. I don't want to allow earthly things to damage my pilgrimage. Amen.

D·A·Y 51

Then I saw in my dream that Interpreter took Christian by the hand and led him in a place where a Fire was burning against a wall. Someone was standing beside it trying to put the Fire out by constantly pouring great amounts of water upon it. Yet the Fire continued to burn higher and hotter.

"What does this mean?" asked Christian.

Interpreter answered, "This Fire is the work of Grace that is formed in the heart. The one who throws water on it to extinguish it is the Devil. But as you can see, the Fire is burning higher and hotter in spite of this; and now you will see the reason why." So he took Christian around to the back side of the wall where they saw a Man with a container of oil in His hand. Secretly this Man was continuously pouring oil into the Fire.

Then Christian asked, "What does this mean?"

Interpreter answered, "This is Christ, who with the Oil of his Grace, continually maintains the work already begun in the heart. Because of this, in spite of what the Devil can do, the souls of His people will continue to walk in His Grace. The fact that the Man was standing behind the wall to maintain the Fire is meant to teach you that it is difficult for those experiencing temptation to see how this work of Grace is being maintained in their souls."

When Christ enters our lives, he ignites our hearts with blazing intensity. We are acutely aware of his loving presence. The devil, despising this work, tries hard to extinguish our devotion. If he can get our enthusiasm down to a spark, he figures he can snuff it out completely. So he douses us with his water. Harassing temptations, trials, distractions, disappointments are all in his bucket. Yet despite his best efforts, he fails. The fire not only continues burning, but it mysteriously burns hotter. How can this be? The Lord secretly feeds the flame with the oil of his grace.

When water is poured on an oil fire, the flames react intensely. They sizzle, hiss, leap, and steam but continue burning. As the devil throws his water at us, we react. It seems he has every advantage, and we are being undone. Yet time goes by, and amazingly we are preserved. Our hearts still burn with love for God; we have grown deeper in faith and more humble and Christlike in character; our desire to serve and follow him is more intense.

Christian is shown the fire by the wall so he will understand that God's grace keeps his people aflame. Because it is his grace, he gets the glory. Thank him for his oil in your life.

Scripture: Romans 8:26-28; 2 Corinthians 12:9-10; Philippians 1:6

Prayer: Dear Lord, thank you for the oil of your Spirit at work in my heart. When I am distressed, help me to trust that you are still pouring it. Thank you, Lord. Amen.

D·A·Y 52

I saw Interpreter again take Christian by the hand and lead him into a pleasant place where a stately Palace had been constructed. It was beautiful to behold, and when Christian saw it, he was greatly delighted. He observed some people walking up on top of the Palace, and they were all clothed in gold.

Christian asked, "May we go in there?"

Interpreter took him and led him up toward the Palace door. A great number of people stood there, all desiring to enter but not daring to try. A man sat at a table near the door with a Book and Pen, ready to take the name of anyone who would go in. Christian saw also that many men in armor stood in the doorway guarding it, having resolved to inflict injury and mischief on those who would enter. Christian was amazed!

At last, after every other person had drawn back in fear, Christian saw a man with a resolute countenance come up to the one seated at the table. He said, "Write down my name, sir," and it was done. Then Christian saw the man draw his Sword and put a Helmet on his head. The man rushed toward the door, and the armed men came upon him with deadly force. Not at all disheartened, he fought back, cutting and slashing with fierce determination. After a bloody confrontation with those attempting to keep him out, he fought his way through them all and pressed forward into the Palace. Then there could be heard pleasant voices from within, even from the Three that walked on top of the Palace. They said, "Come in, come in, Eternal glory you shall win."

So the man went in and was clothed with garments like their own.

Lest Christian think from the example of Patience that he can wait passively for God's blessing, he is taken to this palace to learn that tenaciously confronting obstacles is an important aspect of faith. While many want inside the palace, only one man of resolute purpose fights his way in.

Does this suggest that salvation is less than a free gift of grace? No; salvation is all grace received by faith. But just as the Israelites had to take by faith the land already given them, so we must actively, not passively, receive by faith entrance into God's kingdom. True faith aggressively overcomes the combined resistance of the world, the flesh, and the devil.

Unless we step to the table firmly resolved and boldly approach the gate with burning passion, we will be like those who wouldn't dare to try. Will you pray for increasing faith as you count the cost of a faithful pilgrimage? Then trusting His grace, will you fight the good fight of faith with patient determination? Remember—the reward goes to those who "win" eternal glory.

Scripture: Matthew 11:12; Acts 14:22; Revelation 3:5; Psalm 138:3

Prayer: Dear Lord, I need grace to resolutely overcome the obstacles to my faith. Please grant me more boldness. Amen.

D·A·Y 53

Christian smiled and said, "I'm sure I understand the meaning of this. May I now go on from here?"

"No stay," said Interpreter, "until I have shown you a little more. After that you can be on your way." So he took Christian by the hand and led him into a very dark room where a man sat in an Iron Cage. By all appearances he was very sad. He sat with his eyes staring at the ground and with his hands folded, sighing as if his heart would break.

Christian asked, "What does this mean?"

Interpreter told him to talk with the man. Then Christian asked him, "Who are you?"

He answered, "I am what I once was not."

"What were you before?"

"At one time I was a man who professed Christ and whose faith was pure and growing, not only in my own eyes, but also in the eyes of others. I was, so I thought, fit for the Celestial City and even felt joy when I thought of my arrival there."

"Well, what are you now?"

"I am a man of despair, and I am locked up in it as I am in this iron cage. I cannot get out. Oh, I cannot."

"But how did you get into this condition?"

"I ceased to watch and be sober. I allowed myself to be driven by my lusts, and I sinned against the light of the Word and the goodness of God. I have grieved the Holy Spirit, and He is gone from me; I allowed an opening for the Devil, and he has come to me; I have provoked God to anger, and He has left me. I have so hardened my heart that I cannot repent."

Christian is shown this tragic man to impress him with the importance of staying cautiously watchful. This man, by his own admission, has grieved the Holy Spirit and fallen away from the living God. He has so continued in sin against God that his heart, he believes, is hopelessly hardened and beyond repentance. The Interpreter doesn't say his case is hopeless; sometimes people languish in fear of eternal separation when there is every reason for hope. No one who is truly repentant will end up locked in an iron cage forever. Yet here is a man who perhaps because of double-mindedness or self-hatred finds himself in utter despair, incapable of repentance.

The clear message Interpreter wants to impress upon the young pilgrim is that it is extremely perilous to willfully indulge in sin. We should be careful never to venture even one step from the straight and narrow way. Don't play with your sins. Confess and repent of them quickly.

Scripture: Luke 8:13; 1 Thessalonians 5:6-9; 1 John 2:24

Prayer: Lord Jesus, help me to have a godly fear of leaving your way. May I never wander from your will for my life. Amen.

DAY 54

Then Christian asked Interpreter, "But is there no hope for a man like this?"

"Ask him," said Interpreter.

So Christian asked him, "Must you be kept in the Iron Cage of despair? Is there no hope?"

"No, none at all."

"Why? The Son of the Blessed is very merciful."

"I have crucified Him to myself afresh; I have despised His very Person; I have despised His righteousness; I have counted His blood as an unholy thing; I have shown utter contempt for the Spirit of grace. Therefore, I have shut myself out from all the promises, and nothing remains for me but threatenings, dreadful threatenings, fearful threatenings of certain judgment and fiery wrath which shall consume me as an adversary."

Christian was greatly perplexed. "Why did you allow yourself to be brought into this condition?"

"For the lusts, pleasures, and profits of this world, in the enjoyment of which I promised myself great delight. But now every one of those things bites and gnaws at me like a fiery serpent."

"But can you not now repent and turn around?"

"God has denied me repentance. His Word gives me no encouragement to believe. Yes, He has shut me up in this Cage, and not all the men in the world can free me. Oh, eternity, eternity! How will I ever bear the misery that I must face in eternity?"

Then Interpreter looked at Christian and gave him this charge: "Remember this man's misery, and let it be a caution to you forever."

"Well, this is frightening!" Christian responded. "God help me to watch and be sober and to pray that I might shun what caused this man's misery."

It is tragic but true that the highest purpose for some lives is to serve as warnings to others. For 2,000 years the church has debated the question, "Can one who is truly converted lose his salvation?" Some—Arminians—believe yes, while others—Calvinists—say no. To Arminians, this man was truly born again but subsequently fell away. To Calvinists, he was merely a *professed* believer on the threshold of salvation. Whichever our view, the outcome is essentially the same. Those who openly reject Jesus Christ are unsaved apostates even if they had formerly held the appearance of being saved. "I warn you as I did before," Paul writes, "those who live like this will not inherit the kingdom of God" (Galatians 5:21). Will you take the warning to heart?

Scripture: Hebrews 6:4-6; 10:26-29; 1 Corinthians 6:9-11

Prayer: Dear Savior, I take this warning to heart. While many profess salvation but don't live it, I intend to walk genuinely, by your grace. Amen.

D·A·Y 55

"Sir, isn't it time for me to be on my way?" asked Christian.

"Not yet," said Interpreter. "Stay until I show you one more thing, and then you may leave." So he took Christian by the hand again and led him into a bedroom where someone was getting out of bed. As the man got dressed, he shook and trembled.

Then Christian asked, "Why is this man trembling?"

Interpreter told the man to explain to Christian why he was trembling. So he said, "Last night while I was sleeping, I dreamed, and suddenly the sky became completely black. The thunder roared and the lightning flashed in such a frightening way that I was filled with dread. Then I looked up and saw the clouds moving by at an unusual speed. Next I heard a great trumpet blast and saw a Man sitting upon a cloud, accompanied by the hosts of Heaven. They were all arrayed in flames of fire, and the heavens were aflame as well."

Interpreter introduces Christian to a man who has been seriously shaken by a terrifying apocalyptic dream. Doomsday themes abound today. It seems people are becoming increasingly comfortable with the idea that the world may soon come to an end. While some sacrifice their lives to doomsday cults, many others simply enjoy speculating about the end of the world. Hollywood cashes in by pouring millions of dollars into increasingly dramatic special effects in hopes of securing record audiences. One scene always omitted from Hollywood apocalyptic blockbusters, however, is that of Christ coming back on the clouds of glory. What a scene that would be! What a scene it *will* be!

The Bible promises that the end of the world will be accompanied by Christ's spectacular reentry from heaven into our atmosphere. He will produce, direct, and star in this phenomenal event. But he won't playact, and he won't rely on Hollywood for special effects. He won't command audiences of a few million or even a billion. With the universe as his theater, and with a cast of millions of saints and angels, he will command an unsurpassable record audience—the whole world including all who have ever lived.

Scripture allows for differences in thinking related to some aspects of Christ's coming. What is certain, however, is that his coming will be a cataclysmic surprise to the world, that everyone on earth will see him coming in the heavens, and that we should prepare our hearts and lives—as it may well happen in our lifetime. One church has these words around its clock face: "One of these hours the Lord is coming." Christ's second coming is an indisputable, irreducible, inescapable fact. Are you ready?

Scripture: Matthew 24:26-30; 1 Thessalonians 5:1-3; 2 Peter 3:11-12

Prayer: Lord Jesus, I want to be ready for your coming. What a day that will be! Help me to live in keeping with the truth that you are coming very soon. Amen.

D·A·Y 56

"And I heard a voice saying, 'Arise, you dead, and come to judgment.' With that the rocks split, the graves opened, and the dead within them came forth. Some of them were very glad and looked to the heavens; others tried to hide themselves under the mountains. Then I saw the Man seated upon the cloud open the Book, and He commanded the world to draw near. Yet because of a fierce flame that issued forth from before Him, the dead were set at a distance from Him, like the span between a judge and the prisoners he will sentence.

"I heard it also proclaimed to those accompanying the Man on the cloud, 'Gather together the tares, the chaff, and stubble, and cast them into the burning lake.' And with that, a Bottomless Pit opened near where I stood. From the mouth of the pit spewed forth great amounts of smoke, coals of fire, and hideous noises. It was also commanded, 'Gather My wheat into the barn' [Matthew 13:30]. Then I saw many caught up and carried away in the clouds, but I was left behind. I looked for a place to hide myself, but I was unable to do so because the Man who sat upon the cloud constantly kept His eye upon me. My sins also came to my mind, and my conscience accused me from every direction. After this I awoke from my sleep."

"But what was it that made you so afraid of this sight?" Christian asked.

"Why, I thought that the day of judgment had come and that I was not ready for it. What frightened me most, however, was that the angels gathered some but left me behind. Also, the pit of Hell opened its mouth right at my feet, and my conscience continued to afflict me. It seemed that the Judge always had His eye on me, His face full of indignation."

❦

Life with Christ is our endless hope, but without him life comes to a hopeless end. What vast differences exist between the unbelievers' pseudo-hope based on wishful thinking and the believers' legitimate hope based upon God's unimpeachable promises. Here is a man whose terrifying dream has shattered his false hopes. There is no nirvana, purgatory, or life ending in the grave—only judgment!

All humanity faces history's terminal moment together. Some look upward in joyful expectation; others desperately search for some place to hide. It is an absolute fact of God's Word that there will be inexpressible ecstasy for believers but overwhelming agony for unbelievers.

This flies in the face of the more palatable modern-day "universalist" religions that view all people as ultimately saved. God's Word is, nonetheless, true. Pray today for people in your life who will face this terrible judgment.

❦

Scripture: Matthew 25:31-34, 41; 2 Thessalonians 1:6-10; Revelation 20:11-15

Prayer: Oh Lord, thank you for the glorious hope you've given to those who trust your salvation. I choose to be counted in that number. Amen.

D·A·Y
57

Then Interpreter asked Christian, "Have you paid close attention to all these things?"

"Yes, and they fill me with both hope and fear."

"Well, keep all these things in your mind so that they may be a goad in your sides and prod you forward in the way you must go."

Then Christian tightened his belt and began to make preparations for his journey. So Interpreter blessed him, saying, "May the Comforter always be with you, dear Christian, to guide you in the Way that leads to the City."

So Christian went on his way, saying,

"Here I have seen things rare and profitable
Things pleasant, yet awesome to make me stable.
What I have begun to take in hand
Let me then think on and understand—
That I've been shown truth, so let me be
Thankful, O good Interpreter, to Thee."

Christian will never forget the truths shown him in the Interpreter's house. They will stand out as motivational truths for his entire pilgrimage. He admits that they have combined to cause him *hope* and *fear*. Observing the blessings of the righteous give him hope. The man in the picture gives assurance of godly guidance. The Gospel, sufficient to vanquish sin, will keep his soul from being like a room filled with dust. With Patience, he knows his future reward will be worth the wait. When Satan douses his spiritual fire, the fire against the wall will remind him that the Lord will sustain him. Rather than shrinking in fear, he can take courage from the man who seized his inheritance at the Beautiful Palace. Hope, like an anchor, will keep Christian from floundering in life's storms.

Still a reverent fear will remain with him, too. He won't forget the lessons of Passion's ultimate poverty, of those too afraid to win their place in the palace, of the man in the iron cage, and the man whose terrifying dream brought "a fearful expectation of judgment" (Hebrews 10:27). In that this fear is God-given, wholly unlike that of unbelievers, Interpreter doesn't tell Christian not to fear. While the fear that strikes unbelievers makes them want to flee, the fear we as believers possess makes us run *to* God. It enables us to reverence his authority and obey his commands and to hate and shun evil. It is the "beginning of wisdom" (Psalm 111:10). In what ways do you both hope and fear?

Scripture: Psalm 147:11; 1 Peter 1:13-17; Hebrews 12:28-29

Prayer: Dear Lord, help me to ponder carefully the lessons you provide for me. I pray that they will prod me to both hope and fear. Amen.

DAY 58

Now I could see in my dream that the Highway Christian was to travel on was protected on either side by a Wall, and the Wall was called Salvation. Burdened Christian began to run up the Highway, but not without great difficulty because of the load he was carrying on his back.

He ran this way until he came to a place on somewhat higher ground where there stood a Cross. A little way down from there was an open Grave. And I saw in my dream that just as Christian approached the Cross, his Burden came loose from his shoulders, fell from his back, and began to roll downward until it tumbled into the open Grave to be seen no more.

After this, Christian was glad and lighthearted. He joyfully exclaimed, "Through His sorrows He has given me rest and through His death He has given me life!"

Christian received much illumination at the Interpreter's house. As his hopes and fears have intensified, he is more aware than ever of his need for complete reliance upon God's grace through faith in Jesus Christ. Still burdened with his perpetual sense of guilt, he runs without delay straight up the Highway that is walled by salvation. He sees the cross—the place of deliverance. As he approaches, his burden unfastens, rolls down the hill into a grave, and disappears—forever! The guilt of his former sins is gone. He is forgiven.

Christian receives release from his burden of sin because he trusted in Christ's finished work on the cross. The cross of Jesus Christ is at the heart of the Gospel. "God demonstrates his own love for us in this: While we were still sinners, Christ died for us" (Romans 5:8). Christ, the sinless Son of God, was degraded, humiliated, tortured, and murdered as he paid the penalty for our sins. The paradox of the Christian faith is that God turned the most evil act in history into the greatest possible good for the world. "With his stripes we are healed" (Isaiah 53:5 KJV).

The Scriptures affirm that Christ's crucifixion is the saving event of history. No way exists apart from the cross for dealing with the sin that severed humanity's ability to relate with God. Christ's sacrifice was not a partial payment but a full and perfect payment once and for all time. Through the cross, eternal life is extended to all, and the world is transformed—one soul at a time.

Have you lost your burden at the cross? Isaac Watts, in his great hymn, testified, "At the cross, at the cross, where I first saw the light, / and the burden of my heart rolled away. / It was there by faith I received my sight, / and now I am happy all the day."

Scripture: Isaiah 26:1; 35:8, 53:3-4; Colossians 2:13-14

Prayer: Dear Father, thank you for sending your Son to redeem fallen humanity. I acknowledge that the cross alone justifies me before you. Amen.

D·A·Y 59

Then he stood still for a while to examine and ponder the Cross; for it was very surprising to him that the sight of the Cross alone had brought him complete deliverance from his Burden. So he continued to look and watch until springs of tears welled up in his eyes and came pouring down his cheeks.

Who's this? The Pilgrim! Oh, it's so true,
Old things are passed away; all is now new.
Strange! He's another man, you have my word,
They are fine feathers that make a fine bird.

True converts to Christ, after realizing the dramatic changes taking place in their lives, will stand in awe. There is so much to think about and so many questions they don't have answers for, questions such as: How did this happen to me? What is this incredible power? Why is Christ's love for his enemies so intense that he died for them? Why did he want to see transgressors pardoned, God and sinners reconciled? Why did he choose me? Why is such a costly salvation free? How can all this blessing come simply by relying upon the blood of Christ? Why do I suddenly feel so clean, so light?

Christian has such questions. He is astounded at how easily his tormenting burden is suddenly removed at the cross of Christ. He is set free, converted, a new creation. Everything is different; nothing is the same. He stops and wonders awhile at this amazing cross.

The cross of Christ is powerful. It is not merely an aspect of history to be memorialized. In the cross, untold millions have discovered the liberating power that rescues their souls from the crushing burden of their sins. Such amazing deliverance cannot be taken casually by those who have been so delivered. They stand and "survey the wondrous cross" not once, but over and over again. With Christian, they weep and weep again. Charles Spurgeon said, "No scene in sacred history gladdens the soul like Calvary."

Truly, the cross of Christ is the only ladder high enough to touch heaven. And only those who hear and receive its message can hope to enjoy its salvation. Stop and gaze awhile at the cross. Reflect on all that it means to you; thank God for its liberating power.

Scripture: Hebrews 2:9; 1 Peter 2:24; Zechariah 12:10

Prayer: Dear Jesus, thank you for dying on the cross for me. I give my heart to you afresh and trust in the power of your cross to wash away my guilt. Help me as I point others to your cross that they, too, might come to receive your salvation. Amen.

D·A·Y 60

Then, as he stood watching and weeping, three Shining Ones suddenly appeared and greeted him. "Be at peace!" the first announced. "Your sins are forgiven!"

The second one stripped off his tattered clothing and dressed him in bright, new garments. After this the third one set a mark upon his forehead and handed him a Scroll with a seal on it. He directed Christian to study the Scroll as he traveled and to present it upon his arrival at the Celestial Gate. They then left Christian, and he leaped for joy three times as he went on his way singing,

"I came this far burdened with my sin;
No, nothing could ease the grief I was in,
Until I came here; what a place is this!
Must here be the beginning of my bliss?
Must here the Burden fall off of my back?
Must here the cords that bound it to me crack?
Blessed Cross! Blessed grave! Blessed rather be
The Man who there was put to shame for me."

Oh, happy day! How Christian's life has changed! Now he receives certain gifts to further convince him that he is now a child of God: peace with God through the forgiveness of his sins; a clean garment, representing his salvation; a mark on his forehead, which is the seal of God; a scroll that assures him of acceptance at the Celestial Gate.

The three angels symbolize the work of all three members of the Trinity for our salvation. The Father forgives our sins, the Son strips us of our sinful garments and clothes us with His righteousness, and the Holy Spirit seals us with a mark of ownership and protection and gives us assurance of our salvation.

Christian responds with joy to all the blessings he has just received. His primary focus, however, is not on the blessings but on Christ. When he cries, "Blessed Cross! Blessed grave! Blessed rather be the Man . . ." he indicates the supremacy of Christ in his heart. We should never allow anything, no matter how good or exciting, to displace our love and devotion for Jesus Christ. Christ alone has opened the door to God for us. He is the object of our affections, the center of our lives.

Worship the Lord. Thank him for each special gift you received at the cross.

Scripture: 1 Peter 1:18-19; Colossians 1:20;
Zechariah 3:3-4, Ephesians 1:13

Prayer: Dear Lord, I sometimes forget the enormity of the gift of salvation I have received. Help me to appreciate all you have done for me and to keep you uppermost in my affections. Amen.

D·A·Y 61

After these things, I saw in my dream that Christian journeyed on in this happy state until he came to the bottom of a Hill where he saw, a little off the Way, three men fast asleep with fetters on their feet. One was named Simple, the second was Sloth, and the third, Presumption.

When Christian saw them lying down like this, he approached them to see if he could possibly awaken them. He cried out, "You are like those who sleep on the top of a ship's mast. Can't you see that the deadly sea—a bottomless abyss—is beneath you? Wake up, then, and leave here! Have a willing heart, and I will help you out of your fetters." Continuing his exhortation, he said, "If he who goes about like a roaring lion comes by, you will certainly become prey to his teeth."

Good-will had instructed Christian to stay on the right Way—the Way as straight as a ruler. Now Christian sees, a little off the Way, three careless men sleeping. You do not have to go far to be completely out of the straight and narrow way. Simple, Sloth, and Presumption, though not far off, are in desperate straits. Simple is out of the way because he lacks spiritual depth; Sloth, because he decided to do what most comforted him; and Presumption, because he thinks he can get away with doing whatever he wants.

The worst thing, however, is that these three, each representing their third of humanity, don't even realize their danger. If they believe in an enemy at all, they don't take him seriously. Yet they are right where he wants them. He has already chained their feet, and they lay there like sleeping children cradled in his sinister lap.

Some contend that Jesus' victory on the cross made the devil a toothless lion who can merely roar. Yet if he were toothless, the apostle Peter would not have included in his letter to the churches of Asia Minor a stern warning: "Be sober, be watchful. Your adversary the devil prowls around like a roaring lion, seeking someone to devour" (1 Peter 5:8 RSV). If he were harmless, we wouldn't be advised to soberly guard against him.

The devil, in fact, is still an extremely dangerous creature. While he is no match for Christ, we are no match for the devil. He was the highest of the created beings, and, as such, his power is extraordinary. He is intelligent, deceitful, subtle, hateful, and depraved beyond imagination. Absolutely no room exists in our pilgrimage for simpleness, sloth, or presumption. Take stock of your condition. Do you ever exhibit these faults?

Scripture: Proverbs 22:3; 24:30-34; Numbers 14:44; Hebrews 6:12

Prayer: Dear Lord, I intend to keep awake and alert on my pilgrimage. Help me not to fall asleep because of the temptations to be simple, slothful, or presumptuous. Amen.

D·A·Y 62

At that they looked up at him and began to reply. "I don't see any danger," said Simple.

Sloth yawned as he said, "I just want to sleep a little bit more."

Presumption arrogantly retorted, "Every barrel must stand on its own bottom."

And so they lay down to sleep again, and Christian went on his way. He was troubled to think, however, that men in such danger should have such little respect for one who so freely offered to help them. Not only had he awakened them and offered them wise counsel, but he had also been willing to help them remove their fetters.

❧

With the joy of his salvation experience fresh in his heart, Christian tries to witness to and help these three. Simple, Sloth, and Presumption, each representing a form of religious indifference, are not receptive. Simple doesn't have the wisdom to heed godly advice. Sloth is too lazy to listen, and Presumption is convinced he doesn't need help from anyone. He is content to presume on God's mercies. All three brush godly correction aside as irrelevant. These are not minor but serious errors in judgment. Disobedient to God's expressed will, they allowed themselves to become easy prey for their enemy.

Some people outwardly appear to be pilgrims. They stay near to where the truth is preached; they listen to the Gospel and learn to talk the gospel talk. Nevertheless, their commitment is shallow and their conviction fleeting. Their love for God quickly dies out because they still love the world, comfort, and pleasure. With their sense of spiritual purpose gone, they rest comfortably in their bondage to sin and to Satan. They reject godly counsel and despise making any effort to be faithful. Yet they are confident that all is well with their souls because they presume upon God's grace. If anyone tries to warn them, they retort, "You're disturbing our peace. Mind your own business." So they sleep on, and who can rouse them?

Believers must confess and repent of their sins if they have gotten off track. Help is available to us only when we hear the wake-up call, rouse ourselves from our slumber, and receive our deliverance. Do you hear a wake-up call? How will you deal with these three undesirable traits—simpleness, sloth, and presumption?

❧

Scripture: Proverbs 1:22; 6:9-11; Ephesians 5:14; Psalm 19:13

Prayer: Dear Lord, when I am out of the center of your will, please correct me. If you choose to send a Christian brother or sister for that purpose, help me to receive correction. I do not want simpleness, sloth, and presumption in my life; I renounce them. Amen.

D·A·Y 63

While Christian was still troubling himself over these, he saw two other men come tumbling over the Wall on the left-hand side of the narrow Way; they were able to quickly catch up with him. The name of one was Formality, and the other's name was Hypocrisy. So the three began to converse.

"Gentlemen," asked Christian, "where have you come from, and where are you going?"

They answered, "We were born in the Land of Vain-glory, and are on our way to Mount Zion to receive praise."

"Why didn't you enter at the Gate that stands at the beginning of the Way?" asked Christian. "Don't you realize it is written that 'anyone refusing to walk through the Gate, who sneaks over the Wall, must surely be a thief'?"

Formality and Hypocrisy answered that all the people from their country consider the Gate to be too far away. The usual way was to take a shortcut, just as they had done, by climbing over the Wall.

❧

A new believer first sets out with the idea that everyone on the highway to life is conducting an authentic pilgrimage. Christian is still perturbed over his encounter with the three sleepers when he sees two men enter the Way by an unauthorized method. The home town of Formality and Hypocrisy is a city where the citizens take great pride in their own virtue. Vainglory, however, is empty, unwarranted glory. Take note that people may be quite religious in their outward profession but be lovers of themselves in their hearts. The two men expose their true motives when they claim they are on their way to Mount Zion "to receive praise."

The names of these two further expose their condition. Formalists rigorously practice recognized religious forms and rituals without possessing true salvation. While they may be sincere, their religion is all in vain. Hypocrites, however, are altogether insincere. Deliberately deceiving themselves and others, they profess faith while really having nothing to profess. People like Formality and Hypocrisy can call themselves believers, get baptized into the faith, and devoutly work hard at their religion, but, despite it all, lack saving faith.

The Scriptures warn that in these last days godless people will make an outward show of religion without allowing its transforming power to convert them. We should always resist the tendencies in our own hearts to be "religious" at the expense of true faith. If you similarly met these two men, what would you say to them?

❧

Scripture: John 3:3-6; 10:1; 2 Timothy 3:5

Prayer: Oh, Lord, I hunger for a sincere walk of faith. Let my pilgrimage be true without a hint of falsehood. Let me live solely for your glory and not my own. Amen.

D·A·Y

64

Christian was troubled by this and asked, "But since you are violating His revealed will, won't this be viewed as a trespass against the Lord of the City where we are going?"

They told Christian that he didn't need to worry about that because what they were doing was a custom dating back at least a thousand years, and, if need be, they could produce testimony that would bear witness to the correctness of their approach.

"But will it stand up in a court of law?" Christian asked.

Formality and Hypocrisy replied that a long-standing custom over a thousand years old would by now undoubtedly be deemed legal by an impartial judge. "Besides," they argued, "what does it matter which way we take to get into the Way, just so we are in it? If we are in, we are in. You also are in the Way, though we perceive you came in at the Gate. But we are in the Way, too, though we came tumbling over the Wall. Now in what way is your condition any better than ours?"

Formality and Hypocrisy have embarked on their pilgrimage to do something praiseworthy. Since they want applause for themselves and have no real interest in glorifying God, they look for the easiest way to accomplish that end. They find a shortcut to give them the look of authenticity without having to pay the exacting price of coming in at the beginning of the Way. The Wicket-gate is simply too far from Vain-glory to suit them. Repentance, conversion, and a sincere walk of faith are simply too much trouble. Yet, the Wicket-gate marks a beginning and an end, a before and an after, a decisive turning point without which there can be no true pilgrimage.

These two, as Christian discerns, are violating the Lord's revealed will. Will the Lord simply make an exception for them, or will he view them as trespassers? They justify themselves by explaining that they aren't the first folk to come this way. In fact, everyone from their region has always come this way. They are like multitudes in our day who give little thought to the dubious nature of their religious traditions. "We've always done it this way" is good enough for them. Their ancient rituals and customs, rather than the Word of God, form the basis of authority for their religion.

The vain worship, self-effort, rationalization, and deceit of formalists and hypocrites won't stand up in God's court of law. If you were to stand before God's court, upon what would you rest your case? It is important that you evaluate your beliefs, traditions, and practices in light of God's Word. For he calls you not to religion, but to an authentic relationship—with himself and with others.

Scripture: John 10:9; Jeremiah 7:22-24; Isaiah 3:13

Prayer: Lord, help me to take stock of my walk. I don't want rituals or traditions to replace a genuine vital walk with you. Amen.

D·A·Y
6 5

At this, Christian challenged them. "I walk according to my Master's Rule; but you walk according to your own vain imaginations. The Lord of the Way already counts you as thieves, so I doubt that you will be found to be true men at our journey's end. You have come in by yourselves without His direction, and you shall go out by yourselves without His mercy."

They didn't have much to say to this except to tell Christian to mind his own business. Then I saw that the three men walked on without much discussion with one another, except that the two men told Christian that as to laws and decrees, they would doubtless obey them as conscientiously as he. "Therefore," they said, "except for the Coat on your back, which we trust was given to you by some of your neighbors to hide the shame of your nakedness, we don't see how you differ from us."

Formality and Hypocrisy raise Christian's ire by saying they see no difference between him and them. But he sees a great difference. He is still a babe in the Lord without all the answers, but he possesses, nonetheless, a strong conviction. He calls their vainglorious ideas "vain imaginations," and, noting that their posture robs God of glory, he calls them "thieves." Is he being judgmental? No, he looks to his "Master's Rule" for guidance and sees that *it* judges them.

Even a young pilgrim armed with the truth of God's Word is qualified to represent the Lord in these cases. Christian can tell that these two don't care about the Master's Rule regarding salvation. If they did, they would obey it. They set themselves up as judges when they determine that obedience to the Word is unnecessary for them. In their minds, they know better than God.

The root of all sin is wanting to go our own way, for our own glory. This is an issue of lordship. Obedience is not optional. God demands and expects it. He may require things that seem foolish to us, but our task is to obey him, not to evaluate his wisdom.

To Formality and Hypocrisy, all three men are committed to the same purpose—to reach the Celestial City—and this is what matters. But Christian is right. If we don't start right, we can't expect to end right; if we don't obey God at the beginning of our pilgrimage, we never will. Evaluate your obedience. Is yours an obedient heart and an obedient lifestyle? Commit yourself to walking in full obedience to God's will for his glory.

Scripture: Isaiah 65:1-2; Judges 21:25; 1 Samuel 15:22-23

Prayer: Dear Lord, show me where I am deficient in my desire to obey you. I want my pilgrimage to be one of faithful obedience to you. I open my life to the scrutiny of your Word. Amen.

D·A·Y
66

Again Christian made a swift retort. "Since you didn't come in by the door, you will not be saved by laws and decrees. And as for this Coat on my back, it was given me by the Lord of the place where I'm going. It was given, as you said, to cover my nakedness, and I received it as a token of kindness to me—I had nothing but rags before. Besides this, it encourages me as I journey on. I think to myself, 'Surely when I arrive at the Gate of the City, the Lord of the place will know and accept me because I will be wearing His Coat.' It is a Coat that He freely gave me on the day that He stripped off my rags. Moreover, I bear a mark on my forehead that perhaps you haven't noticed. One of my Lord's most intimate associates fixed it there on the day that my Burden fell from my shoulders. In addition to this, I must tell you that they gave me a Scroll that bore a seal to authenticate it. It was given me to read for encouragement as I journey on the Way. They told me also to present it at the Celestial Gate to prove that I am to be admitted without question. Though you need these things, I doubt you have them since you didn't come in at the Gate."

Formality and Hypocrisy had no answer to the things Christian had said; they just looked at each other and laughed.

While Christian was born again at the cross, Formality and Hypocrisy are content with their own righteousness. Besides the coat Christian received, they see little difference between themselves and him. Despite the coat's uniqueness—representing the righteousness of Christ, received by faith—they show it little regard.

Christian points to the differences existing between them. First, he has the coat, not obtainable by himself. The Lord gave it as a gift. At the Celestial Gate, the Lord will recognize him by the coat. Next the mark in his forehead is another token of the Lord's love and acceptance. Affixed by the Holy Spirit, it cannot be replicated by human efforts. It sets Christian apart for God, distinguishing him as God's own. Then there's the scroll. It reminds Christian of his salvation and assures him of immediate entrance at the Gate.

Formality and Hypocrisy simply laugh. Those like them have a misplaced confidence that will bring a rude awakening. It is up to us to inform them of their lack by exhibiting the life and hope the Lord has given us. Do you struggle with sharing your faith? Perhaps you can begin by telling others of the wonderful things Christ has done for you.

Scripture: Galatians 3:27; Isaiah 61:10;
Jude 23; 2 Corinthians 1:21-22

Prayer: My Savior, you have given me your righteousness, sealed me with the Holy Spirit, and given me assurance. Help me to show others what you have done for me. Amen.

DAY 67

Then I saw that as they continued on their way, Christian went on ahead of the others. He had nothing more to say to them but spoke to himself, sometimes with sighs and sometimes with words of encouragement. He would often refresh himself by reading from the Scroll that one of the Shining Ones had given him.

They all traveled on until they came to the foot of a Hill, at the bottom of which was a spring. In that place could be found two other ways besides the one that came straight from the Gate. There at the bottom of the Hill, one way turned off to the left and the other way to the right. The narrow Way, however, led straight up the side of the Hill, which was called Difficulty. Christian went to the spring and drank from it to refresh himself. Then he began to move up the Hill, saying,

"The Hill, though high, I desire to ascend;
The difficulty will not me offend;
For I perceive the way to life lies here:
Come, be strong, heart, neither faint nor fear.
Better, though difficult, the right way to go,
Than wrong, though easy, where the end is woe."

Early on, new believers face difficulties that try their faith and confirm the reality of their conversion. Christian discovers this for himself. After two fruitless encounters with false pilgrims who refused his witness, he feels some confusion and emotional turmoil. It's not easy to understand those who claim to be on the same path, yet whose lives and beliefs differ in such major ways. It's upsetting when they refuse to take your testimony seriously and when they dispute the truths God has so clearly revealed and confirmed in your life. Christian looks at his scroll often for renewed assurance.

Eventually he reaches a hill called Difficulty. Anyone taking seriously the call to follow Jesus will come to Difficulty. We face situations requiring sacrifice, self-denial, and discipline; misunderstanding from those who mock our decision for Christ; the persistence of our old sinful nature, supposedly dead and buried, rising up to make our past life alluring; emotional turmoil at losing old friendships—and more. We cannot escape Difficulty. God's Way leads straight up the hill.

Christian wisely refreshes himself at the spring of water before moving forward. For needed strength to face the trials ahead, we need daily refreshment in the streams of living water. God is faithful, and as we seek him, he will provide what we need. Drink daily from God's refreshing springs.

Scripture: Isaiah 49:10-11; Philippians 3:12-14; 2 Timothy 2:3

Prayer: Lord, I need to make wise choices as I face trials in my pilgrimage. Help me to rely on your provision, not on fleshly alternatives. Amen.

DAY 68

The other two men also came to the foot of the Hill. However, when they saw that the Hill was steep and high and that there were two other ways to go, they supposed that the three ways might once again converge on the other side of the Hill; therefore, they resolved to go the two other ways. The name of one way was Danger, and the name of the other was Destruction. So one man took Danger and was led into a giant forest; the other went straight up the way to Destruction, and was led into a vast field full of dark mountains where he stumbled and fell to rise no more.

Shall they who begin wrongly rightly end?
Shall they have safety at all for their friend?
No, no, in headstrong manner they first set out,
And headlong they will fall in the end, no doubt.

Formality and Hypocrisy professed to be pilgrims, but they persisted in fashioning their pilgrimage to suit themselves. Having no regard for the authority of the Scriptures, they changed at will whatever they didn't like. Obviously, since they didn't start the journey right, they had no interest in continuing it right. They went as far as the foot of Hill Difficulty, as close to suffering as their religion would ever take them. They did not, however, intend to quit the straight Way altogether but to return to it after avoiding Difficulty. Sad to say, their foolish assumption that the paths would again converge around the hill has robbed them of ever seeing the Celestial City.

It is frightening to think that many who claim to be Christians end up completely off the straight and narrow way, because they want to reach heaven without cost. They lack a reverent fear of God and fail to take seriously the authority of God's Word. "God," they reason, "we know you want us to be satisfied and fulfilled and certainly wouldn't want to interfere with our peace and happiness. So we are going *this* way, and we are *sure* you understand and will be with us and bless us."

In essence, they are saying to almighty God, "Lord, we want you in our lives, but you come follow us." But God is not a mere helper or servant who aids us as we fashion our own feel-good religion. He is our Master and his Word has authority in and over our lives. The consequences are severe for those who disregard his will.

Have you ever foolishly departed from God's will in hopes of avoiding some difficulty? What would you do differently if the situation repeated itself?

Scripture: Proverbs 14:12; Jeremiah 13:16; 2 Timothy 4:4-5

Prayer: Sovereign Lord, your way is the best way. When the enemy tempts me to believe a better way exists that avoids the hardships, help me to go straight forward. Amen.

DAY 69

After this, I looked for Christian and saw him going up the Hill. I could see his pace slow from running to walking—and then from walking to crawling on his hands and knees—because the Hill was so steep. Now about halfway up the Hill was a Pleasant Arbor, a resting place made by the Lord of the Hill to refresh weary travelers. When Christian got there, he sat down to rest. Then he pulled out his Scroll from where he kept it hidden in his Coat next to his heart; he read from it for encouragement. He also looked over the bright new garments that were given to him when he stood at the Cross.

After relaxing for a while, he began to doze and was soon fast asleep. He was detained by his sleep until almost nightfall, and as he slept, the Scroll fell out of his hand.

As he was sleeping, someone came and woke him up, saying, "Take a lesson from the ants, you lazy fellow. Learn from their ways and be wise!" Upon hearing this, Christian suddenly leaped up and hurried on his way, traveling swiftly until he came to the top of the Hill.

So often, as young Christians, we feel like a crusader ready to charge up any mountain for the Lord. We declare, "I want to set the world on fire for you, Lord!" As we begin running, however, we find these hindering difficulties confronting us. Each step takes more exertion, and the difficulties begin to surpass our energy to deal with them. Soon it is with the utmost difficulty that we progress at all. We ask, "Why is this happening to me when only a short time ago I felt so bold?" Yet the Lord uses difficulties to discipline and train us. We should not let them discourage us from our pilgrimage.

Because the Lord is aware of human frailties, he graciously provides some respite. Resting in the Pleasant Arbor, Christian reviews the assurances given him in the scroll and enjoys looking at his new garments. Becoming too relaxed, however, he falls asleep. Often young believers in a season of rest reflect upon God's goodness to them and begin presuming too much about themselves. As a result, devotion suffers, diligence wanes, and suddenly sleep "detains" them. What God graciously provided for refreshment for better meeting life's difficulties instead brings on a careless spiritual drowsiness. Darkness encroaches upon their souls, and the assurances they had held close to their hearts start slipping away. But for the grace of God this condition would abort the pilgrimage. We can thank the Holy Spirit for faithfully sounding his alarm in our hearts. Thank him now for times he has mercifully intervened in your life.

Scripture: Proverbs 6:4, 6; Luke 22:46; Colossians 4:2

Prayer: Dear Lord, thank you for providing times of refreshing. Remind me never to allow those times to cause me to slack off from my spiritual purpose. Amen.

DAY 70

Now when he had reached the top, two men came running up hurriedly to meet him. The name of one was Timorous and the other Mistrust. Christian asked, "Sirs, what is the matter? You are running the wrong way."

Timorous answered that they had been going to the City of Zion and had gotten past this difficult place. "But," he said, "the further we go, the more danger we meet. Therefore we have turned around and are going back again."

"Yes," said Mistrust, "for just ahead of us we saw a couple of Lions lying in the Way. We don't know whether they are asleep or awake, but we couldn't help thinking that if we came within their reach, they would immediately tear us to pieces."

"You are scaring me," said Christian, "but where shall I run for safety? If I go back to my own country, which is awaiting fire and brimstone, I will certainly perish there. If I can get to the Celestial City, I am sure to find safety there. I must take the risk. To go back is nothing but death; to go forward is fear of death, but beyond that lies everlasting life. I will go forward."

Timorous and Mistrust somehow wrestled their way through all their difficulties but fell apart when faced with danger. It is sad how some people will begin their pilgrimages earnestly applying themselves and even depriving themselves. They read the Bible, pray, and even share Christ. Yet when faced with persecution, they imagine the worst and immediately shrink back in fear. Instead of being galvanized to faith, Timorous and Mistrust fall into fear and unbelief. These two in their panic never consider how easily God can restrain even the worst persecutors.

Christian is worried, but to consider going back is out of the question. The same is true for all of Christ's pilgrims. We have made up our minds. Our direction is forward. We cling to our faith in Christ, refusing to entertain thoughts of forsaking him. We fear what is behind much more than what lies ahead. We recognize that sure defeat awaits those who turn back. We keep pressing onward, believing that victory is somewhere ahead. Sometimes we encounter things in our Christian walk that terrify us, but where shall we go? Back to the world, back to sin, back to certain death and destruction? Of course not! We know the futility of such a choice. Why, then, do so many go back?

What things make you afraid of completely surrendering to God's will for your life? What are some actions you can take to counteract them?

Scripture: John 6:68; 2 Timothy 1:7; Psalm 91:14-16

Prayer: Dear Lord, may I never give in to my fears by turning back from your will. When besieging fears confront me, give me strength to press on in faith. Amen.

D·A·Y 71

So Mistrust and Timorous ran down the Hill, and Christian went on his way. Reflecting on what he heard from the men, however, he felt a need to find comfort by reading from his Scroll. He reached into his Coat to find the Scroll, but it was gone. At this, Christian became deeply distressed and didn't know what to do. He knew that he needed the Scroll for encouragement and also to use as his pass into the Celestial City.

Finally, after much turmoil and confusion, he remembered that he had fallen asleep in the Pleasant Arbor on the side of the Hill. He fell on his knees and asked God to forgive him for his foolishness. Then he started back to look for his Scroll. But who could sufficiently express the sorrow in Christian's heart as he journeyed all the way back? Sometimes he sighed, sometimes he cried, and often he chided himself for being so foolish as to fall asleep in the place that was erected only for a little refreshment from weariness.

Christian had been wise in refusing to follow the two cowardly backsliders. Still their terror-breathing words influenced him. The spiritual consequences of this encounter had left him feeling insecure and vulnerable. Indeed, often we don't notice a slippage in our confidence until we need it and it's not there. Christian, feeling his need, reaches for his scroll, but it is gone!

God wants us to be assured of our salvation. He wants us to possess a humble confidence that despite our sin and failure, we are his children. Our assurance is objectively proven by the promises of God's Word. By its authority, believers know Christ died for them, made full atonement for them, and that by opening their hearts to his lordship, he saves them. Assurance is subjectively proven through the deep abiding confidence given by the indwelling Holy Spirit. He, too, convinces us of our forgiveness, adoption, and salvation.

One can be truly saved but lack full assurance. This makes for a miserable Christian existence. Without assurance, we cannot progress very far in our pilgrimage. Our progress depends upon faith in God's promises. Without faith we cannot please God, and without assurance we cannot walk in faith. Christian knows he cannot go on without assurance, so he woefully goes searching for his missing scroll.

How about you? Do you hold your assurance close to your heart? Or by carelessly letting it slip away, do you deprive yourself of needed confidence for withstanding terrorizing fears?

Scripture: Hebrews 10:22-23; 1 John 5:11-13; Romans 8:15-16

Prayer: Dear Lord, the assurance of my salvation is very dear to me. I intend to keep it very close to my heart. Thank you for saving me. Amen.

D·A·Y 72

He traveled in this way until once again he came within sight of the Arbor where he had rested and fallen asleep. But the sight of it compounded his sorrow by reminding him again of the evil of his sleeping. He therefore expressed deep regret for his sinful sleep, saying, "Oh, what a wretched man I am, that I could sleep in the daytime! And that I could sleep in the midst of difficulty! How could I so indulge myself to use that rest to give ease to my flesh when the Lord of the Hill built it only for reviving the spirits of pilgrims! How many steps I have taken in vain! It happened like this to Israel; because of their sin, they were sent back again by way of the Red Sea. And I am now forced to tread these steps sorrowfully three times when I could have happily walked them only once. How far might I have been on my way by this time! But now I am likely to be overtaken by nightfall, for the day is almost gone. Oh, that I had not slept!" Now by this time he had come to the Arbor again, where he sat and wept for a while.

Christian realized the impossibility of going forward without first finding his scroll. In a near state of panic, he returns to where he had last read it. Seeing the Arbor brings no comfort, however. Although he had asked God to forgive him, he begins lamenting and castigating himself for his sinful sleep.

All Christian sees is the trouble he has brought upon himself. It is his fault that instead of simply resting and finding refreshment in the Lord at the Arbor, he carelessly and self-indulgently slumbered. He should have kept alert, gotten up from there full of peace and confidence, and gone on to make good progress. It is also his fault that he didn't make sure his scroll was safely in his keeping. Now he must cover the same ground three times!

God forgave Christian's sins when he confessed them. He continues to lament, however, because without his scroll he feels no assurance that he is forgiven. When we are shaken awake after spiritually slumbering, we can easily lose stability. The result can be a confusing storm of anxious and guilty feelings about ourselves and our relationship with God. Because our progress depends upon what we believe about our standing with God, these feelings will drive us until we accept God's grace to cover our mistakes. Until then, we will experience a loss of heart, a loss of faith, and a loss of spiritual progress. If you feel uncertain about your standing with God, what steps might you take?

Scripture: 1 John 1:9;
Romans 8:1; 1 Timothy 3:13

Prayer: Lord, thank you for your faithfulness in forgiving my sins as soon as I sincerely confess and repent of them. Help me always to hold on tightly to this assurance. Amen.

D·A·Y 73

Finally, while looking under a bench, Christian's hopes were realized—he spotted his Scroll! When he saw it, he hastily grabbed it with trembling hands. How can one describe Christian's joy when he found his Scroll again? For this Scroll gave him the assurance of eternal life and meant acceptance into the Celestial City. Therefore he held it close to his heart and gave thanks to God for directing his eye to the place where it lay. Then with joy and tears he committed himself once again to his journey. And, oh, how swiftly he went up the rest of the Hill!

Yet before he reached the top of the Hill, the sun went down on Christian. This made him again remember the stupidity of his slumbering, and again he began to lament, "Oh, you sinful sleep! Because of you I will probably have to travel at night! I must walk without the sun and with only darkness covering the path for my feet, and I will listen to the sounds of the sad creatures of the night—all this because of my sinful sleep!"

Then he remembered the story that Mistrust and Timorous had told him, how the sight of the Lions had frightened them. He thought, "These beasts roam about in the night for their prey, and if they should meet me in the dark, how could I get them out of my way? How would I escape being torn to pieces by them?"

Christian's scroll now means more to him than ever. Its recovery fills him with joy, at least until the sun goes down. Despite his wonderful restoration, he sees the consequences of his sinful negligence. For the Lord disciplines those whom He loves (Hebrews 12:6). Now, because he must journey at night, he begins doubting and fearing again.

When we lose sight of our assurance, we cry, "Restore to me the joy of your salvation!" (Psalm 51:12). And how is it regained? By renewing our attention to the assurances of God's Word—memorizing, meditating on, studying, and applying them; and by renewing our trust in Christ and devotion to our pilgrimage. We are especially vulnerable when our hearts begin to condemn us. The enemy whispers, "You don't really think God has forgiven you, do you? Your mistakes are simply too great." The only hope of resisting such attacks is by going back to the assurances of God's Word held in our hearts. God's promises convince us of our eternal life and victory in Christ Jesus.

Since the devil can so well exploit our weaknesses, take some time to gather some helpful promises that speak to your particular vulnerabilities. Let them minister to your soul over and over again.

Scripture: 1 Thessalonians 5:7-8; Hebrews 12:12; 1 John 3:21

Prayer: Dear Lord, help me to do all I can to learn the assurances of your Word. I know they will be of great benefit during my times of doubt and fear. Amen.

D·A·Y 74

Christian walked on in this way, but while he was still lamenting his foolish mistake, he looked up and saw a stately Palace ahead of him beside the Highway. Its name was Beautiful. So I saw in my dream that Christian moved quickly toward it, hoping to find lodging there. Before he had gone far, he entered a narrow pass, which was about two hundred yards from the Gatekeeper's Lodge. But then he saw two Lions in the way! "Now," he thought, "I can see the dangers that drove Mistrust and Timorous away." (The Lions were chained, but he was unable to see the chains.) He became very frightened and considered turning back to catch up with the others, for all he could see was death lurking in front of him.

Until now Christian's pilgrimage has been a solitary one. That will change if he is admitted into the Palace Beautiful, as he hopes. The Palace represents the fellowship of believers. But just before he gets there, he suddenly sees the lions that so terrified Mistrust and Timorous. Fearing death, he considers turning around and fleeing as they did.

The lions in the way represent persecution. It is one thing to keep our faith to ourselves; it is quite another to profess our faith openly by publicly joining other believers. To participate in an "illegal" fellowship of believers in many countries invites real persecution, possibly death. In our culture we may not generally face anything so severe, but we can face ridicule and ostracism by friends, family, and associates. The "lions" of persecution are terrifying. Yet they are bound. It is too bad Mistrust and Timorous did not stick around long enough to find out that the Lord had restrained the lions. They fled from beasts that could not even touch them! Persecution sifts genuine believers from those who are not.

What frightens you? Remember that the Scripture's recurring theme is one of standing firm in the face of persecution. The best way to prevail over fears is to face them boldly. Our Lord Jesus warned his disciples of coming persecutions so that they wouldn't be taken by surprise. He promises you, as he promised them, to be with you through every trial. While fear hides the fact that the lions are bound, faith reveals it. We must learn to trust God's Word. The lions are indeed bound, but as 2 Timothy 2:9, inscribed on a Roman catacomb wall, proclaims, "The Word of God is not bound."

Scripture: Psalms 22:20-22; 37:39-40; 1 Peter 3:13-14; Philippians 1:28

Prayer: Father God, I need to trust you when I see ferocious "lions" in the way. Grant me faith to realize that you will protect my soul from them. Amen.

D·A·Y
75

Now the gatekeeper at the Lodge, whose name was Watchful, perceived that Christian had come to a halt as if he would turn back. Calling to him, Watchful said, "Are you so weak and timid? Don't be afraid of the Lions, for they are chained and have been placed there for a test of faith—to distinguish those who have it from those who do not. Keep to the middle of the path, and you will not be hurt."

Difficulty is behind, Fear is before;
He is now up the Hill, but Lions do roar;
A Christian is never for long at ease;
When one fright's gone, another will him seize.

Then I saw that Christian moved on, trembling in fear of the Lions but heeding Watchful's advice. The Lions jumped up and roared, but they did him no harm. After this experience, Christian clapped his hands for joy and walked on.

Fortunately, Christian endures long enough to hear the godly instruction that the Lord provides for him. The Gatekeeper, Watchful, exhorts him to keep moving and explains that this threat is simply a test of faith. Watchful represents the efforts of the vigilant pastor to "keep watch" for souls and to help them enter fellowship. This pastor wards off Christian's fears and admonishes him to press on in faith. He assures Christian that, despite all appearances, the lions will not eat him alive.

A pastor (Greek: *poimen*) is one who tends the Lord's flock. Guiding and feeding, this God-appointed shepherd exerts both vigilant oversight and tender care. God uses pastors to protect and nurture the church as a whole as well as its individual members. Pastors play a significant role in Christ's plan to build and fortify his church.

Today many "Lone Ranger" Christians think they can make the pilgrimage by themselves. They don't think they need anyone watching out for them. Perhaps they simply haven't yet met their "lions," but they will. Far from being easy, the Christian life is plagued by difficulties—"when one fright's gone, another will him seize." God gives pastors to us for our benefit, to spur us on, to keep us growing and faithful. Often, if not for the sensitive prodding of a loving pastor, taking another step forward would seem impossible to us. Will you commit yourself to pray for the pastors who have impacted your life with the Gospel and find ways to show them your appreciation and support?

Scripture: 2 Timothy 4:17-18; Isaiah 41:10; Ephesians 4:11-14

Prayer: Dear Jesus, thank you for the overseer you have provided for my church. I commit myself to support him lovingly and to heed his encouragement. Amen.

D·A·Y

76

Christian arrived at the gate where Watchful stood waiting. Then Christian asked Watchful, "Sir, what is this Palace? May I sleep here tonight?"

He answered, "This House was built by the Lord of the Hill; He built it for the relief and security of pilgrims. Where have you come from and where are you going?"

"I have come from the City of Destruction and am going to Mount Zion, but because the sun is now set, I would like to stay here tonight if I may."

"What is your name?"

"My name is now Christian, but my name at first was Graceless. I am of the race of Japheth, whom God will persuade to dwell in the tents of Shem."

"But why have you come so late? The sun has already set."

"I would have been here sooner, but—I am such a wretched man!—I fell asleep in the Arbor that stands on the hillside! In spite of this, I would have been here much sooner, but while I was sleeping, I dropped the Scroll I received at the Cross. I traveled all the way to the brow of the Hill without knowing it was gone. Then when I felt for it and found it missing, I was forced to return with deep remorse to the place where I had fallen asleep. I found it there, and now I have finally arrived."

Whereas the Interpreter's House represented inner revelations of the Holy Spirit, the Palace Beautiful represents the church and membership in it. Watchful conducts a cautious interview with Christian before deciding to admit him into the fellowship of the faithful.

Christian's original name, Graceless, indicated that he was a Gentile. Noah's son Japheth was father to the Gentiles while through his son Shem came the Jews. Noah promised spiritual blessing to Shem, but he also blessed Japheth. Christian hopes to "dwell in the tents of Shem," meaning he, though a Gentile, hopes to join God's people by faith, thus sharing in Israel's rich spiritual heritage. God promised Abraham to bless all nations through him. Jesus Christ fulfills that promise—for Christian and for all who believe.

When asked the reason for his late arrival, Christian explains. Our fellowship in Christ's body can also be delayed by our sinful carelessness. The Lord wills for his people to come together for prayer, for worship, and to hear his Word preached. When in fellowship, we gain stability and are encouraged to persevere. Our hearts and hands are mutually strengthened, and we provide a united witness to the world. The communion of the saints is a great blessing and privilege. Is anything detaining you from participating?

Scripture: Genesis 9:27; Acts 2:42-47; 1 Thessalonians 5:11

Prayer: Lord, thank you for your church. As it is your will, I commit myself to be involved in a local fellowship of believers. Amen.

D·A·Y 77

"Well," said Watchful, "I will call for one of the young women who lives here. If she accepts what you have to say, then, according to the House rule, she will bring you in to meet the rest of the family." So Watchful, the gatekeeper, rang the doorbell, and a serious but beautiful young woman named Discretion answered and asked why he had called her.

Watchful answered, "This man is on a journey from the City of Destruction to Mount Zion. He is weary, however, and it is dark outside. He asked me if he might sleep here tonight, so I told him I would call for you."

Discretion asked Christian where he had come from and where he was going, and he told her. Next she asked him what he had seen and met thus far on the way, and he answered her. Then she asked him his name.

"It is Christian," he replied, "and my desire to stay here tonight is even stronger because I can tell that the Lord of the Hill built this place for the relief and security of pilgrims."

While the Palace is hospitable, it is also well guarded. Discretion is the one who will make the final decision as to Christian's admittance. She is sent for because she is gifted by nature to decide these cases responsibly. Her circumspection enables her to listen carefully to Christian's answers as she questions him further. Will admitting Christian to fellowship bring helpful or hurtful consequences to the church? Discretion decides.

Old Webster dictionaries[5] define *discreet* as: "Possessed of discernment, especially in avoiding error or evil, and in the adaptation of means to ends . . ." This spiritual application is generally lost in modern English. Nevertheless, the church desperately needs to rediscover and apply this usage. Today we too easily dismiss our duty to establish the legitimacy of candidates. Thinking the matter is between a person and God, we feel we have no place in judging.

This attitude exposes a sub-Christian and irreverent view of Christ's body. Christ esteems his body as a cherished prize; he purchased it with his own lifeblood. Yet we so often treat Christ's body with deplorable irreverence, with no regard for its purity, health, or reflection on Christ's honor. While it is true that God alone can fully judge hearts, he does commission his church to use discernment in determining who should or should not be received as full members. Does this seem like interference to you, or do you welcome godly inquiry?

Scripture: Proverbs 2:11-13; Amos 3:3; Romans 1:11-12

Prayer: Lord, please give me more godly discretion for discerning your will. I pray also for your church. Let there be more discretion in conducting the business of maintaining your body's integrity. Amen.

D·A·Y
78

So she smiled, and tears began to form in her eyes. After a pause, she said, "I will call for two or three more members of my family." So she ran to the door and called for Prudence, Piety, and Charity, who, after a little more conversation with him, had him come join the family. And many of them met him at the entrance of the House, saying, "Come in, man blessed of the Lord. The Lord of the Hill built this House for showing hospitality to pilgrims like yourself." Then Christian bowed his head in appreciation and followed them into the House. After they seated him, they gave him something to drink. Several members of the family—Piety, Prudence, and Charity—were appointed to discourse with Christian until dinner. And so they began to talk.

❦

Legitimate church membership is never automatic. The church is a family, and the members of this family have the right to decide whether an applicant's profession is real. Christian proves his sincerity, and the church gladly welcomes him into its fellowship.

The family members call Christian, "man blessed of the Lord." And indeed he is! He is part of God's eternal family, a member of God's own household. Together the family members enjoy the glorious privileges of the Gospel, and ultimately they will enjoy "an eternal weight of glory beyond all measure" (2 Corinthians 4:17 NRSV). Christ will one day gloriously transport Christian, along with the rest of His family, to the magnificent celestial home he has prepared for them. Christian can call God his Father. He can call God's other children his brothers and sisters. He can call Jesus, not only his Lord and Master, but his elder Brother. How marvelous to be part of the family! How inconceivably wonderful that the holy and almighty God should desire to adopt sinful humans and call them sons and daughters, that the divine Son of God isn't ashamed to call them his brothers or sisters.

Only those born again at the cross of Christ are qualified to enjoy the astonishing benefits of the Gospel. Others may try attaching themselves to Christ's church but only for a season. They cannot know the joy of true fellowship that exists between and among God and his people beginning now and spanning to the farthest reaches of eternity. Having been received into fellowship with his other family members, Christian is "blessed"—and so are we! Reflect on the advantages that are yours in being a part of God's family. Think of some ways you can strengthen the bonds of love with your Christian brothers and sisters.

❦

Scripture: Hebrews 2:10-13; Matthew 12:50; 1 John 1:3, 7

Prayer: Father, thank you for bringing me into your family through the blood of Jesus your Son. I commit myself to treating your family with more love and appreciation. Amen.

Piety first addressed him. "Come, good Christian, since we have welcomed you into our House tonight, let us hear more from you about all the things that have happened on your pilgrimage. Perhaps by listening to you, we can be enriched. What first moved you to take on the life of a pilgrim?"

"I'm delighted that you're interested," answered Christian. "A dreadful sound in my ears drove me out of my native country. I learned that inevitable destruction awaited me if I continued to live there."

"But how did you happen to leave your country to come this way?"

"It was God's will; for when I became fearful of destruction, I didn't know where to go. But fortunately a man named Evangelist came to me as I was trembling and crying. He directed me to the Wicket-gate, which I would never have found on my own. He set me on the way that has led directly to this House."

John Milton said, "God . . . sends His Spirit of Truth henceforth to dwell in pious hearts." Piety is the first member of the family assigned to converse with Christian. Indicating religious devotion and reverence for God, the word *piety* is no longer commonly used. An old Webster dictionary[6] definition for piety is, "Veneration or reverence of the Supreme Being and love of his character; obedient love of the will of God and zealous devotion to his service." Clearly, more of this excellent virtue would greatly enrich our modern fellowships!

True to Piety's nature, she wants to hear Christian's testimony. She knows that God has moved wonderfully in his life to bring him this far. She hopes to hear some enriching stories of God's faithfulness. Her interest delights Christian.

Christian confesses that he didn't simply decide to leave his native country—"A dreadful sound in my ears *drove me out* . . ." He testifies that his leaving death to find life was God's work. "It was God's will." God had everything to do with his decision. By God's grace Christian learned of the impending doom of his city; by God's grace he feared destruction; by God's grace his heart "moved" him toward finding an escape; by God's grace Evangelist came and directed him to the path that has brought him to this present place of fellowship.

Like Piety and Christian, we should attempt to love, reverence, and glorify God together with all our hearts. This is the way to mutually upbuilding fellowship at its best. When was the last time you glorified God by testifying of what he has done in and for you? Decide to do it soon.

Scripture: Psalms 34:2; 66:16; Malachi 3:16; Ephesians 5:18-19

Prayer: Dear Lord, help me to desire piety in my Christian life and fellowship. Also, I want to see my fellow believers edified by what you have done in my life. Please give me opportunities for sharing my testimony. Amen.

D·A·Y
80

"But didn't you see the House of the Interpreter?"

"Yes, and I saw things there that will stick in my memory for the rest of my life—three things in particular. I learned how Christ, in spite of Satan's efforts, maintains His work of grace in the heart. I learned about a man who had sinned beyond the point of hoping for God's mercy. And I saw a man who had a dream while he was sleeping and thought the day of judgment had come."

"Why? Did he tell you his dream?"

"Yes, and I thought it was a dreadful one. My heart ached as he described it, but I'm glad I heard it."

"Was that all you saw at the Interpreter's House?"

"No, he showed me a stately Palace; all the people inside were clothed in gold. A venturesome man came and cut his way through the armed guards that stood at the door to keep him out. Then he was invited to come in and win eternal glory. My heart got so carried away with these things that I would like to have stayed at the good man's House for a year! I knew, however, I had to continue my journey."

Christian goes on sharing his testimony with Piety and the other family members. Piety wonders if Christian somehow missed a significant place. She asks if he had seen the House of the Interpreter (representing the Holy Spirit's instruction). Far from missing it, Christian says he learned things there he will never forget, and he joyfully shares them.

Do you remember how Good-will at the Wicket-gate encouraged him to go and knock at the Interpreter's door? Christian knocked repeatedly until someone finally acknowledged him. Many pilgrims, in a hurry to get where they want to go, come and knock a few times, give up, and scurry away. Even more don't bother stopping at all. Being that the House likely appears modest—the Holy Spirit speaks in a still, small voice—it somehow escapes them that they can gain great treasure once inside. But Christian tarried at the door, and because he did, the Interpreter himself took him by the hand and showed him many vitally important things for his pilgrimage.

Sometimes we are simply too busy with our plans to stop and wait for the Counselor to instruct us. Christian, however, learned precious lessons uniquely fashioned for his life. He cherished this instruction and would have gladly sat soaking it up for a year. Have you taken time recently to let the Holy Spirit instruct your heart? Write down some things you believe you have received from him.

Scripture: John 14:26; 16:13; 1 Corinthians 2:10-11; Proverbs 23:12

Prayer: Dear Holy Spirit, please forgive me for not taking time to sit in your presence and learn from you. Help me to delight in your instruction. I want to do better. Amen.

D·A·Y
81

"What else did you see as you traveled on the way?"

"After going just a little bit further," said Christian, "I saw a vision of One hanging and bleeding on the Cross. The very sight of Him made my Burden fall from my back. Oh, I had groaned under a very heavy Burden, but then it just dropped off! This was a strange experience, for I had never before seen such a thing. Yes, and while I stood looking up—for I couldn't resist staring—three Shining Ones came to me. One of them declared that my sins were forgiven, another stripped off my ragged clothing and gave me this embroidered Coat that you see, and the third one affixed the mark that you see on my forehead and gave me this sealed Scroll."

With that, he pulled the Scroll out of his Coat pocket.

"But you saw more than this, didn't you?" Piety asked.

"The things I've told you were the best. But, yes, I saw other things. I saw three men—Simple, Sloth, and Presumption—just a little out of the Way I was traveling on. They were lying sound asleep with fetters on their feet; but do you think I could rouse them? I also met Formality and Hypocrisy, who came tumbling over the Wall pretending to go to Zion, but they were quickly lost. I warned them, but they refused to believe me. Above all, however, I found that getting up this Hill was hard work; and passing by the Lions' mouths was just as difficult. I'm telling you the truth when I say that if the good man who stands by the gate had not been there, I'm not sure, after all I've been through, that I wouldn't have turned back again. But now I thank God that I'm here, and I thank you for receiving me."

Christian shares his vision of Christ on the cross. If we could look into his eyes at that dreadful moment as he hung gasping and dying for our sins, what might we see? Wouldn't gentle, suffering eyes, welling with compassion greet us? These eyes, even in pain, would plead, not for his own deliverance but for us to look upon him and find ours.

No other knowledge, discovery, or truth is more wonderful than meeting the crucified and risen Savior and realizing that if you were the only one alive, he would have died just for you. He said, "Greater love has no one than this . . ." (John 15:13). Here is the *quod erat demonstrandum*—the truth demonstrated. Upon seeing this supreme demonstration, Christian's burden of guilt tumbled away forever. And that same power has provided him with continuing victory.

Is any knowledge so great as knowing Christ died for you? Gratefully acknowledge all that the Lord's sacrifice means to you.

Scripture: Galatians 1:3-4; 1 Corinthians 2:2; Acts 2:36

Prayer: Dear Jesus, how can I thank you enough for your love so overwhelmingly demonstrated on the cross? I love you. Amen.

DAY 82

Then Prudence wanted to ask him a few questions. "Sometimes don't you think about the country you came from?"

"Yes, but with much shame and abhorrence. It's true that if I had highly regarded the country that I came from, I might have returned at an opportune time. But now I desire a better Country, that is, a Heavenly one."

"But don't you still waver sometimes when you think of the things you were accustomed to?"

"Yes, I struggle, but I don't want to. The inward and carnal thoughts—which all of my fellow citizens and myself delighted in—are especially troublesome. All those things are my grief now. If I could choose to have things my way, I would choose never to think of those former things again. But when I want to do what is best, that is when I find the worst is what motivates me."

"Do you sometimes find that those things have apparently been subdued, but at other times they are your greatest entanglement?"

"Yes, but the former is seldom the case. The hours when I feel free are like gold to me."

Prudence is one who exercises good judgment on the church's behalf. Knowing the world's temptations and the vulnerabilities of the human heart, she wisely evaluates Christian's profession of faith to test its validity. Wanting to study his inner motivations, she knows just what questions to ask.

From Christian's answers Prudence thinks his faith might be too good to be true. Anyone can say the right words to make a favorable impression. She probes deeper. Does part of him remain inwardly loyal to the things he left behind in his old life? Do these things cause him inner conflict? If he answers no, he may be in a serious state of denial, thinking himself already arrived at perfection.

But Christian readily admits his inner struggles with his former life. They even cause him grief. Right when his heart says yes to the right choice, he finds himself struggling with the wrong one. This admission bares the age-old conflict between the believers' two natures. While the new nature delights in God and is committed to the pilgrimage, the old nature seeks to rebel and go its own stubborn, independent way. Shaking off the old sinful nature is no easy task. Clearly, our wills play an important role here as we intentionally yield to the new Christlike nature and renounce the sinful one. Does the old nature unduly influence you? What choices can you make in favor of your new nature, to the defeat of the old one?

Scripture: Romans 7:21-23; 13:14; Galatians 5:16-17

Prayer: Dear Lord, help me to confess my struggles to you honestly. Help me to make godly choices that will keep me from falling back into my old sinful nature's behavior. Amen.

D·A·Y 83

"Can you remember what causes these agitating thoughts to seem to be conquered sometimes?"

"Yes, when I remember what I saw at the Cross, that will do it: and when I gaze at this embroidered Coat, that will do it; and when I read the Scroll that I carry close to my heart, that will do it; and when I meditate upon the place where I am going, that will do it."

"What makes you so eager to reach Mount Zion?"

"Why, there I hope to see the One who hung dead on the Cross alive again; and there I hope to be freed of all the things within me that are such a struggle for me. They say that death doesn't exist there and that I will live there with wonderful companions. To tell you the truth, I love Him because He delivered me from my Burden. And I am so tired of my inward sickness that I long to be where there is no more sin and death and where I will be in the fellowship of those who continually cry, 'Holy, holy, holy.'"

Christian gives many reasons for wanting to reach Mount Zion, the best being that he loves Christ for freeing him from his burden. While he has loved his Savior since the cross, this is the first time he voices that love.

Love is the preeminent virtue of God's kingdom, for God's very nature is love. God showed his love by sending us his Son. That he loves sinful humanity, rebellious and ungrateful as we are, is incomprehensible. How can the perfectly righteous, almighty God love the proud, depraved, mortal dust of the earth? How can Christ—the perfect, blessed forever, only beloved Son of the eternal Father—assign such value to us as to give his life for us? He had no affinity with us; we were enemies; we hated him.

Nevertheless, God perfectly expresses his love in Christ. Can you see Jesus willingly suffering on the cross, bearing the weight of the world's sin, under a curse, heartbroken, alone, dying? And for whom? For undeserving, rebellious, miserable, guilty, broken sinners—for you and me. And why? So we could share in his majestic glory, living forever in his eternal home. Again, why? Only he knows. He is so unlike us. How can we begin to understand a love so pure that nothing we do either motivates or diminishes it? Loving is simply God's choice because it is his nature. Oh, how we should respond to him with fervent love and devotion. "We love because he first loved us" (1 John 4:19). Think of a special gift you can give the Lord just because you love him and want to gladden his heart.

Scripture: 1 John 4:8-10, 16; John 13:1; 14:21; 15:9-13; Psalm 107:43

Prayer: Lord, please forgive me for so often treating your love with nonchalance. I want to love and reverence you much more than I do. Amen.

D·A·Y
84

Then Charity entered the conversation, asking Christian, "Do you have a family? Are you a married man?"

"I have a wife and four children."

"Why didn't you bring them along with you?"

Then Christian began to cry. "Oh, I wanted to! But all of them utterly opposed my going on this pilgrimage."

"But shouldn't you have talked to them and tried to show them the danger they were in by staying behind?"

"I did, and I also told them what God had shown me concerning the coming destruction of our City. However, they seemed to think I was joking and wouldn't believe me."

"Did you pray that God would bless your counsel to them?"

"Yes, and with great love and emotion. I want you to know that my wife and poor children were very dear to me."

❧

The last one to converse with Christian before dinner is Charity. Today the word *charity* generally refers to something given to help the needy. It can also mean an organization established to that end. Thus, *charitable* means being generous in giving money or other aid to needy people. The old Webster definition, however, goes beyond external actions to underlying motives. It speaks of a heart disposition that inclines people to think favorably of others and subsequently to do them good and show them love. *Charitable* in this sense means being full of love and goodwill for others because they, too, are objects of God's love. Love is the heart motive. Charity is love. "And now abideth faith, hope, charity, these three; but the greatest of these is charity" (1 Corinthians 13:13 KJV).

Not surprisingly, in this third conversation, Charity's focus is love. She heard Christian express love for Christ but knows loving Christ also involves loving others. Above all other commands are the ones to love God and our neighbors. And who are closer neighbors than our own family members? To Charity, "Charity begins at home." After all, Paul says of the one who neglects his family that "he has denied the faith and is worse than an unbeliever" (1 Timothy 5:8). Therefore, targeting Christian's love for his family, Charity essentially says, "Wait! You spoke of love, but where is your family?"

Properly representing Christ to our families is a primary life purpose. Pray about this purpose and ask God for wisdom in fulfilling it.

❧

Scripture: Matthew 22:37-40; Ephesians 5:25-33; John 1:41

Prayer: Dear Lord, thank you for your love. May I reflect more of that godly virtue, charity, in my heart and life, especially toward my family. Amen.

D·A·Y
85

"But did you tell them of your own sorrow and of your fear of destruction? For I can imagine how clear the coming destruction was to you."

"Yes, over and over and over. I was so afraid of the judgment hanging over all of our heads that I know they could see the alarm on my face as well as in my tears. But none of this was enough to convince them to come with me."

"But why didn't they come? What did they have to say for themselves?"

"Well, my wife was afraid of losing this world, and my children were enjoying the foolish pleasures of youth. So for one reason or another, they left me to wander in that anxious condition alone."

Love is the chief hallmark of the Christian life and witness. The faith of a professing Christian is suspect if he shows little concern for the salvation of his own family. What is one to do, however, when love for family and love for God pull us in opposing directions? Christian says he tried repeatedly to end the conflict by getting his family to join him. They refused, and they didn't want him to go either. This left him with the unfortunate but necessary decision of choosing between them and the pilgrimage.

Good pilgrims love their families, and yet they love them less than they love their Lord. They recognize a duty to their families. Still their duty to Jesus Christ is of greater importance. They know rejection by their families is preferable to losing him. Middle ground is unacceptable. They must willingly part with the things and with the people that call them back to the world and away from the pilgrimage.

Christian showed love to his family by passionately warning them. Giving in to their wishes would have meant forsaking Christ, losing his witness to them. As it is, Christian went on with his pilgrimage, and his witness to them remained true. We can never hope to inspire our family with what Christ has done in our lives if we compromise the truth for them. The best way to love our family is by continually giving Christ first place in our lives. Then they can see the reality of Christ and his deep impact upon us.

As believers, we must steadfastly love Christ above anything or anyone else. Without a sincere determination to give him first place, we cannot be his disciples. Make a mental list of your loved ones. Put Christ at the head of your list and proceed to make any needed adjustments in the way you relate to those on your list.

Scripture: Hebrews 11:24-26; Matthew 10:37; Micah 7:4-7

Prayer: Lord Jesus, I love you supremely, but I also want to show love to my family and friends. Please show me the best way to witness to them without compromising my position in you. Amen.

DAY 86

"But did your own vain life weaken your ability to persuade them to go with you?"

"You are right; I cannot commend my life, for I am conscious of my many failings. I know that one's own actions can quickly overpower whatever persuasive ability he may have to convince others for their own good. Yet I can honestly say that I tried to be very careful not to be a negative example in any way so that they would have no reason for not joining me on the pilgrimage. But for these very efforts they would tell me I was too exacting, that I denied things (for their sake) in which they saw no evil. No, I think I can safely say that if I hindered them, it was because of my great care not to sin against God or my neighbors."

Charity nodded. "Yes, Cain hated his brother because his own deeds were evil while his brother's were righteous. If your wife and children were offended with you for this, they were showing their own stubborn resistance to what is good. Then you are not responsible for their blood."

Charity wonders if perhaps Christian's life has not measured up to his words. This would have a negative effect on any interest his loved ones might have in joining him. In a large sense, the medium is the message in proclaiming the Gospel. We witness much more by how we live than by what we say.

Rather than defending himself, Christian admits his shortcomings. He assures Charity, however, that he has tried his best to be a good example. He didn't in any way intentionally become a stumbling block for his family. Christian's reply satisfies Charity. It is clear he has done his duty as a loving witness.

We cannot convert our loved ones. This work is between them and the Holy Spirit. Too often, however, our lifestyles are stumbling blocks for our families. We may put leisure, wealth, or success before Christ and wonder why our children prefer playing or working on Sundays to going to church. We may fail to establish a family altar by reading Scripture and praying with our children on a daily basis and wonder why they lack a heart for God. It is said that the Christian faith must be caught, not just taught. Again, how we live impacts others in far greater ways than anything we say.

Pray about your witness. Are there things in your life that might create stumbling blocks to a clear witness for Jesus Christ? Ask the Holy Spirit to help you overcome these things.

Scripture: Deuteronomy 6:6-9;
1 Corinthians 11:1; Ezekiel 3:17-19

Prayer: Dear Lord, please reveal the things in me that muddy my witness. I repent of them in Jesus' name. May my friends and loved ones see you in my life and thereby be drawn to you. Amen.

D·A·Y
87

Now I saw in my dream that this conversation continued until supper was ready. When it was ready, they all sat down to eat at the table, which was spread with rich food and fine wine. Everyone talked about the Lord of the Hill—the things He had done and the reasons He had built the House. I learned that He had been a great warrior and had fought with and killed the one who had the power of death. His victory was not without great sacrifice to Himself, and hearing it made me love Him even more.

Sitting down for supper represents the church participating collectively in the ordinance of the Lord's Supper. It is a family time where the members enjoy a common meal together in honor of "the Lord of the Hill." This Supper was first instituted by our Lord himself. As he celebrated his final Passover meal with his disciples, he presented himself to them as the true Passover Lamb. He offered them the bread and wine as his body and blood and pointed to his forthcoming death as the saving event of history. By the blood of the unblemished lamb, the Israelites were delivered from the spirit of death. By Christ's broken body and poured-out blood, he delivered his people from their bondage to sin and death.

When Christ said, "do this in remembrance of me," he was not instituting a memorial service. After all, he rose from the dead and is present with us. He actually hosts the meal and invites us to sit at the table with him.

Rather than sharing the Supper "in memory of," we partake as lovers calling to mind all that our loved one means to us. We remember his suffering and death and how his sacrifice resoundingly defeated every enemy. We remember his incredible grace and love in paying our debt, forgiving our sins, securing our deliverance, and ushering us into God's kingdom. We are reminded that this supper is a foretaste of the future celestial banquet to which our Lord will welcome us. As we remember these things, our souls stir with fresh love and gratitude; we repent and are washed clean; we renew our commitment to follow and serve Christ. Reflecting on the Lord's goodness makes us "love him even more."

Has the partaking of the Lord's Supper become a dry ritual to you? Ask the Lord to forgive you and to fill your heart with renewed love as you reflect upon all this Supper means for you. Make sure you partake with a clean heart.

Scripture: Exodus 12:7, 12-13;
1 Corinthians 5:7; Luke 22:19-20

Prayer: Lord Jesus, thank you for giving your life for my redemption. It is a joy and privilege to share in your Supper with you and your people. I confess and repent of my sins. Amen.

DAY 88

They related to Christian that [Christ's] victory was accomplished only with the loss of much blood. And the thing that made His gracious sacrifice so beautiful was that pure love for His Country motivated everything He did. Some members of the household told Christian that they had been with the Lord and had even spoken with Him since the time He died on the Cross. They had heard Him say with His own mouth that no one from East to West could be found who loves needy pilgrims more than He.

To demonstrate the truth of their story, they pointed out to Christian how He had stripped Himself of His glory to sacrifice His life for those who needed Him. They had heard Him say that He would not dwell in Mount Zion alone and that He had made into princes many pilgrims who by nature were born to live as beggars in garbage dumps.

The family members continue with the Lord's Supper. As they do, they discuss Christ's sacrificial love. Let us ponder a moment with them. High aloft in his celestial kingdom, all is eternally resplendent majesty, purity, truth, righteousness, joy, and love. However, Jesus Christ, King of the universe, royal Prince of this celestial kingdom, was not content. He looked through heaven's window down to the earth where he saw human beings, made in his image, languishing and dying in the poisonous garbage dumps of willful sin. Amazingly, he loved them and decided to do something bold, something extraordinary. Pure love is like that.

Christ gave up his celestial wealth and glory for our sakes. He stepped out of his celestial garments and took upon himself our humanity. He willingly suffered at the hands of those he loved and came to save, persevering through rejection, ridicule, and finally death. Why were we so special to him, beggars that we were, living in sin? His compassion knows no limits. Seeing our miserable poverty, he chose to share his wealth. We who were dead he has made alive. He has lifted us from the garbage dump of sin and provided a place for us in heaven. He has made us royalty with him and invites us to come and feast at his banqueting table.

Sometimes we grow cold and unfeeling as the trials of life cloud the awesome things Christ has done for us. Partaking of the Lord's Supper draws us back to the marvelous hope we share together in him. Is your passion waning? Remember how he has lifted you out of the garbage heap so that one day you will rejoice with him in the highest heaven. Be thankful.

Scripture: Ephesians 3:17-19; 1 Samuel 2:8; Luke 19:10

Prayer: Dear Jesus, thank you for inviting me to your great heavenly banquet. I look forward to sitting at your table with my brothers and sisters and talking to you face to face. Amen.

D·A·Y

89

They continued to talk until late that night, and after committing their lives to their Lord's protection, they went to bed. Christian was taken to a large upper Room with a window opened toward the sunrise. The name of his Room was Peace. He slept until daybreak, and when he woke up, he sang:

"Where am I now? Is this the love and care
Of Jesus, for the ones who pilgrims are?
How He provides, that I should be forgiven!
And dwell already next door to Heaven!"

❧

Sharing the Lord's Supper and enjoying fellowship in the Lord together until late was a deeply enriching experience for Christian. Committing their lives into the Lord's hands completed the evening. Then Christian spends the night in a very special room called Peace. This room is a sweet place of rest and refreshment. When Christian found new life at the cross, his sins were forgiven, and he enjoyed "peace *with* God," meaning he had been brought into a right relationship with God through faith. Now he knows what it is to enjoy "the peace *of* God."

Many have peace *with* God but don't generally know the peace *of* God. This peace is a blessed sense of being in harmony with God and his purposes, feeling his favor, resting in heavenly hope. It is a peace of mind and serenity of conscience enjoyed as a result of committing our lives (our way, cares, fears, future) into the Lord's hands. It is a peaceful assurance that keeps us from sin, from anxiety, from defeat. As a pilgrim, Christian knows trials exist ahead for him on the path. He can, however, rest in the knowledge that his life is in God's hands.

For most people life is difficult. Perplexing world events along with many personal concerns weigh heavily on our hearts. The Prince of Peace, however, came to give our hearts peace in the midst of life's storms. When we feel concern about a situation, we must learn to spread it out before the Lord in prayer. After this, we entrust it to God. He responds by giving his peace. If you have peace *with* God, he certainly wants you to also walk in the peace *of God.* Do you have fears, anxieties, or stress that hinder your soul's ability to rest in this peace? Lift those things to God in prayer, releasing them to his care.

❧

Scripture: Romans 5:1; Philippians 4:6-7;
John 14:27; Colossians 3:15

Prayer: Dear Lord, trusting you for your peace, I commit my life into your hands, along with all my hopes and fears. In an anxious world, please use my life to point the way to true and lasting peace. Amen.

DAY 90

In the morning they all got up, and after talking some more, they told him that he shouldn't leave until they had shown him some of the rare things preserved there. First, they took him to the Study where they showed him Records of the greatest Antiquity. As I recall in my dream, the first thing they showed him was the Genealogy of the Lord of that Hill, revealing that He was the Son of the Ancient of Days and descended from the eternal lineage. His deeds were fully recorded, along with the names of many hundreds He had received into His service. He had provided them with permanent dwelling places that were not subject to decay by time or nature.

Each room in the Palace represents a facet of the Christian life. The visit to the Study first thing in the morning represents participation in Bible study and a quiet time with God. Unlike some libraries that are mere showpieces filled with volumes collecting dust, the Palace Study generates great enthusiasm. Here Christian learns many valuable things concerning his Lord.

One of the longest, most hard-fought battles in world history is the one over the authority of the Bible, God's Word. The forces of darkness struggle to undermine it because they hate its revelation. From Roman emperors to Chinese Communists, from early heretics to modern liberal theologians, the battle still rages. Who wins is an urgent concern for each generation. The outcome often determines the strength and vitality of the present-generation church, and also profoundly influences the generations to come. There has been a dramatic erosion of faith in the authority of the Scriptures in America over the past generation. While in 1963 two-thirds of American adults believed the Bible should be taken literally, now the numbers have shrunk to one-third.[7] Even so, Christian bookstores sell an average of 34,932 Bibles every day.[8] Evidently while we have plenty of Bibles, our "studies" are largely neglected.

Make it a point each day to spend time with God. Allow his Word to instruct and transform your life. While the world builds its values on quicksand, God's Word can be trusted. Despite every attempt to defeat it, his Word endures because a faithful God stands behind it.

Scripture: Ezra 7:10; Joshua 1:8; Job 23:12

Prayer: Lord, I want to spend more time in Bible study learning about you, your will, and your purposes. I resolve to be one who is faithful to your Word in my generation. I pray that our culture will once again honor your Word. Amen.

D·A·Y
91

Then they read to him the praiseworthy acts that some of the Lord's servants had done—how they had subdued kingdoms, established righteousness, claimed promises, stopped the mouths of lions, quenched the violence of fire, escaped the edge of the sword, been courageous in battle, and caused enemy armies to retreat.

They read further in another part of the Records, where it showed how willingly their Lord would receive anyone with favor—yes, anyone—even though previously that one may have heaped insults against Him and His way. Christian was able to survey the history of many other notable things as well. He learned of things both ancient and modern, along with prophecies and predictions of things that will surely be fulfilled, both to the dread and amazement of enemies and to the comfort and solace of pilgrims.

❧

Christian now studies the courageous lives of great men and women of the Bible. They comprise faith's "Hall of Fame." These ordinary people won outstanding victories by believing in an extraordinary God. The Records don't spruce up anyone's image. Their flaws illustrate the extent to which the Lord "willingly" forgives sinners.

Subsequent generations have gained hope and inspiration by studying these lives. Hosts of unsung heroes have consequently arisen in faith to conquer faith's enemies. Sufficient inspiration is available for us, too. We can experience heroic victories over our enemies. True heroism today consists of battling daily to demonstrate God's love and to establish his truth, standards, will, and purpose in our homes, workplaces, churches, and the world. No doubt studying the Records inspires Christian—and us!—to follow the example of God's heroes.

Christian also learns in the Records things both ancient and modern. Although these Records are of "greatest antiquity," they readily and with great clarity shine light on current events. Numerous prophecies have already been fulfilled, others are being fulfilled, and many await their proper time. They will all take place to the dread of the Lord's enemies and to the comfort of his pilgrims. Some say that because they have read the Bible's last chapter, they know that "God wins!" While gloriously true, we can also go to the beginning of his Word and read straight through to see God's triumph in the lives of his people.

Pick out some of your favorite Bible heroes and reread their stories. Let them inspire you to renewed faith and courage.

❧

Scripture: Hebrews 11; Matthew 5:18; Habakkuk 2:3

Prayer: Lord, thank you for the record you have given us of your faithful servants. Help me to leave a legacy of faith that those who come behind me might find inspiration. Amen.

DAY 92

The next day they took him into the Armory where they showed him all kinds of equipment that the Lord had provided for pilgrims—Sword, Shield, Helmet, Breastplate, All-prayer, and Shoes that would never wear out. There were enough of these to equip many people for the Lord's service—as many as the stars in the heavens.

Christian visits the Armory, a place where military weapons and equipment are stored. Why does a lovely Palace with rooms for fellowship, peace, and study also boast a place indicative of conflict and war? Wouldn't it be better to simply avoid this place? Why can't we just look for peace and harmony? Many today are under the misguided notion that peace-loving people who accommodate everyone's beliefs can achieve peace and harmony in the earth. Many in the church attempt to generate peace by removing military words and references to Christ's blood from lectionaries, hymnals, and even God's Word. Why, they ask, did the Prince of Peace say he did "not come to bring peace, but a sword" (Matthew 10:34)?

Jesus Christ came to make peace between God and sinners through his blood, bring spiritual peace within and among those who would follow him, and send them to preach a Gospel of peace and reconciliation. Nevertheless, when he physically set foot on this planet, it was an act of war against the ruling "god of this world." Although Christ didn't want to create bitter conflict in the earth, he knew Satan and his evil hosts would never simply bow to the arrival of God's truth incarnate. Indeed, the hosts of wickedness rose to face his challenge, and people felt compelled to choose their loyalties. This created divisions as some received Christ and others rejected him. Discord, hostility, and persecution followed. The kingdom of God and the forces of evil have been in violent combat ever since.

We won't see the "peace on earth" we all hope for until Christ comes to earth again to once and for all rid his universe of sin and Satan. Meanwhile, the world visits its own armory and arms itself with its dark and brazen armor of falsehood and unbelief. It behooves us, as believers, to visit God's Armory and take up the weapons of faith available to us. Ask God to take you into his Armory so you can be properly equipped for your spiritual battles.

Scripture: Genesis 3:15; 1 John 3:8; John 7:43; Acts 14:2, 4

Prayer: Dear Lord, I recognize that the cosmic conflict of the ages rages on all about me. Keep me from shying away from the provisions you have amassed in your Armory. Amen.

D·A·Y 93

They also showed him some instruments with which His servants had done incredible things—Moses' rod; the hammer and tent peg used by Jael to slay Sisera; the pitchers, trumpets and lamps used by Gideon to put the armies of Midian to flight. They showed him the ox goad used by Shamgar to kill six hundred Philistines, the jawbone used by Samson to do such mighty feats, and the sling and stone used by David to kill Goliath of Gath. They also showed him the sword with which their Lord will overpower the man of lawlessness in the day of His coming confrontation. They showed him many other excellent things besides, which delighted Christian. After this, they went to bed for the night.

Christian continues his tour of the Armory. The most impressive weapon in the arsenal is the one the Lord will use to destroy the man of lawlessness—the Antichrist—in the last battle. Other implements Christian observes would normally seem inconsequential. In the hands of simple men and women of faith, however, they proved mighty. This should give us hope for our lives and ministries. God can use any person by whatever means he chooses.

Unfortunately, we so often get hung up on implements. We want to do something big for God, so we look to the spectacular. Could something simple really do something great? We doubt it. So we look to the world's ways of winning hearts and minds by promoting, advertising, and televising. We search for just the right technological gimmickry for securing success. Some really exciting implements do exist in our day. We have Plexiglas pulpits, wireless mikes, incredible lighting, state-of-the-art sound systems. We conduct spectacular worship services and offer evangelistic extravaganzas with world-class special effects. Of course these things can tremendously aid our ministries. However, if we feel more anointed and powerful because of them, our faith is misplaced.

Fancy advertising and technical wizardry will never light a candle to simple people of faith, walking by the Spirit's power in obedience to God, carrying very ordinary implements. Who, after all, would consider a rod, a pitcher, or a donkey jawbone anything special? Yet here they are in the Armory as samples of what God uses to do world-changing exploits through his people. Let us focus less on implements and more on growing faith in the one who can use anyone and anything for his glory. Have you hesitated to step out in faith because all you saw at your disposal was a simple implement? Pick it up, then, and remember that your faith is in God, not in implements.

Scripture: 1 Corinthians 1:27-29; 2 Corinthians 6:4, 7; Zechariah 4:6

Prayer: Dear Lord, help me to remember that you can use me to do great things in your name as I take what you have given me and use it in faith. Amen.

DAY 94

Then I saw in my dream that when Christian got up the next day to continue his journey, they again asked him to stay until the next day. "If the weather is clear," they told him, "we would like to show you the Delectable Mountains." They thought that seeing these mountains would encourage him since they were closer to his destination than where he was presently. So he consented and stayed. Early the next morning, they took him to the housetop and told him to look to the south. When he did, he saw far in the distance a very pleasant, mountainous Country, made beautiful by forests, vineyards, fruit trees of every kind, flowers, streams, and fountains—all in all, a most delightful sight. Then he asked the name of the Country. They answered, "That is Emmanuel's Land, and like this Hill, it is to be shared by all pilgrims. When you arrive there, you will be able to see the Gate of the Celestial City. The Shepherds who live there will point it out to you."

Christian feels ready to carry on with his pilgrimage. His friends know better. He needs additional reinforcement to meet the trials on the road ahead. First, they show him the Delectable Mountains so he can keep their memory fixed in his mind during the rough times. These distant mountains are only seen on clear days and from a housetop. Viewing them is a delightful experience. From these Mountains, pilgrims can actually catch a glimpse of the Celestial Gate.

The Delectable Mountains seem to represent the future consolations, joys, blessings, and fellowship with the Lord that are ours if we persevere to maturity. It is "Emmanuel's Land." Pointing to Jesus Christ, the Hebrew name Emmanuel means "God is with us." Jesus graciously promised his followers, "Lo, I am with you alway . . ." (Matthew 28:20 KJV). Through the Holy Spirit, he is with us every step of the pilgrim Way. We have his protection, his provision, his power. His presence is personal, direct, immediate. He is with his pilgrims to save and protect them until they reach that desired haven of abiding peace and joy in him.

Catching a glimpse of the Mountains suggests the reassurance gained by recognizing that not only is God with us as we press forward, but he is leading us to a much deeper experience of his presence. In our times of discouragement when we know he is with us but are forced to "faith it," we need to refocus on God's promises never to leave us. We must keep pressing forward into the life God has for us.

Scripture: Matthew 1:23; John 14:18-20; Isaiah 8:10

Prayer: Lord Jesus, you are Emmanuel; you are with me. Thank you that you are faithfully leading me to a lovely place of abiding fellowship with you. Amen.

D·A·Y 95

Now it seemed to him that it was time to go, and they agreed. "But first," they said, "let us take you to the Armory again." When they got there, they equipped Christian from head to foot with all he would need in case he was attacked on the way.

While Christian was among his godly friends,
Their golden words sufficed to make amends
For all his griefs, and when they sent him to go,
He was clad with steel from his head to his toe.

Christian sees a lot in the Armory, but it is pointless if he fails to apply what he sees to his own life. Before proceeding with his pilgrimage, he needs proper equipping. Far from an intellectual exercise, faith alone can appropriate this vitally important armor. Many dangerous enemies lurk ahead on the path, with a thousand beguiling temptations to seduce unsteady souls. These must be resisted and put to flight. Christian needs full protection if he is to triumph over sin, error, trials, afflictions, and persecutions.

He is, therefore, fitted with armor from head to foot. And what is this armor? First it includes the *belt of truth.* Truth supports the sword and other armor. An upright conscience defeats the enemy's lies. Next comes the *breastplate of righteousness,* which is Christ's righteousness in us that enables us to live godly lives and fortifies and protects us against enemy attacks on our heart. Also *footgear* is included—the readiness to spread the Gospel of peace. This readiness comes from having a clear knowledge of the Gospel, and it motivates us to press on and share our faith in difficult and seemingly hopeless places. The *shield of faith* fends off the enemy's flaming arrows hurled at our hearts. When Satan whispers his temptations, doubts, and fears, standing in faith protects us. We have the *helmet of salvation*, for if the devil can get us to doubt God's salvation, he has defeated us. The *sword of the Spirit* is a weapon of offense as well as defense. Other armor protects; the sword assaults. Wielding it effectively destroys every lie. A single text of Scripture, rightly applied in faith, is a mighty weapon. Finally, we have *All-prayer*, all kinds of prayer—public or private, whispered or shouted, for ourselves or for others, in tongues of men or of angels, confessing or thanking, petitioning or praising. Prayer makes the rest of the armor effective. Without prayer there can be no victory.

Do you have all your armor in place? Which pieces are you using effectively? Where do you need improvement? How could you strengthen your weak areas?

Scripture: Romans 13:12; Ephesians 6:11-18; 2 Corinthians 10:3-4

Prayer: Dear Lord, thank you for the armor you have given me. Help me to learn to secure each piece and use it effectively. Amen.

DAY 96

He then walked with his friends to the gate and asked Watchful, the gatekeeper, if he had seen any pilgrims pass by. "Yes," Watchful answered.

"Please tell me, was it someone you knew?" asked Christian.

"I asked his name," said Watchful, "and he told me it was Faithful."

"Oh, I know him!" said Christian. "He's from my hometown—a close neighbor. How far ahead do you think he is?"

"By this time he should be down the Hill."

"Well, kind sir, may the Lord be with you and bless you greatly for the kindness you have shown me."

As Christian resumed his journey, Discretion, Piety, Charity, and Prudence decided to accompany him to the foot of the Hill. So they went out together, reviewing some of their previous conversations until they reached the place where the Hill began to descend.

Then Christian said, "It was difficult coming up the Hill, and as far as I can see, going down looks treacherous."

❧

The Lord often intersperses challenging difficulties with times of comfort so we will be neither too discouraged nor too confident. After enjoying the Palace Beautiful for a season, it is now time for Christian to make the treacherous descent into the Valley of Humiliation. While experiencing some humbling past failures, this doesn't mean that humility is forged into Christian's soul.

Enjoying a little progress can easily make young pilgrims view themselves more highly than they should. We humble ourselves to receive Christ; we humble ourselves to get through the difficulties. Yet we are often unaware of our tendency to take pride in our humility. Soon, however, we learn how little we really know about being humble. The Lord trains us in humility whether by outward circumstances such as poverty and loss or inward circumstances such as emotional, mental, or spiritual turmoil.

When we achieve true humility, we are broken like a bridled horse; our dependence upon God is complete and childlike; graciously bearing contempt, we bless our persecutors; content with the lowest place, we refuse inordinate recognition; we are receptive to doing God's will; we realize all we have is by grace alone; knowing we are nothing and can do nothing apart from God, our only boast is in him; we live solely for his glory. So the Lord takes us on down to where we can lose our purpose to his, our will in his, to where we can learn unquestioning submission, whether lifted high or laid low. Are you willing to descend into "humiliation"?

❧

Scripture: Proverbs 11:2; 18:12; 29:23; 1 Peter 5:5

Prayer: Oh Lord, I know that humility is a difficult virtue for me to learn. Please help me as I submit to your refining work of humility. Amen.

D·A·Y 97

"Yes, it is," said Prudence. "It is a very difficult thing for a man to go down into the Valley of Humiliation and not slip on the way. That is why we want to accompany you down the Hill." So he began to make his way down very carefully, but even then he lost his footing once or twice.

Then I saw in my dream that when they reached the bottom of the Hill, Christian's dear companions gave him a loaf of Bread, a bottle of Wine, and a cluster of Raisins. And he went on his way.

While humility is a virtue we all assent to, none of us enjoys the process of becoming humble. Discretion, Piety, Charity, and Prudence know how hazardous descending into the Valley of Humiliation can be for pilgrims. Because humbling himself will be so difficult for Christian, they decide to give him moral support by descending the hill with him. Yet the Valley of Humiliation, like any crisis of the soul, is something he must ultimately come through alone.

Going through humiliation can arouse doubts and unbelief, fears and apprehensions, and can quench enthusiasm. It can seem as if our pilgrimage is falling apart and that we might as well die and be done with it. At this point the Delectable Mountains can seem like a distant memory, maybe even a fantasy. A pilgrim may doubt he could ever ascend those heights by descending to these depths.

Believers who have already been this way can be of great reassurance to those who have not. They can remind them of God's promises, all the lessons learned, and that this is a necessary part of a successful pilgrimage. When unsteady pilgrims begin to slip, wise friends can grab their hands and help stabilize them.

As believers, we "must grow up in every way . . . into Christ" (Ephesians 4:15 NRSV). And what was Christ like? For all his greatness, he said of himself, "I am gentle and humble in heart . . ." (Matthew 11:29 NRSV). It should be of great comfort to us to know that Christ, too, has been this route before.

Once Christian reaches the bottom of the hill, his friends give him provisions of bread and the fruit of the vine. These remind us of the Lord's Supper, a symbol of Christ's humbling himself to death for us. Christian will gain strength by feeding upon this provision.

Remember, Christ died for you, and now he wants you to die to yourself. Pray about how he might be calling you to cooperate with his purpose.

Scripture: 1 Peter 3:8; 5:6; Ephesians 4:2; Philippians 2:8

Prayer: Lord Jesus, you walked the way of humility, and I want to be like you. Help me to keep my eyes on you. Help me also to find friends who can encourage me in this desire. Amen.

D·A·Y 98

Poor Christian was having a terrible time in the Valley of Humiliation. He had ventured only a little way before he noticed a foul Fiend, Apollyon, coming across the field to meet him. Christian began to panic and debated whether he should turn back or stand his ground. But then he recalled that he had been given no armor for his back, and he realized that to turn back would give his adversary an advantage. Apollyon would then easily pierce him with his arrows. So he resolved to stand his ground and move forward no matter what. For he thought to himself, "Even if I had no more in mind than saving my own life, this would still be the best choice." So he went on, and Apollyon met him face to face.

The Valley of Humiliation is no picnic. On the contrary, it is an unhappy place to pass through. Here pilgrims are especially vulnerable to giving in to their circumstances. They can feel depressed, lonely, afraid, or discontented. They can begin castigating themselves or even grumbling at God. They can feel a sense of loss for the life they gave up for the pilgrimage and regret the toll they are now paying. They can even feel guilt for their present condition. The devil, well aware of their vulnerability, frequents this place. It is his greatest delight to exploit weakened pilgrims to his advantage.

Christian is in the Valley only a short time before he sees the dark angel Apollyon coming to meet him. Oh, how soon after enjoying such sweet times of refreshment must he face the enemy and test his armor's strength. An encounter of this nature is especially dreadful to one who is inexperienced. Christian's first inclination is to run, but no adequate way of escape exists. No matter how great the danger is in staying and facing the enemy, the alternative is worse. While Christian's armor is complete, it leaves the backside unprotected. His breastplate and shield cover only the front, and who can effectively wield a sword while fleeing? This armor was quite clearly designed only for facing the enemy. No provision at all exists for the pilgrim who turns tail and runs.

Often we shrink from facing our devils and get shot full of arrows as we attempt to find an easier way. Nowhere in Scripture are we encouraged to fearfully take flight in the face of our enemy. After all, the power of almighty God is with us. Have you been running from the fray? Why not take your stand and test your armor?

Scripture: 1 John 4:4; Isaiah 7:9; 1 Peter 1:5

Prayer: Dear Lord, help me to remember to stand and face my enemy when he assaults me. That was your purpose for giving me armor. Thank you that you are with me to bring victory. Amen.

D·A·Y
99

The monster was hideous to look at, covered with scales like a fish (and exceedingly proud of them). He had wings like a dragon and feet like a bear. Fire and smoke came belching up from within his belly, and his mouth was like the mouth of a lion. When he drew close to Christian, he looked down upon him with utter disdain and demanded of him, "Where have you come from and where are you going?"

Christian replied, "I have come from the City of Destruction, which is the place of all evil, and I am going to the City of Zion."

"I can tell by this that you are one of my subjects since that whole country is under my authority. I am the prince and god of it. How is it, then, that you have run away from your king?"

❦

The monster Apollyon is extremely intimidating. He takes his name from the Greek term meaning "The Destroyer" (Hebrew *Abaddon*). The one biblical reference to this name is in Revelation 9:11 where John applies it to the fallen angel from the bottomless pit. Apollyon is the infernal king of hellish squadrons of demons who are under his command.

The malicious king of the City of Destruction is responsible for destroying millions of souls. Destroying is his business, his delight. He diligently works around the clock, driving all the inhabitants in his domain into the same wickedness for which the Lord will ultimately destroy him. Everyone in the City of Destruction is under his power and influence. By his influence, they are all addicted to sin and have little intention of escaping their doom. Apollyon is quick to remind Christian that he has a claim on his life. He holds great sway over his subjects. He certainly doesn't take kindly to anyone trying to escape his domain.

Some contemporary religionists attempt to free us of medieval superstitions concerning Satan and his demons. However, far from being fairy-tale characters, these spirits are real. Satan is the king of all demons. Paul calls him the god of this world (or the god of this age). Jesus called him the prince of this world. Satan boasted to the Lord that as sovereign of the world, he could give it to whomever he wished. We should ever be on our guard against the god of this world. When he and his agents come calling, they are always up to no good.

Have you taken your soul's enemy too lightly? How can you better guard yourself against his temptations?

❦

Scripture: 2 Corinthians 4:4; John 14:30; Luke 4:6

Prayer: Lord Jesus, you successfully resisted the devil's temptations. Help me to stand up and face him in your strength. Amen.

D·A·Y 100

Not waiting for an answer, Apollyon said, "If I didn't believe you might still be of use to me, I would strike you to the ground right now with one blow."

"It is true that I was born in your dominions," replied Christian, "but your service was hard, and your wages were such that a man could not live on them—for the wages of sin is death. Therefore, when I came of age, I did like other people of discernment have done and looked for a way to straighten out my life."

"No prince will take lightly the loss of one of his subjects," countered Apollyon. "Nor will I let you go. But since you complained about your service and wages, go on back, and whatever our country can afford, I hereby promise to give you."

Apollyon's subjects, whether aware of it or not, are nothing more than slaves. They have no rights or freedoms except what their king grants in order to keep them content. When they try leaving, it becomes evident they have no true freedom. Only Christ provides a way of escape, and Christian has found it. He is no longer a slave to sin. Yet Apollyon hopes Christian is not yet aware of the scope of his deliverance.

Apollyon is a clever devil. He begins his confrontation with a war of words. A masterful liar, he will employ every deception and manipulation in his arsenal to convince Christian that he retains authority over his runaway, that Christian belongs to him, and that he must return with him to the City of Destruction. He begins with a not-so-subtle threat to destroy Christian "with one blow" if he remains uncooperative. Christian acknowledges Apollyon's former lordship over his life but objects to his hard bondage and deplorable wages.

Apollyon assures Christian that trying to leave is useless because he won't let him go. After this claim, however, he promises Christian a handsome reward for returning. When hostages become brainwashed into believing their captors are on their side (called prisoner-interrogator syndrome), they even begin to feel grateful for their captivity. Apollyon hopes his generous offer will have this same effect.

As believers, the blood of Christ has redeemed us; we are freed from sin's wages to be God's servants. Our first defense is knowing that we are free. Is there some sinful habit in your life, something you have struggled to overcome and often failed? Take your place with Christ on the cross and reckon yourself dead to that sin. In him you truly are.

Scripture: Ephesians 2:1-3; Romans 6:16-23; 2 Corinthians 3:17

Prayer: Precious Savior, thank you for delivering me from the dominion of darkness. I now have life and hope. I am not about to give up this freedom to the enemy's wiles. I resolve to carry on with my pilgrimage. Amen.

D·A·Y
101

"But I have given myself to another—to the King of Princes—and how can I in fairness go back with you?"

"In doing this you have gone from bad to worse, as the proverb says. But it is typical for those who have professed themselves to be His servants to give Him the slip after a while and return to me. If you will do this also, all will go well with you."

"I have given Him my faith and sworn my allegiance to Him," Christian responded. "How, then, can I go back from here and not be hanged as a traitor?"

"You did the same thing to me, and yet I am willing to forgive it all if you will now turn again and go back."

❧

Apollyon now presents himself as someone of tremendous goodwill as he weaves his deadly web of deceit. Christian isn't so easy to convince, however. Having repented of his former rebellion against God and come to experience his rich saving grace, he feels loyalty and gratitude to the Lord. Apollyon tries to dismiss Christian's concerns by assuring him that abandoning the Lord and his pilgrimage will cause him no trouble. He infers that most who begin as pilgrims change their minds and give it up anyway. Naturally this means that they have come to their senses, that the Lord proved Himself a liar, and benevolent Apollyon has saved them from their folly. He also tells Christian not to worry about the penalty for committing apostasy. Then he presents himself as a better and more forgiving lord.

Our enemy is a smooth operator. While he blinds unbelievers, he cleverly waylays believers. How can anyone be compelled to forsake the Lord? How can one turn from the Kingdom of Light back to the kingdom of darkness? Yet spirits no less vile than Apollyon convince professed believers to return to their bondage to the prince of darkness often without a skirmish. Once back in his grip, they are at his beck and call, enslaved to sin, dooming themselves to eternal death and destruction. Incredible as it may seem, the enemy convinces them that evil is good and good evil.

It doesn't matter how many fall away—we can remain sure-footed and true to the Lord. To withstand the enemy's seductions successfully, we must be alert to his lies and to our own particular vulnerabilities. We must cleave to the Lord, his truth, and his freedom with single-minded devotion, allowing no foothold of doubt. Have you ever naively submitted to demonic temptations that lured you away from God's will? In what areas of your life do you most need to shore up the weak places that you might obey God?

❧

Scripture: Deuteronomy 8:19; 11:16; 26:16-17; Matthew 24:10

Prayer: Blessed Lord, I align myself with you. My loyalty and love are yours. Please keep me from succumbing to enticements to walk in the ways of the world. Amen.

D·A·Y 102

Christian remained undaunted. "What I promised you was before I was of age. Besides, I believe that the Prince, under whose banner I now stand, can free me from my obligations to you and forgive me for what I did in compliance with you. In addition to this, you destroying Apollyon, to tell you the truth, I like His service, His wages, His servants, His government, His company, and His Country better than yours. So forget trying to persuade me further. I am His servant, and I will follow Him."

Apollyon thus far fails in his attempts to intimidate, bribe, and reason Christian back to the City of Destruction. Despite his difficulties and trials, Christian doesn't believe that he has "gone from bad to worse" in leaving the dark domain. He remains resolutely loyal to his new King. Rather than trying to appease the devil, Christian realizes the best way of dealing with the enemy is by making a stand and confronting him with the truth. He lets him know in no uncertain terms that he has absolutely no intention of returning with this demonic spirit to the City of Destruction.

Christian now stands under a new banner declaring allegiance to a new Prince. This Prince, being greater than Apollyon, has the power to forgive and to free him from his former debt. Christian categorically refuses to join the throng of apostates whom Apollyon has lured into turning away from their pilgrimages.

Bravo, Christian! This is the spirit we need when we are barraged with the enemy's cajoling efforts to seduce us out of our resolve to follow the Lord. We refuse the enemy's poison. We emphatically declare that we much prefer Christ and his service. Serving our Lord is not bondage; it is a joy and privilege. His wages aren't death; they are life. His servants aren't evil; they are godly. His government is not tyrannical; it is one of liberty in the Holy Spirit. His presence is not oppressive; it is warm and soothing. His rule is not by force; it is by love. His Country is not Destruction; it is life eternal in the glorious Celestial City. Within our hearts there isn't even a contest. With Christian, we resolutely proclaim, "I am *his* servant, and I will follow *him*."

If you are at all double-minded in your commitment to Christ, you will find yourself harassed much more often than most believers. Make up your mind right now to give Christ 100-percent loyalty, and don't be ashamed of your decision. Instead, boldly celebrate it.

Scripture: Isaiah 9:7; 41:9; 50:7-9; Luke 1:69-75

Prayer: Wonderful Lord, when the tempter comes assailing me with his seductions, I want to make my stand for you. Thank you for the glorious privilege of knowing and serving you. I pledge my allegiance to you and your kingdom. Amen.

D·A·Y
103

Still, Apollyon persisted. "Once you cool down and reality sinks in, consider again what you will likely meet with in the way you are going. You know that, for the most part, His servants come to a terrible end because they are violators of my will and my ways. How many of them have been put to a shameful death! You still believe His service is better than mine even though He has yet to come from where He is to deliver any of His servants from their assailants' hands. But as for me, as all the world very well knows, I have many times—either by power or by fraud—delivered those who faithfully serve me from Him and His servants, though they were taken by them. And I will also deliver you."

William Shakespeare's King Lear says, "The prince of darkness is a gentleman." So we see Apollyon determined to be a gentleman to persuade the stubborn pilgrim back to his way of thinking. He basically tells Christian that, rather than being levelheaded, he is being unreasonable and emotional. If he were looking at reality rationally, he would definitely have second thoughts about this pilgrimage. Apollyon attempts to undermine Christian's resolve by again injecting him with fear. In a pleasant way he lets Christian know that his faith in the Lord to deliver him is ungrounded since those who keep faith come to a shameful death. Not only does he imply that he is more powerful than Christ, but he accuses Christ of abandoning his pilgrims and of not coming to their aid. Apollyon, on the other hand, takes care of his own. He rescues them from their folly and promises to "deliver" Christian safely, too. His arguments sound so perfectly logical.

Deception is the glue that holds Satan's kingdom together. He is a cunning strategist, a master at packaging sin to make it the most appealing. He likes drawing us away from the realm of faith, our greatest strength, into the arena of human reason, his greatest strength. With a God-given brilliant mind turned intensely evil, he uses reason to undermine our faith and confidence. Since Christ demands a narrow way, the enemy tries to open our minds to broader ways of thinking. As he applies his own answers to gospel mysteries, he finds many willing victims. If we hope to survive his schemes, we must dismiss his lies and suspicions and hold tightly to our faith and hope. Faith, not reason, is the victory that overcomes the world. Have any specific reasonings proved problematic for you? Will you renounce them now and conquer them with faith?

Scripture: John 8:44b; 2 Thessalonians 2:9-10; Daniel 11:32

Prayer: Dear Lord, sometimes I don't understand the things I am going through. That's when I'm vulnerable to trying to figure it out instead of trusting you. Please remind me to stand firm in faith. Amen.

DAY 104

Christian answered firmly, "He presently restrains Himself from delivering His pilgrims to test their love and see whether they will cling to Him until the end. And as for the undesirable end you say they come to, that is the most glorious credit to their account. They do not much expect deliverance right now, but they remain true for the glory coming to them—and they shall have it when their Prince comes in His glory and the glory of the angels."

In response to Apollyon's accusation that the King abandons his pilgrims to their enemy's hands, Christian has a ready retort. Seeing through the demon's twist of truth with the perception of faith, he believes God has a higher purpose for the afflictions his pilgrims experience. While for a time the Lord "restrains" his hand from delivering his pilgrims from their enemies, and while the wicked seem to prosper under their master's rule, God is in control.

Christian no doubt recalls Watchful's admonition to press on past the lions outside the Palace Beautiful. Watchful had explained that the lions were there as a test of faith to distinguish those who possessed true faith from those who did not. Christian maintains that all our present trials test our love and faithfulness to the Lord and will work for our ultimate glory before the Lord in his kingdom.

Sometimes God allows testing in our lives to keep us humble, such as with Paul's thorn in the flesh. Sometimes God allows testing, such as with Job, to prove to the enemy a believer's love for him. God uses testings to refine us, to educate us, to teach us more about his sovereignty. The Greek word *dokimazo* used for testing means to test or try with the expectation of approving. God allows afflictions to prepare us for the day when we must give account for ourselves before him in his kingdom. The trials that test us today will prove our faith genuine tomorrow and result in great praise and glory. God looks forward to lavishing his rich rewards upon us; this is why he tests our faith.

With such blessed hope, we should press forward through our trials, desiring to be deemed worthy, trusting that God allows everything in our lives for our eternal profit. List some trials that have discouraged you. Write down next to each a statement of faith based on God's Word concerning them. Refresh your faith by referring to your statement often.

Scripture: Deuteronomy 8:2-3; 1 Corinthians 3:12-14; James 1:12

Prayer: Eternal Father, I want to stand before you victoriously in that day when I must give account. I trust you to weave my trials for your ultimate blessed purpose for my life. Thank you, Lord. Amen.

D·A·Y
105

"You have already been unfaithful in your service to Him," Apollyon sneered. "How do you think you can receive wages from Him?"

"Oh, Apollyon, how have I been unfaithful to Him?"

"You weakened in your resolve when you first set out and were nearly choked in the Slough of Despond. You tried to go wrong ways to get rid of your Burden when you should have stayed on course until your Prince had taken it off. You sinfully slept and lost your treasured things. You were almost persuaded to go back at the sight of the Lions. And when you talk of your journey and of what you have heard and seen, you inwardly desire recognition for all you say or do."

"All this is true," answered Christian, "and much more that you have left out. But the Prince whom I serve and honor is merciful and ready to forgive. Besides, these shortcomings possessed me in your country, where I participated in them and groaned under their weight. I have been sorry for these things and have now received pardon by my Prince."

Apollyon no doubt sees Christ's image in Christian. He despises it and seeks to efface it before Christian becomes too aware of it. He also despises the faith Christian expresses in his new Prince and seeks to overthrow it. If he can weaken the pilgrim's confidence in his relationship with Christ, his resolve will also weaken. Apollyon knows how to accuse God to saints and accuse saints to God. Since he just failed in his attempts to accuse God to Christian, he now tries the other approach. "The accuser of the brethren" catalogued all Christian's sins to use against him at the right time. Surely Christian cannot hope for God's acceptance.

Fortunately, Christian confessed these sins and more besides. He knows he experienced grace and mercy and is confident of Christ's forgiveness. Our enemy's bag of tricks always contains tactics to undermine our confidence in our position in Christ. He exploits our weaknesses and inconsistencies. He reminds us of all our past sins and failures. If we don't continually reaffirm our identity in Christ, we will begin to succumb to the devil's condemnation. We stand our ground against satanic accusations, not because of our goodness but by faith in Christ's grace and mercy. Are you prone to feeling guilt over past sins? When you confessed and repented of them, God forgave you. If the enemy throws them back in your face, throw back in his face your Lord's faithfulness in forgiving you.

Scripture: 1 John 1:9; Zechariah 3:1-4; Psalm 9:10

Prayer: Dear Lord, thank you for your forgiving love that is greater than the sum of all my sins. When the devil comes around to accuse me, help me to remember my position in you. Remind me to point to the blood that covers these sins. Amen.

D·A·Y 106

Suddenly Apollyon erupted into a fierce rage, shrieking, "I am an enemy of this Prince! I hate His Person, His laws, and His people! I have come out with this purpose—to stop you!"

"Apollyon, beware of what you do," warned Christian, "for I am in the King's Highway, the way of holiness. Therefore you had better watch yourself."

Then Apollyon spread himself out in such a way as to cover the entire width of the Way and challenged, "I am without fear in this matter. Prepare to die! For I swear by my infernal dwelling that you shall go no farther. I will destroy your soul right here!"

Apollyon has tried every persuasive tactic in his arsenal to halt Christian's spiritual progress. Having failed, he is out of patience. Erupting in a fit of rage, he furiously spews out a wicked and hostile diatribe against the Lord and his purposes in Christian's life. If he cannot persuade Christian peaceably, he will whip and bully him into line. If that won't work, Christian will die on the spot. At least, that is the threat.

Does Apollyon have power to carry out his threat? After all, the Scripture promises, "Submit yourselves, then, to God. Resist the devil, and he will flee from you" (James 4:7). Christian is certainly submitted to God, and he is clearly resisting his adversary. Even so, the Greek word for "resist," *anthistemi*, is used here in the active voice and imperative mood, indicating it doesn't mean resisting for a time and then stopping. It is an absolute command to solidly fix your position, set yourself against, withstand, and continually oppose the enemy.

No allowance is made for slacking off, but Apollyon wants Christian to do just that. Although the demon is a trespasser without rights to the King's Highway, he menacingly spreads himself out to completely obstruct Christian's view of the Highway, making it look impassable. Christian, however, has no intention of caving in to Apollyon's threats. He has rights. He is on the King's Highway, meaning he is under God's protection, in God's will.

The Lord never leaves us to fight our battles alone. He is with us, but we must consistently resist the enemy. Does he seem invincible to you? He is not, but to prevail, you must turn to God, know who you are and what you have in Christ, have your armor in place, keep sober and alert, fend off intimidation, and stand in faith with unflinching resolve. "You cannot run away from a weakness; you must some time fight it out or perish, and if that be so, why not now, and where you stand?" (Robert Louis Stevenson).[9]

Scripture: 1 Peter 5:9; Ephesians 6:13; 1 Timothy 6:12

Prayer: Dear Lord, I resolve to stand boldly against both the enemy's subtle attacks and his blatant ones. I trust your ability to bring me through into victory. Amen.

D·A·Y 107

At that Apollyon hurled a flaming arrow at Christian's heart, but Christian had a Shield in his hand with which he blocked the arrow. Then Christian drew his Sword and roused himself for the battle. Apollyon, with feverish pace, began throwing arrows as thick as hail. It was all Christian could do to avoid them, and, even so, he was wounded in his head, his hand, and his foot. This caused Christian to retreat somewhat. Seeing this, Apollyon fell upon him with full and sudden fury.

When pleased, the devil can be amiable; when he is angry, however, watch out! Apollyon is enraged! He means to destroy Christian by deadly force as he hurls his first soul-destroying arrow at Christian's heart. Christian fends off this arrow with his shield (of faith). He then draws his sword (the Word of God). Apollyon, in flaming wrath, however, feverishly begins barraging Christian with torrents of his blasphemies until he wounds him. The wounds are to the head, that is, his understanding; to his hand, meaning the faith in God that enables him to wield his sword effectively; and to his foot, suggesting his ability to walk and behave circumspectly. These wounds weaken Christian, and the enemy, noting this weakness, comes at him even more forcefully.

At times like this it appears God has forsaken us. This gives the enemy opportunity to make us doubt God's love and provision. Satan afflicts us with arrows to make us doubt God's truth and our salvation. The shield of faith can repel the fiercest arrows. Sometimes, however, the attack is so feverish that we have trouble avoiding everything thrown at us. No matter how we imagined spiritual warfare, we are unprepared for this. Confusion, dismay, and self-reproach buffet us. We feel so harassed when we pray, read our Bible, or attempt to claim God's promises that for some immediate peace, we are tempted to give them up. We begin to fall back. This is just what the enemy wants. He then pierces us, resulting in a loss of understanding, faith, and firm-footed resolve. At this point some people doubt their convictions and seek solace in some false doctrine, or they retreat to some worldly habit that formerly soothed them.

We must resolve, by God's grace, never to give one inch of ground up to the devil. If we doubt either our cause, our armor, or our King, we will give our enemy an unwarranted advantage. Strengthen your faith by reaffirming the justness of your cause, the adequacy of your armor, and the supremacy of your King.

Scripture: Revelation 12:12; Ephesians 4:27; 6:16-17; Nehemiah 6:9

Prayer: Dear Lord, since I cannot avoid spiritual warfare in this life, please help me to resolve to stand faithfully when under attack. Amen.

D·A·Y
108

Christian regained his courage, however, and resisted as gallantly as he could. This fierce combat went on for more than half a day, until Christian's strength was almost completely spent. Because of his wounds, he grew weaker and weaker. Apollyon saw his most opportune moment and drew up close to Christian. He began to wrestle with Christian and threw him forcefully to the ground. Christian's Sword flew out of his hand.

Gloating, Apollyon said, "I am sure I have you now!" With that, he assaulted Christian nearly to the point of death so that he began to despair of life itself.

❧

Jesus, speaking of the devil, said, "The thief comes only to steal and kill and destroy . . ." (John 10:10). When Christian realizes Apollyon will destroy him if he keeps falling back, he renews his effort to resist Apollyon. Apollyon's temptations and assaults, however, are unrelenting, and Christian increasingly loses heart. Apollyon sees this and moves in for the kill at "his most opportune moment."

When Christ wrestled Satan in the wilderness with the sword of the Spirit, Satan gave up "until an opportune time" (Luke 4:13). That opportune time came when he thought he had nailed Christ to the cross forever.

The devil is an intelligent being who is well aware of his opportune moments. At those times he assails us vigorously until we give up hope and our sword flies out of our hand. With our sword gone, he has a tremendous advantage over us. We are in deep crisis, having lost our chief weapon. If saving faith could completely fail, even true born-again believers would now surely perish. Apollyon has succeeded in ruining many who have set out on a pilgrimage with far less effort. Now, certain of Christian's defeat, he begins to boast triumphantly. Poor unarmed Christian, tending at this point to believe his foe's boasts, begins to despair of life itself.

Often the enemy's opportune time for attacking us has absolutely no bearing on anything we have or have not done. Sometimes, however, we hand him an opportunity to assail us. We must do all we can to resist to his temptations. Rather than losing heart, we need to press on in faith, trusting God for the strength to ultimately overcome our enemy. Do you feel as if the enemy has gone for your jugular? Does the battle seem all but lost? Don't panic; keep believing. God won't abandon you.

❧

Scripture: Ephesians 6:12; 2 Corinthians 1:8-10; Psalm 35:22-26

Prayer: Dear Lord, when I am severely tempted, help me not to falter in my confidence in you. I want to keep wielding the sword of the Spirit—your promises—until the battle is fully won. Amen.

D·A·Y
109

But, as God would have it, while Apollyon was preparing to strike his final blow to annihilate his foe completely, Christian quickly stretched out his hand and grabbed his Sword, saying, "Do not gloat over me, my enemy! Though I have fallen, I will rise again" [Micah 7:8]. With that, Christian gave Apollyon a deadly thrust that made him fall back as if mortally wounded.

❦

"As God would have it . . ." Thank the good Lord that he has a will and purpose for our lives that doesn't fail us in our times of distress. Even when our world seems to spin out of control, even when the enemy seems to have his foot on our neck poised for the kill, God is still on the throne. If we commit our lives to his will, he uses every affliction and trial we go through for our ultimate good.

Still God doesn't do it all for us. Distressing as our situation may be, we must keep believing his promise, trusting that he is with us to help pull us through as we continue to engage our enemy. Thus Christian must fight until he wins, and the only way to win is to recover his sword. As "God would have it," he reaches out his hand and retakes his weapon. While he has to stretch out his hand and take it up, it is the supernatural power of God that enables him to do so.

Christ wielded the sword of the Spirit against Satan in the wilderness, repeatedly quoting Scripture against every temptation. "It is written . . . it is written . . . it is written . . ." Now in a burst of faith, Christian uses Scripture as a declaration against his foe. Being exceedingly powerful, the Word of God seriously wounds Apollyon. While Scripture is the sword, that sword is wielded through faith. As faith rises within Christian's heart and is applied to his sword, it lands a deadly blow. But where does this sudden renewed faith come from? From God's Word. When the Holy Spirit recalls Scripture to our minds, it can powerfully renew our faith. If we resolutely couple that faith with God's promise, no matter how grim our situation, we will be amazed. Our battle will in an instant turn in our favor, and we will pluck victory from the very jaws of defeat. With the sword of the Spirit wielded in faith, we can vanquish demonic armies and batter down the gates of hell. It behooves us to diligently study, memorize, and believe God's Word that when our enemy advances against us, we can cut him down to size.

❦

Scripture: Matthew 4:1-11; Hebrews 4:12; 2 Thessalonians 3:2-3

Prayer: Lord, thank you for the provisions you have given me through your Word—the sword of the Spirit. Please help me to be more diligent in learning how to apply it victoriously to my warfare. Amen.

D·A·Y 110

Seeing this, Christian attacked again, saying, "No, in all these things we are more than conquerors through Him who loved us" [Romans 8:37]. Apollyon then spread his dragon wings and sped away in defeat, and Christian would see him no more.

A more unequal match could there be?
Christian must fight an angel, but you see
The valiant man by wielding Sword and Shield,
Does make him, though a dragon, quit the field.

We are more than conquerors! Christian again thrusts his sword with faith-filled words that Apollyon can no longer tolerate. For all the enemy's threats and boasts, a few duly applied Scriptures send him fleeing. The Greek word for "more than conquerors," *hupernikao*, promises no small victory. It means that we are exceedingly abundantly victorious over our foes.

We are not mere survivors who have somehow held our positions against enemy assault. We are conquerors but not just any conquerors; we are *more* than conquerors over sins of the flesh, over Satan, over trials and afflictions, over worldly influences, over scorn and persecutions. It doesn't mean we simply win victories over these tests and assaults. It means we are better off for going through them. And we are not only better off for going through them; we actually glory in them. We have more faith, more love for the Lord, more joy, more patient endurance because of our battle. Not only this, but we silence our adversaries, put them to shame, and even win some to our side. We encroach upon and conquer long-held enemy fortresses. We even hold our faith firm to the death. Yes, God fights for us as we stand and face our enemy. We suddenly realize that indeed we are *more than conquerors*.

But let us not forget through whom the victory comes—"*through Him who loved us." He* is the one who, through his great love, died for us, equips and helps us to face our enemy, stands with us, picks us up when we fall, strengthens our arm to pick up our sword, apply it effectively, and fight through to victory. *He* is the one who carries us through all our troubles and makes us more than conquerors. *His* is the glory! When was the last time you felt the thrill of victory? Did you give God proper praise and glory? Do it again now, and do it in anticipation of future victories. Praise the Lord!

Scripture: 1 John 5:4; Isaiah 41:11-16; Revelation 12:10-11

Prayer: Dear Lord, thank you for your rich love that enables me to be more than a conqueror. I trust you to train me to be a tried and true victor in your service to your glory. Amen.

D·A·Y 111

No one could imagine, unless he had seen and heard the battle as I did, what yelling and hideous roaring Apollyon made the whole time; on the other hand, what sighs and groans burst forth from Christian's heart. Not once during the struggle did I see Christian look confident until he perceived he had wounded Apollyon with his two-edged sword—and then he actually smiled! It was the most dreadful fight that I have ever seen.

When the battle was over, Christian said, "I will give thanks to the One who has delivered me out of the lion's mouth, to him who helped me against Apollyon." And he did, saying,

"So great Beelzebub, this fiend's captain,
Had devised a plan that I'd never rise again.
He sent him out armed; he was enraged;
In hellish fight we fiercely engaged.
But blessed Michael helped me, and I,
By blow of Sword, quickly made him fly.
Therefore to Christ I'll give lasting praise,
And thank and bless His Name always."

Peeking behind the physical veil, we see opposing spiritual forces warring for Christian's soul. Despite the philosophy of materialists who believe solely in matter, a spiritual realm as real as the physical one exists. God, who is spirit, lives with myriads of angels in this realm. Heaven, a spiritual place, is his home. He created the physical universe like a speck of matter set within the spiritual realm. While the physical dimension seems most real to us, the spiritual one is all around us continually influencing us.

When Satan somewhere in eternity led a host of angels into rebellion, God cast them out of heaven. Since then they have tried to destroy life and inject every evil into our world. The Bible says that Satan, knowing his time is short, is in a furious rage. He vengefully works to drag with him to hell every soul he can. Sad to say, most people ignorantly believe either that spirits don't exist at all or that every spirit is good.

Christ won the decisive victory on the cross, but the war rages on. We must distinguish between spiritual light and darkness and know how to wage spiritual warfare. Every heavenly resource is at our disposal. The next time you feel defeated or discouraged, grasp your sword in faith, trust God for unseen spiritual help, and see the enemy flee. Your trial will have become a means of increased grace and victory.

Scripture: 2 Kings 6:15-18; Revelation 5:11; 12:7-9; Daniel 10:18-21

Prayer: Dear Lord, thank you for graciously sending your angels to help me win my battles. I trust you to bring me victory. Amen.

D·A·Y 112

Then a hand reached out to him, holding leaves from the Tree of Life. Christian took the leaves, applied them to the wounds that he had received in the battle, and was healed instantly! After this, he sat down in that place to eat bread and drink from the bottle his friends had given to him. Feeling refreshed, he prepared to go on with his journey. He kept his Sword drawn in his hand and said to himself, "Another enemy may well be lurking nearby." But he had no more confrontations with Apollyon through the rest of the Valley.

Christian's battle in the Valley of Humiliation with Apollyon and his temptations didn't leave him unscathed. Although he defeated his enemy, it was no proud victory. While more humble and dependent on God's grace, he is also wounded and weary. Consequently, the Lord tenderly and compassionately reaches out with leaves from the Tree of Life. In taking them and applying them to his need, Christian's sins are forgiven, his mistakes corrected, his wounds healed, his soul restored, and his strength renewed.

In the book of Genesis, the Tree of Life indicates paradise lost in the Garden due to sin; in Revelation, the last book, it represents paradise restored in the kingdom of heaven through the grace of our Lord Jesus Christ. In heaven the pure water of the river of life flowing directly from God's throne feeds the Tree of Life with the promises, provision, privileges, and presence of God. Thus its "leaves" are for the healing of the nations (or peoples).

Once in a while we hear of medical researchers discovering medicinal qualities in the bark or leaves of certain plants and trees. For example, slippery elm bark is used for digestion, and ginkgo biloba leaves are used for increased brain function. Even common aspirin derives from willow bark. Not a tree on earth, however, can produce the healing that one "leaf" from the Tree of Life brings. While we won't partake fully of the Tree's fruit until we reach heaven, many of the benefits of God's Tree of Life have already broken through in our lives, providing health, vitality, and the joy of our salvation.

After his healing, Christian partakes of the bread and wine to show humble appreciation for the body and blood of Christ given for him. After this refreshment, however, he realizes he cannot simply rest in the healing he has received. Once we are restored, we must press forward with our journey. Other obstacles and temptations will present themselves, but the Lord will help us through these as well. Do you bear wounds from life's battles? God is offering you healing. Take it in faith.

Scripture: Genesis 2:9; Revelation 2:7; 22:2, 14; Isaiah 57:15

Prayer: Lord Jesus, thank you that when life's battles wound me, I can trust you to bring your healing touch so that I can once again apply myself to my pilgrimage. Amen.

DAY 113

At the end of the first Valley was another Valley called the Valley of the Shadow of Death. It was necessary for Christian to pass through it because it was the only way to the Celestial City. This Valley is a very solitary place. The prophet Jeremiah describes it as a Wilderness, a Land of Deserts and Pits, a Land of Drought and of the Shadow of Death, a Land that no one (except a Christian) is able to pass through and where no one lives.

Here, as you will see, Christian's testings were even more severe than those he had encountered with Apollyon.

Christian is kept from any innate tendencies toward self-congratulation by a new danger. He must pass through the Valley of the Shadow of Death on his way to the Celestial City. This is not death, but the shadow of death, suggesting a fear of death. As a shadow of a lion cannot devour a person, the shadow of death cannot kill. It is, in any case, a most severe deep, dark Valley of affliction and distress.

The Valley of the Shadow of Death must here represent an assortment of inner conflicts, fears, and depression arising from spiritual darkness oppressing and prevailing upon the soul. God's peace has suddenly vanished, and the person's mental, emotional, and spiritual state are all in turmoil. Faith, hope, love, and gratitude are depleted. The believer's spirit feels dull and heavy; prayer seems to fall flat. Because God seems distant and unreal, unbelief sets in. It seems that he no longer cares. The pilgrimage, rather than being a joy and privilege, has become a miserable trial. All former victory seems a delusion. Jeremiah, here quoted, cites the desolate wilderness through which Israel journeyed to the Promised Land. Israel doubted God's provision, feared perishing in the wilderness, and even considered returning to Egypt.

This wilderness, however, is one that no one "except a Christian" passes through. Who but a Christian, after all, has felt the warmth of walking in God's loving presence but then suddenly feels that God has withdrawn? En route to heaven, some believers have a dreadful time here while others pass through with not nearly the difficulty. Whatever their dispositions, few pilgrims have an easy time in this Valley. Despite the circumstance that brings us into this place of seeming death, we must believe that it need not spell disaster. If we trust God, even this experience will bring deeper maturity in our walk of faith.

What will you do if you go through trials that make you feel cut off from the life of God? Will you go forward in faith?

Scripture: Jeremiah 2:6; Psalm 23:4; Isaiah 26:4

Prayer: Dear Lord, I admit I feel ill-prepared for entering this Valley, but I trust you to see me through my struggles no matter how woeful they may become. Amen.

D·A·Y 114

I saw in my dream that when Christian reached the borders of the Shadow of Death, two men met him. They were Descendants of the Spies who had brought back an evil report of the Good Land, and they were in a hurry to go back.

"Where are you going?" Christian asked.

They answered, "Back, back, and we urge you to follow us if you prize either life or peace."

"Why, what's the matter?"

"Matter? We were going along the same way you are going and went as far as we dared, almost past the point of no return. If we had gone just a little further, we would not have made it back here to bring the news to you."

"But what have you met with?"

"Why, we were almost in the Valley of the Shadow of Death, but just by chance we looked ahead of us and could see the danger before we came to it."

After 400 years of Egyptian bondage, God mightily delivered Israel. He planned to give them a bountiful, beautiful, blessed land—the "Promised Land." Upon reaching the land, Moses sent twelve spies to survey it. They came back reporting that it was just as God had promised. Ten, however, believed that possessing it was impossible; the people looked like giants and their cities looked impregnable. They envisioned disaster ahead should Israel attempt to possess it. Faith turned to fear, fear to unbelief, and unbelief to rebellion as these men poisoned the entire community against God and his promise.

Only two spies, Joshua and Caleb, had eyes of faith. Caleb declared, "We should go take possession of the land, for we can certainly do it!" The people listened, however, to the other ten. Infuriated, God kept the roughly two million people wandering in the wilderness for forty years until all the adults died off except Joshua and Caleb. These two alone went in with the next generation to possess the Promised Land.

Christian meets a couple of faithless descendants of the spies. These two fugitives tried the pilgrimage for a while, but the trials of the Valley of the Shadow of Death are too much for them. Not only do they run away, but they excuse their desertion and attempt to inject their unbelief into Christian. Surveying our own actions and attitudes is important. Do we cause faith or doubt to rise in those who hear and observe us? Each of us can influence others for good or for ill. Take a look at your influence. How can you better motivate others to faith and obedience?

Scriptures: Numbers 13:26-33; Hebrews 3:7-19; Psalm 138:6-8

Prayer: Dear Lord, please help me, unlike the ten spies, to be the kind of person who looks past the problems into your bounteous provision. I want to inspire faith, not fear, in others. Amen.

D·A·Y 115

"But what did you see?"

"What did we see? Why, the Valley itself, which is pitch black. We could see Hobgoblins, Satyrs, and Dragons of the Pit. We could also hear in that Valley continual howling and screaming—it sounded like people in indescribable misery who were bound in affliction and chains. We also saw the depressing clouds of confusion hanging over the Valley; and death, with wings spread, was hovering over it all. It is absolutely dreadful and in complete chaos."

"From what you have said," replied Christian, "I'm still not convinced that this isn't the way to my destination."

"Have it your way," they said, "but we won't choose it for ourselves."

So they left, and Christian went on his way with his Sword still drawn for fear that he might be assaulted.

When the children of Israel refused godly persuasion, electing instead to heed the spies, they weren't thinking clearly. They had every reason to go ahead and possess the Promised Land. The almighty God who had already done countless wonders for them had both commanded it and promised it. They should have recounted all his miracles and, with Joshua and Caleb, believed that nothing could stop them with God on their side. They should have discerned the poisonous spirit of doubt and unbelief in the ten spies. How tragic that they chose to view the Promised Land as impossible to attain, themselves as helpless to attain it, and their God as either unable or unwilling to carry out his promises. Their error was inexcusable; God made no allowances for their rebellion.

Fortunately Christian is on his guard. Although it is twilight in his soul, he has accepted that difficulties attend the path of the righteous. Hazards up ahead in no way preclude this from being the right way. They are really irrelevant nonissues in deciding which way to go. The men, like two spirits of fear, try to persuade him to go with them, but he resists their disheartening report.

We need to be careful about the voices to which we listen. They can speak either words of life or words of death into our hearts. Some, while sincere, may approach problems with doubt and unbelief. Even when things look their worst, however, we have every reason to press forward with our pilgrimage. Ours is a great God with great promises. We cannot let fear and unbelief turn us aside from obeying him. What positive and negative voices are in your life? Try listening to the positive ones more.

Scripture: Joshua 14:6-14; Psalm 27:1; Nahum 1:7

Prayer: Father God, help me to have discernment to distinguish between reports that will help and reports that will hinder me in my pilgrimage. I want to faithfully trust you. Amen.

D·A·Y 116

I then saw in my dream that there was a very deep Ditch along the right side of the Valley as far as it reached. It is into that Ditch that the blind have led the blind throughout the ages, and there both have miserably died. I could also see that on the left side was a very dangerous Quagmire; even a good person, should he fall in, will find no bottom for his foot to stand on. King David once fell in here and no doubt would have suffocated had not He who is able mercifully plucked him out.

The pathway was so narrow that Christian had to be very careful. When he tried in the darkness to avoid the Ditch on the one hand, he almost fell into the Quagmire on the other. However, when he tried to escape the Quagmire, unless he used great caution, he nearly fell into the Ditch.

In the Valley of the Shadow of Death, pilgrims become vulnerable to all kinds of fears and insecurities. The Way seems unusually narrow here, and they must take extreme caution as both the ditch on the right and the quagmire on the left are perilously close to where they must walk. Since one could carelessly stumble into either, the safest place is right in the center of the pathway.

The deep ditch into which blind leaders and blind followers fall is a deadly presumption into which they are eased due to pride and false doctrine. Christ said of the Pharisees: "They are blind guides. If a blind man leads a blind man, both will fall into a pit" (Matthew 15:14). Instead of taking the Valley seriously, they are unaware of the danger. Despite what the Scriptures say, they barrel on through, believing they can see better and farther than anyone else. They even think they can lead others to safety. And their followers are no less guilty. Instead of seeking God, they trust unreliable leadership. Neither looks to God or to his Word, and suddenly they disappear together into the ditch.

Extending along the opposite side of the path is the quagmire. It, too, can be fatal. Their troubled Valley experience so upsets some pilgrims that they increasingly lose their bearings. They walk unsteadily, their hearts grow cold, and they think God has let them down. Feeling God won't revive them, they are driven over the edge into this quagmire.

As Christians, we must avoid the extremes of presumption and hopelessness when going through Valleys like this one. Although danger lurks on every hand, we can keep our faith intact by stepping carefully. In dark and dangerous times, has either extreme tempted you? What changes can you make in your attitude and life to keep hopelessness and presumption at bay?

Scripture: Joshua 1:7; Proverbs 4:25-27; Isaiah 30:21

Prayer: Father, I see how in dark and trying times I need to keep to the center of the road. I trust you to bring me through safely. Amen.

D·A·Y 117

Christian went on in this Way, and I heard him sigh bitterly. For, in addition to the dangers already mentioned, the pathway was so dark that often when he picked up his foot to go forward, he had no idea where he should put it down next.

The Mouth of Hell was beside the Way about midway through the Valley.

Poor man, where are you now? Your day is now night.
Good man, don't be downhearted; you are still right—
Your way to Heaven lies by the gates of Hell;
Cheer up, hold on, with you it shall go well.

Christian faithfully presses forward, but he is not a happy camper. As he creeps along, he sighs bitterly. The enemy is no doubt behind all this discouragement. Perhaps the report of the two faithless ones gnaws at him; perhaps he recalls the man with the terrifying dream who fearfully testified of the mouth of hell being right at his feet. Confused and terrified for each step, Christian suddenly sees the gaping mouth of hell near enough to devour him.

When believers suffer some sickness, loss, grief, disappointment, or failure, or when they see wickedness multiplying around them, they can lose sight of God. With hearts overwhelmed with darkness, they enter this Valley of the Shadow of Death experience. Here many sincere Christians born of God's Spirit fear that God has somehow abandoned them. They think of some real or imagined sin that surely must be dooming and consigning their souls to hell. But this is not true at all. Hell exists, but it is for punishing and consuming God's enemies, not his beloved children.

To be sure, God has a furnace of affliction for his people to go through, but it is for a loving purpose. He refines away our dross until he sees his image reflected in our lives. Then he can make of us pure chosen vessels for his special use. And while this furnace may seem like hell, it is not. Through these dark times, we must remember that our destiny is heaven and that this is as close to hell as we will ever find ourselves. Let us keep in mind, too, that the pathway to hell is an easy and broad one to travel. The path of the righteous, on the other hand, is the way of the cross. We can press on with confidence that, despite all appearances, we are still in the center of God's will. When you are in a crisis of faith, seemingly suffering senseless heartaches, losses, and confusion, let God's Word minister hope and comfort to your soul.

Scripture: Job 23:10; Psalm 66:10; 1 Peter 1:7; 4:12-13

Prayer: Dear Lord, with Christian I sigh and moan in my Valley experiences. Help me to understand that this has not come upon me because of my sin or your rejection but for my higher good and your glory. Amen.

DAY 118

So much fire and smoke continually came out, with swarms of sparks and hideous noises (things that gave no heed to Christian's Sword as did Apollyon) that he was forced to put his Sword away and use another weapon called All-prayer. So I heard him cry out, "Oh, Lord, save me!" He continued praying like this for quite awhile, but the flames kept reaching out toward him, and he heard sorrowful voices and rushing sounds around him. Sometimes he thought he would be torn to pieces or trampled down like dirt in the street.

Oh, what can be more terrifying than having your sword pass through some horrifying evil specter leaving it unfazed? Christian's experience is now so distressing to him that even the Word of God seems of little effect. He resorts to the weapon of All-prayer (all kinds of prayer). Unable to pray as he would, he desperately prays as he can—"Oh, Lord, save me!"

Sometimes we find ourselves hemmed in by dark and terrifying temptations. While still believing the Scriptures are essentially true, we are so harassed that we cannot calm down long enough to trust them. The anxious thoughts besieging us deafen us to the promises that brought us victory only a short time before. Relying on heartfelt prayer is our only recourse.

It has already been pointed out that King David fell into the quagmire but was mercifully delivered. He, too, was reduced to a desperate cry to God for mercy. Imagine his desperation as he bawled, "Rescue me from the mire, do not let me sink; deliver me from those who hate me, from the deep waters. Do not let the floodwaters engulf me or the depths swallow me up or the pit close its mouth over me. Answer me, O LORD . . . answer me quickly, for I am in trouble. Come near and rescue me; redeem me because of my foes. You know how I am scorned, disgraced and shamed; all my enemies are before you. Scorn has broken my heart and has left me helpless . . ." (Psalm 69:14-20).

As we pass through our own Valley of the Shadow of Death experiences, we can know that prayer is a powerful weapon. It can reach God from whatever pit we are in. When we are overwhelmed and have little energy for faith-filled praying, he will not despise our simple heartfelt S-O-S. Are you a person of prayer—who doesn't just pray when all else fails? Learn to pray at all times with all kinds of prayer, and you will soon recognize God's Spirit leading you through your dark Valley. Someone has said, "The wings of prayer carry far and high."

Scripture: Ephesians 6:18; Psalms 72:12-13; 77:1-2; 145:18-19

Prayer: Dear Lord, thank you for the powerful weapon you have given your children through prayer. Help me to be a person of prayer, bringing everything in my day to you. Amen.

D·A·Y 119

Christian experienced these terrors of sight and sound continuously for several miles. Then he came to a place where he thought he heard a band of fiends coming forward to confront him. He stopped and began to think about his options. He had half a notion to go back, but then he thought that he might already be halfway through the Valley. He remembered also how he had already met and overcome many dangers. It dawned on him that going back might be much worse than going forward. So he resolved to go on, but the fiends seemed to come nearer and nearer. When they were almost face to face with him, he cried out very vehemently, "I will walk in the strength of the Lord God!" So they fell back and came no closer.

Poor Christian's senses are under continual assault. Emotionally, he is nearly ready to give up. Things become even more alarming as he hears demons, like a pack of ravenous mad dogs, rushing toward him. But instead of panicking, he stops to survey his situation and consider his options.

He first looks back and reviews his progress thus far. He figures he may already be halfway through the Valley. It is hard to understand how some believers, after following the Lord's call for many years, suddenly give it up. Perhaps if they stopped and considered the distance already come, they wouldn't so quickly throw it away. Next Christian notes the difficulties he has already surmounted. Some believers overcome difficult challenges to their faith only to forget it all in a time of weakness. It also occurs to Christian that going back could ultimately bring him more misery than continuing forward. Many believers begin their walk with Christ solidly committed, yet turn away in an hour of temptation. If not immediately, then some time later they see the bitter fruit of their foolish decision.

After regaining a proper perspective, Christian finds the inner strength and resolve to fend off the demonic swarm by declaring God's truth. When we find ourselves severely tempted, rather than panicking, we can calm our hearts and clear our minds in order to remember the ground already gained, the victories already won, the nearness of our goal, and the tragic losses incurred by turning back. Armed with these realities, we can cast off our demons. In his distress Job proclaimed to the devils that were laying him waste, "I know that my Redeemer lives" (Job 19:25).

When you are under severe spiritual attack, don't let your victory be stolen. Take a deep breath, get a grip on reality, and shout out a faith declaration. Keep trusting the Lord and stay true to your course.

Scripture: 2 John 8; Exodus 14:10-15; Psalm 73:26

Prayer: Father, when I am in desperate straits, help me to keep a clear perspective so that I won't succumb to the enemy's temptations to give up. I resolve by your grace to go forward. Amen.

D·A·Y
120

I must not omit one other thing. I noticed that poor Christian had become so confused that he no longer knew his own voice. This is how I noticed it: Just as he was passing the mouth of the burning pit, one of the wicked creatures crept up behind him and whispered many grievous, blasphemous suggestions in his ear. This trial was worse than any of the others because Christian thought these suggestions had come from his own mind. How distressing it was for him to think that he had blasphemed the One whom he had loved so much, but he couldn't help himself. He didn't know enough to close his ears, nor did he realize from where the blasphemies came.

Christian's mind is under attack. Of all the distresses of the Valley, this is the worst. Although the blasphemous thoughts he hears are completely foreign to his way of thinking, he thinks they are his own. This is one of the cruelest and most effective hoaxes Satan perpetrates on vulnerable believers. First, he fills their minds with perverse and blasphemous thoughts; then he further victimizes them by convincingly accusing them of entertaining the thoughts. While those so afflicted abhor these thoughts, they readily conclude they are worthy of God's full condemnation for having them. They believe they are beyond grace, having committed an unpardonable sin.

In his confused state, Christian fails to realize that his distress is in exact proportion to his hatred for the evil thoughts and his love for God. If he didn't hate blasphemy and if he weren't loyal to God, he would feel no distress. Many sincere Christians, especially ones unfamiliar with this demonic device, are easy prey. Filled with anxiety about their spiritual condition, they lament that God can never forgive them for their blasphemous thoughts. A true blasphemer, however, has no place in his heart for repenting or for trusting Christ. Any desire a person has for Christ is proof that he is not truly a blasphemer.

Blasphemy is not an uncommon club that the enemy uses to beat up God's people. John Bunyan himself confessed that he had thought he was demon-possessed because of the blasphemous thoughts that sometimes filled his mind. Have you ever similarly been attacked? The best thing you can do should these suggestions penetrate your mind is to know they are alien thoughts and fight them off. You can do this by praising God, digging into the promises of his Word, reaffirming your commitment to God, and commanding the devil to leave you in Jesus' name.

Scripture: Romans 16:20; 2 Corinthians 2:11; Psalm 17:3, 5

Prayer: Father, please show me when the enemy is harassing my mind. I want to resist his suggestions and fill my mind with your truth. Amen.

D·A·Y
121

After Christian had traveled in this disconsolate condition for quite some time, he thought he could hear a man's voice somewhere ahead of him. The voice was saying, "Even though I walk through the Valley of the Shadow of Death, I will fear no evil, for You are with me" [Psalm 23:4]. Then Christian was glad for a number of reasons: First, he gathered from this that he was not alone but that others who feared God were in the Valley as well. Second, he realized that God was with them even though they were in a dark and dismal state. He reasoned, "Even though I can't feel His presence because of the hindrances in this place, why wouldn't He be with me here, too?" Third, he hoped that if he could soon catch up with someone, he would then have company. So he ventured on, calling out to whoever was up ahead. There was no answer, however; the person evidently thought he, too, was alone.

As the enemy attacks under the cover of darkness in this Valley, pilgrims are hard pressed to resist his horrible suggestions. He quickly convinces them that their mental, spiritual, or emotional upheaval is their own fault and that their heart condition is completely inconsistent with true faith. The darkness only deepens with thoughts such as, "I must be the worst sinner in the world; no one else can be this bad; no one, God included, will ever understand what I am going through." To heighten their feelings of loneliness and isolation, the enemy points out that every other believer, by comparison, "has it together."

Christian needs encouragement. He presses forward but cannot "feel" God's presence. What he does feel is confusion and defeat because of the blasphemous thoughts rattling around in his brain. Suddenly, however, a simple voice in the darkness changes everything. It seems that someone else is fighting his way through the same horrid Valley. Christian's hope rebounds as he thinks about the good things this might mean for him—that his is not an isolated experience, that God is with the other person so he must be with him, too, that perhaps he can gain an agreeable traveling companion.

Little can be of more encouragement to someone struggling in a dark Valley experience than to discover he is not alone. When you find yourself in a similar place, instead of withdrawing, talk to God. Ask him to drive home to you the fact that he is with you. Also talk to others. You may quickly find someone who has experienced or is experiencing afflictions much like your own. This will encourage you, and you may be able to lend great support to each other.

Scripture: 1 Corinthians 10:13; 1 Thessalonians 3:2-3; 1 Peter 5:9

Prayer: Dear Lord, when I am in a Valley experience and cannot even begin to sense your presence, I intend to press on. Help me to remember in those times that I am not alone. Amen.

D·A·Y
122

Before long it was daybreak, and Christian rejoiced. For He turns "the Shadow of Death into the morning" [Amos 5:8 KJV]. Now that there was daylight, he was able to look back, not that he wanted to return, but to see what hazards he had gone through in the dark. He could see more clearly the Ditch on the one hand and the Quagmire on the other. He also saw how narrow the Way was which led between them. He could see the Hobgoblins, Satyrs, and Dragons of the Pit, but they stayed far away after daybreak and would not attempt to come near. He could see these things, however, according to what is written: "He reveals the deep things of darkness and brings deep shadows into the light" [Job 12:22]. He had feared them so greatly, but he could now view them clearly in the light of day. Looking back, he was deeply moved by his deliverance from all the dangers he had encountered on this desolate way.

Praise God! The dark Valley experience doesn't last forever. In due time it must surrender to the light of day. What hope and healing the sunshine brings as it beams forth its life-giving rays. The darkness is swallowed up; all is warm and pleasant. Indeed, "every morning he shows forth his justice, each dawn he does not fail" (Zephaniah 3:5 RSV).

It would be tempting at this point to quickly forget a painful Valley experience and charge ahead to make up for lost time. Christian instead turns around to see where he has been. Christ warned his disciples not to look back longingly to the old life; indeed he deemed those who put their hand to the plow and look back unfit for his kingdom. But Christian's backward look is purely one of reflection upon all he has come through by God's grace.

As he reflects, he sees clearly how the descendants of the spies had been right—the Valley was indeed terrifying. Yet he also sees how their unbelief prevented them from experiencing God's delivering power. While they saw only the flames of hell, he got to see the Man walking in the midst of the furnace protecting his people.

Life brings many painful experiences, and God promises to bring us through them all. Once through them, it is encouraging to look back and see how God worked in our behalf to bring us to safety. Despite the flames, we see how the furnace of affliction removed our dross while leaving us unharmed. Despite the demons, we say with Paul, "I was delivered out of the mouth of the lion" (2 Timothy 4:17 KJV). Take a glance backward and make a record of trials God has brought you through. Praise him for each one.

Scripture: Lamentations 3:22-23; Isaiah 48:10; Daniel 3:24-27

Prayer: Lord, how wonderful it is to realize that you lead me safely through the complicated maze of life's many hazards. Always let me look back and see your loving guidance even in the worst times. Amen.

D·A·Y
123

The sun's rising was also another mercy to Christian, for though the first part of the Valley of the Shadow of Death was dangerous, this second part that he now faced was worse. For from where he now stood, the Way to the end of the Valley was beset on all sides with traps, snares, instruments of torture, nets, pits and pitfalls, deep holes, rocky cliffs, and ledges beneath them. If he had possessed a thousand souls, he would have lost them all if it were still as dark as it had been when he traveled the first part. But, as I said, the sun was rising. Christian said, "He lighted the way before me, and I walked safely through the darkness" [Job 29:3]. In this light he was able to make it to the end of the Valley.

❧

Christian had wisely looked back to reflect upon God's faithfulness in leading him safely through his dark time. Now he must face the trials yet ahead. Thank God that he never tests his pilgrims beyond their limits. In his grace he provides Christian with sunshine for the task.

When we have been going through agonizing times of fear and confusion, during which we have lacked all awareness of God's presence, suddenly finding our fellowship with him restored is of great relief. With the comforting sunbeams of God's Spirit warming our hearts, we can much more easily make our way through the remainder of the Valley. The trials don't let up, however, and we still find that from start to finish, by day or night, malevolent spiritual forces attempt to undo us in a myriad of devious ways. Christian actually finds the second half of the Valley more treacherous than the first!

How strange to find even greater danger in a season of enjoying God's illuminating presence. God, however, doesn't provide the sunshine of his revelation to take away the dangers. He sends it, not to allow us to grow careless, but to help guide us safely through to the end of our Valley. We quickly learn that without this special grace, even if we had a thousand souls, we couldn't save even one of them by ourselves. God's grace is credited with every step of progress, as John Newton's hymn states: "Through many dangers, toils, and snares I have already come; / 'Tis grace that brought me safe thus far, and grace will lead me home."

Thank the Lord for his gracious care in bringing you safely this far. Thank him that he will also continue to work in your behalf throughout the remainder of your life's pilgrimage. Reaffirm your trust in his faithfulness.

❧

Scripture: Isaiah 42:16; Psalms 23; 33:18-19

Prayer: Dear Lord, thank you for the comfort of knowing that you are with me. Help me to press on in faith even when I don't feel your presence. Amen.

DAY 124

I saw in my dream that at the end of the Valley lay blood, bones, ashes, and mangled bodies of pilgrims who had previously traveled this way. While I was pondering the cause of this, I saw a cave nearby where two Giants, Pope and Pagan, had lived in ancient times. By their power and tyranny, they cruelly put to death the men whose bones, blood, and ashes lay there. I wondered why Christian could pass by the place with such little danger, but then I learned that Pagan had long since died, and that—although still alive—the other was very old. He had met with so many skirmishes in his younger days that he had grown somewhat crazy and was stiff in his joints. Now he could do little more than sit at the cave's mouth and grin at pilgrims as they went by and bite his nails because he couldn't go after them.

As Christian traveled on, he saw the old man sitting at the mouth of the cave. He didn't know what to think, especially when he heard him say, "You will never mend your ways until more of you burn." Christian held his peace, however, and went by unharmed.

A martyr is one who chooses death rather than denying his faith. Here two villainous giants have martyred many pilgrims. One giant has died; the other is old and feeble. While Pope represents a corrupted church, Pagan represents unconverted heathens. Bunyan regularly read from *Foxe's Book of Martyrs* and believed that most martyrdoms came by these two powers.

The Roman Catholic pope once possessed great authority. In the thirteenth century, the Inquisition, with papal approval, tried cases of heresy. They tortured and even burned multitudes at the stake for their "heresies." We should recognize, however, that any denomination, religious group, or movement can become corrupt and oppressive. Failure to maintain a pure devotion to Christ or allowing human authority, wisdom, or tradition to supplant biblical authority invites deception. Catholics persecuted early Protestant reformers, but both groups put to death Anabaptists who advocated believers' baptism.

If Pagan died in Bunyan's time, he is resurrected in ours. While church history is strewn with Christian martyrs—some 40,000,000 since the time of Christ—the twentieth century has produced the most. Worldwide some 330,000 Christians are annually martyred for their faith. One out of every 200 Christians can expect martyrdom.[10] We shouldn't allow this to deter us from staying true to our course and reaching our world for Jesus Christ.

Will you pray for the persecuted Christians throughout our world today?

Scripture: Revelation 6:9-11; 12:11; John 16:1-4; Esther 4:16

Prayer: Dear Jesus, please strengthen and protect my persecuted brothers and sisters. Show me how to use my freedom to help their cause. Help us all to persevere to the end. Amen.

D·A·Y 125

Then Christian sang:

> *"Oh, world of wonders (I can say no less),*
> *That I should be preserved in the distress*
> *That I have met with here! Oh blessed be*
> *The hand that from it has delivered me!*
> *Dangers in darkness, devils, Hell, and sin*
> *Surrounded me, while this vale I was in.*
> *Yes, snares and pits and traps and nets did lie*
> *About my path, so that vain, foolish I*
> *Might have been caught, entangled, and cast down:*
> *But since I live, let Jesus wear the crown."*

Now as Christian went on his way, he came to a little Hill placed purposely so that pilgrims could have a view of what lay ahead of them. So he went up the Hill, and from there could recognize Faithful journeying not far ahead. So he called, "Hello! Hold up there! Wait, and I will be your companion!" At that, Faithful turned around and looked. Christian called again, "Wait, wait until I catch up with you."

But Faithful answered, "No, I am running for my life from the avenger of blood who is behind me."

Hallelujah! Christian has come through the Valleys into a bright new day in right relationship with Christ. Christ kept him safe through all the trials, and Christ gets the glory. Praising the Lord brings Christian another mercy—a hill from which he spots another pilgrim. Like Elijah, who wrongly thought himself alone, Christian finds company in his dark Valley experience.

He calls for Faithful to wait, but Faithful is fleeing from an avenger of blood. The Old Testament Law provided no correctional facility for those accused of murder. Instead, justice was left to each family and tribe. An accused killer's only recourse was to flee to a city of refuge for a fair trial before the one who avenged the victim's blood could kill him.

In asking Faithful to wait, Christian risks impeding his brother's progress. Often in the name of fellowship, believers hamper one another's progress. We must be careful not to hinder others or to let them hinder us in our own spiritual growth. Instead, we should catch up with them and walk together in mutually upbuilding fellowship. How can you avoid hindering or being hindered spiritually?

Scripture: 1 Kings 19:14, 18-19; Acts 18:9-10; Romans 15:2

Prayer: Lord, for all your mercies, I offer praise to you in my heart. Help me love my brothers and sisters but not allow anyone to thwart my spiritual progress. Amen.

D·A·Y 126

At this Christian became intent on catching up with Faithful, putting all his strength into the effort. He quickly reached Faithful and even ran beyond him so that the last was first. Then he smiled proudly because he had outrun his brother. While still gloating, however, Christian failed to watch his step and suddenly stumbled and fell. He was unable to get back to his feet again until Faithful came up to help him.

Then I saw in my dream that they went on together in brotherly love, sharing with each other about all that had happened to them on their pilgrimages. Christian said, "Faithful, my brother whom I honor and love, I am glad that I have caught up with you and that God has so unified our spirits that we can walk as companions on this pleasant path."

During Christian's bout with Apollyon in the Valley of Humiliation, the demon accused him of harboring a secret desire for self-glory in his pilgrimage. Christian didn't deny his vulnerability to pride, but, acknowledging it, he declared he would humbly rely upon the Lord to forgive him. It is one thing, however, to humble ourselves when suffering in the Valley of Humiliation and quite another to be humble before our brothers and sisters when back out in the sunshine.

While Faithful's refusal to slow his pace positively inspires Christian to summon his strength and catch up, it also stirs up his pride. Trying to show off his own strength, he reveals his weakness. He catches Faithful, but not content, he proudly runs past him. He smiles, not gratefully to God but proudly at Faithful. However, sinful pride in our own attainments can soon leave us sprawling. Christian's cocky smile and careless feet bring on a humiliating tumble, and it is no easy task for a man in armor to get back to his feet. Faithful, the one he so wanted to impress, must help him.

This experience, humbling as it is, enables the two brothers to become fast friends. Walking together in mutual love and respect, they will never again be found either lagging behind or running ahead of each other. We cannot realize too soon our own need and the strength and support we have to offer one another. Still how can we learn to walk together in harmonious fellowship before learning to need one another? We have to humbly do away with our self-congratulatory smiles and stop trying to impress each other with our victory parades if we want the joy and strength of mutually supportive fellowship.

How difficult is it for you to be humble concerning your strengths and transparent about your weaknesses? How can you deepen your fellowship with others?

Scripture: Proverbs 16:18; Luke 14:11; Ecclesiastes 4:9-10; Romans 15:5

Prayer: Lord Jesus, humbling myself before you isn't easy; remaining humble before others is even harder. Help me to learn humility so I can enjoy real Christian fellowship. Amen.

DAY 127

"Dear friend," said Faithful, "I have wanted your company ever since leaving our town, but since you left ahead of me, I was forced to come much of the way alone."

"How long did you stay in the City of Destruction before you set out after me on your pilgrimage?" asked Christian.

"Until I could stay no longer—for soon after you left, there was a great deal of talk that in a short time fire from Heaven would burn our City to the ground."

"Really! Did your neighbors say this?"

"Yes, it was in everyone's mouth for a while."

"What? Didn't anyone but you come away from there to escape the danger?"

"As I said, there was a great amount of talk, but I don't think they strongly believed it. For in the heat of the debate, I heard some of them speak derisively about you and your 'desperate journey'—that is what they called your pilgrimage. But I believed, and I still do, that fire and brimstone will fall from above to destroy our City; therefore, I have made my escape."

❧

Christian just becomes aware of the stir he caused when he left the City of Destruction. His talk of the city's destruction by fire weighed heavily in Faithful's decision to leave. Yet, despite all the chatter, Christian is shocked as Faithful says he can think of no one besides himself who left the city to find life.

After deciding to follow Christ, we may try hard to reach our friends and loved ones for Christ. If no response is immediately forthcoming, we may feel discouraged. Still God uses our testimony to stir hearts whether or not we ever know it. Christian learns that his witness stirred the city and caused Faithful to leave.

How irrational are those who fear judgment yet deride those who turn to Christ for salvation. They violate their own conscience, brave the dangers of remaining where they are, and hope everything will turn out for the best. Unwilling to repent, they hope God's truth is a mere myth and call our belief a "desperate journey," escapism, or fear. We should not let these discourage us. We should hold to our course, knowing that we haven't yet seen the end of the story. It is likely that by journey's end, many more people, moved by the Holy Spirit, will abandon the City of Destruction.

Have you somehow come to think your witness is fruitless? Don't get discouraged; keep sharing your convictions. While you may never see the harvest yourself, be assured that God will use the seeds you plant.

❧

Scripture: John 4:39-42; 1 Chronicles 16:8-9; Psalm 145:10-12

Prayer: Dear Lord, give me boldness to keep telling others what you mean to me even when the response is disappointing. I trust you to use it to bear fruit for your kingdom. Amen.

D·A·Y 128

"Did you hear any talk of our neighbor Pliable?"

"Yes, I did, Christian. I heard that he followed you until he came to the Slough of Despond, where some have said he fell in. He didn't want anyone to know this, but I am sure that's the kind of dirt that covered him."

"And what did the neighbors say to him?"

"All sorts of people have ridiculed him since his return. People mock and despise him, and he cannot even find employment. Now he is seven times worse off than if he had never gone out of the City."

"But why are they so much against him, since they also despise the Way that he abandoned?"

"Oh, they say, 'Hang him; he is a turncoat; he wasn't true to what he professed!' I think God has stirred up enemies against him; they hiss at him and scorn him because he abandoned the Way."

Pliable received little thanks from his neighbors for returning to the City of Destruction. Not only is he separated from God's people, but those in the city reject him. His sudden change of heart and mind shook their trust in him; all regard him with suspicion. They believe that one who proves himself faithless in one decision will prove himself untrustworthy in others. Neither side comforts him, as he has been true to none. Also, because they view him as a cowardly man without convictions, his neighbors who are committed to their ungodliness, assume a certain superiority over him.

Those who backslide and ultimately commit apostasy in hopes of regaining their old lives can never really return to the way things were. As Jesus explains, "Those who find their life will lose it, and those who lose their life for my sake will find it" (Matthew 10:39 NRSV). If only Pliable had permanently left his old life behind, he would have found life to the fullest. As it is, he ran home to find his life and to take up where he left off, but everything is changed. He is accountable for his decision, and it seems that God is the one behind his woes.

We should let this be a warning when we are tempted to forsake our Christian pilgrimage. We cannot simply return to where we were before meeting the Lord. Instead, in the face of temptation, let us endeavor to keep our eyes and heart fixed upon Jesus and his way that leads to life. Are you ever tempted to give up on the Christian life? Ask the Lord to help you keep fixed in your purpose.

Scripture: Isaiah 48:17-18; Hebrews 3:1; 12:2; Psalm 141:8

Prayer: Dear Lord, I reaffirm my devotion to you and your way. By your grace, I refuse to turn back from my Christian pilgrimage. In your mercy, I pray that you will again find a way to reach those who are backslidden. Amen.

D·A·Y
129

"Were you able to talk with him at all before you left?"

"I met him once in the streets, but he quickly looked away and crossed to the other side, obviously feeling ashamed of what he had done. So I didn't get a chance to speak with him."

"Well," said Christian, "when I first set out, I had great hopes for that man, but now I fear he will perish along with the City when it is destroyed. For it has happened to him according to the true proverb, 'A dog returns to its vomit,' and 'A sow that is washed goes back to her wallowing in the mud'" [2 Peter 2:22].

"Yes, I fear this, too, but who can prevent that which will be?"

Christian won't reply to Faithful's last question. It concerns the difficult age-old debate over the doctrines of human election and free will. Elisabeth Elliot tells of a week-long family vacation where her little brother, despite continual coaxing, refused to go near the water. On the last day, he finally ventured out and discovered all the fun he had been missing. He cried to his mother, "Why didn't you *make* me do it?"[11] So why didn't God simply *make* Pliable do right? Did Pliable have a choice not to return to the City of Destruction? Or was he a victim of predestination?

According to the doctrine of election, only those chosen by God are truly free to receive Christ; the rest are predestined to hell. According to free will, humans ultimately choose their destination by accepting or rejecting Christ. While God would be completely just in consigning us all to hell, that would violate his loving nature. On the other hand, he could hardly open heaven's gates to everyone, thus forcing unrepentant sinners into what their hearts reject. That would violate human freedom. Imagine entering heaven and seeing above the Gate, "Whosoever will to the Lord may come." (See Revelation 22:17.) Passing through, you look back and see above the gate, "Chosen before the foundation of the world." (See Ephesians 1:4.) After all our debate, the truth remains just such a mystery. The Bible seems to hold both views in tension.

While free will offers hope to sinners, election gives assurance to believers. We should extend God's invitation of salvation to everyone. We are urged to pray for everyone because God wants "everyone to be saved" (1 Timothy 2:4 NRSV). We should also be assured that those born again of the Spirit of God are indeed God's elect. Thank God that he chose you, and thank God that you chose him. Then invite someone else into a saving relationship with him.

Scripture: 1 Timothy 2:1-4; Romans 8:29-30; 10:8-13; 1 Peter 1:1-2

Prayer: Father God, thank you for calling and choosing me as your own child. Thank you, too, that I somehow responded to your call of love. Help me to faithfully assist others to respond also. Amen.

DAY 130

"Well, Faithful, my neighbor, let's talk about matters of more immediate concern to our own lives. Tell me about the things you've met with so far in the Way. I know you've had some interesting experiences; if not, it would indeed be a marvel."

"I escaped the Slough that you fell into, and I reached the Gate without much danger."

Falling into gossip about Pliable would be easy to do. The two pilgrims wisely avoid this danger by turning their discussion to their own experiences. Now some readers might study Christian's life and begin doubting their own walk, thinking they, too, should have corresponding experiences in the same order with the same intensity. But Christian is not meant to be the model of true faith. As a matter of fact, conversion experiences defy stereotyping. Faithful, a devout pilgrim, has experiences almost altogether different from Christian's. No crisis experience precipitated his decision. He suffered no crushing burden, he avoided any mishap in the Slough of Despond, and he escaped the terrors of Mt. Sinai. Later he escaped the Hill Difficulty and passed right by the Palace Beautiful. It seems the only thing Christian and Faithful have in common are their common roots in the City of Destruction, their common love for their King, and their desire to reach the Celestial City.

Still the two enjoy sweet fellowship together, a precious gift from God. They have much to learn from each other, as they are individuals with unique perceptions and experiences. We, too, have uniquely fashioned lives and experiences. This gives us an excellent lesson about unity. While the essentials of our faith are vital to true unity, we often let less than significant differences divide us. We should avoid both measuring other people by our lives and experiences, and measuring ourselves by theirs.

No spiritual cookie cutter exists to cut us all into one pattern. As we appreciate the varieties of flowers in a garden, we should learn to appreciate all the varieties of people within Christ's body. Our opinions, experiences, gifts, and spiritual progress will not be alike, but we can love, appreciate, learn from, and draw inspiration from one another. Have you recently traded testimonies with another believer? If not, this might be a good time to do so. Be sure to celebrate both your common faith and the unique ways God has fashioned your lives and faith.

Scripture: 1 Corinthians 1:10; 12:12-30; John 17:21-23

Prayer: Lord Jesus, thank you for my Christian brothers and sisters. I acknowledge that we are all individual creations with whom your work is not yet complete. Give me patience as I grow in learning to appreciate the differing contributions we each have to offer for the upbuilding of your body. Amen.

D·A·Y
131

"But I did encounter someone named Wanton; she made every effort to allure and ensnare me."

"It is good you escaped her net; Joseph was severely tested by her. He escaped her like you did, but it nearly cost him his life. What did she do to you?"

"Unless you have already met her, you cannot imagine what a seductive tongue she has. She pressured me severely to turn aside with her, promising me all kinds of pleasure and contentment."

"She didn't promise you the pleasure and contentment of a clear conscience, did she?"

"No, you know what I mean—only the pleasure and contentment that come from the gratification of carnal and fleshly desires."

"Thank God you escaped her snare; 'he who is under the Lord's wrath will fall into it'" [Proverbs 22:14].

"Well, I don't know whether I fully escaped or not."

"But why do you say this? I trust you didn't consent to her desires."

"No, I didn't defile myself. I remembered an old writing I had seen that reads, 'She leads you down to death and Hell.' So I shut my eyes because I didn't want to be enticed by her seductive looks. She cursed at me, and then I went on my way."

No one escapes temptation. While some believers can avoid some forms, they are susceptible to others. Faithful traveled the pilgrims' highway more quickly than did Christian. Still his own temptations beset him, and he recounts them. Reminiscent of the mythological Sirens who beautifully sang from a rocky island to lure sailors to shipwreck and death, Wanton is a destroyer. Even after escaping, Faithful doubts he is wholly free of her irresistible seductions.

Our current adulterous culture invites Wanton-like spirits to run amok with sexual temptations. Each of us must honestly face our vulnerabilities and plan accordingly. Faithful simply shut his eyes. Job made a covenant with his eyes. Odysseus made his crew plug their ears to escape the Sirens' fatal song. Bunyan admitted he seldom touched a woman's hand. Augustine of Hippo literally ran from a temptress he had known in his pre-salvation days. Joseph likewise fled from Potiphar's wife. Of course, Christian women are also vulnerable to falling prey to sexual advances. They should, nonetheless, be very careful to avoid ever being a tool in Wanton's hand. "The devil hath not all his quiver's choice, an arrow for the heart like a sweet voice" (George Gordon, Lord Byron in *Don Juan*).[12] What is your best strategy for resisting Wanton?

Scripture: Job 31:1; Proverbs 5:1-23; 7:10-20; Genesis 39:11-12

Prayer: Dear Lord, let me honor you with my sexuality. In this sex-crazed society, I want my life to reflect purity. With Job I make a covenant with my eyes against lustful indulgences. Amen.

D·A·Y
132

"Did you meet with any other assaults as you journeyed?" asked Christian.

"When I came to the foot of the Hill called Difficulty, I met a very aged Man who asked me who I was and where I was going. I told him that I was a pilgrim on the way to the Celestial City. Then he said, 'You look like an honest fellow. Will you be content to live with me for the wages that I will give you?' I asked him his name and where he lived. He said his name was Adam the First and that he lived in the town of Deceit. I then asked him what his business was and how much he would pay me to work for him. He said that his work was enjoyment and that his wages would be to inherit all that he had. I questioned further, asking what his House was like and how many others were employed in his service. He told me that his House was full of all the delicacies the world could offer and that his servants were his own children. Then I asked how many children he had. He said that he had only three daughters: the Lust of the Flesh, the Lust of the Eyes, and the Pride of Life, and he suggested that I should marry them if I so desired. I asked him how long he wanted me to live with him, and he said that it would be as long as he himself lived."

Jesus Christ is the last or second Adam. The first Adam is the sinful progenitor of us all. Christ's death on the cross freed us from the consequences of the first Adam's sin. Here, as an extension of Wanton, Adam the First appeals not only to one but to all fleshly appetites. He is the old fleshly, fallen nature driven by sensual appetites and having no affinity for godliness. From the Town of Deceit, this Adam is without conscience. His lustful daughters are likewise corrupting.

The timing of this temptation bears significance. The honeymoon phase of Faithful's pilgrimage is past, and a discouraging prospect of difficult trials looms large. Christian fell asleep at the Arbor on the Hill. Faithful is also tempted to relax, but his temptation comes in a broader, more hedonistic form. Adam the First offers to employ him to work at enjoying himself, indulging his flesh with every rich delicacy.

When the various cravings of the fallen nature incite us to indulge in our old sinful life, we should realize the temptation is coming from "Deceit." God's Word says, "You were taught, with regard to your former way of life, to *put off your old self*, which is being corrupted by its *deceitful* desires" (Ephesians 4:22).

When the road gets hard and the flesh calls for you to take an easier, more appealing way, what most tempts you? How do you respond?

Scripture: 1 John 2:15-16; 1 Corinthians 15:22, 45; Proverbs 10:16

Prayer: Lord Jesus, thank you for delivering me from the first Adam's power. I choose to live for your pleasure and not that of my sinful lower nature. Amen.

DAY 133

"Well," said Christian, "what agreement did you and the Old Man finally come to?"

"Why, at first I found myself somewhat inclined to go with him, for I thought he spoke very sensibly. But then I looked at his forehead as I was speaking with him, and I saw written there, 'Put off, concerning your former conversation, the Old Man'" [Ephesians 4:22 KJV].

"What happened then?"

"Suddenly it came burning into my mind that no matter what he said and how he tried to entice me, I must resist him because his intention was to sell me as a slave. I told him to stop talking to me because I would not come near his house. Then he insulted me and told me that he would send someone after me to cause bitterness to my soul as I journeyed on my way. At that, I turned away from him, but just as I turned, he took hold of my flesh and gave me such a sharp jerk backwards that I thought he had pulled me apart and had part of me in his possession. This made me cry, 'What a wretched man I am!' [Romans 7:24]. Then I went on my way up the Hill."

Faithful had already confessed his vulnerability to Wanton's temptations. His trouble with Adam the First was no less serious. As long as Adam the First kept the discussion going, Faithful lost ground spiritually. The temptation actually made sense to Faithful until the haze suddenly lifted as he looked directly into the tempter's face and saw the words of Ephesians 4:22. Faithful resisted Adam the First when he saw him for the enslaving enemy he is. Used to having control, Adam the First refused to give up quietly. He promised to buffet and torment the pilgrim until he would yield.

Faithful's struggle is not unusual; the "Old Man" troubles us all. He effectively causes many to succumb to the cravings for illicit sex, gluttony, riches, luxury, honor, entertainment—in short, a completely self-gratifying lifestyle. We must decide that when it comes to choosing between gratifying the flesh and gratifying the spirit, we want the spirit. Denying the flesh so that the spirit may have life is much wiser than squelching the spirit so that the flesh may have its way.

This was not an easy victory for Faithful. Along with Paul, he cried out, "What a wretched man I am! Who will rescue me from this body of death?" Have you ever similarly cried out? What can you learn from Faithful about handling this kind of temptation?

Scripture: Romans 6:5-13; 8:5-13; Galatians 5:16-21

Prayer: Dear Lord, when I am tempted to submit to the cravings of my lower nature, help me, without hesitation, to call out for your help. Thank you for the victory I find in you. Amen.

D·A·Y 134

"When I had gotten about halfway up the Hill, I looked behind me and saw someone coming after me, swift as the wind. He overtook me near where the Arbor stands."

"That is the place where I sat down to rest but was overcome with sleep," said Christian. "It was there that I lost my Scroll."

"But, my good brother," continued Faithful, "hear me out. As soon as the man overtook me, after saying only one word, to my surprise, he knocked me out cold with one blow. When I came to, I asked him why he had treated me this way. He said that it was because of my secret inclination toward Adam the First. Then he struck a powerful blow to my chest, and—continuing to punch me—he made me stumble backwards until I again lay at his feet like one dead. When I came to again, I cried to him for mercy, but he said, 'I don't know how to show mercy.' With that, he knocked me down again. He would doubtless have made an end of me had not that One come by and ordered him to stop."

"Who was the One who made him stop?" asked Christian.

"I didn't know Him at first, but as he went by, I noticed holes in his hands and His side; then I concluded that He was our Lord. After that I went on up the Hill."

"That man who overpowered you was Moses. He doesn't spare anyone. He doesn't know how to show mercy to those who break his law."

"Yes, I know that very well," said Faithful, "and this wasn't the first time he has confronted me. Once he approached me while I was still living happily back home; he threatened to burn my house down with me in it if I stayed there."

Moses, representing the Law, came in hot pursuit of Faithful because Adam the First (the old nature) appealed to him. His guilty conscience accused Faithful, and, like a knitted fabric with a stitch dropped, the conscience can quickly unravel. In the words of John Crowne, "There is no hell like a bad conscience."[13] Moses thundered up the hill mercilessly chastising Faithful, trying to beat the problem out of him. While Faithful pleaded for mercy, Moses could show none; he only pronounces judgment.

Christ deals with sin in a way far superior. Faithful cannot meet the righteous demands of the Law, but Christ already has. He suddenly appears to mercifully forgive and restore Faithful. As the one who denied every fleshly temptation—his wounds prove it—he stands in sharp contrast to the lusting flesh of his struggling pilgrim. He commands Moses to stop his beating and restores Faithful to a clear conscience. To the cry, "Who will rescue me from this body of death?" Faithful can join Paul, declaring, "Thanks be to God through Jesus Christ our Lord!" (Romans 7:24-25 NRSV). Is this your confession?

Scripture: John 1:17; Romans 5:14-15; Ephesians 4:22-24

Prayer: Dear Jesus, thank you for your grace and tender mercy that delivers me from Moses' wrath. I love you. Amen.

D·A·Y
135

"I wonder, did you see the House that stood on top of the Hill facing the side that Moses met you on?"

"Yes, and the lions in front of it, too, but I think they were asleep since it was about noon. Because I had so much daylight left, I passed by the gatekeeper and went on down the Hill."

"Yes," said Christian, "he told me that he had seen you go by. I wish you had come to the House; they would have shown you many rare and precious things that you would never forget till the day you die."

The Palace Beautiful represents fellowship in a local church family. We again see how different are the experiences of the two pilgrims. While Christian stopped to join the church, Faithful passed right by. Clearly, belonging to a local church is not requisite to salvation. Some saints decline to enter into fellowship with the church. Perhaps, like Faithful, in the bright sunshine of their experience, they feel content with their spiritual pace. Stopping for fellowship would only serve, in their minds, to slow them.

Yet look at the things Faithful missed—the joy of being lovingly received into the family of God; fellowship and edifying conversation with Discretion, Prudence, Charity, and others; sitting at the table together, learning more about the Lord, enjoying the Lord's Supper; sleeping in the room called Peace; learning in the Study and becoming equipped in the Armory; the view of the distant Delectable Mountains; friends to help him down the hill into the Valley of Humiliation. Perhaps if Faithful had gotten to know Discretion, Prudence, and Charity, he would have found Wanton much less alluring. Christian wishes all the benefits for his brother that he has received through the church. Still the two enjoy fellowship with each other as they agree on the essentials of the faith.

As anti-Christian forces grow and persecutions increase in these last days, neglecting the strength and support of God's family is unwise. Each of us should be a faithful member and participant of a local church, both for our own enrichment and for the support and encouragement of that congregation. Solid, healthy churches are an essential part of the gospel message, reflecting the reality, love, and power of Jesus Christ. Jesus needs us to shine our lights together. What does church membership mean, and what does it entail to you?

Scripture: Hebrews 10:25; Acts 1:13-14; 2:1; 4:32

Prayer: Dear Lord, I acknowledge my need for the family of God. I pray for my church that you will unite our hearts in true fellowship. Show me how I can best serve the interests of your body. Amen.

D·A·Y
136

"But please tell me, did you meet anyone in the Valley of Humiliation?"

"Yes," answered Faithful, "I met someone called Discontent. He tried to persuade me to go back again with him. His reason was that the Valley was altogether without honor. Besides this, he told me that to go this way would offend the sensibilities of many friends, including Pride, Arrogance, Self-conceit, Worldly-glory, and others who he said he knew would be very much upset with me if I were to make such a fool of myself as to wade through this Valley."

"Well," said Christian, "how did you answer him?"

"I told him that although all these that he had named might claim to be my friends and relatives—and it is true, because some of them are my relatives according to the flesh—since I became a pilgrim, they have already disowned me, and I also have rejected them. Therefore, they were now no more to me than if they had never been of my lineage. In addition, I told him that as to this Valley, he had really misrepresented it, because 'humility comes before honor' [Proverbs 15:33; 18:12] and 'a haughty spirit before a fall' [Proverbs 16:18]. So I said to him, 'I would rather go through this Valley to receive what the wise count as honor than to choose what you consider most worthy of affection."

The self-respect that kept Faithful from yielding to Wanton and Adam the First invited new temptations down in the Valley of Humiliation. It didn't take long for him to see that the beliefs he must hold to, the people he must associate with, and the distinct ways he must act will never please the world. The prospect of losing friends and suffering outright hostility may have weakened his resolve. Suddenly Discontent attacks with a sense of brooding dejection. How could the way to life possibly pass through such humiliation?

Fortunately, Faithful refuses to entertain Discontent and fights him off. He asserts that his former associates had already rejected him, so he wasn't going to start worrying all over again about what they think. As to making a fool of himself, he claims that he now lives by a different standard of honor.

Discontent is a dangerous and destructive tempter. Because of discontentment, the Israelites grumbled in the wilderness, Absalom nearly stole his father's kingdom, Judas betrayed the Lord, and Demas abandoned the Lord for the world. We should carefully watch our attitudes for this deadly influence. Ask the Holy Spirit to show you any areas of discontent in your heart. Renounce your discontentment and reaffirm your gratitude.

Scripture: Philippians 2:14-15; 1 Corinthians 10:10-11; 1 Timothy 6:6

Prayer: Father, thank you for the high privilege you have given me in calling me your child. May I always treat my position with gratitude and resist all temptations to complain. Amen.

DAY 137

"Well, did you have any other encounters in the Valley?"

"Yes, I met Shame; but of all those whom I have met on my pilgrimage, he, I believe, most bears the wrong name. After a little debate, others would have backed off some but not so with this boldfaced Shame."

"Why, what did he say to you?"

"What didn't he say! He objected to our faith. He said it was a pitiful, low, cowardly thing for a man to give heed to religion."

❧

Just as Wanton foreshadows Adam the First, so Discontent foreshadows Shame. Faithful managed to shake Discontent and his complaints off with a sound profession of his faith. Nevertheless, he may not yet have come to an unswerving resolution in his heart of hearts. If he had commanded this nuisance to go with finality, he may not have fallen victim to this later round of harassments. As it is, his susceptibility opens the door to Shame, and of all his bold enemies, this one proves the most forcefully persuasive. Sociologist Thomas Scheff calls it the "master emotion," the one hardest to get rid of.

Shame does have its place. When we violate our conscience, we feel shame. God instilled this trait within us so we would instinctively shun corrupt activities. How far we have fallen from the image of God that a reversal of this function can make us ashamed of the things of God! This perverted false Shame argues all the worldly, fleshly reasons against faith in Christ. Everything the world objects to, Shame objects to. This villain's hassling of Faithful, despite his convictions, his arguments, his prayers, leads him to believe that Shame has the wrong name. For Shame has no reticence at all in abusing the gospel truth. Those who tolerate Shame's bold pronouncements remain timidly cautious and private about their beliefs, even when the most favorable opportunities for taking a stand for their faith arise.

We live in a day when disparaging remarks against believers are increasingly sticking in the public mind, making many of us especially vulnerable to shame. Who among us enjoys hearing people belittling them with labels like "phobic," "intolerant," "right-wing," "fundamentalist bigots"? When we hear these remarks, we can be sure Shame is having at us. But we must look to the Lord to fill our need for approval. If he approves of us, we have no reason to be ashamed. When you feel Shame's influence, what do you do—hide out or fight it off? What are some ways you can strengthen yourself against giving in to Shame?

❧

Scripture: Mark 8:38; Matthew 10:32-33; Acts 19:8

Prayer: Dear Lord, help me to resist both the voices of my lower nature and the demonic worldly voices that tempt me to be ashamed to stand tall and proud for you. Amen.

DAY 138

"He said that a tender conscience was unmanly, and that for a man to be careful of his words and deeds would tie him down and rob him of the adventurous liberty to which the truly daring spirits of the times were accustomed. He said that such a person would be the laughingstock of our present-day society.

"He also objected that so few of the truly powerful, rich, or wise men and women were ever of my persuasion, and he contended that, of those of my persuasion, none had ever been powerful, wealthy, or wise prior to their conversion. He thought them to be fools who would voluntarily and eagerly decide to give up all they had for who knows what? He objected also to the lowly, inferior rank and condition of those who were pilgrims. He also said that the pilgrims were ignorant, especially in their understanding of the natural sciences."

❧

While Faithful's guilty conscience caused him trouble with Moses, Shame assaults him for his tender conscience, calling into question his masculinity. In Shame's view, true men are bold and unrestrained. Like wild stallions, they refuse to be harnessed. Furthermore, anyone weak enough to need religion is a dishonorable, pitiable laughingstock. Obviously, a man's man says what he likes, does as he pleases, and will never allow his "adventurous liberty" to be stifled.

A documentary about Billy Graham's life for public television interviews both Billy and a former early friend and colleague in ministry. Their two paths diverged as Billy's friend became theologically liberal and Billy, feeling God's call on his life, committed himself completely to the authority of the Scriptures. Forty-some years later, the former colleague says he feels Billy has missed life in its fullness! This is the nonsensical "adventurous liberty" to which Shame makes his appeal. Those with a worldly orientation see the Christian walk as lifeless and boring no matter how fruitful and exciting it proves to be.

As we shall see in the next passage, Faithful has a definite vulnerability. He is a gentleman and even an aristocrat, and he shows his weakness in wanting honor. Shame knows where to land his punches, carefully distinguishing between Faithful and other pilgrims. He suggests Faithful shouldn't identify himself with them because they are poor, lower-class fools, and he will soon become like them.

We must never let Shame's spurious arguments embarrass us concerning either our walk or our fellow Christians. Have you ever been stung by an embarrassed believer who weakly disowned you or the Lord before non-Christians? What a sad defeat for that person! Always guard your heart against Shame.

❧

Scripture: 1 Corinthians 1:26-31; James 1:9-11; 2:5; Proverbs 19:1

Prayer: Lord, I affirm my joy in being your pilgrim. I refuse to be ashamed of you. I scorn the worldly liberty that ends in spiritual death. Amen.

D·A·Y 139

"He confronted me about a great many more things besides those I have already related. He said that it was a shame to sit whining and mourning under conviction from the message of a sermon, and it seemed a shame to him to see pilgrims sighing and groaning as they returned to their homes. He thought it a shame for me to ask my neighbor for forgiveness for petty faults or to make restitution where I have taken advantage of someone. He said that religion separates a man from those who are great because of their few vices (which he called by finer names), and he said it makes him a member and friend to the lowbrows because of their common religious association. 'Is this not a shame?' he asked."

Faithful either experienced for himself or witnessed other believers emotionally breaking before God. It embarrassed his sensibilities and invited Shame's scorn. The fact is, conversion doesn't automatically deliver us out of sin. We may have died to sin, but it has not yet died to us. In our human frailty, the inclination to sin continues. When we sin, we can feel an awful sense of guilt and impending chastisement as the Holy Spirit convicts our conscience to bring us to repentance. We should gratefully receive this conviction as an act of God's grace. After all, God, before whom we have sinned, is holy, awesome, and fully justified in punishing us. His intention, however, is not to punish but to restore us to right relationship with himself.

Shame, however, perverts our sense of guilt and shame. He insists we should be ashamed of being ashamed for our sins. He would have us burying and hiding our sins like Achan hid the devoted things in the ground. After all, once you start unearthing your sin, who knows where it might lead? Recognizing our sin can be a very intense experience. When godly fear acts upon us, we no longer regard sin indifferently. Convicted and broken, we may cry and groan until we repent and feel God's forgiveness. Such behavior is too much for Shame. Even more appalling, we may stoop to the indecorous behavior of asking others whom we sinned against to forgive us. Then we may further insult ourselves by making restitution. What a shame!

Although we may groan under conviction for a time, the joy and freedom of being cleansed and forgiven are well worth it. Little does Shame know or care that this behavior is precisely what clears the way for true revival. Do you want to see revival? Renounce shame yourself, and pray for today's church to stop entertaining sin and shame so we can have a boldly prophetic voice in our culture.

Scripture: 2 Chronicles 7:14; Joel 2:12; Lamentations 3:40-42

Prayer: Dear Lord, thank you for your Spirit's convicting power that brings me back into right relationship with you. I am not ashamed! Grant all your people repentance in these times. Amen.

D·A·Y

140

"Well, what did you say to him?"

"I hardly knew what to say at first. Indeed, he was so convincing that I felt myself blushing. I felt that his point of view had beaten me. But then I began to consider how 'what is highly valued among men is detestable in God's sight' [Luke 16:15]. And I thought again, 'This Shame tells me man's point of view, but he tells me nothing of what God or the Word of God says.' I thought, moreover, that at the day of judgment we will not be doomed to death or presented with life according to the dictates of the lawless spirits of the world, but according to the wisdom and law of the Almighty. So I determined that what God says is best, even though all the world is against it. I realized then that God is the One who set forward this faith of ours. I saw that God esteems a tender conscience, that those who make themselves fools for the Kingdom of Heaven are wisest, and that the poor man who loves Christ is far richer than the greatest man in the world who hates Him."

Proverbs 3:5 says, "Trust in the Lord with all your heart and lean not on your own understanding." Yet most people interpret life from their own perspective. They rarely bother questioning their viewpoint, though a lifetime of worldly influence has indoctrinated them. But God is the arbiter of all truth and reality, and to please him, we must see from his perspective. Those who find themselves suspended somewhere between two worldviews—God's and the world's—need a "paradigm shift" to God's perspective.

Studying the Scriptures to learn right and wrong "in God's sight" is the solution. God's Word answers Shame's arguments. Faithful recognized how the answers to ultimate questions lay not in worldly logic but in God. He remembered how God favors those with tender consciences toward him, those who look like fools for him, and those who are poor and yet love him. How different is God's perspective!

Shame's influence must be broken! His outlook blinds us to truth, making us adopt cultural views that are corrupt and devoid of God's perspective. Mark Noll says, "The search for a Christian perspective on life . . . is not just an academic exercise. The effort to think like a Christian is rather an effort to take seriously the sovereignty of God over the world he created, the lordship of Christ over the world he died to redeem, and the power of the Holy Spirit over the world he sustains each and every moment."[14]

Have you made a complete shift to God's perspective on life? Let the Holy Spirit convict your heart of any changes in thinking you might still need to make.

Scripture: Isaiah 55:8-9; 1 Kings 11:38; 1 Corinthians 1:20-21

Prayer: Lord, I want a clear perception of your purposes. Help me increasingly to break away from a worldly perspective and see my life through your eyes. Amen.

D·A·Y 141

"Then I commanded, 'Go away, Shame! You are an enemy to my salvation. Should I give heed to you against my sovereign Lord? How would I then be able to look Him in the face when He comes? If I am now ashamed of His ways and His servants, how can I expect Him to bless me?' But this Shame was a bold and persistent villain indeed. I could hardly shake him off. He kept haunting me and whispering in my ear about one or another weakness that goes along with religion. Finally I told him that any further attempts to discredit the faith would be in vain, for it was in the very things he disdained that I was able to see the most glory. So at last I got past this stubborn menace, and having shaken him off, I began to sing:

"Oh, the hard trials that meet us all
Who do obey the heavenly call;
They're many and suited to the flesh
Coming and coming again afresh,
That now or later we by them may
Be taken, overcome, and fall away;
So let the pilgrims, all pilgrims then,
Be vigilant, conduct themselves like men."

With an infusion of biblical truth, Shame's arguments have lost credence with Faithful. He no longer wants Shame hindering him with desires for earthly renown. He enjoys a renewal of spiritual purpose. He in no way wants to compromise his standing with the Lord by being double-minded about his pilgrimage. Faithful resolves to make Shame leave. But Shame is bold and shameless, and merely asking or pleading won't stop his mouth. Faithful must command him to leave.

Temptations come in many forms. Whether Shame is an inclination of Faithful's fleshly nature, an influence from the world, or a demonic personality is irrelevant. The world, the flesh, and the devil all interact to create powerful emotional-spiritual conflicts. All three must be subdued. We conquer them by regaining a godly perspective, submitting to Christ's lordship with single-minded devotion, confessing and repenting of sin, and by verbally renouncing evil influences in Jesus' name.

Faithful found Shame very difficult to shake. With persistence, however, his enemy finally gave up his torments. Are you prepared to show the same great tenacity in shaking off Satan's enticements?

Scripture: James 4:6-8; 2 Timothy 2:12; Matthew 4:10

Prayer: Lord Jesus, when bold temptations assail me, I must be bolder still. Grant me discernment, strength, and determination to deal ruth lessly with them until full victory comes. Amen.

DAY 142

"I'm glad, my brother," said Christian, "that you so bravely withstood this villain. For, like you said, of all our enemies, he seems wrongly named. He is so bold as to follow us in the streets and attempt to make us ashamed before all people. He would have us be ashamed of all that is good. He is Shame, yet if he were not so audacious, he would never attempt to do as he does. But let us keep resisting him, for in spite of all his arrogant intimidation, he exalts none other than fools. Solomon said, 'The wise are promoted to honor, but fools are promoted to shame'" [Proverbs 3:35].

"Well," said Faithful, "I think we must cry for help against Shame to Him who would have us be valiant for truth upon the earth."

"You speak the truth," said Christian. "But did you meet anyone else in the Valley?"

"No, I didn't. I had sunshine all the rest of the way through it and also through the Valley of the Shadow of Death."

Faithful finally succeeded in driving Shame away, but Christian doubts his departure is permanent. He recommends that they keep resisting him. Faithful agrees, saying he thinks they must cry to the Lord for help in maintaining their victory. Indeed, Shame is a powerful tempter. Once even the apostle Peter succumbed to Shame's influence. Although Peter introduced the Gospel to the Gentiles, out of fear of what certain Jews thought, he avoided sitting at mealtime with Gentile Christians. Because the temptation to be ashamed of some aspects of the Christian faith is so often entrenched in the way many of us think and relate, recognizing it for what it is and crying out to the Lord for freedom is essential.

How can we perceive Shame's influence? We are ashamed when we fear letting others know we are Christians. We are ashamed when we evade fellowship with those who would be our dearest friends and heroes but for the derision we fear from others. We are ashamed when we avoid certain behaviors that seem undignified though the Holy Spirit inspires them. We are ashamed when we bypass certain opportunities for ministry because we don't want to be seen doing them. We are ashamed when we dodge taking a stand to preserve godly values in our culture.

Some never do quite shake this false sense of shame. This calls the genuineness of their faith into question. Nevertheless, God has victory for those who hold to his Word, cry out to him for help, and resist temptations to be ashamed. Will you commit to vigilantly fighting off "Shame" at every turn?

Scripture: Galatians 2:11-12; Romans 1:16; Acts 4:29; 28:30-31

Prayer: Dear Lord, keep me alert against every ungodly sense of shame so that I will not shun people with whom you would have me associate or ministries with which you would have me serve. Amen.

D·A·Y
143

"Oh, you were well off. It was far different for me. I had an enduring season of trial. Almost as soon as I had entered that Valley, I had a dreadful battle with that foul fiend, Apollyon. Yes, I thought he was going to kill me, especially when he got me down and crushed me beneath him. It seemed he would crush me to pieces; then he threw me, and my Sword flew out of my hand. He told me his victory was certain, but 'this poor man cried out, and the Lord heard him, and saved him out of all his troubles' [Psalm 34:6]. After this, I entered the Valley of the Shadow of Death and had no light for almost half the way through it. I thought I would be killed there over and over again. But at last the day broke, the sun rose, and I went through the rest of the way with far more peace and quiet."

Christian and Faithful further discover the differences in their pilgrimages. In the Valley of Humiliation, Faithful wrestled Discontent and Shame, but this could hardly compare with Christian's bloody clash with the evil prince, Apollyon. Faithful even enjoyed sunshine most of the way through this valley and all the way through the Valley of the Shadow of Death where he easily walked on through. He could triumphantly testify with David, "Even though I walk through the valley of the shadow of death, I will fear no evil, for you are with me" (Psalm 23:4).

Christian's experience in the Valley of the Shadow of Death bore no comparison with Faithful's. No sooner had he reached the Valley than the two descendants of the spies warned him to flee. They told him all the terrifying sounds they heard and the depression, confusion, darkness, and chaos they saw. Although they couldn't convince Christian to turn back, their negative report left its mark. From then on, his fearful journey through the Valley was all the two men had conveyed and more. Only halfway through did the sun come out and enable him to survive the remainder of his "enduring season of trial."

Here are two pilgrims exposed to temptations of which the other has no experience. Still neither judges the other. Instead, they sympathetically listen to one another's trials as true friends. Often believers suspect, judge, correct, dislike, and even despise each other for their distinctive qualities and experiences. More sympathetic listening will go far in enabling us to complement and help one another succeed in the Christian life. Remember, God's people are all en route to the same destination.

Have you unfairly judged certain fellow believers simply because of irritating differences in personality and experience? How can you better appreciate them? Ask God for his help here.

Scripture: Romans 14:1; 15:1; Colossians 3:13; 1 Corinthians 4:7, 10

Prayer: Dear Lord, help me to respect the differences in experience and perspective we all contribute to your body. I want to listen more patiently and support my brothers and sisters. Amen.

D·A·Y 144

Then I saw in my dream that as they went on, Faithful looked to one side and saw a man whose name was Talkative walking at a distance beside them. For in this place there was room enough for them all to walk. He was a tall man and somewhat more handsome from a distance than up close.

"Friend, where are you going?" called Faithful. "Are you going to the Heavenly Country?"

"Yes, I'm going to that very place."

"Good; then I hope we can share your company."

"Yes, I will gladly be your companion."

"Come on then, let us go on together, and let us spend our time discussing things that will be beneficial to us."

Talkative, too, is on his way to the Heavenly Country and is happy to join Faithful and Christian. Faithful enthusiastically welcomes Talkative. Since relating with Christian has been so enriching, he relishes the thought of another pilgrim joining them.

Interacting with other believers affords us great learning opportunities. Unfortunately, meaningful conversation has diminished as a priority in our culture. At one time a warm summer evening would bring folks together for neighborly front porch visits to converse and to discuss issues of interest. Old-time sitting rooms accommodated neighbors who would pop in to visit. Today the porches and sitting rooms have been retired for rooms packed with electronic gizmos that beg for every spare minute. Even the average married couple in our society now spends only four minutes per day in meaningful conversation.

Many believers today still like to get together to play in the name of fellowship, but true fellowship involves interacting with one another at a deeper level. Faithful appreciates such fellowship and hopes for a beneficial discussion of issues significant to pilgrims. As one who is zealously passionate about his pilgrimage, he has little interest in light, insubstantial small talk. He wants spiritual enrichment. He knows he has much to learn about maintaining a victorious walk, and perhaps this new relationship will prove mutually upbuilding.

We will do well to find friends with whom we can share our views and experiences. How deeply do you relate with other believers? When together, do you discuss real issues or simply shoot the breeze?

Scripture: Deuteronomy 6:6-7; Luke 24:13-32; 1 John 1:7

Prayer: Dear Lord, I need to make room for others in my life. Help me to make friends with whom I can share deep thoughts and feelings, to the end that we become more spiritually mature. Amen.

"Ah," replied Talkative, "this is acceptable to me. I will talk about good things with you or anyone else. I'm glad that I have found ones who like such good conversation. For, to tell you the truth, only a few care enough to spend their time this way while they're traveling. They would much rather choose to speak about things that are worthless, and this has troubled me."

"That is indeed lamentable," said Faithful. "For what is a more worthy use of the tongue and mouth of people on this earth than the things of the God of Heaven?"

"I am going to get along very well with you, for your sayings are full of conviction. And, I might add, what is more pleasant and what is more profitable than talking together of the things of God? What could be more pleasant to a man who delights in wonderful things? For example, if one delights in talking about history or the mystery of things, or if one loves to talk about miracles, wonders, or signs, where will he find things recorded so delightfully and with such pleasing style as in the Holy Scripture?"

"That is true," answered Faithful, "but to profit spiritually from these things should be our main goal in discussing them."

We might gauge a church's spiritual vitality by listening to the conversations out on the front lawn after Sunday services. What are people talking about—yesterday's ball game, the latest gossip, politics? Or do they talk about the Lord Jesus Christ? In Faithful's mind, it is "lamentable" that so few enjoy talking about God. A fellow of boundless discourse who specializes in spiritual talkathons, Talkative fully agrees.

Talkative is certain he will get along nicely with Faithful because both love a good discussion. Yet Faithful wants to qualify something he thinks he might be hearing Talkative say. Discussing theology can be beneficial, but Talkative seems to imply that having a good discussion is some kind of an end in itself. If he means he reads the Scriptures solely to better engage in a stimulating exchange of ideas and interpretations, this is unacceptable. Faithful clarifies the purpose of discussing spiritual things: It should always be "to profit spiritually" from them.

What is the use of talking if we have no intention of learning and growing or blessing the Lord and others in it? The Scriptures exhort us to be filled with the Holy Spirit, speaking "to one another with psalms, hymns and spiritual songs" (Ephesians 5:19). Our conversation should be Spirit-led and grounded in God's Word for the purpose of mutual edification. Evaluate the spiritual value of your conversations. What can you do to relate more meaningfully with your Christian friends?

Scripture: Ephesians 4:29; Proverbs 8:8; 1 Timothy 4:12

Prayer: Dear Lord, fill my heart with such love for you that I cannot help but speak about you with others. I don't want to waste my conversations on irrelevant things. Amen.

DAY 146

"That is what I said. Talking of such things is most profitable, for by so doing a man may gain knowledge of many things, of both the futility of earthly things and the benefit of things above. So in general, but also in particular, by talking, a man may learn the necessity of the new birth, the insufficiency of our works, and the need of Christ's righteousness, among other things. Besides, by this a man may learn what it is to repent, to believe, to pray, to suffer, or the like. A man may also learn through conversing what are the great promises and consolations of the Gospel for his own comfort. Further, he may learn to refuse false opinions, to vindicate the truth, and also to instruct the ignorant."

"All of this is true, and I'm glad to hear these things from you," said Faithful.

Talkative's impressive reply more than satisfies Faithful. Everything Talkative lists as important topics of discussion are central biblical themes and absolutely vital for a sound faith. Many people, ignorant of the great doctrinal truths of our faith, fall prey to all kinds of deceptions. Just as the Bible predicted of the last days, they gravitate to heretical teachers who lead them astray. Cult groups are filled with devotees who were once active yet biblically ignorant members of Christian churches. So discussing issues of doctrinal purity is a worthy activity.

We can easily become entrenched in a faulty belief system if no one ever stimulates us to think otherwise. Through conversing with one another about biblical truth, we sharpen each other's minds and stimulate each other's desire to dig deeper. Still our ultimate purpose is not to gain head knowledge but to make one another wiser and more faithful pilgrims.

Jesus said, "Watch out that no one deceives you" (Matthew 24:4). To escape becoming a casualty, we must understand the core doctrines of our faith well. In this way, we can avoid following every whim or supposed "new revelation" that comes along. Federal agents who specialize in stopping counterfeiters are trained by becoming experts in knowing real money. Likewise we are protected from counterfeit "truths" when we learn the truths of God's Word. Do you know and understand the central truths of the Gospel? While devotional reading is important, the value of serious Bible study must not be underestimated.

Scripture: Colossians 3:16; 1 Timothy 4:1, 13, 16; Titus 1:9-10

Prayer: Dear Lord, I recognize how a proper doctrinal knowledge is important not only for my own walk, but for those whom I will influence. I want to be more devoted to knowing the vital foundational truths of the Christian faith. Amen.

DAY 147

"Alas! The lack of this is the reason so few people understand the need for faith and the necessity for a work of grace in their heart in order to receive eternal life. They ignorantly live in the works of the Law, by which no one can obtain the Kingdom of Heaven."

"But please permit me," Faithful responded. "Heavenly knowledge of these things is the gift of God; no one can attain them by human effort or merely by talking about them."

"I know that very well, for a man can receive nothing, except it be given him from Heaven. All is of grace, not of works. I could give you a hundred Scriptures to confirm this truth."

"Well, then," asked Faithful, "what topic shall we discuss at this time?"

"Ask what you will. I will talk of things in Heaven or things on earth, things moral or things spiritual, things sacred or things secular, things past or things to come, things foreign or things at home, things more essential or things circumstantial—provided that it will be to our edification."

In the original story's sidebar, the author wrote, "Oh, brave Talkative." In other words, Talkative likes to hear himself talk. He impresses himself with his ability to engage in discussions about almost any subject. He knows Christian lingo and easily refers to truths in the Bible: "All is of grace, not of works." (See Ephesians 2:8-9.) He can give a hundred more Scriptures on this point! He seems like a spiritual giant, far superior in depth and knowledge to Faithful.

We shouldn't assume, however, that those who can fluently expound on numerous divine subjects are more spiritual than others, nor should we think that those who say less are less spiritual. Spiritual depth and true apprehension of God's truth aren't necessarily combined with the desire or ability to engage in continuous verbal exchanges. Tolstoy, in his *Invaders*, says concerning one of his heroes, "If a great saying in regard to any subject came into my hero's mind, I believe he would not have uttered it: in the first place, because he would have feared that in saying something great he might spoil a great deed; and secondly, because when a man is conscious within himself of the power to do a great deed, there is no need of saying anything at all."[15]

Talkative's penchant for talking may cover a lack of real depth. He seems most interested in impressing Faithful. We should know God's Word well, but meditating upon and living out God's truth means far more than merely talking about it. Think about your biblical knowledge. Are you allowing it to make a permanent impact upon how you live?

Scripture: 1 Corinthians 2:4; 8:1; 13:2; Ephesians 4:1

Prayer: Father, thank you for the gifts of learning and communication. In addition to discussing my beliefs, however, help me to make a high priority of living them out. Amen.

D·A·Y 148

Now Faithful began to marvel at this man and stepped over to Christian, for Christian had been walking by himself during this time. He said to him softly, "What an admirable companion we've got! Surely this man will make a very excellent pilgrim!"

At this Christian modestly smiled and said, "This man with whom you are so impressed will, with that tongue of his, deceive almost anyone who doesn't know him."

"Do you know him then?"

"Know him! Yes, better than he knows himself."

"Then please tell me, who is he?"

Not only is Talkative impressed with himself, but he staggers Faithful. The young pilgrim had felt some hesitation toward Talkative at first, but in the spirit of being humble and charitable, he decided to believe the best and mistrust his own discernment. Enthusiastic young believers, zealous to learn all they can, are often taken with those who are well studied and versed in the Bible. Since they feel far less impressed with their own knowledge and theological grasp on issues, and these people seem to know everything there is to know, they quickly forego caution. Not surprisingly, you can soon find them hanging on every word of the impressive talker.

However, Talkative's words ring untrue in Christian's ears like the clanging of a cracked bell. To him, Talkative is not only named for his loquacious disposition but for his hot air. While Talkative loves to strut his biblical knowledge, he is simply a vain talker. He easily takes up any doctrinal subject, but his ostentatious talk deludes both himself and his listener. Matthew Henry said, "Those that speak much, speak much amiss." A saying of Jewish rabbis goes, "He that multiplies words brings on or brings unto sin."

The acquisition of knowledge is good. But there are many who love to examine every side of the truth and endlessly dialogue about it without ever committing and conforming their lives to it. Without the commitment to be conformed to God's truths, they are little more than vain talkers. We should cautiously guard our hearts and minds against being taken in by them. Also we should always make sure we are sincerely living out our own faith. Talking about it is all too easy. Are you living your life by the Scriptures? Think of some important ways in which you are conforming your life to God's Word.

Scripture: 2 Timothy 3:1, 5-7; 2 John 9-10; Matthew 7:21

Prayer: Dear Lord, please keep me from being carried away by impressive personalities who may be less than genuine. Also help me to genuinely conform my life to the standards of your Word. Amen.

D·A·Y 149

"His name is Talkative. He lives in our town. I'm surprised you don't know him, but I guess our town is quite large."

"Whose son is he? And in what area of the City does he live?"

"He is the son of a Mr. Say-well. He lived in Prating-row, and he is known as Talkative by all his acquaintances in Prating-row. In spite of his fine tongue, he is a very sorry fellow."

"Well, he seems to be a very impressive man."

"Yes, to those who aren't fully acquainted with him. For he puts on his best image away from home, but at home he is ugly enough. Your saying that he is an impressive man reminds me of what I have observed in the work of an artist whose work looks good at a distance but is displeasing up close."

Talkative lives in a corner of the City of Destruction—Prating-row—where everyone's proclivity for words makes them endlessly chatter. Mr. Say-well, his father, must be a particularly refined man among these talkers. No wonder Talkative takes such pride in his verbosity. According to Christian, however, he has more faults than simply loving to talk. Christian knows him and says he puts on a false image outside his home. In other words, he is a hypocrite. A man of theory and not of practice, he knows how to "talk the talk," while failing to "walk the walk." Christian has already experienced a difficult run-in with one named Hypocrisy from Vain-glory, and he has little interest in conversing with another hypocrite.

The Christian faith must be lived out, not just talked about. Hypocritical vain talkers, however, seek to justify themselves through high-sounding words without actually repenting and without ever truly experiencing the power of those words in their own lives. They think that because they successfully impress themselves and others with their ability to discuss theological subjects, God must also be impressed. In their hearts, they know their lives are less than perfect, but they think that their knowledge makes up for their deficiencies.

Perhaps Talkative doesn't realize his reputation for hypocrisy. He thinks he can disguise his lack of Christlike character. Nevertheless, Christian knows the truth. When we feel spiritually shallow or far away from God, it is tempting to try to conceal our lack. Even Moses put on a veil to disguise the fact that his face no longer glowed with God's glory. Instead of hiding, however, we should shed our veil, confess our lack, and humbly ask for prayer. Are you hiding anything God might have you confess? Do you think God might want you to get prayer concerning your need?

Scripture: Psalm 51:6-7; Proverbs 10:8-10; 18:6-7; Ecclesiastes 10:12-14

Prayer: Lord, help me to be honest and not try to find ways to cover for my lack. No one likes hypocrisy, least of all you. Remove it from my life. Amen.

D·A·Y 150

"But I saw you smile, and I almost think you must be joking."

"I did smile, but God forbid that I should joke in this matter or that I should accuse anyone falsely. I will help you to understand him more fully. This man is ready for any companionship and for any conversation. As he talks with you now, so will he talk when he is at the tavern. And the more alcohol he has in his brain, the more of these things he has in his mouth. True faith apparently has no place in his heart, in his house, or in his way of living. All he possesses lies in his tongue, and his religion is to make a great deal of noise with it."

Christian takes the matter of Talkative's hypocrisy very seriously. He won't joke about it, and he won't falsely accuse. He explains his position to Faithful more fully because Faithful has unwisely assessed the spiritual maturity of Talkative by his words alone. Talkative's life in his neighborhood betrays him. He easily makes friends but doesn't keep them long. He must continually meet strangers since his lifestyle won't support close scrutiny. It matters only a little to most of us what those who don't know us think of us. Yet it matters a great deal what those closest to us think. Talkative's character collapses under the scrutiny of those who know him best.

You can tell a lot about people by the associations they keep. Talkative lets opportunities to talk be his guide. He doesn't care whether he is with saints or sinners if he can find a friendly ear. Thus he has no scruples about frequenting bars. One can always find an audience in a bar. In fact, downing a few drinks loosens the tongue even more.

Unfortunately, so often the last person to recognize hypocrisy is the hypocrite himself. Even a hostile unbelieving world expects Christians to behave differently than unbelievers. The world may denounce Christianity, but it also hates hypocrites. If unbelievers see us drinking freely in bars, they think, *And I thought you were a Christian!* Many of them point to hypocrisy as their primary reason for shunning the Christian faith. We should never be content with merely knowing the right doctrines and the right jargon. We need to be godly examples. Robert Gibson says, "A Christian is the keyhole through which other folk see God." Someone else has said of Christians, "They are the only 'Bible' some people will ever read."

Do you try to live your life as if others are "reading" you? Ask the Lord how you might show Christ more clearly in your behavior.

Scripture: Matthew 5:13-16; Romans 13:13-14; Ephesians 5:8-11

Prayer: Lord Jesus, I want to obey your call to live an exemplary life before others. Help me, therefore, to reflect you in all I say and do. I never want others to use me as an excuse for rejecting you. Amen.

D·A·Y 151

"Well," said Faithful, "if what you say is true, then I am a man greatly deceived."

"Deceived, for sure! Remember the proverb, 'For they do not practice what they preach. For the kingdom of God is not a matter of talk but of power' [Matthew 23:3; 1 Corinthians 4:20]. He talks about prayer, repentance, faith, and the new birth, but he knows only how to talk about them. I have visited his family and have observed him both at home and abroad, and I know what I say about him is the truth."

Deception is no light matter, and Faithful wants to know the truth. Christian explains to him how to recognize whether a profession of faith is genuine or not. A pilgrim who fails to "practice what he preaches" is not an earnest pilgrim. The apostle John says, "This is how we know who the children of God are and who the children of the devil are: Anyone who does not do what is right is not a child of God . . ." (1 John 3:10).

To be effectual, the Gospel comes not only by word, but is also demonstrated through our deeds, in our relationships, and by the power of the Holy Spirit. God's power brings new life to people, deliverance from sin and spiritual bondage, change of inner hearts and outward actions, depth and love to our relationships with others, and strengthening to our faith. These things cannot happen merely by knowledge or impressive talk.

"Do not be conformed to this world," Paul writes, "but be *transformed* by the renewing of your minds" (Romans 12:2 NRSV, italics added). God is far more concerned with the *transformation* of our lives than with the *information* in our heads. Not everyone who professes faith in Christ truly belongs to Christ. There are those who claim to be believers, but they reject the Gospel's power to transform their lives. True faith shows itself in a changed life, day in and day out, "at home and abroad."

When professing Christians fail to exemplify a Christlike lifestyle, the church gives out conflicting and baffling messages to observers. We need to allow the Holy Spirit to transform and empower us so we can be solid and trustworthy witnesses before the eyes of a lost and needy world. Are there any particular areas of inconsistency between how you live your life "at home" and how you live it "abroad"? Ask God to "transform" your life in those areas.

Scripture: 2 Corinthians 10:5; 1 Peter 1:14-16; Ephesians 4:17-18

Prayer: Father, let one message resound from my life—that I am a child of my heavenly Father, redeemed by Jesus Christ, empowered by the Holy Spirit. I pray for more of your transforming power to fall on your church—and on me. Amen.

D·A·Y
152

"His house is as devoid of true religion as the white of an egg is of flavor. He neither prays nor shows any sign of repentance from sin. Why, a poor beast in his own way serves God far better than he. He is the very stain, reproach, and shame of religion to all who know him. Because of him, scarcely can a good word be spoken of religion in all that end of town where he lives. Therefore, the common people who know him say, 'A saint abroad and a devil at home.' His poor family finds it so; he is so unyielding, insolent, and unreasonable with his servants that they don't know what to do or how to speak."

Despite Talkative's sanctimonious words, Christian maintains that this man's home life proves he is not living up to his claims. For the home is the proving ground of faith, and this man's dysfunctional home lacks true faith and character. Talkative apparently jabbers inside the home as much as he jabbers outside the home. But his talk is as tasteless as "the white of an egg." No true family altar exists in this home.

Talkative is mean, self-centered, and stubborn—"a saint abroad and a devil at home." He won't pray, he resists allowing God's Spirit to touch his heart; he refuses to repent of sin. His faith is a sham! How then can his children come to know of a loving and righteous God? What he teaches them about God from the Scriptures is denied by the example of his life. Tragically, his children will probably be just like him. God only knows how many children are lost to his kingdom because of such hypocritical fathers who lecture incessantly but who fail to live the life their families desperately need to see.

We live in a disintegrating society. Almost every societal problem points back in some way to a problem with the family. The role of fatherhood desperately needs to be restored, and until it is, the moral fiber of our society will continue to unravel. Men of God need to rise up and reclaim their God-given responsibility for providing compassionate and godly leadership in their homes. Unlike Talkative, we should make every effort to cultivate healthy families by loving and honoring one another and by showing our children authentic Christian living. We should pray and read God's Word together and seek to glorify God in all aspects of our marriage and family life.

In light of so many shattered families in our society today, how can you ensure that your family will be a solid witness to those who observe it?

Scripture: Romans 2:21-24; Colossians 3:19-21; 1 Peter 3:7-10

Prayer: Dear Lord, help me to honor the role you have given me within my family and to do what I can to strengthen my family life. Also with your help, please enable our family to be a positive witness and blessing to others. Amen.

D·A·Y 153

"Those who have any dealings with him say that it is better dealing with a pagan than with him, that a pagan would deal more fairly than he. This man Talkative, if given the chance, will manipulate, deceive, defraud, and take advantage of them. Besides all this, he is bringing up his sons to follow in his footsteps. And if he finds in any of them a 'foolish fear of danger' (for this is what he calls a tender conscience), he calls them fools or blockheads; further, he won't employ them much or recommend them to others."

How do you feel toward someone who professes to know God but lives like the devil? Probably angry and disgusted. Talkative's conduct disturbs and confuses everyone associated with him—his children, associates, those working for him. The effect upon unbelievers is particularly destructive. They decide they prefer dealing with unbelievers like themselves rather than with a so-called believer who manipulates and cheats them.

To be effective witnesses, we as believers need to exemplify to unbelievers our peace, love, patience, joy, and humility. They should feel stirred by the mystery and the miracle of our testimonies and inspired as they see God's transforming power displayed in and through our lives; hopefully, they would desire that Christ change their lives, too. They should not, however, be forced to puzzle over the contradiction between what we say and how we act. They have legitimate grievances toward those of us who try to calibrate pious words with devilish behavior.

Talkative, who has ruined his own conscience, is now ruining his sons'. A sensitive conscience has no place in his definition of manhood. According to the Scriptures, one of the distinguishing characteristics of the end times will be seared consciences (1 Timothy 4:2). People will no longer care about right and wrong. We see the fulfillment all around us. A survey of 7,000 American youth found that young people are "lying, cheating, and stealing in unprecedented numbers." Largely, however, those who admitted to regular unethical behavior considered their personal ethics "very good or excellent." Not to imply that adults were any less guilty, the survey cited the poor example of adults as a probable leading factor for this moral crisis.[16]

By contrast, true believers must lead exemplary lives in this world if we expect unbelievers to embrace Christ as their Savior. Do you keep your conscience tender with regard to your ethical choices?

Scripture: Leviticus 20:26; 1 Peter 2:9-12; Ephesians 6:4

Prayer: Dear Lord, I want to take the moral high ground in my life. Please help me to be completely fair and honest in all my dealings. Thank you for showing me where I err. Amen.

DAY 154

"In my opinion, by his wicked example he has caused many to stumble and fall, and if God doesn't prevent it, he will be the ruin of many more."

"Well, my brother," responded Faithful, "I am obliged to believe you, not only because you say you know him, but also because when giving an account of the facts concerning people, you speak as a Christian should. I cannot believe that you speak these things out of ill will but because it must be as you say."

Christian has faced the issue of hypocrisy often. Not only has he met other hypocrites on the way, but in the Valley of Humiliation Apollyon forcefully accused him for his own hypocritical motives and behavior. Has he now become too sensitive to this issue or given it too much consideration? In saying so many terrible things about Talkative, is he giving in to a judgmental spirit? Faithful thinks not. He knows the serious consequences of hypocrisy. After all, Talkative's religiosity nearly mesmerized him. While some might criticize Christian for being too judgmental, Faithful commends him for speaking "as a Christian should."

Faithful knows Christian would be the first to "bear with the infirmities of the weak." Nevertheless, hypocrites must be shown for what they are. Many who think shallowly about this issue fail to understand the serious consequences of allowing hypocrites to go unchallenged. Clearly Christian has given much thought to these ramifications and believes turning the light on them is the best policy. The issue of authenticity is simply too important to ignore. Choosing to run the risk of seeming uncharitable and harsh, he candidly speaks his mind. Those who disgrace the faith not only mislead the immature, but they also cause those who are seeking the truth to stumble, and they give ammunition to the enemies of the Gospel. Such hypocrisy within the church must be exposed. "Have nothing to do with the fruitless deeds of darkness," Paul writes, "but rather expose them" (Ephesians 5:11).

We should never speak against anyone unnecessarily. But sometimes even sincere Christians exhibit hypocrisy and need to be confronted. When the apostle Peter was too ashamed before Jewish Christians to eat with Gentile Christians, Paul publicly exposed that hypocrisy. Peter repented, and the church was spared serious consequences. When the truth of the Gospel or the health of the church is at risk, we may need to speak up. Is there hypocrisy you should confront for the Lord's sake?

Scripture: Galatians 2:11-16; Leviticus 19:17; 1 Timothy 5:20

Prayer: Dear Lord, show me the best way to unmask hypocrisy when I see it. I don't want to be judgmental, but I do want to speak up when I see your kingdom discredited by vain talkers. Amen.

D·A·Y 155

"Had I known him no longer than you," added Christian, "I might have thought of him as you did at first. Yes, if I had received this report from the lips of the enemies of our faith, I would have thought it to be mere slander falling from an evil person's mouth upon a good person's name and faith. But from my own knowledge I can prove him guilty of all these things, yes, and a great many more as bad. Besides, good people are ashamed of him; they are unable to call him either brother or friend. Even his name called out among them causes embarrassment."

Just as Talkative should be able to prove his boasts, Christian should be able to prove his allegations. He wisely attests that not only does he personally know Talkative and the trouble he has wrought, but he can prove Talkative's guilt on all counts. He reaffirms his unswerving loyalty to speak only the truth. He does not expect Faithful simply to believe his opinion but will provide verification. His words, "I can prove him guilty," show he is not just repeating some rumor. If Christian could not stand behind his claims, he would be a gossip and slanderer, as bad or worse than Talkative.

Christian says that were he unable to prove these allegations, his report would be suspected of being contrived by an enemy of the faith. Often enemies do indeed begin such rumors. Why are we so quick to believe the worst about our fellow Christians and not the best? What in our fallen nature relishes tidbits of gossip, perhaps lies? We need to be much more careful about passing on unverifiable "facts." Many of us are too often prone to pick up a false rumor and run with it.

Over recent years millions of Christians have believed and repeated falsehoods from news of a well-known atheist's alleged attempts to ban religious broadcasting to social security checks stamped with 666 whose recipients must be marked in their hand or forehead to cash them. Then there are the multitudes of smaller rumors that many of us pass along on a daily basis. Increasingly, we are becoming a society that loves rumors. Competing political parties constantly "leak" rumors; tabloids flourish because "inquiring minds want to know."

This is where extreme care must be exercised within the Christian community. Reputations are at stake. False rumors ruin many upright Christian people. Have you ever been hurt by a rumor? What can you do when someone passes on a rumor to you?

Scripture: James 3:5-10; Proverbs 12:18; 20:19; Leviticus 19:16

Prayer: Dear Lord, I know you are a God of truth and only want truth spoken. Help me to use great discretion in passing along information I hear. Amen.

DAY 156

"Well, I see that words and deeds are two different things, and from now on I will make a better observation of this distinction."

"Indeed, they are two things and are as diverse as are the soul and the body. For as the body without the soul is but a dead carcass, so words, if they are alone, are nothing but a dead carcass as well. The soul of true religion is the part that puts it into practice. 'Religion that God our Father accepts as pure and faultless is this: to look after orphans and widows in their distress and to keep oneself from being polluted by the world' [James 1:27]. Talkative is not aware of this; he thinks hearing and speaking, in and of themselves, will make him a good Christian; he thus deceives his own soul. Hearing is merely the sowing of the seed, and talking alone is not sufficient to prove that fruit is truly in the heart and life."

A human body may have the appearance of life, but if its soul has departed, it is in reality stone-dead. To be truly alive, it needs both its body and soul. Similarly, if you remove good works from a profession of faith, you effectively remove that faith's soul, and it is dead. Professed faith in Christ without good works is dead faith, just as much as good works without true faith are but dead works. Works, in and of themselves, do not prove the existence of true faith. Yet uttering pure words without the accompanying good works makes for an impure religion. These words are like a dead and putrid carcass.

An acceptable faith, therefore, shows itself in observable ways. Widows and orphans, for instance, are cared for and not just talked about. Someone with Talkative's persuasive skills could effectively champion the cause of the poor and powerless, but he is too preoccupied with promoting himself to express genuine care for others.

Acceptable religion also means keeping our souls unpolluted by the world and its soul-corrupting values. "Do not love the world or anything in the world," writes John. "For everything in the world—the cravings of sinful man, the lust of his eyes, and the boasting of what he has and does—comes not from the Father but from the world" (1 John 2:15-16). We are taught to separate ourselves from worldly ways, denying self-centeredness and lustful desires in order to live righteous and holy lives for the Gospel's sake.

Faithful is now much wiser, and from now on he intends to make a more careful distinction between words and deeds. Will you be careful to do the same?

Scripture: James 2:14-17, 26; Luke 6:46-49; John 15:14

Prayer: Dear Father, I want to be filled with your life. Please cleanse me from false religiosity, and show me how, specifically, you want me to practice my faith. Amen.

D·A·Y 157

"Let us be assured that on the day of judgment, all people will be judged by their fruit. They will not be asked, 'Did you believe?' but, 'Were you doers, or merely talkers?' God will judge them all accordingly. The end of the world is compared to a harvest, and you know that those who do the harvesting care about nothing but the fruit. Of course, this does not mean that deeds, by themselves, which do not arise from faith are of any value either; I say this to you to show you how insignificant Talkative's words alone will be on that day."

If the tree is bad, it bears worthless fruit; if it is good, it produces good, succulent fruit. We may think it is the fruit that makes the tree good, but it is the tree's goodness that makes the fruit good. The tree is first good, and then it produces good fruit. Likewise, we may assume that good fruit in a life makes a person good, but this reverses the facts. The person is already good, or he wouldn't be bearing acceptable fruit. Fruit that God considers good comes only from his life within us. When this good fruit is born, it is because God, who is good, has already transformed our lives.

God wants us to be trees of righteousness, bearing the good fruits of righteousness. Empty words and good intentions cannot produce this fruit. Some folks, like Talkative, deceive themselves by their own talk, but they cannot deceive God. For he looks for good fruit, not lofty words, to gauge the true quality and life within a person's heart. Thus Christian points to Judgment Day when God will carefully evaluate the quality of our lives, not by the right words, but by examining the fruit of our lives. We can *say* we believe, but as James so incisively pointed out, even the demons "believe and tremble" (James 2:19 KJV).

Those like Talkative blossom prettily with their words. A bountiful yield of wholesome fruit seems forthcoming. When it ripens, however, it is inedible! The real evidence of our belief is seen in how we live out that belief. Do we say we love Jesus? Do we show it by displaying his glory, grace, and power in our lives? Do we offer his love in practical ways to others? Do our actions really separate us from talkers? Believers should consistently bear good fruit. We should daily examine our lives and our fruit. Think about the kind of fruit you want to produce. How can you better assure a good yield?

Scripture: John 15:4, 8; Matthew 7:16-20; James 1:22-25

Prayer: Dear Lord, I want to produce righteous fruit for your kingdom and glory. Therefore, please help me to let your purity and life nourish me. I want you to be pleased when you examine the fruit of my life. Amen.

D·A·Y
158

Then Faithful replied, "This brings to my mind Moses' description of animals that are clean—those that part the hoof and chew the cud. Those declared clean are not those that part the hoof alone or chew the cud alone. The hare chews the cud but is still unclean because it doesn't part the hoof. This truly resembles Talkative. He chews the cud, seeking knowledge, chewing on the Word, but he does not divide the hoof. He professes true faith with his mouth, but he does not live what he professes. He refuses to part company with the way of sinners, and thus he is unclean."

Faithful makes a most unusual observation from the Old Testament Law. The Lord instructed Moses and Aaron in the kinds of meat Israel could and could not eat. Lest there be any misunderstanding, he forbade them from even touching the animals he deemed "unclean." Why were some animals "clean" and some "unclean"? God wanted to stamp in his people's hearts that a distinction exists between what is holy and what is not. In contrast to their wicked pagan neighbors, God wanted his people to live a "holy," set-apart, unique lifestyle according to his standards. He limited them to eating certain "clean" foods, thus keeping them a distinct and separated people. Differing from the people around them, God's people, who were "clean," ate only clean food. Clean animals included those that both parted the hoof and chewed the cud, while unclean animals bore either one or the other characteristic.

Talkative "chews the cud" with his mouth, but fails to "part the hoof" by his walk. Thus, because he only satisfies the first part of the requirement, he is unclean. Unclean peoples are disobedient to God, and they have no real reverence for his holiness. Because they won't abhor uncleanness, they fail to avoid temptation.

Under the terms of the New Covenant, God declares "clean" those once considered "unclean." He has redeemed us, set us apart as his holy, chosen people. We must, therefore, come out from what is unclean and worldly among us, separated from sin and devoted to God. Anyone in Israel who ate unclean food was considered unclean by it. Those of us who want to be clean in God's sight must keep ourselves from idle talk and truly consecrate ourselves for his holy purposes. How "clean" are you today in your spiritual life and witness? Confess any defilement and receive God's cleansing.

Scripture: John 13:11; 2 Corinthians 6:17; Revelation 21:27; Acts 11:1-18

Prayer: Dear Lord, thank you for declaring me "clean." I feel privileged in being set apart for your purposes! Keep me from all uncleanness and make me an effective example of your holiness. Amen.

D·A·Y
159

"I know you have discerned the true spirit of the gospel," said Christian, "and I will add another thing. Paul describes such people—those known as great talkers—as resounding gongs and clanging cymbals. Elsewhere he calls them lifeless things, giving off only sound, strangers to true faith and the grace of the gospel, and consequently, though their voices sound like the voices of angels, they will never be received into the Kingdom of Heaven among those who are the true children of life."

Eliza Doolittle in the classic musical *My Fair Lady,*[17] shouts in exasperation, "Words, words, I'm tired of words; show me!" This is the sentiment of our two pilgrims towards Talkative. They have been discussing the difference between words and deeds, seeking knowledge and living it out. What is the "true spirit of the Gospel" for which Christian commends Faithful's discernment? It is the Gospel radically transforming your life, faith being put into practice—not just talked about. And what motivates us to go beyond our talking? Love. It is our motivational force, the underpinning of all we do, the Gospel in action. Without love, words and actions are empty and ineffective. As Paul says, "If I speak in the tongues of men and of angels, but have not love, I am only a resounding gong or a clanging cymbal" (1 Corinthians 13:1).

Talkative represents those in every age who delight in gaining knowledge so they can talk about it. Yet they lack the love of Jesus in their hearts. Talkative's speech is not an outgrowth of love. He refuses to give up his sinning because he lacks a true relationship with God. If he really knew God, he would love God, and out of that love, he would forsake his sin. True faith always works itself out in love. As it is, Talkative, void of love, is as fruitless as a noisy gong or a clanging cymbal.

We may have great minds, eloquent tongues, and great persuasive abilities. Nevertheless, if we are devoid of love, our most eloquent oration about God is useless noise. To believe that our words and actions can be separated from the motivation of love in our hearts is to distort the Gospel. As we walk through life, let us always bear in mind the great difference between mere words and flighty feelings on the one hand and a genuine commitment to love on the other. True love produces tangible actions. We will never cease bearing good fruit in our lives if we walk in God's love. Which do you do more of—living the Gospel or talking about it? How much of what you do for Christ is purely out of love?

Scripture: Ephesians 5:1-2; 1 Peter 1:22; 1 Corinthians 13:1-8, 13

Prayer: Father, thank you for the love you demonstrated through Christ and the love you express to me through your Holy Spirit. Help me to live and walk in your love. Amen.

DAY 160

"Well, Christian, I am sick of his company now. What can we do to be rid of him?"

"Take my advice. If you do as I say, you will find that he will soon be sick of your company too, unless God should somehow touch his heart and change it."

"What do you want me to do?"

"Return to him and get involved in some serious discussion with him about the power of religion. Once he affirms the power of the Gospel, and he certainly will, ask him whether or not he has experienced these things in his own heart, or in his home, or in his way of life."

When we converse with those who say they are believers but live dishonorably, we should have two considerations—either breaking fellowship or trying to convince them to turn from their error. The easiest choice for Christian and Faithful would be to chase Talkative off by rejecting him. They have hopes, however, that he might yet have a change of heart. Since he loves discussing theology, perhaps if they engage him in a serious discussion and he hears the truth presented straightforwardly and persuasively, he will respond favorably.

Like Formalist and Hypocrisy before him, Talkative is "holding to the outward form of godliness but denying its power" (2 Timothy 3:5 NRSV). To him, talking about godliness suffices for godliness. Christian hopes that getting Talkative to intellectually acknowledge the reality of the Gospel's transforming power will cause him to realize his need for that power in his own life.

Sometimes the loving thing to do is to tactfully correct an erring brother or sister. This can be stressful, because we have no guarantee that the one being confronted will respond well. When Christian involved himself with Simple, Sloth, and Presumption, they told him to mind his own business. For like reason, many prompted by God's Spirit to offer correction shrink back in fear that they will seem intrusive or cruel. But small problems left unattended usually grow to disastrous proportions. It is rarely effective to simply ignore problems and hope they will go away. Those who do so usually live to regret it. We need to speak the truth in love, endeavoring to bring every person into a growing, healthy walk with Christ.

Suppose you knew someone with Talkative's spiritual need and you felt the Lord wanted you to offer correction. What would you say, and how would you say it?

Scripture: Colossians 1:28; 2 Corinthians 7:8-11; 2 Timothy 2:25-26

Prayer: Dear Lord, please help me first to be open to receiving correction. Next grant me love, humility, and boldness in bringing correction if you should call upon me to do so. Amen.

DAY 161

Faithful then walked back over to Talkative and asked, "How is it going now?"

"Well, thank you," answered Talkative. "But I thought that by now we would have enjoyed a great deal of conversation."

"Well, if you want, we can talk now. Since you left it with me to choose the subject, let it be this: How does God's saving grace reveal itself when it is in one's heart?"

"I perceive, then, that our talk will be about the power of things. Well, it is a very good question, and I am willing to answer. Briefly stated, first, where God's grace is in the heart, it causes a great outcry against sin. Second—"

"No, hold on; let us consider one point at a time. I think it might be better to say that it shows itself by inclining the soul to abhor its sin."

"Why, what difference is there between crying out against and abhorring sin?"

"Oh, a great deal. A man may make it his policy to cry out against sin, but he cannot really abhor it unless he has a godly aversion to it. I have heard many preachers cry out against sin from their pulpits while allowing it to abide safely within their own hearts, homes, and lifestyles. The wife of Joseph's master cried out against him with a loud voice as if she were quite righteous. In spite of this, however, she would have committed adultery with him. Some cry out against sin, like a mother crying out against the child in her lap, calling it a 'naughty girl.' And yet, later, the same mother is seen hugging and kissing the child."

The word *hypocrite* derives from the Greek term *hupokrinomai*—to speak on stage, to impersonate, play a part, feign, pretend. Ancient Greeks called their actors hypocrites, and when Christ came along, he applied it to religious pretenders. Because Talkative decries evil and mimics the language of faith, Faithful must get beneath his words to unmask his hypocrisy.

To Talkative an outcry against sin, the louder the better, proves grace resides in one's heart. Yet Faithful argues that we must abhor sin, that crying out can be staged. Indeed, some of the worst hypocrites holler the loudest. Who can forget the TV evangelist who railed on America's sins but was found with a prostitute? Or how many political candidates who vow to right some wrong actually keep their promise? Crying out against evil is still just talk. What matters is a change of heart that causes us to abhor evil. The wife of Joseph's master hypocritically cried out against sin while righteous Joseph abhorred and fled from it. May we choose to follow Joseph's example. Think about authenticity versus playacting. How genuinely do you relate with others?

Scripture: Genesis 39:2-15; Matthew 6:5; Mark 7:6

Prayer: Lord, show me the sinful places in my life and help me to abhor them as you do. Rather than playacting on life's stage, I want to be a genuine lover of your truth. Amen.

D·A·Y 162

"It seems that you are trying to trap me," said Talkative.

"No, I'm not. I am only trying to set things straight. Now what is the second thing by which you would prove a work of grace in the heart?"

"Great knowledge of gospel mysteries."

"I believe this sign should have been first, but first or last, I believe it is also false. For knowledge, even great knowledge, may be obtained concerning the mysteries of the Gospel, and yet lack a work of grace in the soul. Yes, even if a man has all knowledge, this doesn't guarantee that he is a child of God. When Christ taught His disciples, He made it clear that it wasn't enough simply to understand these things; He said, 'Now that you know these things, you will be blessed if you do them.' [John 13:17]. He makes it clear that they will be blessed, not because of their knowledge, but because of their doing. There is a knowledge that produces no doing. Indeed, there are those who know the Master's will but do not do it. A man may have knowledge like an angel of God and still not be a Christian. So I must say that your sign is not true. To know is something that pleases talkers and boasters, but to do is what pleases God."

Faithful sees Talkative's second proof of God's grace in one's heart, great knowledge of gospel mysteries, as similarly flawed. He asserts that knowing is one thing while doing is quite another. Of course, saving faith involves knowledge of the Gospel and an assent to its truth, but it is much more than that. Since Talkative shows great regard for Scripture knowledge, Faithful offers Scripture as evidence. He cites Jesus' words after washing his disciples' feet. Jesus had spent much time instructing them, but he wanted them to understand that living the message was more important than knowing it. He explained that he had just set them an example of kingdom living and that they weren't above him in doing it. He didn't say knowing was bad; but he did say the blessing comes in doing, not in knowing.

Faithful next alludes to Jesus' parable of the wise and faithful servant. The Master, upon returning from a long trip, will promote to a high rank the servant whom he finds faithfully carrying out his instructions. Yet he will severely punish the servant who fails to do what he knows is right.

Finally Faithful seals his argument by touching on Paul's words, "If I have . . . all knowledge . . . but have not love, I am nothing" (1 Corinthians 13:2). Clearly, knowledge without love-in-action is meaningless. The ones who live an authentic gospel lifestyle will be blessed. Is there a situation in which you professed love but now want to more fully express it with deeds?

Scripture: 1 John 2:3-6; John 13:12-17; Luke 12:42-48

Prayer: Jesus, I want not only to voice your Gospel, but I want my life also to show it. Help me to carry out your purposes lovingly and obediently. Amen.

D·A·Y
163

"Of course, a heart cannot be good without knowledge, for without it the heart is lost. Therefore, there is knowledge and there is knowledge. One kind of knowledge rests in mere speculations about things; the other is accompanied by faith and love that moves a person to do the will of God from the heart. The first of these will serve the talker, but a true Christian cannot be content without the other. 'Give me understanding, and I will keep your law and obey it with all my heart'" [Psalm 119:34].

Feeling somewhat uncomfortable, Talkative answered, "You are once again trying to catch me in a trap. This conversation is not edifying or uplifting."

"Well then," answered Faithful, "why don't you propose another sign of how this work of grace shows itself in a life."

"No, I can see that we won't agree."

"Well, if you won't, will you allow me to give my proof?"

"You are free to do so."

Faithful admits that conversion cannot take place without knowledge. Nevertheless, a distinction exists between two kinds of knowledge—one spiritual and the other speculative. Spiritual knowledge comes by believing and responding to God's revealed truth. This produces a humbling, cleansing, transforming love for God and his revealed truth. It ushers one's soul into fellowship with God and produces joyful obedience.

Speculative knowledge, on the other hand, is based on ideas and fanciful impressions of spiritual things. This knowledge doesn't lead souls to God, but it can actually lead them away from him. It allows for professing knowledge of God while continuing to live a carnal, sin-entrenched, self-righteous life. It enables persons to create their own definitions of holiness, permitting them to form conclusions based on conjecture and supposition without heeding the practical applications of God's Word.

The psalmist cried out to God, promising his undying obedience if only God would grant his heart "understanding." It was spiritual knowledge that he was crying for. Talkative and those he represents, however, flee from such knowledge, fashioning their religion after their own desires. We should with the psalmist cry out to God with all our hearts for true spiritual understanding so that we will genuinely let his will be our guide. Think about spiritual versus speculative knowledge as they impact your life. How can you better discern between them and cultivate the first as you impede the latter?

Scripture: Psalm 119:97-102; Proverbs 15:14; 18:15; Philippians 3:7-11

Prayer: Oh Lord, I want the kind of knowledge you would give me, not my own fanciful notions. I cry with the psalmist for a heart of spiritual understanding. I want to know you and your ways better. Amen.

D·A·Y 164

"A work of grace in the soul shows itself either to him that possesses it or to those standing by. To the one who has it, it brings conviction of sin, especially of the defilement of the old nature and of the sin of unbelief for which he will surely be damned if he does not find mercy from God's hand through faith in Jesus Christ. This experience of grace works in him a deep remorse and shame for sin. In addition, it is revealed to him that Jesus Christ is the Savior of the world, and he becomes aware of the absolute necessity of agreeing with and submitting to Him for eternal life. Consequently, he finds himself hungering and thirsting after Him who alone can satisfy those hungerings and thirstings as He has promised. Now in proportion to the strength or weakness of his faith in the Savior, so will be his joy and peace, his love for holiness, his desire to know Him better and to serve Him more effectively in this world.

"Now even though I say that the work of grace shows itself within him, it is only seldom that he can perceive this work. The struggles with his own inner corruption, along with his distorted capacity to reason, cause his mind to misjudge the matter. So it is that very sound judgment is required before he can conclude with certainty that this is, indeed, a work of grace within him."

Faithful finds Talkative's two signs of God's saving grace at work in a heart—crying out against sin and acquiring great knowledge—superficial and therefore unacceptable. A true work of grace is recognizable, and Faithful proceeds to show how.

First comes conviction of sin and of eternal condemnation. The sinner has broken God's Law and realizes that no true salvation exists apart from faith in Jesus Christ. The pride, rebellion, aversion to goodness, and love for sin that previously caused resistance to this great salvation now bring deep remorse and shame. Thus, when invited to receive Christ's salvation, he submits his life to God. The new believer not only yearns for salvation but hungers and thirsts to know Christ, to walk in personal relationship with him, and to serve him effectively.

Sometimes inner conflicts and wrong thinking make it difficult for us to recognize God's grace for what it is. But after a while we see what God has been doing in our lives. Have you noticed God doing a work of grace in your heart? If you find yourself in turmoil, perhaps God in His loving grace is allowing the pressure to bring about the ultimate good of a closer walk with him.

Scripture: Titus 2:11-14; 1 Peter 5:10-12; Matthew 5:3-6

Prayer: Dear Jesus, thank you for your grace working in my heart that restores my fellowship with you. Please allow me more of this grace that I may walk ever closer with you. Amen.

D·A·Y
165

"Observers can first witness this work of grace in the believer's life through his experiential confession of faith in Christ. Next they must see a life that is consistent with that confession. This calls for a life of holiness—holiness in his own heart and life, holiness in his family life (if he has a family), and holiness in his conduct in the world. Thus he trains himself to abhor and deal with his own secret sins, to subdue sin in his family life, and to promote and exalt righteousness in the world. None of these can be attained by talk alone, as a hypocrite or a talkative person may try. On the contrary, there must be a practical submission of the heart, in true faith and love, to the power of the Word."

Faithful continues to explain a true work of grace in the heart. It begins with a verbal confession of faith in Christ, but it doesn't end there. A person's life must conform to his confession. This requires a transformation from sinful ways to righteousness and holiness, which in turn will influence how we live and relate to people in every area of our lives. But this transformation is not automatic. We must train ourselves by the Holy Spirit's empowerment to walk in holiness. We intentionally abhor and renounce personal sins, arresting sin in our homes and in our conduct before the world. We cannot talk our way into this lifestyle. It takes Christ's work of grace in our hearts as we consciously yield to God's Spirit.

Unfortunately, too few believers allow God's transforming grace to have its full effect. We greatly mar our witness before the world by too much talking and too little right living. As evidenced by a Roper poll, the behavior of born-again Christians after their conversion experience is not much different from what it was before. In fact, the survey showed that adultery, illegal drug use, and drinking actually increased after conversion! For instance, 2 percent said they had indulged in illicit sex before being born again, while 5 percent had done so after. Five percent abused drugs before conversion and 9 percent did after. Four percent said they drove while intoxicated before conversion while 12 percent said they did so afterwards. Don Otis, leader of the organization that commissioned the poll, said this indicated a real moral decline in the U.S. church.[18]

Have you allowed the transforming work of the Holy Spirit to train you in holiness? A lost world needs to see believers living out an authentic faith. People need to see our lives changed, not merely hear empty words.

Scripture: 1 Thessalonians 1:5-7; Romans 15:18-19; 2 Timothy 2:20-21

Prayer: Dear Lord, I want to live my profession consistently. Grant me a heart that embraces your correction when I begin to err from a holy walk with your Holy Spirit. Amen.

DAY 166

"And now, sir, as to this brief description of the work of grace and also the means by which it can be perceived, if you have any objection, then object; if not, then please allow me to propose to you a second question."

Talkative replied, "No, my part is not to object now but to listen. Go ahead and ask your second question."

"It is this: First, have you truly experienced this first work of grace? And also are your life and conduct consistent with that experience? Or does your religion stand on the power of word and tongue alone but not on the power of actions and truth? Please, if you decide to answer me in this, say no more than what you know God above will say 'Amen' to and also nothing except what your conscience can justify. 'For it is not the one who commends himself who is approved, but the one whom the Lord commends' [2 Corinthians 10:18]. Besides, to say, 'I am thus and so' when my conduct and all my neighbors tell me I am lying is great wickedness."

Living in the shallow realm of head knowledge, Talkative is just a little "squirt" who thinks he is a "fountain" of wisdom. Words stream from his brain out through his mouth, but unfortunately they have never soaked down to the heart level. Faithful seeks to cut through the smoke screens, urging Talkative to be honest about his spiritual experiences. He urges him to answer only what God and his own conscience can agree is true. He closes his appeal by saying that the one truly approved is the one whom God commends, not the one who commends himself.

There are some in Christ's church who commend themselves by claiming what doesn't belong to them. They learn to talk "Christianese" and recite the testimonies of others as if they were their own. But something is missing. There is a hollowness, a lack of authenticity, a life not matching the words. To Faithful, such hypocrisy is "great wickedness." If we are tempted to "talk" beyond where we really are spiritually, let's be honest with ourselves and with God about it. We don't grow spiritually by faking it but by humbling ourselves before God and others, acknowledging our need of his grace and strength.

When we talk about ourselves, let us make sure God will put his "Amen" to our words. How wonderful to be approved by God, to hear, "Well done, good and faithful servant. . . . Come and share your master's happiness!" (Matthew 25:23). Whose approval do you strive most to gain?

Scripture: 1 John 3:18-19; 2 Corinthians 10:12; Proverbs 27:2

Prayer: Dear Lord, let my life be the example of one who lives my faith in deed and in truth. May I never sacrifice your commendation for some form of self-promotion. Amen.

D·A·Y
167

Talkative started to blush, but he recovered and replied, "You have now come around to the issues of experience, of conscience, and of God, and to our appealing to Him for justification of what we speak. I did not expect this kind of discussion. I am not inclined to give an answer to such questions because I don't see that I am bound to do so, unless, of course, you take it upon yourself to be my teacher. But even if you should do so, I can still refuse to allow you to judge me. Will you please tell me, however, why you have asked me such questions?"

"Because I saw that you were eager to talk, and I didn't know whether or not you possessed anything more than mere notions. To tell you the entire truth, I have heard of you, that you are a man whose religion lies in talk, and that your conduct says that your mouth lies. It is said that you are a blemish among Christians and that your ungodly lifestyle has hurt the reputation of our faith. I have heard that some have already stumbled over your wicked ways and that because of this more are in danger of destruction. It is said that your kind of religion is compatible with the frequenting of bars, with covetousness and impurity and swearing and lying, with keeping bad company, and the like. If this is true, the proverb that says a whore is a shame to all women is also true of yourself; you are a shame to all who profess Christ."

Faithful sounds very judgmental as he attacks Talkative's problem with the unseasoned zeal of a young, "faithful" believer. Won't he do more harm than good with this approach? Perhaps. Before dismissing him, however, let us remember the prophet Nathan's straightforward confrontation of David's self-deception: "You are the man!" The healthiest way to deal with David's hypocrisy was to confront it head on.

Often, rather than confronting another believer, we fear being harsh or judgmental, so we opt for the easier, more polite, more "loving" way. But in so doing, we risk perverting God's love into a false mercy that condones sin. Christ forgives sinners and shows incredible mercy to the humble and repentant. Yet he *never* condones sin. In his love for sinners and hatred of sin, he perfectly unites both truth and love. Some Christians are by nature gentle and merciful while others tend to be more harsh. We need to yield to Jesus, and allow his Spirit to work in us the balance he exemplifies.

Healthy reproving is a biblical directive. We should be willing to receive it as well as give it. Have you been unbalanced in your approach to correcting others? What might the Lord have you do differently?

Scripture: 2 Samuel 12:1-13; Psalm 141:5; 2 Timothy 4:2-4

Prayer: Dear Lord, I want to emulate you as you perfectly love people. It's harder when that love means correcting a brother or sister. Give me courage to honor both love and truth. Amen.

D·A·Y 168

"Since you are so ready to listen to rumors and judge so rashly," Talkative countered, "I cannot help but conclude that you are a faultfinding, unpleasant, and depressed person, not worthy of my conversation—so good-bye."

After Talkative had left, Christian approached his brother and said, "I told you how it would happen. Your words and his lusts could not agree. He would rather leave your company than reform his life. But he is gone, as I said, so let him go. The loss is no one's but his own. He has saved us the trouble of leaving him. For if he goes on as he is, and he most likely will, he would have been a blot to our fellowship. Besides, the apostle tells us concerning such men to 'keep away from them'" [Romans 16:17].

As believers, we try to take spiritual and moral responsibility for one another. Being accountable to one another serves to protect and strengthen us. It enables Christ to keep his body healthy and his individual followers on the right path. But whereas the Holy Spirit wants to produce in us teachable and submissive spirits, the sin nature recoils at such things, wanting to assert self over Christ and others.

When confronted with the truth, many tend to backpedal and sometimes even reject it. When God calls upon us to offer loving correction to a wayward brother or sister in Christ, we need to do our best and trust him with the results. The person may decide to leave, crossing a line that releases us from personal responsibility for him or her. Talkative tragically crosses such a line, and Christian tells Faithful to "let him go." Inevitably faithful hearts grieve as numbers of our fellow believers reject wise, straightforward counsel of true friends and then seek "counsel" from others who will comfort and caress them in their sins. At this point, after doing what God has asked of us, we must release them to God. Even our Lord, straightforwardly speaking the truth to the rich young ruler, let him go. If only we could have seen the sadness in his loving eyes as he watched the young man turn and walk away from Truth incarnate.

When friends choose sin and reject us for telling them the truth, we need to let them go. If they persist in sin, we dare not allow them to spread their poison within our fellowship. Until they are ready to repent, we should avoid them. However, this doesn't mean we should give up wrestling for their souls in prayer.

How important is it to you to keep the integrity of Christ's fellowship? What can you do to promote integrity both within your personal life and within your church?

Scripture: Romans 16:17-18; 1 Corinthians 5:6-13; 2 Corinthians 1:12

Prayer: Lord, often you bring correction indirectly through Christian friends and leaders. I want to be teachable and open to correction. Please help me to make my life accountable to them. Amen.

"But I am glad we had this little discussion with him," said Faithful. "It may happen that he will think of it again. But if he doesn't, I have been honest and straightforward with him, and if he should perish, my conscience is clear."

"You did well to talk so openly with him. There is not enough of this kind of faithful dealing with people nowadays. It is no wonder that religion stinks in the nostrils of so many. Fools like to hear themselves talk. They reduce their religion to words alone, while their lifestyles reflect only corruption and worthlessness. The fact that such people are welcomed into the fellowship of the godly is a confusing mystery to those in the world; it produces a dark blemish upon the name of Christianity and a deep grief in the hearts of sincere believers. I wish that all brothers and sisters would deal with such people as you have done. They would then be forced to become either more obedient to the faith, or else the fellowship of the saints would be too hot for their comfort."

Then Faithful said,

> *"How Talkative at first shows off his plumes!*
> *What a show of words; oh, how he presumes*
> *To persuade all who hear him! But just as soon*
> *As I speak of heart-work, then like the moon*
> *That's past its full, will his light wane and go;*
> *So it is with those who don't heart-work know."*

Did Faithful fail with Talkative? Some might agree with Talkative that Faithful was overly critical and doesn't know how to carry on a pleasant conversation. To Faithful, however, getting through to Talkative with good-humored words held no promise. His criticism may still penetrate Talkative's heart, perhaps later bringing repentance, and he has faithfully fulfilled the role of Ezekiel's watchman.

Christian finds Talkative altogether irksome. Professing Christians who don't obey Christ end up disgracing Christ and defiling and grieving the entire Christian community. Some become brazen and rebellious. Jude calls them "blemishes" and "wild waves of the sea, foaming up their shame" (Jude 12, 13).

We need a proper reverence for Christ that extends to his body, the church, for which he shed his blood. The church cannot afford spiritual laxity. Holding truth in love, we must exercise church discipline and even withdraw fellowship from those willfully living sinful lives. What is God saying to you in this regard?

Scripture: Ezekiel 33:7-9; Isaiah 56:10; Jude 4-13

Prayer: Dear Lord, help me to have such high regard for your church's integrity that I will not tolerate sin either in myself or in others of my Christian family. Amen.

D·A·Y 170

So they went on, talking of what they had seen on the way, and this made their travels more enjoyable. No doubt the journey would otherwise have been tedious because they were now going through a Wilderness. When they had passed nearly all the way through it, Faithful happened to glance back and saw someone coming after them who looked very familiar. "Oh! Who is approaching us?" he asked.

"Why, it's my good friend Evangelist," replied Christian.

"Yes it is, and he is my good friend, too; for he is the one who sent me on the way to the Gate."

So Evangelist came and greeted them, saying, "Peace, peace to you, and peace to your helpers!" [1 Chronicles 12:18 RSV].

"Welcome, welcome, Evangelist, my friend," said Christian. "Seeing your face reminds me of all your kindness and patient effort for my eternal good."

Then Faithful greeted him. "And a thousand welcomes, dear Evangelist! How desirable your company is to us needy pilgrims!"

After spending time with an empty talker, the two pilgrims find themselves in a wilderness, but their close fellowship helps alleviate the dullness they feel. When their mutual friend Evangelist appears, they excitedly greet him—the one to whom both owe their very souls—and they eagerly invite his fellowship.

Young believers have many needs, and sometimes they forget that ministers also have needs. The affectionate greeting Evangelist receives must warm this lonely Christian servant's heart. Any uneasiness he might have felt concerning the pilgrims' appreciation for his ministry are laid to rest by their fond affirmations. How encouraging it must be for him to see that these two pilgrims whom he led to Christ are still walking faithfully with the Lord, and, not only that, they have found each other and are progressing together. Little could be more gratifying to Evangelist, especially after Christian's earlier problem when he disregarded instruction and searched for the house of Legality.

When you see those who have invested in your spiritual well-being, how do you greet them? Does your gratitude show? If it doesn't, how will they know where you stand? Perhaps instead of waiting for them to approach you and do something more to bless your life, you could make some extra effort to show them your appreciation. What are some ways you can show them respect for their leadership?

Scripture: 1 Thessalonians 5:12-13; Isaiah 52:7; Psalm 133:1; John 13:34-35

Prayer: Dear Lord, thank you so much for faithful ministers like Evangelist who show up at the right time. May they never consider their ministry a thankless task. Help us all to think of ways to bless and encourage them. Amen.

D·A·Y
171

"How has it been going with you, my friends, since the time we last parted?" asked Evangelist. "What have you encountered, and how have you conducted yourselves?"

Then Christian and Faithful told him about all the things that had happened to them in the way, and how and with what difficulty they had come to their present position. "I am very happy," said Evangelist, "not that you have met with trials, but that you have been victors. In spite of having many weaknesses, you have continued in the Way to this very day. Yes, I am happy for both my sake and yours. I have sowed, and you have reaped. 'What joys await the sower and the reaper, both together!'" [John 4:36].

Evangelist wants the rundown on all the pilgrims have experienced. After reporting their conflicts and struggles, they might have expected him to shake his head at their immaturity and weakness. Instead, he delightedly calls them what they would refrain from calling themselves—"victors." He explains that their weaknesses have no bearing on his judgment, because he considers them victors for their endurance.

What a joyful moment for Evangelist as he hears how the pilgrims are learning to patiently endure their trials. He shares the apostle Paul's concern when Paul prayed that the Colossian Christians would be strengthened to have "great endurance and patience" (Colossians 1:11). The Greek word Paul used, *hupomone,* means patient continuance. It suggests unswerving devotion to one's purpose, staying loyal to one's faith, even in the greatest suffering and trials. Those who are trained in this quality will hold fast, never flee, and bravely bear every misfortune.

Knowing the importance of perseverance, Evangelist is happy for the pilgrims' sakes, not because of their trials, but for the strength of character being produced within them. He knows that they will need even more endurance for the trials still ahead. Evangelist has sown the seeds of the Gospel into their hearts, and they are reaping its benefits. Now all can rejoice together.

Perhaps you are suffering in a season of trial. Rather than focusing on your weaknesses and difficulties, look to God's strength to carry you through. He wants to produce the quality of endurance in you that you will be a "victor" in your pilgrimage. Refresh yourself in the joyful hope that awaits you, and rejoice in how far you have already come.

Scripture: Romans 5:3-4; 8:24-25; James 5:7-11

Prayer: Dear Jesus, I admit that learning endurance is no delight to me. However, I know I need endurance to follow you through this weary and pain-filled world. Grant that I, too, will be a victor for your glory. Amen.

D·A·Y
172

"However, 'Let us not become weary in doing good, for at the proper time we will reap a harvest if we do not give up' [Galatians 6:9]. 'Run in such a way as to get the prize. Everyone who competes in the games goes into strict training. They do it to get a crown that will not last, but we do it to get a crown that will last forever' [1 Corinthians 9:24-25]. Some set out to attain this crown, and after they have gone a good distance for it, they allow another to come in and take it from them. 'Hold on to what you have, so that no one will take your crown' [Revelation 3:11]. You are still within gunshot of the devil. 'In your struggle against sin, you have not yet resisted to the point of shedding your blood'" [Hebrews 12:4].

Evangelist reveals his ongoing love and care for his converts. Far from thinking that his work is done in their lives now that they believe, he takes on the role of pastor and exhorter. After expressing joy over their endurance, he now urges them to continue running the race until they have attained the victor's crown.

Using athletic imagery, he hones in on his theme of patient endurance. Yes, the pilgrims are victors, but these were only preliminary heat victories. They must keep training if they want to win the much-coveted victor's crown in the final round of competition. Greek athletes won corruptible olive branch crowns, but the crowns that persevering pilgrims win will never perish. Evangelist warns that many contestants go some distance but then simply give up and allow someone else to seize their prize. The crown was theirs, but because they did not persevere, they lost it.

We are in a spiritual race with spiritual competitors. The devil eagerly desires to sabotage the race. As pilgrims, we must be continually alert until we are outside his range, for he wants to ascend the winner's platform himself, robbing us of our prize.

Evangelist knows of what he speaks, for he, too, is sowing a harvest, running to win, wrestling an enemy. No doubt Evangelist in his travels to win lost souls throughout the countryside has sometimes had to force himself to persevere. He has learned to press on, to faithfully carry out his ministry, and thus he can exhort these young pilgrims to do the same.

Are you "weary in doing good?" Keep pressing in and pressing on. You will reap a harvest; you will win the crown if you persevere.

Scripture: Hebrews 12:1-3; 1 Corinthians 15:58; 2 Peter 3:13-14

Prayer: Heavenly Father, again I confess my need of endurance in the calling you have given me. I pray that by your grace I will one day stand before you wearing the victor's crown. Amen.

D·A·Y
173

"Let the Kingdom be always uppermost in your minds, and believe unflinchingly in the things that are unseen. Let nothing that is on this side get within and attach itself to your hearts. Above all, be very careful of your own hearts and the lusts that can hide there. 'The heart is the most deceitful thing there is, and desperately wicked' [Jeremiah 17:9]. So remember the words, 'Therefore have I set my face like flint, and I know I will not be put to shame' [Isaiah 50:7]. Don't forget that you have all the power of Heaven and earth on your side."

❦

Evangelist urges Christian and Faithful to continue giving first place to God's kingdom. The kingdom must capture their affections and be their hearts' treasure, their highest prize. They must meditate on, speak of, and affectionately yearn for it. Its concerns must be their concerns. Only the kingdom, what *comes from* it or is *going to* it, should concern them. For they no longer belong to this present world but to the kingdom. Shortly they will reach their heavenly country; this should be their overriding and all-encompassing priority. The enemy will try to pull them away from the kingdom, but they must set their minds and hearts with unflinching resolve.

Oh, the things on "this side" will try to deceive and grab hold of their hearts—earthly things, temporal pleasures, riches, honors, possessions, carnal lusts. Shouting and clamoring for their attention, these things can so worm their way inside the mind and heart without warning that they ultimately deceive and enslave the entire person.

Evangelist warns the pilgrims to set their faces like flint on their goal. Flint is a hard stone. If something comes up against it, it does not yield. If the pilgrims determine to give the goal first priority, they will not yield to the evil pressures and persuasions to fall away. Referring to Matthew 28:18, he also reminds them that Christ's power—"all power in heaven and earth"—is also theirs. Their King is omnipotent with power to provide for their needs, to forgive their sins, to keep them from the evil one, to support them in trouble, to deliver them from temptation, and to preserve them from falling away.

Let us resolve to keep our King and his kingdom uppermost in our minds and hearts as we travel the pilgrim way, to set our faces like flint, unresponsive to the world's enticements. And let us remember the powerful resources that belong to us in Christ Jesus our Lord. In what area of your life do you need to renew your commitment to God and his purposes?

❦

Scripture: Colossians 3:1-4; 2 Corinthians 4:18; Luke 9:51

Prayer: Dear Lord, free me from the earthly entanglements that have wound themselves around my heart. May these things fall powerless as I reflect upon your rich promises. Amen.

D·A·Y 174

Then Christian thanked Evangelist for his exhortation but added that they would like to have him speak to them further so that they could be strengthened on the rest of the journey. They perceived that he was a prophet, so they asked him what dangers might lie ahead in the Way and how to best resist and overcome them.

So Evangelist began to speak all that was on his mind. "My sons, you have heard the truth in the words of the Gospel, that 'we must go through many hardships to enter the Kingdom of God' [Acts 14:22]. With Paul you can say, 'prison and hardships are facing me' [Acts 20:23]. You cannot expect to be able to go very far on your pilgrimage without facing hardships in one form or another. You have already experienced some of the truth of this testimony, but more will soon follow."

The wise counsel of veteran ministers can lend great wisdom to young believers. Evangelist knows God's Word concerning the hardships we must go through to enter God's kingdom. He relates this to the pilgrims but then begins prophesying.

Prophecies are the communications of divine messages through human messengers called prophets. Prophets in Old Testament days were held accountable to strict standards of accuracy. While the Lord's true prophets were consistently accurate in proclaiming God's message, those who prophesied falsely were to be stoned to death. Early Christian prophets were powerful persons in the church who stood next to the apostles in importance. The New Testament mentions Agabus, Jude, Silas, and Philip's four daughters as prophets, along with Paul, Barnabas, and others. These prophets were often itinerant preachers who moved from church to church, strengthening believers in their faith. Sometimes prophets like Agabus, who warned Paul against going to Jerusalem, foretold hard times ahead. Similarly, God has sent Evangelist to prepare the pilgrims for their trials. Supporting his prophetic word with scriptural admonitions, he begins to warn them of their coming ordeal.

Christians in our affluent society generally expect everything to go their way and are shocked when things don't. Angry and resentful, they sometimes even turn away from God. Trustworthy prophetic words that speak directly into our particular circumstances can help prepare us for meeting what lies around the bend. We can thank God for prophetic gifts while remembering to carefully evaluate the prophecies by God's Word and those who give them by the fruit of their lives. How do you treat prophecy?

Scripture: Amos 3:7; 1 Corinthians 12:10, 28; 14:1-5, 39; Ephesians 4:11-12

Prayer: Thank you, Lord, for those with prophetic gifts. Since false prophets bring deception and true prophets prevent deception, help your people to know the difference and to invite true prophecy. Amen.

D·A·Y

175

"See, you are almost out of this Wilderness, and you will shortly come to a town lying in front of you. There enemies will severely hem you in. They will try hard to kill you, and, to be sure, one or both of you must seal the testimony you hold with his blood. For our King says, 'Be faithful, even to the point of death, and I will give you the crown of life' [Revelation 2:10].

"Whoever dies in that place, even though he will be murdered and will possibly suffer greatly, will be better off than his brother. For not only will he have arrived at the Celestial City sooner, but he will also have escaped the many miseries that the other will still face on the rest of his journey. After you have come to that town and the things I have related to you are fulfilled, then remember me, your friend, and remember my words. Persevere to the end like true men, and remember this word, 'So then, those who suffer according to God's will should commit themselves to their faithful Creator and continue to do good'" [1 Peter 4:19].

The pilgrims will soon catch their first glimpse of a bustling city. Seen from the wilderness, it might seem inviting. After all, cities are full of fascinating people, sights, and activities. But Evangelist has a hard word for the two. They must be their Lord's witnesses even to death if God wills. The Greek word for "witnesses" in Acts 1:8 is *martus,* from which we get our word *martyr*. At least one of the two, they are told, will die for his faith.

Hearing such words, how many of us would flatly say, "I don't feel led?" Would we simply dismiss this as false prophecy? We might decide instead to "retire" from the Christian life and stay in the wilderness. But what, then, becomes of all the truths we thought we believed? If we avoid living them out, how are we better off than Talkative? The King calls, "Be faithful, even to the point of death," and we must respond, "Yes, Lord."

How much does your faith mean to you? Would you die for it? Why do we so often view such death as a tragedy? While death is a great loss to an unspiritual man, for a true believer it is gain. Paul proclaims, "For to me, to live is Christ and to die is gain" (Philippians 1:21). By it, we escape all the evils of this life—the indwelling sin, doubts, fears; the sicknesses, pain, grief; the oppressions, temptations, persecutions. We give this up to go directly to an eternal kingdom of peace, light, and glory! Wow! Yes, the one who dies in the Lord *is* better off! So, on to the city!

Scripture: Philippians 1:20-21; Acts 21:10-14; Romans 8:35-39

Prayer: Lord, help me not to fear your call. I want to say with Paul that if I live, I will live for you, but if I die, that will be far better. Amen.

D·A·Y

176

Then I saw in my dream that when the two had reached the end of the Wilderness, they could see a town stretching before them. The name of that town is Vanity, and in that town there is a perpetual fair called Vanity Fair. It bears this name first because the town where it sits is as superficial as vanity, and also because all that is bought and sold there is meaningless vanity. The saying of the wise is true, "Vanity of vanities, all is vanity."

This fair is no newly erected enterprise; it is a thing of ancient standing. Let me tell you of its origin. About five thousand years ago, two honest pilgrims were walking to the Celestial City. Beelzebub, Apollyon, and Legion, together with all their companions, saw that the path the pilgrims were traveling on to the City passed through this town of Vanity. So they devised a plan to set up a fair within it, a fair in which all kinds of worthless vanity could be sold all year long.

Vanity is the City of Destruction in its most sensual and alluring party attire. Its fair, Vanity Fair, runs perpetually. It is a never-ending party, full of meaningless pleasures designed to distract and preoccupy passersby. Representing the emptiness of life without God, it is a microcosm of the sinful world and its alluring temptations. Think of the Las Vegas strip with its perpetually blinking lights, blaring music, buffets, slot machines, and entertainment. Vanity Fair's appeal is even broader and more powerful. Far from a mere entertainment center, it is the brainchild of Satan and his demonic hordes and exists specifically for the purpose of ruining pilgrim souls. When the devils noticed that the pilgrims' path passed through Vanity, they set up the fair to distract and seduce pilgrims into ending their pilgrimage.

People go to fairs for amusement. Beelzebub, like a stage manager, makes sure everyone is continually amused. Where the love of pleasure takes priority, Beelzebub rules easily. The amphitheaters of the former Roman Empire attest to the effectiveness of this approach. As long as the masses remained content with their entertainment, they were diverted from real issues.

We live in an entertainment-driven, hedonistic society. Just look at entertainers' and sport celebrities' salaries! We, as Christians, need to take serious stock of our motivations. Do we delight more in worldly entertainment or in pursuing the knowledge of God? The dictionary calls entertainment a diversion. We need to examine our hearts, to be careful that the demonic atmosphere of the "fair" doesn't divert us from God and his purposes for our lives. What do you see in your heart?

Scripture: Ecclesiastes 1:2; 12:8; Isaiah 6:10; John 8:12

Prayer: Oh Lord, help me to untangle myself from worldly pleasures that sap and swallow my spiritual passion. I want to be available for your purposes, not distracted by a perpetual parade of exciting but empty diversions. Amen.

DAY 177

To this day all kinds of merchandise are still sold there—houses, lands, jobs, positions, honors, promotions, titles, countries, kingdoms, lusts, pleasures. And there are also enjoyments of all sorts to suit one's preferences—whores, prostitutes, wives, husbands, children, masters, servants, lives, blood, bodies, souls, silver, gold, pearls, precious stones, and more. In addition, at this fair one always finds deceptive trickery, cheating, gambling, games, plays, amusements, fools, frauds, knaves, and rogues of every type—not to mention the numerous thieves, murderers, adulterers, and false witnesses of the basest sort.

Other fairs of less consequence have several rows and streets called by proper names that identify where certain items are sold. Likewise, here rows and streets are named by countries and kingdoms where the desired merchandise can be found. There is the British Row, the French Row, the Italian Row, the Spanish Row, the German Row, and so forth. All sorts of vanities are sold in these places. But as in other fairs, one commodity is chief of all at the fair. So the wares of Rome and her merchandise are greatly promoted at this fair. Only our English nation, with some others, have taken a dislike to it.

What a fair this is! Noisy crowds push and shove as they cavort from one place to the next. They laugh, curse, and scream as they covet, pursue, and contend for the things of this life. It is the "whole world lying in wickedness," the wretched state of things spanning the ages and in all nations. Some pursue their desires respectably, others corruptly. Some are harmless, others dangerous. All are enthralled with the fair.

The pleasures and profits in this fair are trifling and transient. Solomon, trying everything here, deemed it all "vanity of vanities" (Ecclesiastes 1:2 RSV). Despite this, the traffic never lets up. Why? Because the lower nature is never satisfied. No matter how greatly indulged, it continues craving more. And the Fair has suitable commodities to keep feeding these lusts.

Ever since our first parents went the way of Vanity in the garden, we have idolatrously sought happiness in the creation rather than in the Creator. Satan has continually enticed humankind to "ignore such a great salvation" (Hebrews 2:3). The Scriptures alert us that the cares of this world, the deceitfulness of riches, the lusts and the desires for other things will choke our spiritual lives. (See Mark 4:19.) They warn us against loving the world and the things of the world. (See 1 John 2:15.) They even condemn those who are friends of the world as adulterers against God. (See James 4:4.) Let us pray seriously about our desire for worldly vanities. Instead of pursuing these, will you find your delight in the Lord?

Scripture: 1 John 2:15-17; Ephesians 2:1-2; John 12:40

Prayer: Lord Jesus, keep my heart true. I do not want to be corrupted through chasing worldly vanities. You are my Lord. Help me to find my delight in living for you. Amen.

DAY 178

Now, as I have said, the way to the Celestial City passes right through this town where the lusty fair is held, and he who would like to bypass this town on the way to the Celestial City would have to leave the world altogether. The Prince of Princes Himself, when on earth, went through this town on His way to His own Country. I believe it was Beelzebub, the chief lord of the fair, who invited Him to buy from his vanities. Indeed, Beelzebub offered to make Him lord of the fair if only He would pay him homage as He went through the town. Because He was such a person of honor, Beelzebub took Him from street to street, in a short time showing Him all the kingdoms of the world. He tried to allure the Blessed One into buying some of his vanities and by that cheapening Himself, but He had no interest in the merchandise. He left the town without buying so much as one penny's worth. So you can see that this fair is ancient; nonetheless, its alluring power is still very great today.

Why must the pilgrims' Way pass through Vanity? Our Lord doesn't permit us to "put our light under a bushel" any more than he allows us to "bury our talents in the ground." Nor does he permit us to avoid this city by moving to cloistered communes in the wilderness. We are to be salt and light *in* the world, but not *of* it. So we all pass through this city and its accompanying temptations.

Even our Lord, the Prince of Princes, found no alternate route around this city. Since Beelzebub, the god and prince of this world, governs Vanity Fair, he tried tantalizing the Lord with everything the Fair had to offer. He was a persuasive master, packaging evil to make it look extremely appealing. However, Jesus effectively resisted these enticements without compromising at all. When the devil offered him sovereignty over all earthly kingdoms in exchange for worship, Christ responded, "Be gone!" Christ was on a mission He was determined to fulfill. Thus he kept his course, refusing to heed worthless vanities.

We are weak and vulnerable creatures. Martin Luther admitted, "My temptations have been my masters in divinity." The Lord knows our need, and, passing this way before us, he became our example. Resisting this world's vanities, Jesus resolved to obey his Father's will. Continually filled with the Holy Spirit, he relied on the power of God's Word.

To overcome the powerful array of demonic seductions in Vanity Fair, we must wholeheartedly follow Christ's example, relying on his strength and the power of his Word to give us victory. What actions are you willing to take to avoid succumbing to the powerful allurements of this world?

Scripture: Matthew 4:8-11; 6:32-33; Hebrews 11:24-26

Prayer: Thank you, Jesus, for faithfully resisting every temptation. Please grant me the grace to follow your example as I pass through the vanities of this life. Amen.

D·A·Y
179

Now Faithful and Christian would have to go through this fair, and so they set out. Even as they first entered the fair, however, all the people took notice. In fact, the entire town came together in a great commotion around them. There were several reasons for this.

First, the pilgrims' clothes were so different from those traded at the fair that the people just stood and stared at them. Some said they were fools; others said they were lunatics; still others said they were very strange.

Second, just as the people marveled at their clothing, they also wondered at their speech, for only a few could understand what they said. This was because the pilgrims naturally spoke the language of Canaan, but those at the fair were people of the world. So from one end of the fair to the other, the pilgrims were thought to be uncivilized foreigners.

Third, the pilgrims showed little interest in the items displayed for sale, something not at all appreciated by the city's merchants. The pilgrims didn't care enough even to take a look, and when the merchants called upon them to buy, they would put their fingers in their ears and cry, "Turn my eyes from looking at vanities" [Psalm 119:37 RSV]. They would look upward, signifying that the only things of interest to them were in Heaven.

Two strangers enter a strange land. They don't try to stand out; they don't parade their piety. Still they cannot avoid notice. Because the pilgrims are in some ways conspicuously nonconforming and peculiar, they create an immediate stir. Three things seem to prick the townsfolk's consciences:

The pilgrims' clothing offends the well-dressed people of Vanity. While the citizens of Vanity Fair apparently wear clothing that grabs the eye, our two pilgrims are less concerned with finery than with the humble robes of righteousness given them at the cross of Christ.

Their conversation betrays them as foreigners. While Vanity's folk think nothing of profanity and blasphemy, no evil talk passes from the pilgrims' mouths. The wholesome, meek, guileless "language of Canaan," is so unknown to those in Vanity that they pass the pilgrims off as uncivilized foreigners.

Christian and Faithful also draw scorn by showing no interest in Vanity's amusements or wares. They shun the very things that these folks are utterly devoted to. Turning away from these earthly things, they look toward heaven where their true citizenship lies. Their unfeigned godly priorities and behavior quickly alienate these worldly-minded people.

Do you humbly seek to live a godly life in Christ? Don't be surprised if people take offense.

Scripture: 1 Peter 1:17; 1 John 4:5-6; Philippians 3:20-21

Prayer: Lord, I do not wish to offend the world, but I do want unbelievers to see the difference between us. Help me be the best example I can be. Amen.

One merchant, after observing them for a time, mockingly asked, "So, what will you buy?" But looking intently at him, they answered, "We will buy the truth." This gave the people a reason to despise them even more. Some began mocking the pilgrims, taunting them and discrediting them, and they called on others to beat them up. At last the situation became out of control, and the commotion in the fair was so great that all order was lost. Word then reached the manager of the fair, who quickly came down and appointed some of his most trusted friends to take the men into custody for questioning since they had disrupted the entire fair.

Christian and Faithful have no use for Vanity's worldly merchandise; the only commodity they want is truth. Not surprisingly, their simple declaration of loyalty to truth immediately draws outrage. Someone has said that "truth makes the devil blush." So more often than not, the devil's children who live by lies also despise truth.

Paul's allegiance to truth caused him trouble nearly everywhere he went. He so provoked the pagan silversmiths of Ephesus by his persuasive presentations of the truth that a riot broke out. In Jerusalem a near riot erupted again when he proclaimed the truth. Martin Luther, whose revelation of truth sparked the Reformation and a firestorm of controversy that has shaken the church for centuries, proclaimed, "Peace if possible, but truth at any rate."

Our society has diminished the importance of truth and distorted its meaning. Relativism has reduced truth from fact and reality to opinion and preference—"my truth, your truth"; no longer is there widespread belief in absolute standards of right and wrong. "Tolerance," understood today as accepting all values as equally valid, now outranks truth as the essential virtue. To believe in Christ, however, is to believe that he *is* Truth; that everything he taught about God, humanity, sin, judgment, salvation—everything—is true; that he is indeed Truth incarnate at every level, in every dimension.

We who embrace Christ must not shrink back before the dilettantes of spurious truths. We must overcome our fears of being labeled closed-minded by a world that despises truth. We must keep a confident faith in him and in the truth of his Word. God entrusts his truth to us, and we must lovingly yet unabashedly commit ourselves to it. Silvio Pellico puts it this way: "Of all duties, the love of truth, with faith and constancy in it, ranks first and highest. To love God and to love truth are one and the same."

Have you been persecuted for your loyalty to God's truth? If not, you might wonder why not.

Scripture: Acts 19:23-41; Proverbs 23:23; Psalms 25:5; 43:3

Prayer: Lord Jesus, your truth is "the" truth, and I am not ashamed of it. Help me to stand tall for you and your truth. Amen.

D·A·Y 181

So the pilgrims were interrogated. They were asked where they had come from, where they were going, and why they were dressed in such unusual garb. They answered that they were pilgrims and strangers in the world, and that they were on their way to their own Country, the Heavenly Jerusalem. They explained that they had not given the townsfolk or the merchants any reason to abuse and detain them from their journey. They went on to explain that when asked by a merchant what they would buy, they answered only that they would buy the truth. However, those conducting the examination would not believe that the pilgrims were anything better than troublemakers and madmen. How else could they have brought the entire fair into such a state of confusion? Therefore, taking Faithful and Christian, they beat them and smeared them with dirt. They put them into a cage made for criminals and made them a spectacle for everyone at the fair.

❧

Christian and Faithful were minding their own business when incited to make a candid declaration of their principles. When they spoke up, those looking for trouble began a ruckus. The interrogators, however, are not interested in finding the truth. They think, "We had no disturbance before they came!" Thus, while scoundrels go innocent, the pilgrims bear the blame.

King Ahab blamed the prophet Elijah for his problems, saying, "Is that you, you troubler of Israel?" (1 Kings 18:17). Officials reported to King Zedekiah that the prophet Jeremiah was seeking Israel's ruin. They urged, "This man should be put to death" (Jeremiah 38:4). Amaziah, the priest, blamed the prophet Amos to King Jeroboam, saying, "Amos is raising a conspiracy against you in the very heart of Israel" (Amos 7:10). In Philippi, the owners of a slave girl dragged Paul and Silas before authorities, saying, "These men are Jews, and are throwing our city into an uproar by advocating customs unlawful for us Romans to accept or practice" (Acts 16:20-21). Again in Thessalonica an angry mob shouted concerning them, "These men who have caused trouble all over the world have now come here . . ." (Acts 17:6). Our Lord stood before Pilate as his accusers insisted, "We have found this man subverting our nation. . . . He stirs up the people all over Judea by his teaching" (Luke 23:2, 5).

Have you ever similarly drawn fire for honoring God's truth? You should not feel surprise or alarm at such times. Instead, you can take courage and appeal to him for strength to carry on. In that Christ promises us abundant reward for our faithfulness, we can even rejoice! Remember, too, that in experiencing these conflicts, you stand in the best of company.

❧

Scripture: Luke 6:22-23; Matthew 5:11-12; 1 Peter 4:1-4, 12-16

Prayer: Dear Lord, I know I cannot expect the world to treat me kindly. When I am misunderstood and persecuted for my beliefs, please strengthen me with your presence. Amen.

DAY 182

So Christian and Faithful sat in the cage for quite some time and were made the objects of any passing person's amusement, bullying, or revenge. The manager of the fair kept laughing at all that had befallen them. But the men were patient and, holding their tongues, refused to return evil for evil. On the contrary, they returned blessing for insults, offering good words in exchange for bad, and kindness for injuries inflicted.

Refusing to conform to Vanity's principles and conscientiously living out the values of their pilgrimage are the pilgrims' only crimes. For this they are treated like criminals. "Indeed, all who want to live a godly life in Christ Jesus will be persecuted" (2 Timothy 3:12 NRSV).

Instead of giving the devil any opportunity, however, the pilgrims use their situation to their best advantage. They understand that the purpose of their pilgrimage is not to keep them from trials but to produce the necessary character to meet trials victoriously. In the midst of dehumanizing jeering, they "let steadfastness have its full effect" (James 1:4 RSV) by not only refusing to return evil for evil, but by returning blessing for evil.

Sad to say, although Jesus commanded it, this type of behavior among Christians is often lacking. He said, "Love your enemies and pray for those who persecute you" (Matthew 5:44). He left us his own example to follow as Peter attests, "When they hurled their insults at him, he did not retaliate; when he suffered, he made no threats" (1 Peter 2:23). Paul, testifying of his and the other apostles' efforts to follow this pattern, says, "When reviled, we bless; when persecuted, we endure" (1 Corinthians 4:12 NRSV). He encouraged the Roman church to do likewise, saying, "Bless those who persecute you; bless and do not curse" (Romans 12:14). Peter urged persecuted believers of the dispersion, "Do not repay evil with evil or insult with insult, but with blessing . . ." (1 Peter 3:9).

The Lord would have us approach conflict much differently than the world does. Do you ever see worldly movie heroes turning the other cheek to their enemies? Typically, they win by being brash, violent, tough guys. God's heroes, however, win with humble, self-giving love. They are not proud, brash, and violent. Patiently representing God to sinners, they love, bless, and forgive. They pray for their enemies to see the error of their ways so they might repent and receive his grace. They even rejoice in their persecutions. This is courage in its finest form! Pray for more of this kind of courage.

Scripture: Matthew 5:38-48; 1 Thessalonians 2:2; James 1:2-3

Prayer: Dear Lord, I will need special grace to love my enemies in the face of persecution. I ask for more of your Spirit's character in my life. Amen.

D·A·Y 183

Some people at the fair who were more observant and less prejudiced than the rest began to correct and confront the more depraved types for their continual abuse of the two men. This caused the ruffians to angrily attack them in return, accusing them of being as bad as the men in the cage and in league with them. They said their behavior warranted their being tossed into the cage along with the two pilgrims. The defenders answered that all they could see was that the men were quiet and serious-minded, intending nobody any trouble. They said that many who traded in the fair were far more deserving of being put into the cage than these poor, abused men. After much more angry argument, while the pilgrims continued to conduct themselves wisely, the opposing sides finally came to blows and began to harm one another.

After this, they dragged the two poor pilgrims before their examiners again, this time charged with causing this latest ruckus. The examiners beat them mercilessly, and, putting them in iron chains, they led them by the chains up and down the streets of the fair as an example and deterrent to others who might try to speak up on their behalf or, worse yet, join them.

See Vanity Fair! The pilgrims there
Are chained and stoned beside;
Even so, our Lord passed here,
And on Mount Calvary died.

Christian and Faithful tried to avoid provoking their enemies. Yet their situation worsens as a brawl breaks out. Many at this point might despair, thinking, "Well, I tried it God's way, and things are worse!" But let's look at their predicament through eyes of faith.

God intends for His servants to "silence the ignorant talk of foolish men" (1 Peter 2:15). Thus he gives the pilgrims a public forum, albeit a painful one, to show their character. Sure enough, their punishment backfires on its perpetrators as onlookers see and awaken to its injustice.

Those of us who suffer for Christ's sake should resolve to imitate these faithful pilgrims. In behaving with grace and humility amid persecution, we provide a powerful testimony of faith. Good triumphs over evil whenever blinded consciences suddenly see genuine faith exhibited. Thus Stephen witnessed to Saul of Tarsus and the three Hebrew lads to Nebuchadnezzar. How do you respond under fire? Ask God to make you Christlike in this area.

Scripture: Galatians 6:9; Acts 7:54-8:1; Daniel 3:16-18

Prayer: Lord, help me stand firm under fire. I want my life to witness for you both in good and in painful times. Amen.

DAY 184

But Christian and Faithful conducted themselves even more wisely in the face of all the deep, personal disgrace and humiliation heaped upon them. They responded with such meekness and patience that it won to their side (though only few in comparison) some of those in the fair. This put the opposing side into such a great rage that they concluded that these two men deserved the death penalty. They angrily presented their case that neither cage nor chains would do any good in reforming them, and that only death would do justice for all the damage and delusion that they had caused the fair. They then ordered the pilgrims back to the cage to await further action. Once the captives were inside the cage again, their feet were locked in chains.

The pilgrims cannot simply mind their own business, for the devil despises their business. He powerfully influences those of Vanity with his hatred of Christ and the pilgrims. When all efforts to reform Faithful and Christian seem to fail, the people are incensed. They conclude that the pilgrims are incorrigible and that the only way to keep the poison from spreading is to put them away—for good.

What is it about our two pilgrims that the folk of Vanity resent so vehemently? Christian and Faithful have been released from the power of worldly lusts; they are no longer motivated to seek after things of transient value; they are no longer subject to the bondage of sin or Satan. Therefore, their enemies hate them. Their strategy, however, fails to work. They may chain the pilgrims' bodies, but who can chain their souls? As Paul and Silas sat chained in jail and singing praise songs at midnight, they were the ones who were free, while their jailer was bound.

Most who live an authentic Christian life will suffer persecution in one form or another. Sometimes it means reviling and reproach; sometimes it means confiscation of property or restrictions upon the free exercise of their faith; and sometimes it means imprisonment, torture, or even death. Nevertheless, we are free! The evil one trembles at the liberating power of the Gospel we carry. Paul asserted that his enemies could chain his body but never God's Word. (See 2 Timothy 2:9.) Instead of feeling undone by our troubles, we need to let those in real bondage see our eternal freedom and victory. Do you feel free? Remember, even under the worst spiritual attack, eternal life is yours in Christ. That's freedom!

Scripture: John 8:36; 16:33; Philippians 1:12-14, 27-30

Prayer: Dear Jesus, when I begin to feel like a victim in life, help me to remember the freedom you have won for me. I am not a victim but a victor, no matter what the world thinks, says, or does to me. Amen.

D·A·Y 185

So the pilgrims called to mind what they had heard from their faithful friend Evangelist. Recalling his words encouraged them and confirmed to them that their way and their sufferings were not mistakes. They also comforted and reassured each other that if one of them were chosen to suffer and die, that one would have the higher blessing. So each man secretly desired that position. But, committing their lives to the all-wise will of Him who rules over all things, they contentedly waited for the further unfolding of His will and purpose.

If Christian and Faithful ever took Evangelist's words lightly, his words mean life to them now. They can remember the scriptural admonitions he gave—to allow no one to seize their crowns; to keep the kingdom uppermost in their minds; to believe unflinchingly in things not seen; to set their faces like flint, not trusting even their own hearts. They especially recall the prophetic word concerning their suffering and possible death in Vanity. It is a hard word, yet in their present circumstance, it is like a compass in the storm. It tells them their suffering is not some meaningless, random mistake. God has a purpose, and he sent Evangelist to encourage them in it. This makes their plight much easier to accept.

In their present suffering, each secretly yearns for the higher blessing of dying for their Lord and going straight to the Celestial City. Yet it would be a mistake for them to waste their energy speculating about how their present trial will end. Instead, they obey Evangelist's further exhortation to commit their lives fully into God's hands. In that the pilgrims believe that he has an "all-wise will" and that he "rules over all things," they find themselves able to rest in his unfolding purpose.

Our God truly is the supreme and almighty Ruler, the King of Kings and Lord of Lords who reigns over the entire universe. He will carry out his every purpose and plan. At the same time he is our loving Father who promises to bring about ultimate justice for us. Often, however, we are blinded by our fears or desires and by our inability to fathom his ways or understand his purposes. This is why it is best to simply trust his love and commit our lives to his purpose. If we would have peace amid our fiery trials, we must believe and trust in his absolute sovereignty and undying love.

Do you sometimes feel that your suffering is purposeless, due to some divine mistake? In trusting God's sovereignty, you will gain a more mature outlook. Also you will gain much peace by committing your life to the "all-wise will of him who rules over all things."

Scripture: Acts 17:24-28; Jeremiah 23:24; Psalm 139:7-12

Prayer: Dear Father, sometimes, in the storms of life, I have trouble trusting that you really do control my destiny. Help me to trust your sovereignty better and to commit my trials to your care. Amen.

DAY 186

They were appointed to stand trial at a time convenient to the court. When the time had come, they were brought before their enemies and arraigned. The judge's name was Lord Hategood. Though varying in form, the testimony was basically the same in substance. The content of the indictment handed down was this: That they were enemies and disturbers of their trade, that they had made a commotion and caused divisions in the town, and that they had won a group to their own most dangerous opinions in contempt of the law of their king.

Then Faithful began to reply to the charges.

Now, Faithful, play the man, speak for your God;
Don't fear the wicked's malice nor their rod;
Speak boldly, man, the truth is on your side;
Die for it, and to life in triumph ride.

Christian and Faithful are bound over for trial on three counts. First, they are charged with disturbing Vanity's trade; second, with disturbing the peace; and third, with winning over several citizens to their "dangerous" opinions. The trouble first began when the pilgrims said they would only buy truth and not sell it again. Now they stand as public enemies before a court that should embody the pursuit of truth and justice; however, with a presiding judge named Lord Hategood, we see little hope for justice. "For truth is precious and divine, too rich a pearl for carnal swine."[19]

Nevertheless, Faithful bravely takes the stand. If he should give in to anger, act rashly, or become contentious, he would ruin his witness. His accusers would have some ammunition against him, and the devil would be delighted. Yet if he boldly holds out the truth, faithfully maintaining his witness for Christ, he will "heap burning coals on their heads" (Romans 12:20 NRSV).

In situations like these we must trust God's guidance. Jesus promised that when people unjustly drag us to court, "the Holy Spirit will teach you in that very hour what you ought to say" (Luke 12:12 RSV). There will certainly be times in our lives when we are called upon to take our stand faithfully for Christ. Let us be sure to rely upon the Holy Spirit to guide our testimony; for our faithfulness, he promises an eternal crown of life. If, however, we try in the flesh to appease our enemies by compromising our faith, we will win nothing. How can you better prepare your soul for victory in the event you must stand for Christ?

Scripture: Matthew 10:17-20; 24:9; 1 Peter 3:15-16; Revelation 2:10

Prayer: Dear Lord, I feel so weak, but I resolve, by your grace, to represent you faithfully before my accusers when they call me to give account for my faith. Please use me for your glory. Amen.

D·A·Y 187

"I have set myself only against that which has set itself against Him who is higher than the highest. And as for disturbance, I have made none, being a man of peace. The persons who were won to our side were won by seeing our honesty and innocence, and they are only the better for it. And, as to the king you speak of, since he is Beelzebub, the enemy of our Lord, I defy him and all of his angels."

Then a proclamation was made that if anyone had anything to say for their lord the king against the prisoner at the bar, they should appear forthwith and give their evidence.

❦

Before opening their mouths, the pilgrims' presence alone rebuked and convicted the people of Vanity. By merely saying, "We will buy the truth," an uprising ensued. Now the time has come to speak up again. Realizing their danger, most in similar straits would probably try to say something conciliatory to avoid further conflict. But Faithful, as his name implies, must remain true to his convictions. Uninterested in saying what the court wants to hear, he unashamedly presents a simple declaration of the truth. He is clearly much more concerned for the Lord's honor than he is with securing his own release.

Today the church could use more moxie—the ability to face difficulty with spirit and courage. Faithful faces his accusers with "holy moxie," and so can we. When people persecute us for righteousness' sake, we should give an account of our faith with humility and yet with boldness. Paul enjoined Timothy to "not be ashamed to testify about our Lord" (2 Timothy 1:8). Even before a Lord Hategood we should give a straightforward answer as did Stephen before the Sanhedrin and Paul before Felix and Agrippa.

Testifying for the truth doesn't take a spiritual giant or super saint, as some might think. God knows our frailty, and he understands our tendency toward fear. That is why so often we see in Scripture the admonition, "Do not be afraid." He will provide the courage and strength we need when he calls us to stand for his honor and truth. Remember, our strength for the task is proportionate to our dependence upon him.

Does the thought of testifying for your faith frighten you? Ask God for more "holy moxie" to overcome your fear and to count it a privilege to bear a witness for your Lord. Commit yourself to standing for your Lord in some way today.

❦

Scripture: Luke 21:14-15; 2 Timothy 1:8-12; Ephesians 6:10-13

Prayer: Sovereign Lord, who am I that you should approve me to stand and testify for you, the God of the universe? Yet you choose human instruments. Thank you for the privilege of testifying for you. I rely upon you for the needed strength. Amen.

D·A·Y 188

So three witnesses came in—Envy, Superstition, and Talebearer. They were then asked if they knew the prisoner at the bar and what they had to say for their lord the king against the prisoner. Envy stepped forward and said, "My lord, I have known this man for a long time, and I will attest upon my word before this honorable bench, that he is—"

"Hold up there! Give him his oath," the judge interrupted.

So they swore him in, and the man continued, "My lord, this man, in spite of his credible name, is one of the most disgusting men in our country. He regards neither prince nor people, law nor custom; on the contrary, he does all he can to influence people everywhere with his disloyal notions, which, in general, he calls principles of faith and holiness. But specifically, I myself once heard him affirm that Christianity and the customs of our town of Vanity were diametrically opposed to one another and could never be reconciled. By such a statement, my lord, in one breath he not only condemns all of our praiseworthy ways but condemns us for following them."

"Do you have anything more to say?" asked the judge.

"Your honor, I could say much more, but it would only become tiresome to this court. Yet if you need me, when the other gentlemen have given their evidence, if anything is lacking, I will return and enlarge my testimony lest this man be freed." So he was told to stand by.

Solomon said of envy, "Wrath is cruel, and anger is outrageous; but who is able to stand before envy?" (Proverbs 27:4 KJV). Indeed, envy is a powerful and destructive force. It led Cain to kill Abel, Joseph's brothers to sell him into slavery, Herod to kill the infants of Bethlehem. Envy filled Satan's evil heart when he coveted God's position and led heaven's mutiny. And the religious establishment of Jesus' day, envious of Jesus' popularity, conspired to nail him to the cross.

Now Envy comes to court as a character witness against Faithful. How ludicrous! Envy cares nothing for Vanity's people, laws, or customs. He has seen Faithful's peace and tranquillity, his righteousness and integrity, his faith and hope. These qualities are a silent indictment of Envy's wickedness, and he gladly joins the conspiracy against Faithful.

We must be careful to allow envy no foothold in our hearts. James warned, "For where you have envy and selfish ambition, there you find disorder and every evil practice" (James 3:16). Indeed, once given expression, envy destroys lives, ministries, and churches. Can you find envy in your heart? Repent of it now.

Scripture: Proverbs 14:30; Matthew 27:18; Psalms 56:5-6; 57:4-5

Prayer: Dear Lord, help me to uproot all envy from my heart. When I see others giving in to this sin, give me freedom to offer a gentle correction. Amen.

D·A·Y
189

Then they called Superstition and charged him to look at the prisoner. They asked him also what he could say for their lord the king against the defendant. They swore him in, and he began his testimony. "My lord, I am not very familiar with this man, nor do I want to get to know him better. However, I do know from talking with him in town the other day that he is a very dangerous fellow. I heard him say that our religion is nothing and that no one could please God by it. In saying this, my lord, you very well know what must follow—that we still worship in vain, are yet in our sins, and will eventually be damned. This is all I have to say."*

*Obsolete definitions of superstition include the excessive adherence to religious rites that God has not commanded.

Vanity has a religion, and Superstition is its courtroom advocate. Martin Luther said, "Superstition, idolatry, and hypocrisy have ample wages, but truth goes a begging."[20] Indeed, when Superstition comes to the stand, truth is nowhere to be found. Superstition professes to be religious, but he rejects the truth. His is a religion of outward ceremonial observances that has no connection with the heart, conscience, or intellect. He is an unenlightened ritualist following human traditions, ideas, and opinions. Not having a true and loving relationship with the living God, he considers genuine, living faith dangerous. He shares guilt with the religious rulers to whom Jesus said, "You have a fine way of rejecting the commandment of God in order to keep your tradition!" (Mark 7:9 NRSV).

Although Superstition allegedly conversed with Faithful on one occasion, he obviously gained no true insight into Faithful's life and character. Jesus said, "You will know the truth and the truth will set you free" (John 8:32). Superstition heard the truth from Faithful but declined to know it. He shallowly prides himself in upholding his religion and imagines himself qualified and worthy to speak against God's true servant. Just as Jesus predicted, he thinks "he is offering a service to God" (John 16:2).

There are many religious people like Superstition who believe themselves righteous but are actually enemies of the Gospel. Rejecting the key biblical doctrines of salvation, they don't worship God in Spirit or in truth. Their religion is vain, useless, deceptive, empty, lifeless, powerless, and unacceptable to God. Remember that there is *no* substitute for a vital personal relationship with the true and living God. We should beware of those who claim otherwise. Do you have an intimate friendship with God? Or do you merely know about him? He wants to be more than an acquaintance to you.

Scripture: Mark 7:5-13; 1 Timothy 4:7; John 17:3

Prayer: Dear Jesus, I commit myself to getting to know you with my heart, not just with my head. Help me spend time with you, getting to know you better. Amen.

D·A·Y 190

Then Talebearer was sworn in and charged to say what he knew in behalf of their lord the king against the prisoner at the bar. "Your honor," began Talebearer, "and all you ladies and gentlemen, I have known this man for a long time and have heard him speak things that he should not have said. For he has insulted our noble Prince Beelzebub and has spoken contemptuously against all of his honorable friends whose names are Lord Old Man, Lord Carnal-delight, Lord Luxurious, Lord Desire of Vain-glory, old Lord Lechery, Sir Having Greedy, along with all the rest of our nobility. Furthermore, he has said that if everyone was of his frame of mind, there would remain no living for any of these upstanding citizens in this town. Besides this, he has not been afraid to revile you, my lord, who are appointed to be his judge. Why, he has called you an ungodly villain, along with other slanderous names with which he has besmeared most of the aristocracy of our town."*

*Originally called Pickthank, an obsolete word meaning an officious fellow who does something he shouldn't for the sake of gaining favor.

How painful to hear your faithful words twisted by a slanderer. Talebearer makes a habit of malicious gossip for his own gain. A man without religious principles, he regards neither the superstitious nor the spiritual worshiper. He will advocate anything if it promotes his own self-interest. Although he sees nothing in Faithful to incite him to rage or envy, he joins the attack since the tide is against the accused. A whispering parasite of a man, he wants to impress his leaders. Therefore, he gives his testimony out of personal greed and ambition, fawning over the most loathsome of characters to get ahead in this world.

Unlike Superstition, Talebearer says he has known Faithful for a long time. However long, he watched the whole time for an opportunity to foment trouble against the pilgrim. He now polishes the apples of Vanity's power brokers including the wicked fiend, Beelzebub, by further decrying Faithful's views. Naming these "honorable friends" by name, he alleges that the nervy pilgrim insulted them by protesting against their vices.

Seeking human affirmation is a risky business. In times when religion is fashionable and one can gain credit in its participation, hypocrisy is born. In times when religion is denigrated and credit can be lost in its participation, apostasy is given birth. Rather than hoping for human recognition, honor, and praise, we should always seek the honor that God gives to those who honor him. Do you seek to please people rather than God? Repent, and ask God to help you look for his praise instead.

Scripture: John 5:44; 12:43; Philippians 2:3; 1 Thessalonians 2:5-6

Prayer: Dear Lord, if people esteem me, I will feel doubly blessed. But your favor is my first concern. Help me humbly to live only for your honor and glory. Amen.

D·A·Y
191

When Talebearer had finished his story, the judge directed his speech to the prisoner at the bar, saying, "You renegade, heretic, traitor! Have you heard what these honest gentlemen have witnessed against you?"

Faithful answered, "May I speak a few words in my own defense?"

"Sir, you don't deserve to live a minute longer. You should be put to death on the spot! Yet so all may see my fairness, let us hear what you have to say."

"First, I say in answer to what Mr. Envy has spoken, I never said a thing except that any rules, laws, customs, or people who are not in harmony with the Word of God are in reality diametrically opposed to true Christianity. If I have said something amiss in this, convince me of my error, and I will publicly recant.

"As to the second witness, Mr. Superstition, and his charge against me, I said only that to truly worship God, divine faith is required, but there can be no divine faith without a divine revelation of the will of God. Therefore, whatever is included in the worship of God that is not in agreement with divine revelation cannot be done except by a false human faith, which is not beneficial for eternal life.

"As to Mr. Talebearer's charges, I have avoided terms that are insolent and abusive. But I did say that the prince of this town, along with all the rabble that this gentleman named, are more fit for being in Hell than in this town and country. And so may the Lord have mercy on me."

Did Faithful botch his own defense? Only as Christ did! Christ gained no friends among those he told, "You belong to your father, the devil, and you want to carry out your father's desire" (John 8:44). Why did Christ sabotage his own popularity? Because the Pharisees needed to hear the truth. Their smug self-righteousness blinded them, and he had to point out their sinfulness and their need for a Savior—himself!

If ever the church needed to stand up and herald the truth, it is today. Yet how can we offer a prophetic voice to our bankrupt culture when in recent years the church has been rocked by enormous moral and financial scandals? Sometimes we even sell out the true gospel message for one more appealing to unbelievers. Let us repent of giving the world mixed messages. May we be faithful representatives of truth to lost and deceived sinners. Let this be our scandal! As Peter said, "It is better, if it is God's will, to suffer for doing good than for doing evil" (1 Peter 3:17).

How can you be more straightforward with the truth without being discourteous?

Scripture: John 7:7; 8:42-50; Ephesians 6:19-20

Prayer: Lord, I need more courage. I ask that you will fortify my heart to stand solidly as a Christian, clearly and wisely enunciating and demonstrating my faith in every occasion. Amen.

DAY 192

Then the judge called to the jury (who were listening and observing all the while). "Gentlemen of the jury, you see this man about whom so great an uproar has been made in this town. You have also heard what these worthy gentlemen have testified against him, and you have heard his reply and confession. It lies in your hands whether to hang him or save his life, but I think it is fitting for me to give you some instruction in our law.

"A decree was made in the days of Pharaoh the Great, a servant of our prince, that in order to prevent those of a contrary religion from multiplying and growing too strong for him, their males should be thrown into the river. A decree was also made in the days of Nebuchadnezzar the Great, another of his servants, that whoever would not fall down and worship his golden image should be thrown into a fiery furnace. Further, a decree was made in the days of Darius, stating that whoever called upon any God but him should be thrown into the lions' den. Now this rebel has broken the substance of these laws, not only in thought, which cannot be allowed, but also in word and deed, which is absolutely intolerable.

"Now Pharaoh's law was based on supposition of what might happen, to prevent trouble, though no crime had yet been apparent. But in this case, it is clear to all that a crime has been committed, and, as you have witnessed, he admittedly disputes and denies our religion. For the treason that he has confessed, he deserves to die."

Wait! Are there no defense witnesses? Evidently not in Lord Hategood's kangaroo court. The judge, a self-professing religious man, knows enough of God's Word to be dangerous. His inspiration for interpreting the Scriptures is no doubt the spirit of antichrist. To condemn Faithful, he cites as precedents the decrees of Pharaoh, Nebuchadnezzar, and Darius. All three of these ancient rulers sentenced to death the faithful servants of God who refused to compromise God's truth or disobey his will.

The outcome of this trial is a foregone conclusion, but who is really on trial? As Christ stood before Pilate, it was the sinful world, not Christ, being tried. And while the judge condemns Faithful, he actually condemns himself.

When it seems the whole world is arrayed against you in judgment, remember the Judge who has final authority and who stands by your side. Yours is the ultimate vindication. Ask him for the grace to see your troubles from his perspective and for the strength to stand courageously for him. This may be your finest hour for bringing him glory!

Scripture: 1 Timothy 6:12-16; Jude 14-15; Romans 1:28—2:2, 5

Prayer: Dear Lord, the world can get quite mean and nasty. I pray for grace to always keep my eyes on you. No matter how hard my enemies press me, help me to stand firm for you. Amen.

D·A·Y
193

Then the jury went out to deliberate. Their names were Mr. Blind-man, Mr. No-good, Mr. Malice, Mr. Love-lust, Mr. Live-loose, Mr. Heady, Mr. High-mind, Mr. Enmity, Mr. Liar, Mr. Cruelty, Mr. Hate-light, and Mr. Implacable. All these expressed their opinions in the jury room and then agreed to return a unanimous verdict of guilty.

First, Mr. Blind-man, the head juror, spoke and said, "I see clearly that this man is a heretic."

Then Mr. No-good said, "Away with such a man from the earth."

"Yes," said Mr. Malice, "for I hate the very looks of him." Then Mr. Love-lust added, "I could never endure him."

"Nor I," said Mr. Live-loose, "for he would always be condemning my ways."

"Hang him, hang him," demanded Mr. Heady.

"He is a miserable bum," said Mr. High-mind.

"My heart swells with anger against him," said Mr. Enmity.

"He is a worthless person," said Mr. Liar.

"Hanging is too good for him," snarled Mr. Cruelty.

"Let's put him out of the way," suggested Mr. Hate-light.

Then Mr. Implacable said, "If all the world were offered me for reconciling with this man, I would be unable to. Therefore, let us immediately recommend the death penalty."

It's "an ill company where the devil bears the banner." Like a rogues' gallery, lowlifes comprise this jury. Under the power and influence of their wicked prince, they support his cause and do his bidding. How unjust that these are granted the right to condemn a man whose only crime is his innocence of crime. They treat Faithful as the worst and vilest of creatures, as the scum of the earth, and offscouring to be swept quickly out of their way.

Some believers suffer far greater hardships than do others. Though many might think something terribly wrong with those who draw angry persecution, the apostles would beg to differ. For they experienced terrible afflictions, and most suffered excruciating deaths. Of course, those who simply adapt to the surrounding culture escape much trouble and enjoy relative ease. But these shouldn't be our role models. Rather, we should look to those who are filled with the Holy Spirit, consistently displaying godly character, and boldly defending God's truth with his love in their hearts. As with their sinless Lord, they may provoke uncomfortable and even distressing opposition that might end in death. While largely unsung, they are today's real heroes—don't you agree? How can you emulate their example?

Scripture: 2 Corinthians 6:3-10; Hebrews 11:32-38; 1 Peter 2:21-23

Prayer: Dear Lord, help me to appreciate those who suffer greatly for simply living for you. Help me to be more faithful, too. Amen.

D·A·Y 194

And so they did. Faithful was condemned to be put to death by the most cruel means that they could invent.

> *Faithful, so brave in what you've done and said,*
> *Judge, witnesses, and jury have, instead*
> *Of overcoming you, only shown their rage.*
> *When they're dead, you'll live from age to age.*

So they brought him out to do with him according to their law. First, they whipped and beat him; then they cut him with knives and swords; after that they stoned him with stones; and, last of all, they burned him to ashes at the stake. Thus, Faithful came to the end of his earthly life.

Well done, heroic Faithful! You lived up to your name. You never fretted nor complained over the injustice dealt you. You shot through your enemies' falsehoods with arrows of truth. In suffering, you set your eyes on the Lord's example, honoring him and fulfilling his will. Dear brother, you loved not your life to the end. Oh, could we all be so faithful! No wonder they wanted to destroy you! The Lord has news for you, city of Vanity! His servant's life is only beginning!

All earth and hell are powerless to touch a child of God until he has accomplished God's purposes. Thus Jacob escaped from Esau, Moses from Pharaoh, Elijah from Jezebel, Paul from the Jews, and Peter from Herod. But Faithful has finished his earthly task. Therefore, God let his persecutors expedite his entry into his heavenly inheritance. So also it happened with Stephen, James, and our Lord Jesus Christ. John Milton writes, "Servant of God, well done! well hast thou fought / The better fight, who single hast maintain'd / Against revolted multitudes the cause / Of truth."[21]

Today's easy gospel makes unpalatable the thought of a loving God not rescuing his servants from persecution. Yet our faith was conceived in Christ's martyrdom, and martyrdom has attended its path ever since. Like the early Christians, we need to count it a privilege to suffer for our Lord. If we are unwilling to die for Christ, how can we really live for him? Fear of death and love for this life are enemies of true faithfulness. Reaffirm your utmost loyalty to him.

Scripture: John 15:19; 1 John 3:13; Matthew 10:28; Revelation 2:10

Prayer: Dear Lord, I pray that my earthly life will end in resounding victory, that I will never falter in my trust in and devotion to your sovereign design for my life. You are worthy! Amen.

D·A·Y 195

Then I saw that behind the crowd stood a chariot driven by horses waiting for Faithful, who, as soon as his enemies had finished with him, was ushered inside. With the sound of a trumpet, it immediately carried him up through the clouds—the nearest way to the Celestial Gate.

As for Christian, he was given a temporary delay and ordered back to prison where he remained for a time. But He who overrules all things, having power over their rage in His hand, made it possible for Christian to escape. After Christian had escaped, he went on his way singing:

"Well, Faithful, you have faithfully professed
Your Lord, by whom you will surely be blessed;
When faithless ones with all their vain delights,
Are crying out under their hellish plights,
Sing, Faithful, sing, for your name will survive,
For though they killed you, you are yet alive!"

Glory! Faithful's death was no disadvantage to him. His enemies took a poor mortal body that would perish anyway, but they couldn't touch his immortal soul. Angels took him to join the other martyrs around God's throne. He will never see this troublesome world again but will know the endless joy prepared for him.

This said, however, we should never take injustice toward fellow Christians lightly. Chinese and Egyptian believers are regularly imprisoned and tortured. Thousands of Christians have been killed in Nigeria's religious riots. Pakistan invokes a death penalty on anyone who "defiles" Mohammed's name. Saudi Arabian officials often arrest Christians for meeting privately Uzbekistan Christians are harassed and pastors threatened. Police raid evangelical churches in Vietnam. North Korea permits no religion. Sudanese Christians face genocide for refusing to convert to Islam. Persecution comes in Christ's name, too. Russia's Orthodox Church is behind attempts to outlaw "unregistered" churches, for example.

We should thank God for our relative freedoms. Less fortunate believers throughout the world desperately need us to pray and to speak on their behalf. Ask God how he might use you to help persecuted brothers and sisters in Christ.

Scripture: Revelation 6:9-11; Isaiah 57:1; Psalm 12:1; John 11:25

Prayer: Lord, thank you for our precious religious freedoms. Help us to preserve them. Also, grant my persecuted brothers and sisters your grace, strength, and deliverance. Amen.

D·A·Y 196

Now I saw in my dream that Christian did not have to go very far by himself. One whose name was Hopeful joined him, having become so by observing the examples of Christian and Faithful in what they said and did during their sufferings at the fair. The two of them entered into a covenant with one another, vowing to be companions. So following the death of one who died bearing testimony to the truth, another was raised up out of his ashes to be a companion with Christian in his pilgrimage. And Hopeful related to Christian that before long many more people from the fair would set out to follow them.

The "blood of the martyrs is the seed of the church." Those who courageously endure suffering provide powerful sermons that cannot be easily forgotten. Christian and Faithful made a profound impact upon this man who says he became Hopeful and left on his pilgrimage after observing their lives in Vanity. How remarkable that the horrid scene in Vanity could somehow produce hope. All the same, the reason is clear. In contrast with the selfishness, superficiality, and insincerity of Vanity, our heroes were Christ-centered and earnestly committed to the truth. They were willing to suffer and even die if faithfulness to God's call required it. This so impressed Hopeful that he seriously considered their claims and became a pilgrim himself. Now, full of hope, he enthusiastically shares his certainty that many others will in time follow as well.

Hopeful's friendship with Christian is a much-needed gift from God at a time of loss. Christian needs encouragement right now, and Hopeful has it to share. He is of a different disposition than was Faithful, illustrating that, just as believers have unique conversion experiences, so believers are themselves unique. While Faithful underscored the importance of faithfulness to the pilgrimage, Hopeful emphasizes the importance of maintaining hopefulness. Where Faithful was serious-minded, Hopeful is more the cheerful optimist. Hopeful, however, is not a mindless optimist whose hope rests on nothing. His hope springs from his newly found relationship with Jesus Christ.

We can thank God for those who, like Faithful, steadfastly exhibit their faith before a skeptical world. We can also give thanks for those like Hopeful who always expect the best because God is good. Don't we have a whole lot to learn from both? Think about people you know who inspire faith and hope in others. Ask God to help you incorporate their attitudes and actions into your life.

Scripture: 1 Thessalonians 1:3;
1 Corinthians 12:7, 20-21; 1 Peter 4:10

Prayer: Lord Jesus, your church is comprised of so many people with different personalities and gifts. Help me to appreciate those whom you have placed in my life. May we draw strength from one another as we journey together. Amen.

D·A·Y 197

Not long after they had left the fair, I saw that they overtook one who had been traveling ahead of them. They asked him, "Where are you from, sir? And how far are you traveling this Way?" He answered that he had come from the town of Fair-speech and that he was on his way to the Celestial City.

"From Fair-speech?" asked Christian. "Are there good folks living there?"

"Yes, I certainly think so," he answered.

"Tell me, sir, what may I call you?" asked Christian.

"Oh, I am a stranger to you, as you are to me. If you are going to be traveling this Way, I will be glad to have your company, but if not, I must be content."

"This town of Fair-speech," Christian said, "I have heard of it; as I recall, people say it's a wealthy place."

"Yes, I assure you that it is, and I have many rich relatives there."

"Who are your relatives there, if you don't mind my asking?"

"Well, almost the whole town. Let's see, some more notable ones are Lord Turn-about, Lord Time-server, and Lord Fair-speech (from whose ancestors the town first took its name); also, there are Mr. Smooth-man, Mr. Facing-bothways, and Mr. Any-thing."

❧

The genteel citizens of Fair-speech talk so pleasantly that their words flow like a balmy breeze over their town. No rude, unkind words toward anyone can be heard here. Despite their pleasantries, however, these folk use their refined speech to keep up an impressive but misleading appearance of righteousness. Learning to be tactful, diplomatic, and gracious in our speech is certainly wise. But refinement of speech is no guarantee that what is being said is wise, good, or true. While an appreciated virtue, courtesy can be shallow and lacking in substance.

Representing varying forms of affected spirituality, the citizens of Fair-speech live, as John Kelman describes it, in "the heartbreaking borderland of church membership." They are religious opportunists who cherish faith for what they gain by it. Thus Lord Turn-about quickly changes his opinion and allegiance; Lord Time-server conforms to the prevailing opinions of the moment; Lord Fair-speech knows how best to express himself; Mr. Smooth-man's finish gleams like well-polished silver plate; Mr. Facing-bothways holds every opinion without seeming inconsistency; Mr. Any-thing embraces anything and everything.

Confess any inconsistencies in your Christian life. Thank God that he truly loves you, that his commitment doesn't "change like shifting shadows" (James 1:17).

❧

Scripture: Proverbs 26:25; Romans 16:18; Jeremiah 7:4, 8

Prayer: Dear Lord, you care more about inward character than outward manner. Please help me to be inwardly pure and authentic. I want to be one whom you can count trustworthy. Amen.

D·A·Y
198

"Our pastor, Rev. Two-tongues, is my mother's own brother. To tell you the truth, I have now become a gentleman of high standing, although my great-grandfather was only a boatman—looking one way and rowing another. Actually, I received most of my estate from those of the same occupation."

"Are you a married man?" asked Christian.

The man smiled proudly. "Yes, and my wife is a very fine and virtuous woman who is also the daughter of such a woman. She is Lady Feigning's daughter and so comes from a very honorable and prestigious family. She has acquired such a high degree of poise and sophistication that she knows precisely how to conduct herself with both prince and peasant alike."

❦

There is a church in Fair-speech whose pastor is this gentleman's uncle. Striving to keep his esteemed position among his parishioners, the double-tongued Rev. Two-tongues has sold himself to say what everyone wants to hear. He lets his church members rest in their illusion of righteous gentility when, in fact, their fine speech and demeanor merely cloak the serious character flaws so deeply ingrained within them.

When the same requirements for attaining status in society are introduced into the church, then refinement, breeding, education, wealth, and worldly attainments become prominent gauges for distinguishing people. Hypocrisy becomes entrenched, and goodness rests more on outward form, fashion, and pleasantness than upon truth.

This man, a professed believer, illustrates the deception. He obviously sees himself as a refined, well-bred, educated gentleman of the privileged class. His climb to the aristocracy began with his beloved great-grandfather, who began his career as a double-minded boatman. He improved his lot even more through an "honorable" alliance with the prestigious Feigning family. His wife, a true soul mate to her husband, is a role-player who knows how best to conduct herself with everyone.

Unfortunately, the whole town, as in the tale of *The Emperor's New Clothes*, has embraced deception. Like the Laodicean church, their religion seems royally clad, but it is nonetheless naked. When we see such superficiality and hypocrisy in our lives and within the church, we need to expose them. Granted, *how* we are to speak is "in love." Yet *what* we are to speak is the truth. (See Ephesians 4:15.) Do you see areas in your life or in your church that cannot stand up to the searchlight of truth? Lay them before the Lord, and ask for his grace.

❦

Scripture: Luke 6:26; Jeremiah 6:13; Revelation 3:14-18

Prayer: Oh Lord, help me to see through outward appearances to what is truly relevant in life. I want to be courteous and gracious and, more importantly, sincere and honest in my conversations. Amen.

D·A·Y
199

"It is true, our faith differs in some respects from those of the stricter sort, but only in a couple of minor points. First, we go with the flow; we never strive against the wind or current. Second, we are always more zealous for religion when it is refined and elegant—wearing silver slippers, so to speak. We love to walk boldly in the streets with religion when the sun is shining upon it and people are applauding it."

❧

The gentleman seems to think his theology differs with orthodoxy on only a few minor points. First, unlike Christian, who has often had to swim upstream, this man and his family always go with the flow. They follow the prevailing winds and currents. What could be easier? When they must make a decision concerning faith and practice, the best way is the easy way. It is such a simple, uncomplicated principle. It makes perfect sense to them.

What gets this man's religious heart pumping? What makes him "zealous for religion?" He says, refinement, elegance, wealth. He and his relatives love to march down the street with heads uplifted, the sunshine brightening their faces, and people applauding them. When this is the case, they can imagine that God is smiling upon them and the Holy Spirit is pouring into their hearts the happy emotions they feel.

What a false and fallen gospel this is! Here this man advocates compromise and "safety first" on the heels of Faithful's giving up his life and Christian's suffering torture for his faith. Doubtless, since this stranger is on the pilgrim Way, he passed through Vanity just ahead of Christian and Faithful. Yet he fearlessly paraded on through without creating a stir. How so? Because, like the chameleon he is, he closely resembles its inhabitants. Does this illustrate a difference of minor points of faith?

But here we have it. Many churches in our land are full of fair-weather Christians, the fashionably religious sort who love the worldly culture but are strangers to God's culture, unwilling to pay the price of becoming true disciples of Jesus Christ. Let us deplore such false and disloyal religion, keeping it far from us. Wisdom tells us to keep our eyes on our Lord and on the way he lived and on the way his disciples lived. Far better to go to heaven barefooted than to wear silver slippers into hell!

How is the worldly culture influencing you to live a self-centered lifestyle? How can you put it off to better embrace God's culture?

❧

Scripture: Mark 8:34-37; Luke 14:26-33; John 12:25-26

Prayer: Dear Lord, I want to follow you. Please help me to stay grounded carefully in your truth, neither swerving to the right nor the left. Help me also to beware of embracing smooth, easy solutions in the difficult tasks to which you have called me. Amen.

D·A·Y 200

After hearing this, Christian stepped aside to talk to his friend Hopeful. "It dawns on me that this man may be Mr. By-ends from Fair-speech. If it is, we have in our company as tricky and deceitful a person as lives in all these parts."*

"Well, ask him," said Hopeful. "I don't think he will be ashamed of his name."

So Christian returned to him again and said, "Sir, in listening to you talk about yourself and your views, if I am not mistaken, I have a pretty good idea who you are. Are you Mr. By-ends of Fair-speech?"

"That is not my name, but, yes, it is a nickname that some who cannot stand me gave to me. I must be content to bear it as a reproach just as other good people have had to before me."

"But did you ever give anyone good reason to call you by this name?"

"Never, never! The most I ever did to give reason for calling me this name was that I have always had the good luck to be able to adjust my views to the present trends of the times. Whenever I have had a chance to gain, I have employed this ability, and if I have prospered in this way, let me count it a blessing. But do not let those who are malicious burden me with their scorn."

*Probably from the obsolete word *bye-end,* meaning "a private end or interest, secret purpose or advantage."

This well-spoken gentleman finally admits his nickname, By-ends. Some who could not stomach his motives pinned it on him. He does feel some embarrassment about it. Thinking his flexibility of belief is a virtue, he feels unfairly accused. How deceived he is!

Why did this man even bother leaving on a pilgrimage? No doubt because he sees some advantage in doing so. In his mind, the end always justifies the means, and he would not be on this path if it didn't somehow satisfy the end he hopes to accomplish.

What are some less-than-Christian reasons for which people join churches and profess Christ? Many reasons exist, but most boil down to lust and greed. Some look for financial gain, either in the ministry or through business contacts. To others, recognition, respectability, and attention are as good as money. Still others like the power and glory they achieve by climbing the leadership ranks.

Lest we become like Mr. By-ends, having ulterior motives for our acts of worship and service for Christ, we should regularly examine our motives. Ask God to point out any area of hypocrisy in your heart. Be sure to renounce it and receive His purifying grace.

Scripture: Matthew 21:13; Titus 1:11; 2 Corinthians 7:1

Prayer: Lord, please show me any impure secret motives in my heart. I want to be done with them so I can follow you wholeheartedly. Amen.

D·A·Y 201

"I thought you were the man I had heard of," Christian responded. "Let me tell you what I think; I fear this name is more appropriate for you than you are willing for us to believe."

"Well," said By-ends, "I cannot help what you think. You will still find me a good traveling companion if you allow me to continue walking with you."

"If you will travel with us," said Christian, "you will have to go against the wind and current, and I believe this is contrary to your belief. You must also embrace this faith not only when it wears silver slippers, but also when it is dressed in rags. You must stand by it when it is cast into prison and also when it parades triumphantly through the streets and receives applause."

If By-ends wants to fellowship with serious pilgrims, he must expect to pay the price of it. First, to partner with Christian and Hopeful, he must row against the wind and current. The worldly flow is always downhill and away from the Celestial City, so it takes a continual determined effort to push against this current. By-ends, however, shows how little he thinks of his faith, since he stakes nothing on it. With regard to the pilgrimage, he lives by one principle—the avoidance of struggle and danger at all times.

Christian also makes it clear that if By-ends wants to fellowship with them, he must be willing to hold to the faith not only in good times, but also in bad. Sometimes there may be silver slippers but at other times rags. True pilgrims learn to trust God and rejoice as did Paul who learned contentment in every situation. While sometimes the Christian walk may allow for parading triumphantly through the streets, at other times remaining true to the faith may mean imprisonment. When our Lord triumphantly paraded into Jerusalem, he fully recognized that a short time later he would be nailed to a cross.

We should not unduly concern ourselves with how little or with how much we have. Nor should we worry about how kindly or unkindly the world treats us. These things do not determine the measure of blessedness in a Christian life. A blessed walk with Christ is independent of either external wealth or poverty. True wealth or poverty is unseen and eternal, a matter of an internal work of the heart. We should avoid considering outward advantage as a sign of being right with God or as a principal motivation for serving him. Have you honestly and realistically considered the cost of following Christ? Have you sincerely committed yourself to a faithful pilgrimage regardless of what it may require of you?

Scripture: Philippians 4:11-13; 1 Corinthians 4:9-13; Psalm 119:14

Prayer: Dear Lord, help me to have the maturity to realize what constitutes true blessedness. Let me walk a blessed life with you as the true Sovereign of my heart. Amen.

D·A·Y 202

"But you should not impose your views on me nor lord it over my faith," responded By-ends. "Allow me to walk in my liberty and at the same time continue with you."

"No," said Christian. "Unless you intend to do what I have presented to you, as we intend to do, we won't be traveling another step together."

Then By-ends said, "I will never desert my old principles; not only are they harmless, but they are also very profitable for me. If I cannot go with you, I must continue on as before and go by myself until someone comes along who will enjoy my company."

Insincere professors of Christ recollect one Scripture well and love to quote it: "Don't judge!" Here By-ends adds another used in the same spirit, as he admonishes Christian to let him be. He quotes Paul's words to the Corinthians, "Not that we lord it over your faith . . ." (2 Corinthians 1:24), insinuating that Christian and Hopeful are overbearing and judgmental. He then seals his argument with a reference to his personal freedom in Christ. Paul did indeed say that God calls us to freedom. Yet if By-ends cared to read on, he would notice that Paul goes on to say not to use our freedom for self-indulgence. (See Galatians 5:13.)

By-ends's obvious manipulation of biblical truth fails to convince Christian, who lets him know that if he refuses to repent, they cannot walk together another step. By his own admission, this is not the first time By-ends has been confronted. Yet he still refuses to change his ways. Instead, he sees himself as a persecuted and misunderstood victim who is forced to go it alone—as if no difference exists between suffering for true faith and suffering as a reproach to true faith!

Christian does right to choose his companions carefully. He does not owe it to By-ends to walk with him. Nor do we owe it to half-hearted Christians to walk with them. The Bible even says, "From such turn away" (2 Timothy 3:5 KJV). Of course, we are to reach out in love to unbelievers. But we must do so in spiritual strength, and that strength comes in large measure from fellowship with other strongly committed Christians. We should always want to find fellowship that will aid our spiritual progress. Do you need to make some changes in the type of fellowship you enjoy? Why not submit this need to the Lord right now?

Scripture: Matthew 23:27-28; Titus 1:16; Proverbs 12:26; Ephesians 5:7

Prayer: Dear Lord, I want to run with those who are serious about their Christian faith. Please protect and deliver me from those who drag me away from a faithful walk with you. Help me instead to maintain fellowship with those who will spur me on in my pilgrimage. Amen.

D·A·Y 203

Now I saw in my dream that Christian and Hopeful left him and went on ahead, keeping their distance from him. After awhile, one of them happened to look back and saw three men following Mr. By-ends. As the men caught up with him, they greeted each other warmly. Their names were Mr. Hold-the-world, Mr. Money-love, and Mr. Save-all. Mr. By-ends had known all of them previously. In their younger years they had been schoolmates and had been taught by Mr. Grasp-man. He was a teacher from the town of Love-gain, a center of commercialism in the northern county of Coveting. This teacher had trained them well in the art of getting ahead by whatever means, whether by violence, cheating, flattery, lying, or by putting on an external appearance of religion. These four had excelled to such a degree in their teacher's art that each of them could have run such a school by himself.

Mr. By-ends did not have to walk alone for long. The path is smoother here, and where rest is given to the church, hypocrites often multiply more quickly than true believers. Three old friends with whom By-ends has a great deal in common soon catch up with him. Like birds of a feather, they trained together under their mentor, Mr. Grasp-man from the wealthy town of Love-gain in Coveting County. The four money mongers now live to try to get more money. They either hoard it or use it to purchase possessions, pleasure, or power for themselves.

Often in the church, especially in affluent cultures like ours, there are many who profess Christ but whose primary allegiance is to money. While money is a blessed gift God provides to meet our needs and to fulfill his plans on the earth, it can also be the source of many spiritual snares. Wealth can blind us to our true spiritual condition; it can lull us into spiritual slumber. Our need for it can become an obsession that has more influence in our lives than God's Spirit.

Ours is a society where the rich are getting richer and everyone, it seems, lusts for more money. Those who are rich are seen as "successful." They buy their way into the corridors of power and often have undue influence even within the church. Have you found yourself affected by the lust of those who cloak greed and covetousness in religious terms? In what ways have their theology and methods influenced you? To maintain a sincere passion for God's kingdom and purposes, we must carefully keep ourselves untainted from greedy seductions.

Scripture: Hosea 12:8; Psalms 37:16; 119:72

Prayer: Dear Lord, please free me from this society's lust for wealth. Knowing that "it is more blessed to give than to receive," help me find greater joy in giving money away for your kingdom's work than in receiving it. Amen.

DAY 204

After they had greeted one another, Mr. Money-love asked Mr. By-ends, "Who is on the road ahead of us?" For Christian and Hopeful were still within view.

Mr. By-ends replied, "They are men from a distant country who are, in their own way, going on a pilgrimage."

"Too bad! Why didn't they wait so that we could enjoy their company?" asked Mr. Money-love. "After all, aren't we all going on a pilgrimage?"

"Yes, we are indeed, but those men up ahead are very rigid and dogmatic. They love their own opinions to such an extent that they have precious little regard for anyone else's. A person could be very godly, but if he doesn't agree with them on every point, they will thrust him completely out of their fellowship."

Christian and Hopeful would certainly be labeled "intolerant" today by many in the church. Since "all" are on a pilgrimage, why would the two pilgrims prefer to walk apart from the others? Mr. Money-love wonders why they cannot simply walk together. Mr. By-ends, not understanding the significance of their differences, criticizes the two pilgrims. From his perspective, they are so rigid and dogmatic that everyone who would walk with them must agree with them on every point. To him, these "points" are completely unworthy of disrupting unity over.

These four men hold to a theology based upon greed, a theology that, when followed, always draws people away from Christ and his will. To walk with Mr. By-ends and his friends means to fellowship with them, to consent to them, to approve of them, to commit the same sins. It is contrary to a true pilgrim's character to walk with them.

Today, we increasingly hear cries for unity. To be sure, God wants unity, for there exists one Lord, one faith, and one baptism. And Christ in John 17 prays fervently for Christian unity, for it is an essential part of our witness for Christ. Nevertheless, pilgrims must distinguish between true unity and false unity. Legitimate Christian unity is based upon truth. A unity that cannot stand upon gospel truth and that values it beneath tolerance must be rejected.

Charles Spurgeon deplored false unity, saying, "a chorus of voices keep harping the unity tune. . . . Such teaching is false, reckless, and dangerous. Truth alone must determine our alignments. Truth comes before unity."[22] Are you eager to maintain unity within Christ's body? Have you ever made the mistake of trying to keep unity at the expense of gospel truth? What might have been a better approach to take?

Scripture: 2 John 10-11; Galatians 1:8-9; Philippians 1:27

Prayer: Lord Jesus, please give me discernment to distinguish between true and false unity. Show me how to foster unity within your church without sacrificing our fellowship's integrity. Amen.

DAY 205

"Well, that is bad," said Mr. Save-all. "However, we have read about some who are overly righteous. The extreme legalism of this type of person drives him to judge and condemn everyone else. But please tell me, on what and on how many points did you differ?"

Those who neglect the essential elements of a true pilgrimage, who avoid the cross and preserve their worldly ambitions and interests, easily judge faithful pilgrims as "overly righteous" or as "extreme legalists." Thus miserly Mr. Save-all, who hoards all his money to himself, thinks he can judge the pilgrims.

Like Mr. By-ends, Mr. Save-all knows enough Scripture to use it for his purposes. His statement about the overly righteous refers to Solomon's words: "Do not be overrighteous, neither be overwise—why destroy yourself?" (Ecclesiastes 7:16). Originally intended as a rebuke against academic, hard, hypocritical righteousness, the enemies of true righteousness pick it up and run with it.

With his charge of legalism, Mr. Save-all manipulates the truth. He insinuates that the pilgrims preach justification by works, rather than faith in Christ's finished work. True legalists trust in their own good deeds to earn them right standing with God. The pilgrims, however, trust Christ's salvation but also know that the Lord calls them to live honest and obedient lives. Isn't it ironic how a balanced, grace-filled Christian life will appear legalistic to those who are worldly and worldly to those who are legalistic? These men are worldly, so Christian and Hopeful seem to them legalistic. The legalistic Pharisees, on the other hand, looked at Jesus and considered his spending time in the homes of sinners scandalously worldly.

Christian understands legalism better than these accusers, however. Didn't he stand trembling under Mt. Sinai in search of one named Legality? Subsequently, he discovered that the only one in heaven and earth with power to remove his burden was the one who hung on the cross for him. He now stands, not in his own goodness, but in the loving grace of his Savior, the Lord Jesus Christ.

As victorious Christians, we are neither legalistic nor worldly. Far from being legalistic, we rest in God's grace, knowing we belong to him, are of him, and live in and for him. Far from being worldly, by his Spirit within, we live wholesome, holy, and happy lives free of worldly motives. The warped and greedy Mr. Save-alls of this world may criticize us, but what have they to do with us? They have no share in God's kingdom. Thank the Lord that you are not subject to their opinions but to Christ's.

Scripture: Ephesians 5:3-5; Luke 12:30-32; Romans 8:31

Prayer: Dear Lord, protect me from worldly opinions. I know I stand in your grace alone. May I be a devoted and obedient Christian, lovingly and faithfully keeping your commandments. Amen.

D·A·Y 206

"True to their headstrong manner," replied Mr. By-ends, "they have concluded that it is their duty to rush forward on their journey no matter what the weather; I, on the other hand, am for waiting for favorable wind and current. They are for risking all for God at the snap of a finger; I am for taking advantage of every opportunity to secure my life and estate. They are for holding to their ideas although all the world would be against them; I, however, am for religion insofar as the times, conditions, and my safety allow it. They are for religion when walking in rags and abuse; I am for it when it walks in silver slippers, in sunshine, and with applause."

In the company of his distinguished friends, Mr. By-ends candidly offers his opinion of Christian and Hopeful. It seems clear to him that they are very foolish. He explains in "plausible words of wisdom" why he thinks their perspective is wrong. The pilgrims suffer unnecessary discomfort when they could be comfortable; they impetuously risk their lives and fortunes for God when they should appropriately safeguard them; they persist in their notions no matter how unpopular they become; they stick to their commitment despite which way the tide turns.

Mr. By-ends considers this behavior absurdly ridiculous. He thinks these pilgrims would come to embrace his sensible point of view if only they were not so "headstrong." Sad to say, he is typical of many Christians today who believe that *God* exists for *our* purposes rather than that *we* exist for *God's* purposes. His premise is that his health, safety, comfort, and wealth are the highest good, while God exists to meet those needs. Far from his being accountable to God, God is accountable to him!

Mr. By-ends is a "fair-weather Christian," someone who follows Christ only when it is in his interest to do so. When the "weather" gets rough, he forsakes God. His god is false, his religion bogus. How, then, can we even try to reconcile his worldly perspective with the Christian one? In light of eternity, we should incline ourselves more to the perspective of the martyred missionary, Jim Elliot, who declared, "He is no fool to give what he cannot keep to gain what he cannot lose." Have you committed all that you are and all you have to God, now and forever, in order to gain what cannot be lost?

Scripture: 1 Corinthians 4:10; 2 Timothy 2:19; Proverbs 3:13-14

Prayer: Lord Jesus, please teach me your wisdom so I can interpret life not from a worldly perspective but from a biblical one. Worldly people may deem me a fool, but they are the fools. I am willing to be called a fool for your sake. Amen.

D·A·Y
207

At this, Mr. Hold-the-world spoke up. "Ah, yes, Mr. By-ends, hold to your position. In my opinion, whoever has the freedom to keep what he possesses but is unwise enough to lose it is a fool! Let us 'be wise as serpents' [Matthew 10:16]. Make hay when the sun shines. And can't you see how the bee lies still all winter but rouses herself again only when she can enjoy her gain? Sometimes God sends rain and sometimes sunshine; if they are such fools as to go through the rain, let us be content to take the good weather along with us. As for me, I like that religion best that will favor the security of God's good blessings to us."

Hold to your position! This is the cry of those who conspire together against the truth. They are familiar with the Bible, but their perspectives are warped by their sinful desires. They twist Scripture, using it to support their corrupted priorities rather than conforming their lives to its truth. How wily they are as they so seriously recite God's Word—"Let us be wise as serpents, brothers!"

In such practice we find the genesis of almost every cult group. "Hold to your position!" Mr. Hold-the-world exhorts. But to what position do they hold? You can discover it in Mr. Hold-the-world's name. You can determine it from his words—"In *my* opinion" and "As for *me*, *I* like that religion best that. . ." This is their position: They are "me-centered." They staunchly hold to the root sin, the one of self-aggrandizement. It is this sin that exalts self above God, causing misinterpretation of the Scriptures to justify a self-centered existence.

Paul advised Timothy that in the last days, "People will be lovers of themselves, lovers of money . . . rather than lovers of God" (2 Timothy 3:2, 4). How aptly Mr. By-ends and his friends fit this description as they rationalize their sacrifice of truth on an altar of self-worship.

It is good to hold to your position if that position is rooted in a true worship of God in accordance with his Word. As believers who live in the last days before Christ's return, it is imperative that we study God's Word diligently and learn how to interpret it responsibly. Deceptions will continue to increase, and while those who cleave to false hopes will be swept away in their lies, those who know and cleave to the truth of God's Word will be victors. "Hold to Scripture's position!" This should be our cry. Is it your pastor's cry? The cry of your Christian friends? Your cry?

Scripture: Isaiah 28:15-18;
1 Thessalonians 5:21-22; 2 Peter 1:19-21

Prayer: Blessed Lord, I want to hold to your position, not my own nor anyone else's. Your Word is authoritative. Help me to search it honestly, not for my will but for yours. Amen.

DAY 208

"Can anyone who listens to the dictates of common sense imagine that God, who has bestowed on us the good things of this life, does not want us to keep them for His sake? Abraham and Solomon grew rich through their religion, and even Job says that a good man shall 'lay up gold as dust' [Job 22:24 KJV]. But these great men differ from those two ahead of us if they are as you have described them."

"I think we all agree concerning this matter, so there is no need to discuss it any further," concluded Mr. Save-all.

Mr. Money-love agreed. "No, we need not waste any more words over this matter. For he who believes neither Scripture nor reason—and we have both on our side—neither knows his own liberty nor seeks his own safety."

How can people become so deluded? Reasoning with these men would be an exasperating chore. Without conscience, they keep cutting and shaping Scripture to suit their own me-centered theology. Meanwhile God's Word warns of the "deceitfulness" of riches. Riches often delude people, leading them out of the true Way, causing them to err from sincere faith. Money becomes their real god. Instead of spending their wealth on the Lord's concerns, they either hoard it or spend it on themselves and their families. Then they quote Scripture to hide their idolatry. How do they justify their sin? Primarily by interpreting the Scriptures by their "common sense." It is important to realize that our deepest values shape and define what to each of us is common sense. Thus common sense to those who are radically committed to Christ is very different from what it would be to those who live for their own selfish desires.

Mr. Hold-the-world sanctifies his greed by saying it is all for "His sake." But how can greed be for God's sake? Perhaps he sees himself parading down the street wearing luxurious clothing and jewelry, with people saying, "Wow! Did God ever bless him. Glory to God!" Indeed, some popular preachers today do proclaim, "God wants you rich for his glory!"

What a different spirit our dear Savior, the Man from Galilee, possesses! Born to simple peasants in a wretched stall, that first night our infant King had no cradle, only a trough; as an adult, things changed little, for he admitted he had no place to lay his head. He lived his life owning nothing. His sole earthly possession, his garment, was raffled off at the cross. This is the founder of the faith these four money mongers claim to follow! How do you feel when you observe Christ's life as he really lived it and his teachings as he really taught them? How does "common sense" tell you to respond?

Scripture: Mark 4:19; Malachi 3:8-9; Luke 12:16-22

Prayer: Dear Lord, please help me never to rationalize sin by saying it is for your sake. I want in all honesty to surrender all and live for your glory. Amen.

DAY 209

"My brothers," said Mr. By-ends, "as you know, we are all going on a pilgrimage, and for a positive diversion from unpleasant things, allow me to propose this question: Suppose a person—a minister, a businessperson, or other—should have an opportunity to get the good blessings of this life. However, the only way he can attain them, it seems, is to become extraordinarily zealous in certain religious matters in which he had previously shown no interest. Can he still be an honest man while taking advantage of this means to achieve his end?"

Mr. By-ends poses a theoretical question. Of course, he already knows his answer. His entire company will agree that a person can use religious means for worldly gain and be better for it. Oh, but let us look at our Lord Jesus Christ. With his charismatic personality, unequaled wisdom, and miracle-working power, he had "the opportunity for getting the good blessings of this life." People became so enamored with him that they wanted to force him to be their earthly king.

Yet our Lord never needed to blush over false motives. He never had to hide his face in shame for discovering some selfish ambition in his heart. Anxious thoughts of wealth or success found no place to settle within him. Earthly power and applause awakened no secret longing in his heart. Instead, he met them with avoidance or disdain. Our Lord told his disciples not to worry about food or clothing because God would take care of them.

So what was our Lord's underlying motive? What was he "extraordinarily zealous" for? What end was he trying to achieve by the means he applied? He simply wanted to please his Father. Zeal for his Father's house consumed him. He passionately sought his Father's glory. Every day his only concern was to speak on his Father's behalf, to express his Father's compassion, to draw souls into his Father's kingdom, to accomplish his Father's will. Hearing his Father say, "I am well pleased with my beloved Son" was all he needed or wanted for himself.

Shouldn't we desire more of the Lord's heart beating within our hearts? The only way this can happen is for us to allow him to remove the idols from our hearts. Then there will be sufficient space for him to further glorify his Father in and through us. Have you surrendered each of your idols to him?

Scripture: Luke 9:58; John 4:34; 5:30; Ephesians 5:10

Prayer: Lord Jesus, you are so incredibly wonderful. You are Lord of the universe, yet your desires are so pure and uncomplicated. Help me to love the Father as you do. I praise you for bringing me into relationship with him. Amen.

D·A·Y
210

At this, Mr. Money-love quickly replied, "I can see your purpose in asking this question, and if you gentlemen will permit me, I will propose a suitable answer. First of all, I would like to speak to your question as it concerns a minister. Suppose a minister, a worthy person, has received very little compensation but has set his sights on a much higher standard of living. Suddenly he has the opportunity of getting it—but by being more studious, by preaching more frequently and zealously, and by altering some of his principles in order to accommodate the disposition of his listeners. As far as I am concerned, I see no reason why a man may not do this, and even a great deal more, provided he has a calling from God."

Mr. Money-love's "worthy" minister is discontented with his pay. He decides to find a way to improve his financial picture. Instead of seeking first the kingdom of God and his righteousness, he decides to seek first a rich monetary reward for himself. To attain his goal, he will do what he has been doing but much better. He wants to become a well-known preacher, perhaps even getting on radio or TV. To achieve his goal, he must study his craft harder than ever, drum up more preaching opportunities, preach like a fireball while still telling his listeners what will most please them.

Mr. Money-love thinks this minister's ambitions are worthy if he can say he is called by God. But he has traded his calling for a business enterprise, one that may well reap material dividends but end in spiritual bankruptcy. His preaching is no longer Holy Spirit-inspired. As a merchant selling his wares, he sells himself with feigned and contrived words to cover his true motives. Just how many ministers similarly adulterate their calling for personal profit? Scandalous numbers. Some become so desperate for new angles at self-marketing that they create gimmicks and schemes, sometimes falling into pernicious heresies.

Paul calls them corrupt who claim to serve God and yet "think that godliness is a means to financial gain" (1 Timothy 6:5). He gave up everything to follow Christ while these serve their own selfish interests. We live in a materialistic society where many serve money. While churches should seek to provide adequately for their pastors, we need our ministers to be exemplary in their values, priorities, and lifestyles. We should all carefully check our motives for serving Christ and for choosing our spiritual leaders. Have you prayed for your spiritual leaders recently—for purity of heart and purpose?

Scripture: 1 Peter 5:2; 1 Timothy 3:1-3, 8; 2 Corinthians 2:17

Prayer: Dear Lord, please grant my minister faith to trust you for his needs and keep him from temptations that muddy his motives. Raise up ministers with pure hearts. Amen.

D·A·Y
211

"He is still a man of integrity, and these are my reasons why: First, no one can argue the legality of his desire for greater compensation, and God Himself has set before him the opportunity to improve his lot. So, then, he may get it if he can do so without any question of conscience.

"Second, his desire for more money makes him more studious, and thus a better teacher and a more zealous preacher. He has therefore greatly improved himself and is a better man for it—and this is obviously in accordance with the will and purpose of God."

Mr. Money-love thinks this minister, for whom personal gain is the first order of business, can still be considered a man of integrity. Why does he think this? Because he knows that wanting proper compensation is perfectly legal for God's ministers. Indeed, God's Word says, "Do not muzzle the ox while it is treading out the grain" and "The worker deserves his wages" (1 Timothy 5:18). Obviously, providing for yourself and your family is important. However, since Mr. Money-love wants to argue legal issues, we could remind him of the commandment upon which all the Law rests—"Love the Lord your God with all your heart and with all your soul and with all your mind" (Matthew 22:37). This leaves no space for secretly harbored idols.

Next, Mr. Money-love thinks that despite this minister's greedy underlying motives, he better fulfills God's purposes now that he is a more effective minister. Again the end justifies the means; the good results sanction the motives. Notwithstanding, wherever service for God improves solely for motives of personal gain, that service is seriously flawed. No matter what their pretensions, these ministers cannot truly serve God. They may say they love, trust in, and worship him, but in reality theirs is another hope, another allegiance, and another lord. How, then, can they bear anything but imperfect fruit?

Truly wise ministers know that they "cannot serve both God and Money" (Luke 16:13). This would be like trying to take orders from two conflicting commanders. Once God's servants displace their affection for Christ, they soon neglect their orders and abandon his service.

Avid study of the Scriptures and keen ability to teach should not be confused with true godliness. Many gifted Christian leaders and teachers have strayed from a sincere devotion to Christ without even noticing. Are you certain you love and serve one Master? Let us examine our motives and be careful that our service for Christ is first and foremost for his gain and glory, not for our own.

Scripture: Proverbs 30:8; Hebrews 13:5; Malachi 2:2

Prayer: Dear Lord, please help us to renounce the temptations to love money. Let us love and serve you with all our hearts. Purify my heart. Amen.

"Third, his accommodation to the dissenting opinions of his people by yielding some of his principles in order to serve them will exemplify a self-denying spirit and a gentle yet winning demeanor. Thus he will demonstrate that he is all the more fit to fulfill the obligations of ministry.

"Fourth, I will conclude by saying that a minister who exchanges a little for much should not be judged as covetous for doing so. Rather, since he has improved his lot in life and, in so doing, has also improved his level of competence in his work, then let him be viewed as one who diligently pursues his calling and makes the most of every opportunity that has been given him to do good."

Mr. Money-love continues to champion the cause of his hypothetical minister. Besides studying harder and applying himself to become a better preacher, this minister learns the art of diplomacy. Of course this is a helpful skill for anyone in ministry. Knowing how to accommodate others in nonessential matters for the sake of unity is important. Yielding sometimes, knowing that your perspective may not always be the best one, carries with it a certain element of wisdom. Surely the admonition to "be subject to one another out of reverence for Christ" (Ephesians 5:21 NRSV) includes ministers. A successful ministry depends upon diplomacy.

This man's *savoir-faire*, however, is a sellout. He cares little about what is best for God's kingdom or his people. The love of money steers his ministry. Thus his accommodating manner arises from selfish ambition. He playacts to impress; his winsome demeanor is mere window dressing.

Mr. Money-love believes we should push motives aside when evaluating this man's life and accomplishments. He believes this man's people-pleasing false motives have actually brought a better result for himself, his flock, and God's kingdom. Observe, however, the apostle Paul's heart, as he says, "For what we preach is not ourselves, but Jesus Christ as Lord, with ourselves as your servants for Jesus' sake" (2 Corinthians 4:5 RSV). God's servants never violate their call by preaching to impress their listeners so they can amass wealth to themselves. They trust God to provide their needs and preach as grateful servants *for Jesus' sake*. Their supreme mission in life is to glorify their awesome Lord and King.

Shouldn't we pray for this kind of selfless freedom? Shouldn't we support those who sincerely and sacrificially labor to exalt Christ alone? Shouldn't we seek to emulate them? Let your answer be yes.

Scripture: Galatians 1:10; 1 Thessalonians 2:4; 2 Timothy 3:10

Prayer: Lord, I do not want to impress others with my spiritual savvy. Rather, I want to impress them with your greatness in my life. Help me to possess the freedom that comes from purity of heart. Amen.

"And now to the second part of the question, concerning the businessman you mentioned. Let's suppose his business has been meager in this world, but by becoming religious, his market may improve dramatically. He may be able to get a rich wife or more numerous and perhaps wealthier customers. I am of the opinion that there is no reason why this could not be legitimately done, and this is why: First, to become religious is commendable, regardless of the means by which a person does so. Second, there is nothing wrong with getting a rich wife or more and better customers. Another way of looking at it is that the one who receives these blessings by becoming religious gets good things from good people by becoming good himself. So here we have a good wife, good customers, and a good livelihood—all by becoming religious—and that is good! My conclusion, then, is that it is a very good and profitable objective to become a devout person for receiving all these benefits."

Mr. Money-love now goes on to offer his rationalizations concerning a greedy businessman. This man belongs in the greedy minister's church since they share so much in common! His business efforts bring him little return until he decides to go to church to meet a wealthy wife and clients. This seems good to Mr. Money-love because the man is now a good religious man with good customers, a good wife, and a good financial bottom line. Since everything is so good, what can possibly be bad?

Where, however, is God in this man's affairs? His sudden turn to religion, while commendable in people's eyes, can bring no commendation from God. For he has not humbly turned from his sins and offered his future to God. He shows no heart for God. Instead, he uses God in much the same way the merchants and money-changers of Jesus' day did in the temple. God's house became a place of business transactions rather than of worship.

Now that everything is so "good" in this upstanding layman's life, we should ask him how he intends to invest his blessings. Will he invest them to magnify the Lord's name in the earth, to promote his Gospel, to expand his kingdom? Or will he spend it on himself, his ease, his honor, sacrificing a pittance for Christ's sake?

When we come to church humbly seeking to give our lives to God in worship rather than trying to solicit something from others, we may miss some advantages in the short run. Yet those who choose God over selfish gain will one day receive heavenly wealth beyond measure. Perhaps right now you can reexamine your reasons for attending church.

Scripture: Ezekiel 33:30-31; 1 Timothy 6:6; John 4:23-24

Prayer: Dear Lord, I do not want to use you or the church to my personal advantage. Please free my heart of every such impurity and let my worship be true. Amen.

DAY 214

Mr. Money-love's answer to Mr. By-ends's question was well received and highly applauded by all of his companions. They heartily endorsed all of his conclusions and thought them to be extremely insightful and profitable. The thought occurred to them that no one could refute these arguments. And because Christian and Hopeful were still within earshot, and because of their earlier opposition to Mr. By-ends, they all decided to catch up with Christian and Hopeful quickly so they could present the same question to them. So they called after the two until they stopped and waited for them.

Meanwhile, as they were walking to meet them, they decided that old Mr. Hold-the-world would pose the question to them instead of Mr. By-ends. They didn't want Christian and Hopeful's answer to be influenced by the heat of controversy kindled between them and Mr. By-ends at their earlier parting.

How wise these four think themselves! Although their arguments are as weak as water, they think them absolutely irrefutable. The men keep on building their theological houses on sand, completely unaware of the diseased condition of the foundation. Convinced that their position is right and that their spiritual state is good, they are unaware of the ditch they are about to slide into, a ditch of their own making.

Due to the "deceitfulness of riches," people who have become wealthy often think very highly of themselves. They think they are somehow more discerning, sounder in judgment, and more farsighted than those of modest means. Those who think themselves wise, however, should humble themselves, take an honest look at their hearts and acknowledge God. They should embrace the true Gospel, take up the cross of Christ, and follow him. Renouncing worldly wisdom and earthly security, they should learn to wholly rest and rely upon Christ and his eternal life.

Unfortunately the likelihood is stronger for convincing lost sinners of the error of their ways than for changing the minds of these four self-willed men. Their desire and commitment to money far outweigh their commitment to God and pursuit of spiritual maturity. Yet living for God is either a means toward other ends or an end in itself. Unless it is an end in itself, our faith is not genuine. True faith allows God to take hold of our lives and transform us.

What occupies more of your heart—God or money? It has been said that our checkbooks are theological documents that tell a lot about what we believe about God. If Jesus sat down with your checkbook, how would you feel—wise or foolish, sad or joyful? Our commitment to God often meets its match in money matters.

Scripture: 1 Corinthians 3:18; Luke 16:15; 1 Chronicles 29:16-18

Prayer: Dear Lord, help me to follow you, not the worldly wise who so easily deceive themselves. I submit my money to your will and pray that the Holy Spirit will occupy more of my heart. Amen.

D·A·Y
215

The group caught up with the two, and after a friendly greeting Mr. Hold-the-world posed the question to Christian and his friend, inviting them to answer it if they could.

This was Christian's reply: "Even a baby in the faith can answer ten thousand such questions. For if following Christ for loaves and fish is wrong—as it is—how much more an abomination it is to use Him and religion as a means to get and enjoy the world!"

❦

Christian is poised to undo the gentlemen's earthly wisdom with spiritual wisdom. Even a babe in the Lord instinctively knows not to follow Christ for selfish reasons. Christian refers to Christ's feeding of the five thousand with a few loaves and fish. Some of those who enjoyed the meal went out after the Lord in their boats, not because they were seeking spiritual truth, but because they wanted him to repeat the miracle for them. Their appetite for free bread so drove them that it mattered not to them that the Bread of Life stood among them offering them eternal sustenance for their souls. Because of their appetite, they could barely notice that the miracle they experienced meant their Prophet and Savior had appeared. All they could remember by the next day was that their stomachs were growling again. This drowned out all the Lord's gracious teaching; it kept them from thinking of the honor and glory due him, and it kept them from considering the enrichment he could provide their immortal souls. All that mattered to them was that he could fill their bellies.

Far worse, says Christian, are money-hungry Mr. By-ends and his friends. Theirs is not just a desire to satisfy physical hunger, but an insatiable appetite for wealth that spurs them to continually crave more and more. Far from being a mere matter of loaves and fish, it is the practice of using Christ and his church to amass worldly riches to satisfy their greed. As Christ minced no words with the money-loving Pharisees, Christian confronts these hypocrites.

You might ask yourself: Do I tend to look more at the loaves and fish or more at the Miracle Worker? Do I seek first the gift or the Giver? Do I lustfully crave worldly advantage or wisely renounce its temptations? Be careful not to let your soul go hungry while you are busy seeking fleeting earthly gain.

❦

Scripture: Isaiah 55:1-3; John 6:26-27; Proverbs 28:11

Prayer: Precious Lord, you mean more to me than any miracles, any gifts, any benefits, any gain I could receive from you. I never want to lose sight of you. Help me always to feast upon your living bread and drink from your living water. Amen.

D·A·Y
216

"Only pagans, hypocrites, devils, witches, and sorcerers are of such an opinion. Let me explain: First, let me tell you about pagans. Hamor and Shechem wanted Jacob's daughter and his cattle as well, but they saw that there was no way for obtaining them except by being circumcised. They told their friends, 'If every male among us is circumcised as they are, won't all their cattle, money, and everything of theirs become ours?' In seeking to obtain daughters and cattle, they used religion as a pretense to get what they wanted. You can read the whole story."

Mr. Hold-the-world had earlier conveniently cited the examples of some Old Testament notables—namely Abraham, Solomon, and Job. So Christian begins with a stinging rebuttal from the Old Testament story of the Shechemites.

When Jacob and his family camped within sight of the city of Shechem in Canaan, a young man named Shechem abducted and raped Jacob's daughter Dinah. Jacob's sons, in a furious rage, negotiated with Hamor, the young man's father, an agreement to allow Shechem and Dinah to marry. Hamor invited Jacob's sons to intermarry with them and to live, trade, and acquire property in their land. Jacob's sons, however, would never violate their covenant with God by intermarrying with uncircumcised people. Because circumcision sealed the covenant, they told the men they would allow the marriage if all the men in Shechem were circumcised.

Jacob was very wealthy by this time, and when Hamor went to the men of the city to encourage them to submit to circumcision, he exposed his greedy motives. He told them that if they all live together harmoniously as one people, it would be to their financial advantage since Jacob's wealth would also become theirs. Unfortunately for them, two of Jacob's sons took revenge and killed them all before they could gain anything from Jacob.

Jesus said that the pagans (those outside the faith) spend their lives on worldly concerns but that we, as his followers, should busy ourselves with seeking his kingdom and righteousness. We can trust our provision to our loving heavenly Father who knows better than we do what we need. Hamor's plan for gaining more wealth through submitting to a religious observance backfired, and so will Mr. Hold-the-world's. Do you habitually spend more time investing in "pagan" concerns or kingdom concerns? Can you trust God to provide for your needs?

Scripture: Genesis 34; Matthew 6:31-33; 2 Chronicles 1:11-12

Prayer: Dear Lord, please protect me from thinking I need to strive and maneuver for financial well-being. Help me instead to entrust my life into your care, remembering that you know what is best for me. Amen.

DAY 217

"Then there are the hypocritical Pharisees. They were of this same faith. Long, impressive prayers were their pretense, but their intent was to cheat widows out of their houses. God will judge them with greater damnation."

Now in answer to the question of whether a person can become religious for financial gain and still be justified, Christian moves to the New Testament. He begins his argument by citing the example of the Pharisees. These men were of a dominant Jewish religious party that shaped Judaism at the time of Christ. They had little use for the Lord, reacting angrily at much of his teaching. Jesus had many run-ins with the Pharisees during his ministry, and he served up some of his most scathing "Woe-to-you" rebukes to them.

The implication of Scripture is that some members of the Pharisee party took advantage of widows by convincing them that it was in their best interest to sell their houses and give them the money. While they cheated these poor widows, they made prolonged unctuous prayers as if they were very holy. It may have been that they made these long prayers for the widows in exchange for their substance. If this is the case, these Pharisees, like huntsmen hiding behind their horses while stalking their game, used their devout religiosity to cover their avarice. Such oppression directly opposes God's expressed will to care for widows and orphans.

These hypocrites will receive "greater damnation" than open sinners because of their voracious appetites for wealth, their greedy cheating, their hypocritical use of religion as a cover, and for rejecting Christ's calling them to account for their injustice. Because people held them in high honor, the Pharisees felt safe and secure in their wealth and greed. Yet the Lord saw through the pious image straight into their wicked hearts.

Today those who lust for more power, money, and status are no more hidden. When we step on others to "get ahead," act piously for the sake of gaining some material advantage, or find ourselves sacrificing our personal integrity, we need to seriously repent. Jesus Christ has no kinder words for scheming hypocrites in our day than he did back in first-century Jerusalem. Ask the Lord to show you areas of pharisaism in your own life and in that of your church or ministry. Are there instances when you have sought your own advantage at others' expense? Conversely, how often have you sought to enrich others at your own expense?

Scripture: Matthew 23:14; Luke 16:14; 20:47; Isaiah 56:11

Prayer: Dear Lord, please deliver your church from those who hypocritically abuse their privileges for gain. Open our eyes and give us the will to remove greed from our midst. Amen.

D·A·Y 218

"Third, there are the devils of which Judas was one; he was also of this religion. He was religious so that he could carry the common purse, hoping that he might possess what was inside. But he was lost, cast off, the very son of perdition."

❧

Judas, one of the Lord's closest associates, used religion for financial gain. Perhaps his desire for money began long before he betrayed Jesus for thirty pieces of silver. He may have had mixed motives to begin with, thinking that Jesus was on his way to becoming rich and powerful and that, as a disciple, Judas was, too. During the years of itinerant ministry, he was the one who volunteered to hold the purse in which were kept donations for the needs of Christ and his band of followers. The apostle John called him a thief who regularly helped himself to the till.

When Mary, Lazarus's sister, poured a pint of expensive perfume on Jesus' feet, Judas was there objecting. He thought she had wasted it and that they should have given it to the poor. "It was worth a year's wages!" he barked. Jesus flatly told Judas to leave her alone. Judas did not really care about the poor; he cared about himself. Perhaps this incident finally brought it home to Judas that Jesus would never meet his expectations for wealth and power. He didn't care about money—he never had and never would. Jesus would remain poor, and so would he.

So Judas decided to cut his losses, jump ship, and get what he could out of his three-year investment. His secret sin finally found him out on the evening Satan entered his heart. He stole over to the enemy camp and betrayed the Son of God with a kiss. For what? A lousy handful of silver coins. Later Judas was stricken with remorse and hanged himself.

Money has great power to lead us into tragic paths we never dreamed possible. When we allow money to displace God in our hearts, we begin serving it. It can so control our lives that it harms others and destroys our relationship with God. It can prove a very cruel master. Christ, on the other hand, is a loving Master who grants peace of mind and eternal life when we put him first. He deserves our highest loyalty. Unlike Judas, Mary lovingly gave the best she had to Jesus. How can you be more like Mary?

❧

Scripture: John 12:3-6; 13:27-30; Matthew 26:10-16

Prayer: Lord Jesus, I see the danger in loving money more than I love you. Help me to assess my heart's condition with all honesty and to give you my wholehearted devotion. Amen.

D·A·Y 219

"Then, fourth, are the witches and sorcerers. Simon was of this religion, for he desired to receive the Holy Spirit only for the money he hoped to gain with His power. Peter sentenced him accordingly."

Offering money to buy religious pardons, power, and position is called *simony*, after a Samaritan man who tried to use religion for his own advantage. This man called Simon Magus—for he was a magician—so allured the Samaritans with his magic arts and sorceries that they were wholly addicted to him. He used enchantments and divinations as had Balaam and the magicians of Egypt. He so astounded princes and peasants, educated and uneducated alike, with his feats that they considered him a divine person or perhaps even the Messiah. They said of him, "This man is the great power of God!"

Then Philip came into town with the Gospel of the true Messiah, backing his claims with manifestations of God's power. How awesome is God's grace! The entire city converted to Christ, and Simon, accustomed to power, stood amazed. What he witnessed was far more dramatic and real than anything he had ever done. As a result, he professed belief in Christ and got baptized. Staying close to Philip, the man with the miracles, he seemed like such a devoted disciple.

The secret ambition of Simon's heart, however, was soon flushed out. He did not care about growing in Christian character. His eyes were on the external manifestations—the fact that the Holy Spirit was given through the laying on of hands, that people began prophesying, speaking in tongues, working miracles, and healing diseases. He coveted this power for the wealth and prestige he might gain from it. Thinking, "Everything has its price," he tried to purchase the Holy Spirit's power from the apostles so he could then resell it for a profit as people would hungrily flock after him. His proposal appalled Peter, who immediately exploded, "May your money perish with you!"

Simon had cheapened the grace of God and proved himself in violation of true saving faith. His motives were wrong for coming to Christ, wrong for following Christ. When tempted to merchandise the Gospel, can you unhesitatingly show that God's favor is not up for sale?

Scripture: Acts 8:4-23; Psalm 119:36; Matthew 10:7-9

Prayer: Lord, some people follow you for wrong reasons. I want to follow you for right ones. Please anoint me with the power of your Holy Spirit for your glory, not my own. Amen.

D·A·Y
220

"Fifth, I cannot help but believe that the person who takes up religion in order to gain the world will also throw it away just as quickly to gain the world. Judas, for example, hoped to gain the world by embracing the faith, but he subsequently sold his faith—as well as his Master—for the same purpose. Therefore, to answer this question affirmatively, as I perceive you have done, and to say that such a motive can be viewed as acceptable and authentic faith, seems to me to be pagan, hypocritical and devilish. If you adhere to this position, your reward will be according to your works."

Christian warns the four greedy gentlemen that they must repent of their pagan, hypocritical, devilish doctrine. With this, he rests his case against them, and it is up to them to respond.

In observing this assortment of professed believers, we note that while all made "decisions for Christ," not all were "converted to Christ." Christian and Hopeful look back on their former principles and conduct with shame and disgust. Seeking salvation, they also aim to glorify God. They follow the Lord no matter what troubles beset them. The other men, however, excuse their sins, citing God's grace and their liberty. They profess faith to win friends, customers, or applause. Renouncing nothing, they hope to gain everything. They are fair-weather friends to Christ, who will conceal or deny their faith when they experience the least bit of discomfort.

The gospel of hypocrites is one of cheap grace, false mercy, and artificial salvation. It excuses sin away, saying things such as, "In their own way, they are living for God," "They simply need a clearer understanding of the truth," "Judge not," "Jesus understands and forgives." This gospel reduces God to a friendly adviser, strips the cross of its power, ignores the heart's depravity, and doesn't challenge it to repent. Yet the true Gospel of grace is costly. It deems sin so serious that it cost Christ his life. If he hadn't suffered the death penalty for us, we would never be forgiven.

God's love is unconditional in that he extends it to all people without distinction. He sets conditions, however, upon individual commitments. His love demands wholehearted repentance and committal of our lives to God. It requires faith, discipleship, and stewardship. Unfortunately, the modern church, largely set within a narcissistic culture that no longer believes in sin, is greatly imperiled with the false gospel and false conversions. Think about the changes Christ has brought to your life. Since making your decision for him, have you literally allowed his Gospel to transform your life?

Scripture: Galatians 1:6-7; Revelation 3:18; Romans 12:2

Prayer: Dear Lord, I embrace your Gospel of grace that calls me to a life accountable to you. I submit my life to your transforming power. Amen.

D·A·Y 221

At this, they just stood staring at each other! No one knew how to answer Christian, so there was a prolonged silence between them. Hopeful was pleased with the soundness of Christian's reply, but Mr. By-ends and his friends lagged behind in order to keep a good distance between Christian and Hopeful and themselves. Christian said to his brother, "If these men cannot stand before mere mortals, how will they stand before God? And if mere earthen vessels silence them, what will they do when the One whose tongue is a consuming fire rebukes them?"

After posing what they considered an unanswerable question, Christian leaves the four men dumbfounded. Undeniably, God uses the lowly to stop the mouths of the wise. It happened just as Christian said: "Even a baby in the faith can answer ten thousand such questions."

The resulting prolonged silence is the silence of spiritual conviction. Now that truth has pierced their deception, they should honestly take stock of their condition. They should realize their false perspective, the sad stains on their character, the foolishness of their pursuits. They should be frightened at being linked with Shechemites, Pharisees, Judas Iscariot, and Simon the Sorcerer. They should admit their crazed desire for worldly mammon.

Yet look what happens! Instead of repenting, they withdraw like the Jews who quietly slunk away after Jesus showed them they had not stumped him after all with the woman caught in adultery. The Jews' tactic backfired in their own faces.

Christian wonders how these men hope to stand before God with their shallow arguments if they cannot even stand before him. The men should heed Job who said of God, "If one wished to contend with him, one could not answer him once in a thousand" (Job 9:3 NRSV). Jesus told a parable about another man who stood in stunned silence. After sneaking into a wedding feast, he was asked why he wore no wedding clothes. He said nothing in his defense. Everyone could see that he had not properly prepared himself for the wedding. Like this man, the four hypocrites will be as silent at the judgment as they are right now.

Our natural pride makes it hard for us to look at our false motives. Nevertheless, when we are confronted with our sins, instead of withdrawing in silence, we should take the opportunity God affords us to repent and be rid of them. This is by far the best choice. Do you have previously self-justified and glossed-over sins that you need to repent of right now?

Scripture: Isaiah 30:27-30; 1 Corinthians 1:27-29; Matthew 22:11-12

Prayer: Dear Lord, I confess that I don't like to take correction. Yet I want to yield my sins to you right now as you reveal them. Please forgive and cleanse me from every hidden sin. Amen.

D·A·Y 222

Christian and Hopeful continued on their way until they came to a lovely plain called Ease. They were very happy to travel there, but the plain was small, and they passed through it quickly. At the far side of the plain was a little hill called Lucre, and in that Hill was a Silver-mine. Some of those who had gone that way had previously been attracted by the mine's uniqueness and had turned aside for a better view. Having gone too near the edge of the pit, however, the ground underneath them was deceptively untrustworthy, and it had given way. Some had fallen to their deaths, while others had been maimed for life.

The Lord provides the plain of Ease to balance the hardships of the Way with some pleasure. Pilgrims come through this season of outward peace and well-being quickly because God does not provide too much ease. Nevertheless, it affords enough time for those who become unwary in their relaxed state an opportunity to sightsee at Lucre. From the Latin, this word means "illicit gain." Inside Lucre is a silver mine that has lured many into incapacitating accidents and even death.

Lucre's attraction is no recent development. Samuel's sons, Joel and Abijah, while judges in Israel "turned aside after lucre" (1 Samuel 8:3 KJV). Delilah betrayed Samson for 1,100 pieces of silver. (See Judges 16:5, 18.) Except for Esther's intervention, the Jewish nation would have been annihilated after Haman's bribe of ten thousand pieces of silver to King Ahasuerus. (See Esther 3:8-9.) Lucre also caused trouble for the early church as false teachers led whole households astray for filthy lucre (Titus 1:11 KJV). Christian leaders were strongly urged to avoid the destructive influence of "filthy lucre" (1 Timothy 3:3, 8 KJV). Paul tells us that those who pursue wealth "fall into temptation and are trapped by many senseless and harmful desires that plunge people into ruin and destruction" (1 Timothy 6:9 NRSV).

During times of persecution or other difficulties, lucre can seem so out of reach as to nearly lose its attraction. In times of ease, however, pilgrims are presented with greater opportunities for gaining worldly riches and are therefore much more susceptible. How many would-be missionaries never make it to the field because they are sidetracked by the lure of material things? How many missionaries on furlough lose their vision for the field, trading their mission for material comfort?

God gives us times of ease in our lives, for recharging our enthusiasm for our pilgrimage. In our enjoyment of them, let us not be carelessly lured into covetous pursuits. Is anything sidetracking you from fully embracing God's call upon your life?

Scripture: 2 Peter 2:14-15; Jude 11; Psalm 32:10

Prayer: Dear Lord, thank you for the easy times you provide along my way. Help me to use those times to press in to know you instead of wandering over to more lucrative ventures. Amen.

D·A·Y 223

Then I saw in my dream that a little way off the road, close by the Silver-mine, a distinguished-looking man named Demas stood ready to call travelers to come and take a look. He called to Christian and Hopeful, "Hello, there! Turn aside over here. I have something to show you."

"What is so important that it warrants our going off the Way to see it?" Christian replied.

"This is a Silver-mine, and some are digging in it for treasure. If you come, with a little effort you can provide richly for yourselves."

"Let's go see," said Hopeful.

"Not I," said Christian. "I have heard of this place before and of the many who have died there. Besides, that treasure is a snare to those who seek it, for it hinders them in their pilgrimage."

Then Christian called to Demas, "Isn't this place dangerous? Hasn't it hindered many in their pilgrimage?"

"Not really," Demas replied. "It's only dangerous to those who are careless." But he blushed as he spoke.

Temptations from without are powerless unless a corresponding desire exists within. Hopeful resisted the persuasions of Mr. By-ends and his friends. But now he might blindly turn aside. Somehow this distinguished gentleman impresses him, and the short jaunt to where the treasure hunters are digging seems harmless enough. Wisely discerning a dangerous trap, Christian resists the temptation.

Because Lucre stands only a little off the path, going to the silver mine seems a minor departure to many. Satan, however, has baited his hook, and for the poor deluded souls who bite, it means death. The Lord allows this temptation to prove pilgrim hearts. Will they stay true or choose worldly treasures?

Demas reassures Christian that only the careless need be concerned. This sounds like the rationale of those who claim the Bible says nothing against money, only against loving it. They deceive themselves and confuse others as they amass wealth.

Most of us are vulnerable to such temptations. Simply observing the wealthy in their gorgeous homes and expensive cars may make us start coveting. We should remember, however, that while lucre appears fascinating and attractive, it never satisfies the soul. Mother Teresa told Billy Graham that she pitied Western Christians, so wealthy in material things yet so poor spiritually. Is worldly glitter becoming dull and unattractive to you? If so, you are on your way to true riches.

Scripture: Ecclesiastes 5:15; Matthew 6:19-22; Luke 16:11

Prayer: Dear Lord, I live in a culture filled with silver mines. Cleanse my heart and help me, by your grace, to keep to my pilgrimage. Amen.

D·A·Y
224

Then Christian said to Hopeful, "Let's keep on our way and not take even one step toward him."

"I agree with you, brother, but I'll just bet you that when By-ends comes here and receives the same invitation, he will go there to look."

"No doubt," said Christian, "for his principles lead him that way. A hundred to one that he dies there."

Then Demas called to them again, saying, "But won't you come over and take a look?"

So Christian bluntly answered, "Demas, you are an enemy of the righteousness of the Lord of this Way, and one of His Majesty's judges has already condemned you for your own turning aside. Why are you seeking to bring us under a similar condemnation? Besides, if we turn aside at all, our Lord the King will certainly hear about it. We would then stand before Him ashamed, whereas we could have stood before Him with full confidence."

Fortunately, Hopeful trusts Christian more than he does Demas or his own muddled instinct. He quickly agrees with Christian not to take even one step toward Demas.

Demas had been one of the apostle Paul's closest associates. He traveled with such kingdom notables as Mark and Luke. Paul closes his prison letter to the Colossian church with greetings from Luke and Demas. In his letter to Philemon, he closes with greetings from Epaphras, Mark, Aristarchus, Luke, and Demas. What a wonderful thing for this man to be so noted twice in God's Word. No doubt Demas had stood with Paul through his trying time in prison. He probably preached the Gospel, enduring abuse for the kingdom.

Yet Demas had a vulnerability. He deserted Paul, renounced his pilgrimage, and disgraced the Gospel. No doubt this caused Paul and the whole church great grief. What sad news Paul confided to Timothy as he said, "Demas, because he loved this world, has deserted me" (2 Timothy 4:10). If only he had remained faithful, his name would be immortalized as a dedicated Christian leader and a reliable companion to Paul. Instead, his name serves only as a perpetual warning for believers to beware of the potent enticements of this present world.

So what is your vulnerability? In times of temptation will you keep trusting God, or will you look to worldly securities? Would you stick with Paul or follow Demas?

Scripture: Philemon 23-24; Colossians 4:14; Matthew 24:12-13

Prayer: Dear Lord, the thought sobers me that once committed Christians can cave in to the allurements of this world. Help me always to lean hard upon your grace to keep me true to my pilgrimage. Amen.

Demas cried again, pleading with them to understand that he was also one of their brotherhood, and that if they would but stay a little while, he would walk with them.

"What is your name?" asked Christian. "Isn't it the same as I called you?"

"Yes, my name is Demas; I am a son of Abraham."

"Well, I know you; Gehazi, Elisha's servant, was your great-grandfather, and Judas was your father. You are walking in their footsteps. Your father hung as a traitor, and you deserve no better. Be assured that when we come to the King, we will inform him of your behavior." After this, they went on their way.

Demas promises to rejoin the pilgrimage, if only the pilgrims will join him for a while so he can finish with his first order of business. Christian responds by linking him to Gehazi who compromised his calling for money and to Judas who betrayed his Lord for thirty pieces of silver.

Gehazi had the honorable distinction of working with God's powerful prophet Elisha. He was there as the Shunammite's son rose from the dead and even gained an audience with the king of Israel. He lived day in and day out witnessing Elisha's power and character. Yet this did not prevent him from getting sidetracked and cashing in on his calling.

Gehazi's failure began with a miracle. Naaman, the powerful commander of his nation's army, journeyed to Israel to find healing for his leprosy. As Elisha commanded him, he dipped in the Jordan River seven times and was restored. Acknowledging that Israel's God was the true God, he wanted to give Elisha a monetary gift. Elisha refused to take any compensation for God's miracle, and Naaman left.

Gehazi, however, regretted rubbing shoulders with kings and commanders and remaining poor. Coming up with what he thought was a great idea, he ran after Naaman. Upon reaching him, he explained that Elisha had changed his mind and needed money after all. Naaman gave him two bags of silver. His covetousness, however, did not escape Elisha, who confronted him. As a result, Gehazi received Naaman's leprosy, finding out the hard way how off base his thinking had been.

So many have betrayed Christ and the Gospel because of greed. Has the allurement of riches deceived you in some way? When God should receive all glory, are you tempted to cash in? Money has an alluring power that can lead us away from God into sin. We should pray for a clean heart and right spirit, free of covetousness, ambition, and hypocrisy.

Scripture: 2 Kings 5:15-27; Haggai 2:8; Exodus 20:17

Prayer: Dear Lord, I see that covetousness has serious consequences. Show me any places where I betray my calling by coveting worldly goods for myself. Amen.

D·A·Y 226

By this time By-ends and his companions were again in sight. At Demas's first call, they went over. Now I am not certain whether they fell over the edge of the pit or whether they went down inside to dig, or whether the gases that commonly arise from the bottom asphyxiated them. One thing I observed, though, was that they were never again seen in the Way.

Then Christian sang a song:

"By-ends and silver-hearted Demas both agree;
One calls and the other runs, that he may likewise be
A sharer in his lucre, so promptly he'll also
Leave the Way for the world, and no farther go."

Now we see the dismal end of the four foolish money mongers as they run to worship their real god. How different was their orientation than that of the Lord Jesus Christ. God the Son already possessed unfathomable riches in his eternal kingdom. All power, glory, riches, and honor were his. When he came to earth, he came not to amass material wealth but to give us his heavenly riches. When offered by the devil the riches and power of the kingdoms of the world, he renounced them to be true to his Father's will and to himself. He gave everything up to seek and save lost humanity.

Wouldn't you think that the King of Kings would enter this world in the highest estate? Instead, he accepted the lowest estate and submitted himself to the trials of extreme poverty. He did this not only to humble himself as our example, but to show us the foolishness of seeking worldly wealth. In the light of the glorious estates awaiting us in heaven, he wants us not to be distracted by worldly riches.

Christ deems anyone who sets worldly prosperity for his goal as unfit to be his disciple. Unfortunately, many are deceived into thinking they have some divine right to worldly wealth. Christ tells us by word and example just the opposite. While many who are wealthy become Christians, they are to see themselves as stewards of what belongs to God. They are to spend their wealth according to his will, not in self-indulgent lifestyles. Jesus instructs us to store our treasures not on earth but in heaven by giving to the poor and to the mission of building his kingdom. For where we store our treasure discloses our heart's true loyalty. Which excites you more—soaring investments on Wall Street or soaring investments in God's heavenly storehouses?

Scripture: Matthew 6:24; 8:19-20; 2 Corinthians 8:9; 1 Timothy 6:10-11

Prayer: Oh, Lord, as your disciple, I am at your service. Help me to follow you and to invest in the heavenly revenues of glory, not in the fleeting treasures of this life. Amen.

D·A·Y 227

Now I saw that on the other side of this plain, just beyond the Silver-mine, the pilgrims came to a place where an old Monument stood along the roadside. Upon seeing it, they were both intrigued by its appearance. For apparently it had been a woman who was now transformed into the shape of a pillar. They stood there gazing at it, not knowing what to make of it. Eventually, Hopeful noticed some unusual writing above its head, but he could not make it out. After careful scrutiny, Christian could decipher these words: "Remember Lot's wife" [Luke 17:32]. They both concluded that this must have been the Pillar of Salt that Lot's wife had been turned into when, fleeing for safety, she had looked back upon Sodom with a covetous heart. It was an incredible sight.

"Oh, my brother," said Christian, "this is certainly a timely sight. Its appearance so suits the invitation Demas gave us to come over to view Lucre Hill. If we had gone over as he wanted us to—and as you, my brother, were inclined—we may well have turned out like this woman, a spectacle to all who come after."

Before destroying Sodom and Gomorrah, God rescued Lot, his wife, and two daughters. By his grace, he had two angels lead them by the hand away from their home in Sodom. The angels commanded the family to run for their lives and not to look back. Unfortunately, as fire fell from heaven on the cities, Lot's wife turned around to look. Evidently, this disobedience stemmed from an unwillingness to turn completely away from her old life. Though she had left Sodom physically, she had not left it spiritually. She had too much of her security tied up in Sodom, and her heart was divided. She looked back longingly and disobediently. Immediately she became a pillar of salt.

If Lot's wife merely yearned for the possessions and life she left behind in Sodom, what will be the end of those of us who, professing Christ, chronically chase worldly pursuits? What a dreadful warning Jesus gave—"Remember Lot's wife!" The immediate context of these words is Jesus' reference to his sudden second coming. He makes it clear that our hearts must not be attached to earthly possessions but to him alone. Are you ready for Christ to return? Are you pressing forward with your pilgrimage, setting your affections on Christ's interests? Are you willing to go wherever he wants to lead you? Or is your heart too entwined with the things of this present world?

Scripture: Genesis 19:15-26; Luke 9:62; 17:25-36

Prayer: Blessed Lord, help me not to look back wistfully when you call me to move forward. I give my life to you so that I can embrace the future you have planned for me. Amen.

D·A·Y
228

"I'm sorry I was so foolish," said Hopeful, "and it's a miracle that I'm not like Lot's wife now. For what is the difference between her sin and mine? She only looked back, but I had a desire to go and see. Let grace be cherished, and let me be ashamed that such a thing was ever in my heart."

"This lesson may be of future usefulness, Hopeful. Let's take note and not forget what we see here. This woman escaped one judgment—the judgment that fell on Sodom—yet she was destroyed by another. May we always remember this Pillar of Salt."

"Yes," Hopeful answered. "She should be both a caution and an example to us. A caution because we should shun her sin, and an example of the judgment that will overtake those who disregard the caution. Likewise, Korah, Dathan, and Abiram, along with two hundred and fifty others perished in their sin and became an example telling all to beware. But one thing I marvel at above all others is how Demas and his friends can so confidently look for that treasure when this woman, only looking behind her—we don't read that she stepped one foot out of the Way—was turned into a Pillar of Salt. The judgment that overtook her is an example within plain sight of them all, and they can't help but see her if they look up."

Lot's wife looked back at Sodom and was instantly struck dead. Rather than falling to the ground, however, she stood upright as a pillar of salt. Hopeful, unlike Demas, Mr. By-ends, and his friends, has a repentant, teachable spirit. Seeing the pillar humbles him. It strikes godly fear in both his and Christian's hearts.

About 2,000 years before Christ, God left the pillar of Lot's wife as a poignant example to his people. The Apocryphal book, Wisdom of Solomon, written around the time of Christ, speaks of "a pillar of salt standing as a monument to an unbelieving soul" (10:8). The Jewish historian Josephus (c. A.D. 37-100) claimed that it actually continued standing until his day and that he saw it. Early church fathers Irenaeus and Tertullian also spoke of its existence in their times.

Sometimes God provides signs to encourage and bless us, like the rainbow, for example. At times he also provides signs to warn us, like the pillar of salt. Some react at such "fear tactics." But God's warnings are not "tactics"; they are desperately needed warnings about real dangers that have eternal implications. Lot's wife standing as a pillar of salt is a warning to all generations: Do not allow possessions to possess you! Allow no idols in your heart! Love God above all else! Be ready to go when he says "Go!" Will you take his warnings to heart?

Scripture: 1 Corinthians 10:6-12;
Hebrews 4:11; Luke 12:15; Jonah 2:8

Prayer: Dear Lord, thank you for your warnings. Help me always to be ready to part with earthly securities so I can heed your call. Amen.

Christian added, "It is a mystery, and it goes to show that their hearts are in a desperate condition. I don't know whom best to compare them with—one who pickpockets in the judge's presence, or one who greedily grasps for more gain while on his way to being executed. It is said that those in Sodom were terrible sinners because they were sinners 'before the face of the Lord' [Genesis 19:13 KJV], that is, within His eyesight—and this in spite of all the kindness He had shown them, for the land around Sodom at that time was like the Garden of Eden. This provoked the Lord even more to jealousy and caused their plague of fire from Heaven to be as hot as the Lord could make it. It must be concluded that those who sin in the sight of God, despite many examples to warn them to the contrary, will come under the severest judgments."

"You have doubtless spoken the truth," said Hopeful. "But what mercy God has shown us, that neither you nor especially I have made such an example of ourselves. Let us thank God right now and fear Him, and let us always remember Lot's wife."

How do you figure someone who steals in a judge's presence or covets more money on the way to his execution? How do you explain those who take no thought of Lot's wife or think the lessons of Scripture are meant for someone else? To Christian, such behavior stems from hearts in a "desperate condition." So bent are these folk on their own desires that they don't even notice the warnings, let alone heed them. They see only what they want to see.

So, too, did the people of Sodom act. God blessed them with a beautiful land, but they did not seek to honor or know him. Instead, they sinned grievously against him by continually throwing their sin in his face. They so recklessly hardened their hearts that he finally came upon them with burning wrath.

Why did they choose to sin continually "before the face of the Lord," the pilgrims wonder. In light of such perplexities, Hopeful can only thank God for his mercy toward them that they have been spared from being made a similar example. He has the proper perspective toward himself and toward God. We do not respond to God out of some inherent goodness in our hearts. Even our desire to respond to him is an act of God's grace for which we should continually give thanks. Can you thank God for his grace in preventing you from becoming a negative example and a warning to others?

Scripture: Genesis 13:10-13; 2 Peter 2:6-10; Romans 1:18-25

Prayer: Dear Lord, thank you for sparing me from calamity and mercifully enabling me to keep my heart true to my pilgrimage. I rely upon your grace to make my life a positive example for your sake. Amen.

DAY 230

Then I saw that they went on their way to a pleasant River, which King David called "the River of God" and which the apostle John called "the River of the Water of Life." Since their way went alongside its bank, Christian and Hopeful walked there with great delight. They drank from the pleasant water in the River, and it revitalized their weary spirits. In addition to this, there were green trees with all kinds of fruit lining the banks of the River. The leaves were edible and beneficial like medicine for the healing of various maladies.

When Abraham gave up the best choice of land to his nephew Lot, the Lord immediately blessed his victory with glorious promises. The pilgrims, in like manner, resisted indulging in Lucre, and now wonderful consolations follow. The "River of God" represents the everlasting love of God expressed through the Holy Spirit. All believers partake of the Spirit's divine influences in some measure, but there are times when he unveils his presence and shares his blessings in much fuller measure.

Christian and Hopeful now bend down and drink from this delightful river with its inexhaustible supply of living water. The pure, crystalline water refreshes and revives the drooping pilgrims. What love, life, peace, joy, energy they now feel! They are elated in the renewed knowledge of their redemption, forgiveness, adoption, regeneration, and calling. Experiencing afresh the power of their salvation and enjoying sweet fellowship with their God, they quickly forget the former pains and difficulties of their pilgrimage. Losing all sense of the guilt, sin, and demonic temptations they have struggled with, they wonder how they might have ever thought God had abandoned them.

Jesus said, "How much more will your Father in heaven give the Holy Spirit to those who ask him" (Luke 11:13). Do you need to be refreshed in the Holy Spirit? To be renewed in his love and joy and peace? To be charged up by his mighty power? To be restored in your spirit or healed in your body or soul? "If anyone is thirsty," Jesus said, "let him come to me and drink" (John 7:37). This includes you. Why not come to the river and enjoy his blessings right now?

Scripture: Psalms 36:7-8; 46:4; John 7:37-39; Revelation 22:1

Prayer: Dear Lord, thank you for your invitation to come and delight myself at your river of life. I surrender to your Holy Spirit's life and fullness. Please come now and fill me. I reach out and receive the blessings. Amen.

DAY 231

On both sides of the River were perpetually green meadows covered with lovely lilies. They lay down here and slept awhile because here they had found safety. When they awoke, they gathered some fruit to eat, and they drank again from the water of the River. Needing more rest, they once again lay down to sleep. They continued this routine for several days and nights, and they sang:

"See here how this crystal River does glide,
To comfort pilgrims by the Highway side.
The meadows are green with a fragrant smell,
Yielding refreshment, and they will soon tell
What pleasant fruit and leaves these trees do yield;
They will soon sell all to purchase this field."

When they were ready to go on (for they were not yet at their journey's end), they ate, drank, and set out once again.

In this time of refreshing the pilgrims forget former trials and prospects of future ones. Their hearts, stayed on the Lord and his grace, joyfully anticipate the glories to be revealed. They relish the deliciously green meadows where no fences keep them out and no warnings hamper their consciences.

Because of the peaceful confidence, the pilgrims feel secure in God's love—different from every kind of worldly security. They completely abandon themselves to the fair meadows. They alternately lie down to sleep, then awaken to eat and drink again. Feasting upon the blessings and promises of Christ, they find renewed hope. What satisfaction, what replenishment they enjoy; what safety, what security they feel in this quiet resting place. Ah, what a foretaste of their eternal rest.

This renewal experience follows the pilgrims' successful resistance of worldly temptations. These wondrous treasures and pleasures they would not have experienced had they followed the alluring riches of the world that offer only a counterfeit and fleeting joy and peace. Resisting the worldly culture's temptation in favor of the Holy Spirit's leading in our lives brings God's smile. We enjoy new discoveries of his love, fresh manna from his Word, and sweet consolations from his Spirit when we honor our commitment to him. Do you want this renewal? Keep to the pilgrim path, and it will shortly lead you to this place.

Scripture: Psalm 23:2; Ezekiel 34:13-14; Matthew 13:44

Prayer: Lord, please spark revival in my heart. You are my portion. I will sell all to purchase your field. Lead me into these sweet meadows. Amen.

DAY 232

Now I saw in my dream that they had not gone very far when the River and the Way parted for a time. This made them very sorry, yet they dared not go out of the Way. Now the Way from the River was rough, and because their feet were already sore from their travels, they became very discouraged. They continued to press on but began to wish for a better way. Before long they saw lying in front of them on the left side of the road a Meadow; it was called Bypath Meadow. Then Christian said to his brother, "If this Meadow lies alongside our way, let's go into it." He climbed up some steps that led over a fence so that he could take a good look. There he saw a path that lay parallel to the Way but was on the other side of the fence. "This is the way I want to go," he said, "because it will make our traveling much easier. Come on, Hopeful, let's go on over."

❧

Christian and Hopeful think trouble and danger are behind them, so they grow careless. They quickly learn, however, that even in the path of duty and supported by the Holy Spirit, trials keep coming. After reveling in the meadow, the two are suddenly caught off guard. This is not to say, of course, that we should never enjoy happy seasons of comfort and ease. The problem for the pilgrims does not lie in the good times they enjoyed but in their present mood. They are unhappy with keeping on the right Way now that it has led them away from the green pastures and refreshing waters. Their discontentment can only open a door to Satan.

Their feet have grown accustomed to the cool tender grass of the riverside. Returning to a colorless, rough, dry path of righteous perseverance quickly wearies and discourages them. When they should be reassuring themselves that they are on the Way, they are found caught up in their own desires. Pitying their feet, remembering the pleasant meadows, they hope for an easier way. Suddenly they see Bypath Meadow. Christian peeks over the fence and sees what he thinks is their solution. "I *wish* for a better way," has become "I *will* have a better way."

Troubles, sicknesses, and losses hit us all. Whatever the reason might be for God's way becoming difficult, it is best not to argue with it. The only thing that really matters is that it is the right Way, the safe Way, the biblical Way, and that our feet are blessed to be on it. Can you thank God for both the happy times and the difficult ones?

❧

Scripture: Numbers 21:4; 32:7-9; Hebrews 6:15; 12:7

Prayer: Dear Lord, thank you for the spiritual time-outs you provide for renewing my strength. Help me to remember, however, that I am still at war and must cautiously stick to your Way. Amen.

D·A·Y
233

"But what if the trail over there leads us out of the Way?" asked Hopeful.

"That's not likely. Look, doesn't it go alongside the Way?"

So Hopeful was persuaded by his friend and followed him over. Once they were inside, they found it was very easy on their feet. Soon they could see a man ahead of them walking the same path. His name was Vain-confidence. They called out to him and asked him where this way led. He replied, "To the Celestial Gate."

Christian turned to Hopeful and said, "See, didn't I tell you? Now you can be sure that we made the right decision."

So they followed, and he kept ahead of them. But soon night began to overtake them, and it grew so dark that they lost sight of the man. Vain-confidence, not being able to see the way clearly, fell into a deep pit. The owner of the grounds put it there on purpose to catch presumptuous fools, and there Vain-confidence would die. Now Christian and Hopeful both heard the man fall. They immediately called out to find out what had happened, but there was no answer, only a faint groaning.

It is probably not coincidental that this temptation comes immediately after an empowering and refreshing experience in the Holy Spirit. Jesus, too, was tempted after the Spirit came upon him at his baptism. Unlike Jesus, however, Christian trusts appearances rather than praying or relying upon Scripture. Wanting an easier way, he rejects Hopeful's concern and leads them both astray.

No one resisting God's path will escape a temptation to leave it. Satan knows right when to offer us the means for satisfying our sinful desires. Thus the way over the fence coincides with the pilgrims' desire for it. Nevertheless, it takes at least some special effort for the pilgrims to deny their consciences. To get into the bypath, they cannot simply cross over but must climb over.

Opportunities for escaping God's will have lined the entire Way. While these were not previously tempting, this latest alternative suddenly seems like God's provision. The pilgrims easily justify their sin by ascribing signs to it, subconsciously hoping to force God into the bypath with them.

Seeing a strong believer like Christian succumb to the temptation first to leave the Way and then presumptuously to rely upon "Vain-confidence" should cause us to be ever mindful of our desperate need for God's guidance and grace. We should guard our hearts from complaining about our hardships. A humble song of praise will serve us much better than will peering over fences into forbidden places. Have you any areas of discontentment that you need to turn over to God?

Scripture: Proverbs 16:17-18; Psalm 119:104, 128; Romans 12:9

Prayer: Dear Lord, I give you my dissatisfaction. Please steady my heart and keep me from looking for an easier way around your will. Amen.

DAY 234

"Where are we now?" cried Hopeful. Christian remained silent, fearing that he had led them both out of the Way. Then a dreadful storm came with rain, thunder, and lightning, and the water began rising quickly.

Hopeful groaned to himself, saying, "Oh, that I had kept on the Way!"

"But who could have thought that this path would have led us out of the Way?" Christian asked.

"From the very first I was afraid of it," replied Hopeful, "and that is why I gave a gentle caution. I would have spoken more forcefully, but you are older than I."

"My dear brother, please don't be offended with me," pleaded Christian. "I'm sorry I have brought you out of the Way and led you into such imminent danger. Please, brother, forgive me, for I didn't do it with an evil intent."

Now that Christian and Hopeful are in trouble, they see their error. They should have prayed earnestly for increased faith and patience instead of looking for an easier way. They should have sought direction from God instead of relying on their own wisdom and insight. Each wrong step led them farther away from God's will and brought more temptation and sin.

Unbelief, ingratitude, self-will, and presumption always bring painful consequences. The pilgrims followed a blind guide who died in a pit. Now, stripped of their boldness, they seem like two lost children who know they are in extreme danger. The path is cold, the adventure gone. They thought the right Way was discouraging, but look at them now as they cower in the dark chill of guilt and uncertainty.

Hopeful here learns a painful lesson in trust. He had trusted the example of his older and more spiritually mature companion. But now he realizes that it is a mistake to unreservedly trust any person other than Christ. Even the finest human leaders can make mistakes. The apostle Peter led Barnabas and others into a bypath when, among certain Jews, he refused to eat with Gentile believers, thus distorting the message of the Gospel. Being the younger believer, Hopeful saw Christian as a spiritual giant. Lacking confidence in his own perceptions, he violated his conscience and followed Christian into sin.

When we blindly follow others instead of learning to recognize our Shepherd's voice, we risk grave danger. We should know God ourselves and trust the wisdom of others only as it is consistent with biblical truth. Before making important decisions, do you make an adequate effort to find the Lord's will?

Scripture: Galatians 2:11-13; Psalm 118:8-9; Matthew 24:4-5

Prayer: Dear Lord, I know other believers can be important guides in confirming your will. Yet I realize I am ultimately accountable for my own soul. Help me to listen for your voice and obey your word. Amen.

"Take comfort, Christian, my brother, for I forgive you, and I believe that this will work out for our good."

"I'm glad I have such a merciful brother with me, but we must not stand here like this; let's try to go back again."

"But let me go first," said Hopeful.

"No, please let me go before you so that if there is any danger, I might come to it first since this is all my fault."

"No," replied Hopeful, "I cannot let you go first because your mind is troubled, and it might lead you astray again."

Then they heard a voice, and they were encouraged as they heard it say, "Let your hearts be toward the Highway; the same Way that you came, turn back to."

Hopeful reflects his nature as he forgives Christian and encourages him with his belief that, despite their foolhardy error, this predicament will somehow work for their good. He and Vain-confidence exhibit two diverse types of optimism. Hopeful has a genuine hope in God, and his conscience made him hesitate at going this way. Now that he sees his error, he remains humble and trusts God. Vain-confidence, on the other hand, trusted only in himself.

Hopeful, demonstrating genuine spiritual growth, quickly forgives his brother. Also he learns a lesson in balancing his gentle and hopeful nature with strength and discernment. No longer blindly following, he takes initiative and recognizes he is in better shape to lead at the moment than is Christian. The youthful believer is becoming a man.

Christian, on the other hand, is completely demoralized. He seems a mere shadow of the man he had been earlier as he argued with Hold-the-world and resisted all attempts by Demas to rob him of his victory. That so many people in life choose bypaths is tragic enough, but it is all the more gut-wrenching to find one like Christian fallen into such a state. Still, he has the desire to get back over to the right Way. The Holy Spirit, seeing the pilgrims' repentant hearts, does not condemn them but gently affirms their desire and encourages them to return to the King's Highway.

When we stumble and lose our way, let us not get into deeper trouble by trying to find our own solutions. We should instead resolve to return to where we made our departure and seek the Lord for full restoration. If you have veered out of God's will in some area of your life, how about returning right now?

Scripture: Romans 8:28; Isaiah 30:21; Jeremiah 31:21

Prayer: Dear Lord, grant me a heart that never strays from you. Nevertheless, thank you that even when I do stray, I can trust you to encourage me back to your Way. Amen.

DAY 236

But by this time the waters had risen greatly, which made going back very dangerous. (Then in my dream, I thought to myself that it is easier going out of the Way when we are in it than it is going in when we are out of it!)

Now the pilgrims seek to gratify the flesh,
But by seeking its ease, Oh! How they afresh
Find many new griefs they've plunged head on into.
Seek pleasing the flesh, and your life you'll undo.

So they ventured back, but it was so dark and the flood so high that they nearly drowned nine or ten times. Not only that, no matter how they tried, they couldn't get back that night to the steps that led over the wall. Finally they found a little shelter and decided to sit there until daybreak. Being very tired, however, they fell asleep.

After hearing the encouraging word to return to the King's Highway, you might think the pilgrims would quickly go back. Looking back to where they left the Way, however, is dangerous business. Seeing their ungrateful, rebellious hearts is traumatic for them. Their consciences bear such guilt and their souls such darkness that they nearly perish in a flash flood. The chasm between them and the pilgrim Way seems immeasurably widened and God unwilling to restore them. Every victory won and lesson learned seems forever washed away. They can barely keep their heads above the whelming flood, let alone gain back lost ground. And to think that so shortly before they were drinking from the tranquil waters of the River of Life!

Despite their resolve to return to the Way, recovering their former walk seems too difficult. Discouraged, they lose the heart and energy to keep fighting their way back. They don't recognize Satan, but he is there, making their situation appear hopelessly bleak and God inexorably ungracious. So they find a temporary solution—a little shelter just above water level. But shouldn't they stay up all night, if need be, crying out to God and fighting to get off this cursed ground?

Sometimes believers, having wandered into sinful bypaths, do some good deed to alleviate their conscience short of fully returning to Christ. Feeling less alarmed, resting until morning makes more sense than thrashing it out all night. Oh, but we should never rest content while still in the place of sin! Can you decide right now that the next time you sin, you will refuse to accept a temporary Band-Aid for your problem? Instead, will you press on into God's will until you are fully restored?

Scripture: Psalm 88:7, 17; Hebrews 12:5; 1 Thessalonians 5:17

Prayer: Dear Lord, if I should venture into a sinful bypath, I pray for the will to not rest until I am once again going securely in your Way. Amen.

DAY 237

Not far from the spot where they were sleeping was a castle called Doubting Castle. Its owner was Giant Despair, and it was on his property that they were sleeping. The Giant got up early the next morning, and walking up and down his grounds, he spotted Christian and Hopeful sleeping there. Then with a fierce, threatening voice, he woke them up and demanded where they had come from and what they were doing on his property. Christian and Hopeful answered shakily that they were pilgrims and that they had lost their way.

Then said the Giant, "You have committed an offense against me by trampling in and lying on my property last night. Therefore, you must come with me." So they had no choice but to go with him because he was much stronger than they.

God did not tell the pilgrims to stick around Bypath Meadow. Nevertheless, Christian and Hopeful decided to rest in the little shelter until morning. Better that, they reasoned, than to stay up all night fighting the ravaging flood. In so doing, however, they worsened their dilemma. What caused them to think they could put off dealing with their sinful condition? How could they think they would escape harm by resting away from Christ's path? Is there any safe place apart from him? When David fell into sin, he earnestly sought the Lord for mercy; when Jonah sinned, he cried desperately to him for restoration. Situations like this require special effort. How, then, can the pilgrims hope for restoration without wholehearted repentance, persevering prayer, and a commitment to obey all that God is calling them to do?

Foolish pilgrims! Just as the disciples lay down in the garden "exhausted from sorrow" on the night of Christ's betrayal, the pilgrims fall short in their opportunity to "watch and pray." They sleep, hoping everything will look better in the daylight. Yet daylight comes with no solace, only the enablement to see their sins more clearly. With their burden of sins immense, their situation is desperate. Before they can think straight, Giant Despair is upon them, telling them what they already know in their hearts—they are trespassing on the wrong soil. He seizes them and leads them farther from the path, deeper into darkness and confusion.

Can you think of times when you chose to ignore your sins? Didn't you find that this just added to your troubles? When the Lord calls us to repent, we had better immediately respond and not rest until we once again rest in his peace.

Scripture: Ephesians 5:13-17; Luke 11:1-8; 22:45-46

Prayer: Dear Lord, please help me never to allow myself to carelessly rest in forbidden territory. I want to avoid getting seized by spiritual enemies. Amen.

DAY 238

They also had little to say in their own defense since they knew they were guilty. The Giant forced them to walk in front of him until they reached the castle. There he threw them into a very dark dungeon, which the two men found disgustingly foul and smelly. They lay there from Wednesday morning until Saturday night without even a crumb of bread or drop of water; there was no light at all, and they had no one to ask what would become of them. They were, therefore, in a very evil situation, far from all friends and acquaintances. Christian felt doubly sorrowful because it was his ill-advised haste that had brought them into this distress.

Christian is no stranger to trouble: the frightful feelings in the City of Destruction, the consternation of the Slough of Despond, the horrors of Mount Sinai, the burden he carried to the cross, the panicky feelings as he clashed with Apollyon, the horrors of the Valley of the Shadow of Death, the nightmare of Vanity. All these had seriously tried him, but none prepared him for this present ordeal.

Despair, like an ugly giant, will eventually seize every unbeliever's soul, and Christian fears he is numbered with them. In fact, both pilgrims feel like doomed hypocrites. They feel the Giant has legal right to do with them as he will. After all, not only have they sinned, but they feel powerless to pray or even read the Scriptures. Thus they listlessly let the Giant march them into his Dungeon of Despair.

Getting into Doubting Castle is easy. Any conviction of sin without corresponding hope in Christ's mercy can immediately drive a soul there. Some come by pride and self-righteousness, suddenly realizing their own efforts and merits cannot justify them. Others come through some favorite sin or self-indulgence. Some come through spiritual sins, others through sensual ones. For some, unguarded sleepiness and coldness cast them here. Others have a more natural disposition toward melancholic feelings, of which Satan takes advantage. Distorted views of God's Word, speculations, or false doctrines lead many there. Still others, misunderstanding grace, are driven by fearful thoughts of judgment. Some come by conformity to the world, others by the cares and pressures of life. Most who come here have somehow neglected spiritual disciplines. Yet even spiritual disciplines may drive us here if we are not trusting Christ. How regrettable that so many ways exist for getting into this castle!

Have you noticed how easily "small" sins left to themselves give rise to huge spiritual dilemmas? You should let *nothing* separate you from your fellowship with Christ.

Scripture: Job 19:1-11; Psalm 143:3, 7; Romans 15:4

Prayer: Dear Lord, please keep me from falling into my own spiritual dungeon. Should I find myself in such a place, deliver me quickly. Amen.

D·A·Y 239

Now Giant Despair had a wife, and her name was Distrust. When the Giant went to bed, he told his wife that he had taken a couple of prisoners and cast them into the dungeon for trespassing on his grounds. Then he asked her what else he should do to them. She asked who they were, where they were from, and where they were going, and he told her. Then she advised him that first thing in the morning he should beat them unmercifully.*

So when he got up he took a wooden club and went down to the dungeon. Although they never said a word to provoke him, he started ridiculing and insulting them as if they were dogs. Then he beat them fiercely and mercilessly, and he so devastated them that they could do nothing to help themselves. They were unable even to roll over on the floor. When the Giant had finished his attack, he left them there to mourn and grieve in their misery and distress. That entire day was spent in nothing but sighing and bitter lamentations.

*Originally called *Diffidence*. In modern usage, the term primarily indicates one who lacks self-confidence, is shy or timid. The obsolete meaning, however, primarily indicated a distrust, suspicion, and lack of confidence in others. Thus we call her Distrust.

Oh, the distress these two servants of Christ feel. Until this misadventure, they carried themselves faithfully along the pilgrim Way. Only a short time ago they felt such joy and victory in the Holy Spirit that they thought they had almost reached heaven. Now they are stricken with passivity and paralyzed with fear. This powerful husband/wife team, Despair and Distrust, seem bent on destroying them. The pilgrims must feel somewhat like Paul when he despaired of life itself or when a "messenger from Satan" afflicted him after an abundance of revelations.

Yet the pilgrims know that, unlike Paul's situation, their despair does not proceed from walking in the center of God's will; their demonic oppressions and assaults are due solely to their own presumption and foolishness. No doubt they cry with David, "For I know my transgressions, and my sin is ever before me" (Psalm 51:3 NRSV). As with Adam and Eve, their sin results in "distrust" of God's compassionate grace and mercy. Their stricken consciences become completely unreceptive to God's grace, and they are horrendously assaulted by the "despair" they think they must bear.

Satan gains tremendous advantage over believers when we think we deserve his abuse. We must remember that when we turn to Christ, confessing and repenting of our sins, we can trust him to forgive and restore us, knowing that his grace will carry us through. Why not confess your sins and give your doubts and fears to God now?

Scripture: 2 Corinthians 1:8-9; 12:7-10; 1 John 3:21; Psalm 56:3

Prayer: Dear Lord, please help me to remember to trust—not distrust—your ability and willingness to restore me when Satan tries to drive me to despair. Amen.

D·A·Y 240

The next night, talking with her husband about them further and finding out that they were still alive, the Giant's wife further advised him to counsel them to kill themselves. So when morning came, he went to them in a fierce manner as before. Seeing that they were in pain from his beatings, he advised them that, since they were likely never to come out of that place, their only option would be to do away with themselves immediately. "I am leaving you a knife, a rope, and some poison; you choose which means of death you prefer. Why should you choose life, since it involves so much bitterness and pain?"

They begged and pleaded with him to let them go, but he only glared at them with frightening eyes; then he rushed at them again. He would doubtless have killed them himself, but he suddenly fell into one of his seizures, which he sometimes had in sunny weather. This caused him to lose the use of his hands for a time, so he once again left them to themselves. Then the two prisoners consulted between themselves about what they should do. Should they take the Giant's advice or not?

Distrust is the real power behind the throne of Doubting Castle. She has the brains and her husband the brawn. Although she does nothing to harm the pilgrims directly, she advises her husband. He always comes running to her because she knows exactly how to make the pilgrims doubt their Lord and their salvation.

The attacks of depression seem to hit the severest in the early morning hours, since that is when the Giant comes to beat his prisoners. As much as he wants to kill them, however, he cannot. For quite independently of either him or his prisoners, the sun comes out, causing him paralyzing seizures. These glimpses of the sun are like little rays of hope protecting the pilgrims from succumbing completely. Yet Giant Despair tries to convince them that their situation is so hopeless that they should enter into a suicide pact. He even offers them the means to carry it out.

Why, if the Lord so graciously provides sunny weather, doesn't he provide complete deliverance? Perhaps before this whole episode, the pilgrims viewed themselves as victorious champions, invincible in the face of spiritual attack. God shows them their vulnerability, providing them an opportunity to learn true humility and reliance upon him. Sometimes he allows severe trials, not so he can discover what is in our hearts, but so *we* can. Only then can we learn to deal with our doubt and unbelief and trust him for our deliverance.

The next time you go through severe trials, take note of the shards of sunlight God provides for your encouragement.

Scripture: Ecclesiastes 2:20; Habakkuk 1:2-4; Psalm 42:5-6

Prayer: Dear Lord, when despair comes to beat me down, I pray for sunny times so that I can gain a better glimpse of your reality. Amen.

"Oh, my brother," said Christian mournfully, "what shall we do? The life we are now living is miserable. As for me, I don't know whether it is best to live like this or to die on the spot. My soul would rather choose to die than to live, and the grave will be easier for me than this dungeon. Shall we live our lives in bondage to this Giant?"

"Indeed, our present condition is dreadful," replied Hopeful, "and death would be far more welcome to me than living like this for the rest of my life, but let us reconsider for a moment. The Lord of the Country to which we are traveling has commanded that we shall not murder anyone. How much more, then, are we forbidden to take this counsel and kill ourselves."

Christian, poisoned with despairing unbelief, sees only two options—life with despair or death by suicide. He wonders whether he and Hopeful should not just get it over with and take the Giant's advice. Fortunately, for Christian, he has Hopeful for company and not Job's wife who encouraged her husband to do away with himself.

Christian seems to experience everything intensely. His battles are never simple skirmishes, his conquests never light achievements, nor his mishaps minor setbacks. Now in this dungeon, where he neither sees nor feels any hope, he thinks the idea of suicide has much to be said for it. Hopeful, on the other hand, possesses inner springs of hope that stabilize him. Even in this depressed state, the thought of suicide is so far from his thinking that it startles him.

Hopeful begins to counter the dark mind-set of his friend. He begins by citing their accountability to God. According to the Ten Commandments, murder is impermissible. Killing yourself may even be the worst type of murder since it affords no opportunity for repentance. Many today condone and even encourage suicide in certain hopeless circumstances. But "with God all things are possible," so who can say that a believer's plight is ever totally and irredeemably hopeless? Further, on what basis do we justify playing God, terminating our lives, when God, the giver of life, is also the Judge to whom we are accountable?

Hopeful contends that taking one's own life denies God's authority and denigrates the intrinsic value of a human life. We, too, should always affirm the value of human life, including our own. We shouldn't allow the anti-life bent of our culture to sway us at all. Can you see how circumstances are never so bad that we should consider suicide? Think of ways that you can champion life.

Scripture: Exodus 20:13; 1 John 3:15; 1 Corinthians 6:19-20

Prayer: Dear Lord, if I become depressed and despairing, please remind me that my situation is never hopeless and that deliverance will come as I trust you. Help me to cultivate more hope in my life. Amen.

DAY 242

"Besides, he that kills another can only kill his body, but he who kills himself, kills his body and soul together. Furthermore, my brother, you speak of ease in the grave, but have you forgotten the Hell where all murderers will certainly go? 'You know that no murderer has eternal life in him' [1 John 3:15].

"Let us also remember that all authority does not lie in the hands of Giant Despair. As far as we know, others may have been taken by him and yet escaped out of his hand. Who knows but that the God who made the world may cause the Giant to die, or that at some point the Giant may forget to lock us in, or that he may shortly have another seizure and lose the use of all his limbs? And if this ever happens again, I am resolved to take courage like a man and try my utmost to get out from under his hand. I was a fool that I didn't try to do it before. So, my brother, let's be patient and endure for a while. The time may come that will give us a blessed freedom, but let's not be our own murderers."

With these words Hopeful stabilized Christian's mind. So they continued sitting together in the darkness in their sad and despondent condition.

Hopeful continues with more reasons against resorting to suicide. This Giant may kill their bodies, but he cannot touch their souls. Yet if they resort to killing themselves, they will kill body and soul. And killing your soul may well mean eternal death in hell with other murderers. This prospect is more terrifying than anything Despair can do.

Furthermore, God is greater than the Giant. Although the pilgrims are presently at Despair's mercy, he is a usurper with no ultimate authority. Hopeful challenges Despair's right to seize his life and inheritance. He also thinks it possible that others may have escaped the Giant's hand. The enemy always tries to make us think we are alone in our suffering, that no one has ever sinned as we have, and that no case could be more hopeless. Yet we will find encouragement in remembering that countless others endure and fight and come through similar battles victoriously.

Hopeful reminds his brother, too, that God may yet intervene for them. Because his mercy triumphs over judgment, he may open an opportunity for them to make their escape. All these thoughts settle Christian's mind. When your soul is depressed, list reasons for keeping your hope in God alive. Perhaps you can start a list of your blessings now to refer to in dark times.

Scripture: Psalms 42:11; 77:7-12; Habakkuk 3:2; James 2:13

Prayer: Dear Lord, if I begin feeling hopeless because of my circumstances, please remind me to keep holding on to hope for a better day. I know you will not leave me sitting in a shadowy dungeon for long. Amen.

Toward evening the Giant went down into the dungeon again to see if his prisoners had taken his advice. But when he came, he found that they were still alive—but barely. Because they had been given no food or water, and because of the wounds they had received when he beat them, they could do little more than breathe. Even so, upon seeing them alive, the Giant fell into a terrible rage, screaming that since they had disobeyed his counsel, it would be worse for them than if they had never been born.

They trembled greatly at this, and I think Christian even fainted; however, when he came to again, he and Hopeful renewed their discussion about the Giant's counsel, wondering whether taking it might not be best.

The tyrannical brute Giant Despair is bent on destroying all hope in the pilgrims. Both prisoners suffer almost to the point of death under his merciless hand. Still, they are alive, and where there is life, there remains hope. With the latest threats, however, despair almost completely conquers them.

The Giant likewise has many captives in our current society. Feeling the stress of end-time birth pangs, a culture of despair has emerged, evidenced by a rampant suicide problem. Paul Kennedy of Yale University says, "Far from (being) a stimulus to preventive actions, global trends are so large as to induce despair."[23] Instead of offering true hope for living, however, many advocate the suicide solution. While "Dr." Jack Kevorkian wants physician-assisted suicide legalized, heavy metal music groups with names such as Suicide Machines and Suicide Commandos can convince youth to go ahead and try it.

Every seventeen minutes an American dies from suicide—the ninth ranking cause of death in the country. Among older Americans it ranks fourteenth and among teenagers, third. Every year half a million Americans attempt suicide. A survey among Presbyterian young people revealed that 86 percent knew someone in their age group who had either attempted or committed suicide.[24] On one Indian reservation forty youths attempted suicide (six died) in a six-month period. Then there are examples of religious extremism—from 900 dead in Jonestown's People's Temple to 39 dead in San Diego's Heaven's Gate cult.

While so many consider the suicide solution, many more soothe themselves with false hopes. God's people, however, have true hope. We never need succumb to despair. Those of us who have avoided or survived Bypath Meadow and its hideous trials must offer true hope to those who so desperately need it. Can you think of someone to whom you can give some special encouragement?

Scripture: Job 6:11; 17:15; 1 Thessalonians 4:13; 2 Corinthians 1:3-4

Prayer: Lord, may I help others who suffer under giants of despair. Help us stop the tide of suicides and other forms of killing in our society. Amen.

Now Christian again seemed in favor of doing it, but Hopeful made his second appeal, saying, "My brother, don't you remember how brave you have been before? Apollyon could not crush you, nor could anything that you heard, saw, or felt in the Valley of the Shadow of Death. What hardship, terror, and consternation you have already gone through! And now are you just a bag of fears?

"You see that I'm in the dungeon with you, and I'm a far weaker man by nature than you are. This Giant has wounded me as well as you, and I have no bread or water either. I mourn without the light along with you, but let's exercise a little more patience. Remember how you stood tall at Vanity Fair; you weren't afraid of chains, the cage, or even of a bloody death. If only to avoid shame—which is not proper for a Christian to be found in—let's bear up under it patiently as well as we can."

Oh, the unbearable misery of an accusing conscience! Again self-destructive thoughts assail the pilgrims. Hopeful rebounds while Christian, it seems, draws near the very gates of hell. Again he is ready to do away with himself and seems more like the Interpreter's Man in the Iron Cage than the victorious Christian we once knew.

Perhaps Christian is the most deeply afflicted because he was the most eminent of the two and led them both into sin. In any case, Hopeful continues to spread hope even within the Dungeon of Despair. The last thing Christian now needs is harsh moralistic sermonizing. So Hopeful renews his gentle corrections. He calls to Christian's mind his former bravery, reminding him that he never dreamed of destroying himself while fighting Apollyon. Apollyon's best efforts could not defeat the stouthearted pilgrim. Then all the wicked forces that so terrorized him in the Valley of the Shadow of Death proved powerless against him. Even in Vanity awaiting a death sentence, he never entertained thoughts of suicide.

Hopeful also reminds him that he is with him. Both are suffering together, and a sorrow shared is a sorrow halved. He encourages Christian to exercise a little more patience in hopes that, just as God had seen him through other trials, he will see them through this one. At the least, if they must die, they should not disgrace themselves and their God by killing themselves.

We should be very patient with those who suffer under similar afflictions. We may try a quick fix, but they need hope, encouragement, and patient and loving support until they can find their way out of their dungeon. Can you commit to being more patient with those you know who are suffering?

Scripture: Job 17:11; 1 Thessalonians 5:14; Hebrews 10:23-25

Prayer: Dear Lord, help me to remind the distressed to remember the victories already seen, progress already made, and grace that is always sufficient for their failures. Amen.

DAY 245

It was nighttime again, and the Giant and his wife were in bed. She asked him if the prisoners had taken his counsel. He replied, "They are sturdy rascals; they choose to bear all the hardship rather than to do away with themselves."

Then she said, "Take them to the castleyard tomorrow and show them the bones and skulls of those we've already killed. Make them believe that before a week ends, you will tear them to pieces as you have done to those before them."

So when morning came, the Giant returned to them. As his wife had told him, he took them to the castleyard, showed them the bones, and said, "These once were pilgrims like you, and they trespassed in my grounds as you have done. When I thought it a fitting time, I tore them to pieces. Within ten days I will do the same to you, so get back down to your quarters and wait." With that he kicked and beat them all the way down to the dungeon. They lay there all day Saturday in a terrible state.

Despite the Giant's best efforts, the pilgrims hang on. Although drowning in unbelief and distress, they refuse to completely give up. Research shows that religious people are generally healthier individuals than the nonreligious. Numerous suicide studies conclusively show that people with religious faith are less likely to take their lives. Nevertheless, research also suggests it is very unhealthy for those holding strong religious convictions if they do not live according to them.[25] So it is with the pilgrims who are continually reminded that they chose Bypath Meadow and that Doubting Castle cannot even be seen from the King's Highway. Pathetic and broken, they fear they have so terribly failed God that they have little hope of ever escaping their misery.

Yet things are rarely as hopeless as they seem. The Scriptures spill over with examples of those who found themselves in utter despair. David flagrantly sinned, Asaph bewailed God's unjust treatment, Job was afflicted beyond comprehension, Elijah despaired at Jezebel's threats, Jonah wanted to die after God spared his enemies, Peter denied his Lord. Yet these were ultimately rescued. The despairing Philippian jailer nearly killed himself after the earthquake released Paul and Silas. Yet he chose life, and that night he and his entire family were eternally saved!

No matter how deep our pit, we should keep hanging on, hoping against hope for God's solution to our troubles. As Betsy ten Boom told her sister Corrie in the Nazi concentration camp, "There is no pit so deep that he is not deeper still." Will you, too, choose a hope-filled outlook?

Scripture: Psalm 142:7; Romans 4:18; 1 Peter 4:19

Prayer: Oh Lord, help me when I am down to gather strength from remembering those who, despite their woeful circumstance, saw ultimate victory. Amen.

D·A·Y
246

Now when night had come and Giant Despair and his wife, Distrust, had gone to bed, they renewed their discussion of the prisoners. The old Giant wondered why he couldn't bring the pilgrims to an end either by his blows or his counsel. His wife said, "I fear that they live in hopes that someone will come to set them free. Or maybe they hope to find a way to pick the lock and escape."

"Since you mention it, my dear, I will go down and search them in the morning," the Giant replied.

But it so happened that Saturday at about midnight the pilgrims began to pray and continued in prayer until almost daybreak. Then Christian, a short time before daylight, became astounded and passionately exclaimed, "What a fool I am! Here I lie in a stinking dungeon when I could be walking in complete liberty! I have a Key in my pocket called Promise that I am sure will open any lock in Doubting Castle."

"That's great news, my brother!" cried Hopeful. "Get it out right now and try it!"

God never withdrew his promises. The pilgrims simply forgot them or lost faith in them. Even when they did see glimpses of daylight, they could scarcely keep hoping because of overwhelming feelings of despair. Feelings can be treacherous, and trusting them can be our undoing.

The pilgrims' strength never came from feelings, but from an abiding trust in Christ. When they sinned and failed to come to the throne of grace, they began relying upon feelings. Thus feelings of isolation told them they were completely cut off from Christ, his Way, and his people. Decimating their faith, these horrid feelings made them lose hope. Although they tried, they could not regain their balance. It seemed too much to believe God would ever claim them back again.

At first when Moses came to Egypt to offer the children of Israel deliverance, they could not believe him. Their cruel bondage had conditioned them to feel hopeless. Yet God delivered them. Christian and Hopeful might stay in their dungeon forever, too, but for God's grace. God has allowed them to come to the end of themselves and motivated them to wrestle all night in prayer. Following this prayer, Christian stops listening to his own reason, and his faith is reborn. He remembers what was close to his heart all along—the Key of Promise.

God's promises are true, but until we get back into right relationship with Christ through faith, we will not experience them as a "yes" in our hearts. Are they a "yes" in your heart? Can you now reaffirm your faith in God's promises?

Scripture: Psalm 143:8-12; 2 Corinthians 1:20; 5:7; 2 Samuel 22:31

Prayer: Dear Lord, when I begin to rely upon my thoughts and feelings more than upon your promises, please restore me to a sound walk. Amen.

D·A·Y
247

So Christian pulled it out and went to the prison door. He put the Key in the lock and turned it, and the door flew open easily. Christian and Hopeful both stumbled out. Next they went to the outer door that leads into the castleyard, and Christian used his Key to open that door also. Finally they went to the iron gate and put the Key in that lock, and although it was extremely stubborn, it too opened. As they thrust open the gate, it made such a loud noise that it awakened Giant Despair, who hastily arose to pursue his prisoners. One of his seizures struck him, however, and his limbs failed so that there was no way he could go after them. Then they went on until they got to the King's Highway, and so, being out of the Giant's jurisdiction, they were safe once again.

It is Sunday, the Lord's Day, the day on which Jesus Christ broke out of the tomb providing release to all prisoners. Now Despair's two prisoners take a giant leap of faith, using God's promises in hopes of escaping. The key turns in the lock! The door flies open! Hallelujah! The pilgrims stagger out of the dungeon into the pure reviving air. The Key of Promise will open every other lock on the premises, too. Yet not every lock so easily gives way. The one to the outer gate is extremely difficult to turn because of the remaining doubts, unbelief, and guilt that stubbornly continue to resist God's promises. The pilgrims' backsliding has rusted this lock, but it too must open in compliance with the key's demand.

Through their suffering, the pilgrims have learned many valuable lessons that will stay with them until the day they die. What have they learned? That no matter what befalls them in the pilgrim Way, enduring it is better than departing from the Lord and his calling; that despite the attractiveness of the bypath, it will prove far more intolerable than the roughest place on the pilgrim Way; that they must walk much more cautiously without complaining over hardships; that walking in the light of God's presence is too dear to jeopardize; that they must trust themselves less and cast themselves more upon Christ; that sin is devastating, but God's grace is sufficient; that his promises are absolutely reliable. In every way the pilgrims are wiser for their experience. It may take some time, however, before they can say, "It was worth it all."

When we believe God's promises, we can expect miracles. Not only will prison doors swing open, but God will use our suffering for our ultimate good. Will you now take up one of God's promises and claim its provision for an area of defeat in your life?

Scripture: Isaiah 49:13-16; Mark 11:22-24; Romans 4:20-21; 2 Peter 1:4

Prayer: Dear Lord, thank you for your faithful promises that bring health and deliverance. I choose to believe them for my life. Amen.

DAY
248

Now after they had gone back over the steps they had originally come in on, they began to plan what they should do to prevent those who would come after them from falling into the hands of Giant Despair. So they agreed to build a Monument and engrave this sentence upon it: "Take these steps over the wall, and you will be on your way to Doubting Castle, which is kept by Giant Despair, who despises the King of the Celestial Country and seeks to destroy holy pilgrims."

Many, therefore, following them, read what they had written and escaped the danger. This done, they sang the following:

"Out of the Way we went, and then we found
What it was to tread upon forbidden ground;
So let them that come after please take care,
Lest heedlessness makes them, as we, to fare;
Lest they, for trespassing, his prisoners are
Whose Castle's Doubting, and whose name's Despair."

Christian and Hopeful wish their bitter experience upon no one. As soon as they get out of their enemy's jurisdiction and back into the safety of the Lord's blessed Highway, they begin to think about the safety of others. No longer ignorant of their enemy's devices, they understand full well the dangers of leaving the Way. Recognizing how Despair had robbed them of their hope and joy, they make a monument at the steps to warn others.

Fortunately, because of this compassionate act, many pilgrims who came behind the two successfully avoided the temptation. How important it is to be humble enough to listen and learn from one another the nuggets of truth and hope we glean not only from our victories but also from our mistakes and failures. God powerfully uses the testimonies both of our struggles through gloomy, despairing times and of his faithfulness to bring us back to a vibrant, restored faith.

Most believers at one time or another visit Doubting Castle. If you should somehow find yourself there, begin praising the Lord. This is another testimony in the making! Although the devil seeks your ruin, the Lord has life for you. His promises are the keys of faith that bring freedom from every dungeon of despair. Believe. Receive. And don't forget to point the way to hope and victory for others.

Scripture: John 10:10; 1 Corinthians 10:13; Ezekiel 3:21

Prayer: Lord, I offer this prayer in the words of an anonymous pen: "Dear Shepherd of Israel, thou knowest that to err is human. Keep us from erring; guide us continually; and when we do stray, O Lord, reclaim us."

D·A·Y
249

Christian and Hopeful went on their way until they came to the Delectable Mountains, which belong to the Lord of the Hill. So they went up to the Mountains to look at the gardens and orchards, the vineyards, and the fountains of water. They drank of the water and washed themselves in it, and they freely ate from the vineyards. Upon the mountaintops, close to the Highway, Shepherds were feeding their flocks.

The Mountains Delectable they now ascend,
Where Shepherds are, which to them do commend
Allurements and cautions; learn to keep clear;
Pilgrims are kept steady by faith and by fear.

How wonderful, how marvelous, how full and free is God's grace in Christ to the repentant! No sooner do the pilgrims escape the bypath and erect their monument than God balances their suffering with refreshment and joy. They find themselves at the Delectable Mountains, the same ones that Christian had viewed from afar much earlier in his pilgrimage.

God's servants all experience trials and testings. At times they make mistakes and suffer for it. But God is faithful to deliver them when they cry to him, and he is faithful to encourage, bless, and reinvigorate them after bringing them through the suffering and trials. In Psalm 40 David relates one of his "Delectable Mountain" experiences: "He (the Lord) lifted me out of the slimy pit. . . . he set my feet on a rock and gave me a firm place to stand. He put a new song in my mouth, a hymn of praise to our God" (vv. 2, 3). The apostle Paul, after two weeks of utter hopelessness in a storm at sea, suddenly appears encouraged and refreshed as he assures all those on the ship that they will live. How did he recover faith and hope? "Last night," he said, "an angel of the God whose I am and whom I serve stood beside me and said, 'Do not be afraid, Paul . . .'" (Acts 27:23-24). He, too, had been to the "Delectable Mountains."

Even Jesus, after being battered for forty days by Satan's temptations and assaults, was given a walk in the "Delectable Mountains." We are told, "Then the devil left him, and angels came and attended him" (Matthew 4:11). They encouraged his spirit and renewed his strength.

Are you in a period of testing or suffering? Remember God's faithfulness. As you cleave to him, he will deliver you, and more—he will comfort and encourage you as you walk together in his "Delectable Mountains."

Scripture: Isaiah 55:12; Ephesians 1:17-19; Colossians 1:9-12

Prayer: Dear Lord, thank you for bringing me through the hard times in my life. I know I can trust you for encouragement and refreshment when fiery trials sap my faith and strength. Amen.

D·A·Y 250

The pilgrims approached the Shepherds, and leaning upon their staffs (as is common with weary pilgrims when they stand to talk with any on the Way), they asked, "Whose Delectable Mountains are these, and whose sheep are you feeding?"

They replied, "These Mountains are Emmanuel's Land, and they are within sight of His City; the sheep are also His, and He laid down His life for them."

"Is this the Way to the Celestial City?" asked Christian.

"Yes, you are right on the Way."

"How far is it from here?"

"Indeed, too far for any but those who will get there."

"Is the Way safe, or is it dangerous?"

"It is safe for those for whom it is to be safe, 'but sinners trying it will fail'" [Hosea 14:9].

Leaning upon their staffs—that is, trusting God in anticipation of future blessing—the pilgrims ask about the mountains. They are told these are Emmanuel's Land and are within sight of the City. Emmanuel, the Lord Jesus Christ, is the great Shepherd who owns them. The sheep are his, too, because he ransomed them with his life. The under-shepherds who tend the sheep are pastors.

Christian observed these same mountains early in his pilgrimage from the Palace Beautiful. At that time they were but a distant vision. Nevertheless, detecting their lush beauty and bounteous fruitfulness greatly encouraged him. As one who would experience ups and downs in his walk on a near daily basis, every remembrance of this sight would renew his hope for the truly abundant life that Christ offers those who follow him. He could trust that faithfulness and perseverance in obedience to God would eventually produce the fruit of peace and joy and spiritual maturity. Now he has found it true—special blessings and consolations come with maturity. From this new vantage the pilgrims will look ahead with even greater assurance and anticipation toward Emmanuel's City, which may even be seen from here.

As we grow older, images of our heavenly home become far more prominent to us. Experiencing the depths of God's blessings and consolations as we mature in Christ, we get more intense glimpses of how wonderful heaven will be. These visions give us the inspiration we need for holding to our course, finishing the race, and keeping the faith. When you get discouraged, you can gather hope from thinking of the joyous seasons still ahead in your pilgrimage.

Scripture: Hebrews 11:8-10; Philippians 3:12-15; 2 Corinthians 3:18

Prayer: Dear Lord, how I thank you for your blessings and consolations. They give me a taste and a glimpse of how wonderful heaven will be. Amen.

D·A·Y

251

"Is there anywhere for weak and weary pilgrims to find rest and renewal?"

"The Lord of these Mountains has given us a charge that we 'not forget to entertain strangers.' Therefore, every good thing of this place is set before you."

The charge the Lord gave to these shepherds is the same one he gives to all his people, recorded in Hebrews 13:2 (NRSV): "Do not neglect to show hospitality to strangers." The Greek word used here, *philoxenia*, literally means "love to strangers." The Lord wants all who come to him to feel at home, so the shepherds make every traveler on their mountains feel welcome.

Hospitality is an essential ministry, not only on the Delectable Mountains, but also within the church at all levels. Respect should be shown to the members of our church community and even beyond them to the visitors and strangers. Both the unconverted people who are strangers to Christ and the saints who are strangers to this world need hospitality. As the shepherds offer "every good thing" their fellowship has—the love, acceptance, community, comfort, care, counseling, prayer, material resources—so should we. It is not an optional ministry to be ignored but a scriptural mandate. In the Old Testament God informed his people that because he loves strangers, they must also. (See Deuteronomy 10:18-19.) In the New Testament hospitality is listed before teaching as a responsibility for bishops. (See 1 Timothy 3:2.) Only widows who demonstrated hospitality qualified for receiving aid. (See 1 Timothy 5:10.) The entire church was to be "given to hospitality" (Romans 12:13 KJV).

Even the pagans of Malta showed "unusual kindness" to Paul and other shipwrecked prisoners (Acts 28:2, 7). How much more should we show love to strangers. Unfortunately, we often neglect this loving service today. We prefer to insulate ourselves in a comfortable cocoon that provides for *our* needs but leaves others out in the cold. Doug Erlandson says, "Beneath our excuses is a root cause. We are selfish. Hospitality requires giving ourselves to others."[26]

There are lonely, hurting people all around us who need a loving touch, a sense of belonging. Can you seek God for a welcoming heart? The Chief Shepherd takes this ministry very personally and will even use it to distinguish between sheep and goats on the day of judgment.

Scripture: Matthew 25:37-46; Job 31:19, 32; Isaiah 58:6-8

Prayer: Dear Lord, I see your heart toward strangers. Thank you that when I was a stranger, you invited me to your banqueting table. Help me to be hospitable to others. Amen.

D·A·Y 252

I also saw in my dream that when the Shepherds realized that the men were travelers, they questioned the pilgrims about where they were from, how they had gotten into the Way, and how they had persevered thus far. For only a few who begin on the Way are ever seen in these Mountains. When the Shepherds heard their answers, they were very pleased, and they looked upon the pilgrims with love and favor, saying, "Welcome to the Delectable Mountains."

The Shepherds, whose names were Knowledge, Experience, Watchful, and Sincere, took them by the hand, led them to their tents, and served them a meal. Then they said, "We would like you to stay here for a while that we might get better acquainted and also to allow you to gain more solace here on these Delectable Mountains." So the pilgrims agreed to stay, and they then went to bed because by this time it was quite late.

❦

These shepherds are pastors. In the New Testament, the Greek word for shepherd, *poimen*, is used metaphorically of Christian pastors. Like all shepherds, these four not only feed their flocks, but they tend them, too. Their names—Knowledge, Experience, Watchful, and Sincere—describe vital characteristics of a spiritual pastor.

When evaluating pastoral leaders, often the tendency is to focus more on charisma, eloquence, or credentials. Though these are important assets, a pastor proves sadly deficient without knowledge, experience, watchfulness, and sincerity. *Knowledge:* Do our pastors know God and his Word in a way that glorifies him and saves and nurtures souls? *Experience:* Have they experienced the transforming power of the Holy Spirit in their lives and applied the faithful promises of God's Word to their lives? Do they demonstrate a maturity in Christ that grows out of walking closely with him over a number of years? Does their ministry effectively bring their flock into spiritual victory? *Watchful:* Are they diligent to caution their flock against errors and snares that might defile and deceive them? Do they keep awake spiritually to guide and guard the flock from attack when others might slumber? *Sincerity:* Do they truly know that Christ has called them? Do they look out for Christ's interests, not their own? Do they sincerely love the flock God has given them? Will they care for the wounded and sick sheep and seek to find and recover the lost or trapped ones? Do they "practice what they preach," or do they simply enjoy preaching?

We should pray that God raises up more Christian leaders who are spiritually knowledgeable, experienced, watchful, and sincere. How can you better develop these qualities in your life?

Scripture: Titus 1:7-9; 1 Samuel 16:7; John 7:24

Prayer: Dear Lord, I ask that Christian leaders will receive your grace to develop these qualities; I also want my own life to exemplify these characteristics for your glory. Amen.

D·A·Y
253

Then I saw in my dream that in the morning the Shepherds beckoned Christian and Hopeful to walk with them upon the Mountains. So they went off together, enjoying the lovely views on every side. Then the Shepherds said to one another, "Shall we show these pilgrims some wonders?" They decided to do so and carefully escorted them to the top of a mountain called Error. It was very steep on its farthest side. They told them to look down to the very bottom. So Christian and Hopeful looked down and saw at the bottom several dead bodies that had been dashed to pieces; these had fallen all the way from the top.

❧

Now we see that even on the Delectable Mountains, there is a place of grave danger. Mt. Error refers to doctrinal error. It slopes upward innocently, but its far side is a precipice. Discontented with the limits of revealed truth on the narrow Way, people see the tall peak and curiously climb it to get a better view of heaven and earth. Once they get to the top, rather than watching their step, they busy themselves with their new vantage point and carelessly walk right off the precipice. Falling in the midst of their speculations brings their pilgrimage to a sudden and disastrous end.

Sometimes in church history, the least departure from established doctrines was decried as damnable heresy. Now the pendulum has swung toward indifference to the point that theological truth no longer seems like something vital to safeguard. Not wanting to be maligned as narrow-minded bigots within a broad-minded society, many find openness and impartiality more comfortable than strong convictions. Those who "contend for the faith that was once for all entrusted to the saints" (Jude 3) seem embarrassingly dogmatic and hard-line. Thus the truth revealed through prophets and apostles, the truth Christ proclaimed and incarnated and for which he and many millions of his followers have been martyred, seems of trifling significance. So errors proliferate—and the fall off the precipice today is no less destructive than yesterday.

Does your heart gravitate toward "new revelations"? Are you drawn to exciting new movements? Are you bored with your faith? If so, you could be in real danger if you do not stay firmly centered in the balanced truth of God's Word. In your joyous sojourn through the refreshment of the Delectable Mountains, be careful that you don't become careless with doctrinal truth.

❧

Scripture: 2 John 9; 2 Corinthians 11:3; Psalm 131:1

Prayer: Lord Jesus, help me to avoid sightseeing in places of error. Your old, old story in all its simplicity and beauty is good enough for me. Amen.

D·A·Y 254

"What does this mean?" asked Christian.

One of the Shepherds replied, "Haven't you heard of those who listened and were deceived by Hymenaeus and Philetus, who promoted a false doctrine concerning the resurrection of the body?"

The pilgrims answered that they had. Then the Shepherds said, "Those whom you see dashed to pieces at the bottom of this Mountain are they. To this day they remain unburied, as you can see, as an example for others to heed. Climbing this Mountain can be treacherous, especially when one goes too high or ventures too near the edge."

The bodies at the bottom of the mountain are examples, not of the propagators of error and heresy, but of those who submitted to their influence. This is why Paul had such contempt for Hymenaeus and Philetus, two principal authors and spreaders of error and heresy in the early church. Although they never denied the resurrection of Christ, they corrupted the true doctrine of his resurrection and upset the faith of many.

While none of us sees perfectly, no error is completely harmless. Little errors often lead to larger ones, and some errors delude multitudes. Many factors contribute to professing Christians starting up Error Mountain—self-exaltation, ignorance, curiosity, rebellion, resistance to truth, counterfeit experiences, listening to false teachers, presumptuously "leaning upon their own understanding." Many believers spend so much time on their speculations that they lose interest in the core issues of the Christian life. They ultimately swerve from the faith, ending up at the bottom of the precipice.

Paul took the error of Hymenaeus and Philetus so seriously that he likened it to gangrene. This spreading disease in a human body so corrupts, consumes, and blackens the flesh that the only recourse is amputation. In like manner, the errors and heresies of false teachers spread through the body of Christ, feeding upon souls, consuming faith, bringing spiritual sickness and threatening spiritual death. With the life of the entire body at stake, these teachers must be opposed and cut off.

Mt. Error is a popular attraction in these last days. When we hear curious teachings, we should approach them as the Bereans did who studied the Scriptures together to make sure what they were hearing was true. We should not want to take one step up Mt. Error. How tragic to come so close to the destination only to be ruined. What will you do to assure yourself safety from the perils of doctrinal error?

Scripture: 2 Timothy 2:15-18; Acts 17:11; Colossians 2:18-19

Prayer: Dear Lord, help me neither to undervalue your Word nor to overvalue human opinions. Please keep me and the other members of my Christian family from error. Amen.

D·A·Y
255

Then I saw the Shepherds take them to the top of another Mountain, the name of which was Caution. They told them to look far off in the distance. When they did, they thought they could see several people walking up and down among tombs that were there. Because of the way they sometimes stumbled over the tombs and could not seem to find their way out from among them, the pilgrims deduced that they were blind. Then Christian asked, "What does this mean?"

One of the Shepherds answered, "Did you notice a short distance below these Mountains on the left side of the Way some steps that led over a fence into a Meadow?"

They answered, "Yes."

The shepherds next take the pilgrims to a second mountain, Caution. This mountain is so named for the effect it produces in climbers when they look at the view from its peak. They feel a strong sense of caution at what they see. Generally, caution can mean both vice and virtue to pilgrims. The walk of faith forbids some types of caution. Those who cautiously calculate and scheme their way along so they can maintain the best of both worlds are far from a true biblical walk. At the same time, the dangers of the path cannot be understated. They demand caution. This mountain's cautions are of this latter variety.

From the mountaintop's vantage point, the pilgrims clearly observe far off from Caution the plight of the spiritually blind. These stumble through a hopeless labyrinth of spiritual darkness and confusion among the graves of the spiritually dead. When the pilgrims ask the meaning of this spectacle, a shepherd answers with a question of his own—one the pilgrims would just as soon not hear. How they wish they had never noticed the steps on the left side of the Way! The painful memory of their departure from the true path still stings them with pain and embarrassment.

Although it is difficult to be reminded of such dismal failures, it is important that we come to grips with them. Have we learned our lessons well so we won't be vulnerable again? Has the experience taught us to be wisely cautious? Has our self-righteous pride been dethroned, replaced by a humble heart and mind?

We should never "throw caution to the wind" in our spiritual pilgrimage. Instead, we should always welcome the Lord's cautions through our spiritual leaders, never forgetting our own propensity for spiritual calamities. Have you shunned wise cautionary advice offered you by a spiritual leader? What do you think God wants you to do about it?

Scripture: Proverbs 14:15, 18; 27:12; Leviticus 18:4-5

Prayer: Dear Lord, I humbly thank you for the cautionary guidance you give through pastors and other spiritual leaders. Help me to respect their ministries and to take their guidance to heart. Amen.

D·A·Y 256

"From the steps, a path leads directly to Doubting Castle, which Giant Despair owns." Then one Shepherd pointed at the men among the tombs and said, "All these people were once on a pilgrimage to the City, as you are now, until they came to those steps. Because the right Way was rough in that place, they chose to go out of it into that Meadow, and Giant Despair took and cast them into Doubting Castle. After they had been kept awhile in the dungeon, he at last put out their eyes and led them among the tombs, where to this very day he has left them to wander so that they might fulfill the saying of the wise man: 'A man who strays from the path of understanding comes to rest in the company of the dead'" [Proverbs 21:16].

Then Christian and Hopeful looked at one another and burst into tears, but they said nothing to the Shepherds.

Christian and Hopeful see that those among the graves are reckless souls who had once professed Christ. These lost ones sought to escape discomfort by turning aside from an obedient walk, but far from finding relief by flouting the King's Way, they brought upon themselves spiritual disaster. How unfortunate for them that they wickedly forsook the holy Highway to undo everything they ever learned thereon. They foolishly gave themselves over to delusions and returned to their former company with those dead in sin.

Who are these hapless souls wandering blindly and aimlessly among the graves? Surely they would have included Christian and Hopeful but for the wonderful grace of God who reached out to rescue them. No wonder they are speechless. They look into each other's faces through streams of tears. They see others lost in ruin by the very same sins from which God had rescued them. Surely the pilgrims think, *Why are we any different? Why did we not suffer a similar fate? How merciful God has been to save us from such blindness and destruction!*

How often, it seems, we escape by the skin of our teeth some sin over which others stumble never to rise again. Somehow after our own sinful departures, God lovingly rescues us from our folly by granting us faith to escape the lost condition of those doomed to wander in futility. Seeing their examples should cause our hearts to overflow with godly sorrow and with gratitude for his amazing mercy and grace.

Should we find ourselves on spiritual mountain heights, we should know we have not "arrived" at all. God's grace and mercy alone have brought us. Express your gratitude to him right now.

Scripture: 2 Corinthians 7:8-11; Micah 7:18; 1 Chronicles 17:16

Prayer: Blessed Lord, I give you all the glory for every footstep of spiritual progress I make. I humbly thank you again for rescuing me from my sins—yesterday's, today's, and tomorrow's. Amen.

D·A·Y
257

Then I saw in my dream that the Shepherds took them to the bottom of the Mountain. There was a door in the side of a Hill. The Shepherds opened the door and told the pilgrims to look inside. When they did so, they saw that it was very dark and smoky inside. They also thought they heard a sound like a roaring fire and the eerie cries of people suffering in torment. In addition, there was a strong odor of sulfur.

"What does this mean?" asked Christian.

A Shepherd answered, "This is a By-way to Hell, a way through which hypocrites enter—namely, those who sell their birthrights along with Esau; those who sell their Master along with Judas; those who blaspheme the gospel along with Alexander; and those who lie and hide under false appearances along with Ananias and Sapphira."

Even the fairest places in this world have passages to hell. Now the pilgrims breathe a bit of hell's infernal smoke through the By-way to Hell. This is not Christian's first such encounter. His experience with "the mouth of hell" as he went through the Valley of the Shadow of Death nearly scared him witless.

This door to hell is reserved for hypocrites who pretend to be true pilgrims. These hypocrites include those who sell their birthright as Esau did. Disregarding the value of their spiritual lives, they trade them away for some desire of the soul or flesh. Other hypocrites, like Judas, sell their Master. Hypocrites like Alexander, named with Hymenaeus, blaspheme the Gospel. While refusing to remain true to the faith, they insist upon sticking around to drain the church dry spiritually. Finally, hypocrites like Ananias and Sapphira lie to the Holy Spirit. Since authenticity means so little to them, they feel no qualms about giving false impressions, deceitfully trying to impress others with their piety.

Why do the shepherds take Christian and Hopeful here? Since only God can really see human hearts, our ability to distinguish between true and false believers is not always possible. Who really knew Esau's heart before he sold his birthright? And who knew the heart of Judas, Alexander, or Ananias and Sapphira prior to their downfalls? There may be subtle yet deadly sins working beneath the surface in our own hearts or in the hearts of our Christian companions. Thus warning even the most esteemed saints among us is wise and proper. For, perhaps thinking they are standing firm, they might fall. Since you cannot even know your own heart, open it completely to the Holy Spirit's scrutiny. Ask him to expose sins hidden even from you.

Scripture: Matthew 23:25, 27; Luke 12:1; Psalm 26:2

Prayer: Holy Spirit, I take comfort in the fact that you know my heart better than I know it myself. Please purify my heart and keep it untainted from hypocrisy in all its forms. Amen.

D·A·Y
258

Then Hopeful said to the Shepherds, "I perceive that each of these appeared to be on a pilgrimage, even as we are now. Is this true?"

"Yes," said one Shepherd, "and they held that appearance for quite some time, too."

"Well, how far did they succeed on their pilgrimage before they came to such a miserable end?"

"Some got farther than these Mountains and others not so far."

Then the pilgrims said to each other, "We have a great need to cry to the Strong One for strength."

"Yes," added another of the Shepherds, "and you will need to use all that He gives you, too."

If our two pilgrims had begun to see themselves as standing, they are snapped back to reality. They can still fall! It seemed at first that their arrival upon the pristine mountain heights meant that they had finally attained spiritual maturity. The ugly storms of youth seemed far behind in the valleys. Now, however, it is clear that even in the Delectable Mountains, they are in a battle for their souls and can never let their guard down. Doctrinal error and presumption can still lead to carelessness and sin. A reminder of their past failure awakens them from any tendency to slacken spiritually.

Now peering into the fires of hell, they are sobered by the realization that its population includes many would-be pilgrims who lacked the sincerity to keep their commitment to Christ. This quickens the spirits of both Hopeful and Christian. Are their hearts sincere? Will they avoid making such devastating mistakes? Shocked and mystified, they realize they cannot understand their own sinful tendencies, let alone anyone else's. Seeing the danger, their only recourse is to "cry to the Strong One for strength." Their own strength and wisdom are not enough.

Oh, these troublesome Shepherds! Why can't they simply soothe and stroke us? Why must they trouble us with their warnings of danger and hell? While we may want buttercups and daisies without unhappy visits to unfriendly mountains and doors to hell, faithful pastors must do more than console and soothe us; they must also warn us of the consequences of unfaithfulness and error. They know that to reach "the full assurance of hope until the end" (Hebrews 6:11 RSV), we must give careful attention to every part of our pilgrimage. Do you show your spiritual leaders adequate respect?

Scripture: 1 Timothy 5:17; Colossians 1:28; Acts 20:27-28

Prayer: Lord Jesus, thank you for the tireless efforts of your shepherds who faithfully represent your truth. They often carry intense concern for your people's spiritual well-being, and I want to honor their leadership. Amen.

D·A·Y
259

By this time Christian and Hopeful had a desire to go forward in their pilgrimage, and the Shepherds also desired this for them. So they walked together toward the end of the Mountains. Then the Shepherds said to one another, "Let's show the pilgrims the Gates of the Celestial City from here—that is, if they have the skill to look through our perspective glass."

So they led them to the top of a high Hill called Clear and offered the glass to them. The pilgrims gladly accepted it, and both attempted to see through it. Because of the memory of the last thing shown them, however, their hands shook. Although they could not look steadily through the glass, they did think they saw something like the Gate and perhaps even some of the City's glory.

Glory! The Shepherds don't leave the pilgrims buried in fear and caution after all. They take them to Mt. Clear's heights for a season of intense spiritual insight to see more clearly above and beyond the temporal landscape. From here the most delectable sight of all may be seen—the Celestial City! Yet a clear perspective must be received by faith. St. Augustine explains, "Faith is to believe what we do not see, and the reward of this faith is to see what we believe." Unfortunately, because of the pilgrims' weak human nature, their faith is too limited to see clearly what they believe. Thus a telescope-like "perspective" glass is provided them.

Still, it takes steady hands to see past myopic dull visions, and their hands continue trembling from their experience at the By-way to Hell. Did the Shepherds err in showing the pilgrims that sight? Not at all. When filled with faith and enthusiasm from our mountaintop experiences, we often lack humility and caution. A peek inside the door of hell provides valuable introspection and godly fear. While seeming to weaken our faith and lessen our confidence in our inheritance, these attitudes are nonetheless worthwhile. Christian and Hopeful, after all, nearly destroyed themselves by blithely climbing into Bypath Meadow when their confidence ran high. The best we can do, therefore, is to maintain a godly tension between faith and fear—". . . *you stand by faith.* Do not be arrogant, *but be afraid*" (Romans 11:20).

Despite their frailties, the pilgrims do see something, just a glimpse. Yet it is real. It is the City! This alone is enough to ravish any heaven-bent pilgrim's heart. We should cherish our glimpses into glory. We should also appreciate the sum total of all our experiences, as they prepare us for the Celestial City. Perhaps your glimpses of glory are fewer than you desire. Will you praise God anyway?

Scripture: 1 Corinthians 2:9-10; 13:12; Psalm 31:19

Prayer: Blessed Lord, thank you that rather than leaving us reflecting at hell's door, you also take us to see the gates of heaven. Help me to live a sober life balanced with joyful expectancy. Amen.

DAY 260

After this, they began to descend the Hill, and the pilgrims sang this song:

> *"Thus by the Shepherds secrets are revealed,*
> *Which from other men are kept quite concealed;*
> *Come to the Shepherds, then, if you would see*
> *Things deep, things hid, and that mysterious be."*

When they were about to resume the pilgrimage, one of the Shepherds gave them written instructions to guide them on their way. Another told them to beware of the flatterer. A third told them to be careful not to sleep on the Enchanted Ground. Then the fourth wished them God's blessing on the journey. So then I awoke from my dream.

Although the pilgrims saw little more than "through a glass darkly," the vision set their hearts singing. Such heavenly glimpses, seen particularly as the destination draws nearer, are wonderfully sustaining. Trials seem smaller and more bearable, hope brighter and more tangible. How dull, how empty earthly things look in heaven's light! Yet we cannot always be in this frame of mind. God doesn't give these visions to bring us to our eternal rest immediately. He wants to make us so desire it that we will fight through until we reach it.

Thus the pilgrims must press on. As they leave the Delectable Mountains, the four Shepherds (indicating four primary pastoral attributes) offer their final admonitions. *Knowledge* offers the pilgrims written instructions to guide them. His plea is that the pilgrims continue to educate themselves thoroughly as they carry on. *Experience* tells them that head knowledge alone will not keep them safe, but they must remember from experience to avoid deceivers—namely, "the flatterer." *Watchful*, who has been watching the pilgrims, seems to think it most necessary for them to guard their souls against carelessly falling asleep on the Enchanted Ground. Unpretentious *Sincerity,* reminds them simply to look to God. His blessing will bring a happy end to their pilgrimage.

Having accepted their instructions, the pilgrims leave the Delectable Mountains greatly enriched. We, too, should take to heart the instructions of godly pastors. Too often we follow their advice only when their counsel agrees with us and makes us feel good. Yet because God appoints shepherds to watch over our souls, we should take their admonitions very seriously. Thank God for the pastors who have loved you enough to speak truth to you, whether fully welcomed at the time or not.

Scripture: Jeremiah 3:15; 23:4; John 21:15-17

Prayer: Dear Lord, help me to heed the admonitions of my spiritual leaders. You are my primary Guide, but I know you appoint them to watch over me as well. Grant me a submissive heart. Amen.

D·A·Y

261

I again fell asleep and had a dream. I saw the same two pilgrims going down the Mountains along the Highway toward the City. Now a little beyond these Mountains on the left hand lay the Country of Conceit. A little crooked lane came from that country and joined the Way in which the pilgrims were walking. At that junction they met a very lively young man from that country whose name was Ignorance, and Christian asked him where he came from and where he was going.

He replied, "Sir, I was born in the country that lies over there, a little to the left, and I am going to the Celestial City."

Now a new dream begins. Many have thought that perhaps this little break in the narrative marks Bunyan's release from jail. In any case, we enter a perilous stage of the pilgrimage—for dangers are hardly over in this advanced stage of life. On this easy descent from the Mountains to the level stretch preceding the City, pilgrims must still exercise utmost caution, as we will see. For while coming down the mountain is easier, climbing up it is safer.

In this relatively easy-to-travel region, the aging pilgrims meet the bright and energetic young man, Ignorance. At first glance, this impressive young man appears to be a person who could make the pilgrim Way seem attractive and fashionable to other young people, for he could easily influence many to come along and join him.

Yet his name betrays him, exposing how deficient he is in true spiritual understanding and judgment. His country also is a problem, indicating how sufficient he considers his wisdom and knowledge. Ignorance must be the most common name in the land of Conceit. For conceit and ignorance go together as inescapably as do wisdom and truth. Paul understood the correlation. As he explained to Gentile believers that God had graciously grafted them into his family, he added, "I do not want you to be *ignorant* of this mystery, brothers, so that you may not be *conceited* . . ." (Romans 11:25, italics mine).

Beneath the Delectable Mountains, a little off the pilgrim path, the country of Conceit spreads out impressively before descending pilgrims. None like Ignorance ever makes it to the peaks to learn from God's shepherds. With such ignorance in Conceit, you would think no learned pilgrim would ever be tempted to visit. We are most vulnerable to pride, however, as we descend from our peak spiritual times. How hard is it for you to avoid conceit after having been on the mountaintop? In what ways can you preserve and maintain a humble spirit?

Scripture: Psalm 125:5; Philippians 2:15; Ephesians 4:18

Prayer: Dear Lord, when I enjoy spiritual revelations and special manifestations of your grace, help me to guard my humility carefully. Amen.

D·A·Y 262

"But how do you think you will get in at the Gate?" asked Christian. "You may find some difficulty there."

"I will get in as other good people do."

"But what do you have to show at the Gate so that it may be opened for you?"

"I know my Lord's will and have lived a good life. I pay back every debt, I pray and fast, pay tithes and give to charities, and I have left my country behind in order to reach my destination."

❦

As Ignorance steps out of his happy little lane into the King's Way and sees the two battered old pilgrims limping along, they could not impress him less. How odd they seem to him. Why, you would rarely see a greater contrast anywhere in these parts. For Ignorance, by comparison, stands tall, dresses sharply, and thinks he knows all about the business of salvation. To him, these two weather-beaten pilgrims seem somehow out of tune and out of touch.

Yet the two elderly men are far from dried up. Ignorance could learn much from these seasoned veterans of the King's Highway. They have wisdom of experience in Christ of which the young man never dreamed. They have endured sloughs, battles, hills, and mountains. They have experienced hunger, thirst, cold, and imprisonment. They have also known the joys of salvation and seen glimpses of the City that the young man hopes to reach.

While many reject Christ altogether, multitudes more, like Ignorance, hold to some form of Christian faith short of true salvation. They may presume that because they think well of themselves and their friends think well of them that God must think well of them, too. They ask themselves, "What can a couple of broken-down strangers teach me? I will get in just as other good folks do. Just look at my life!" Ignorance is a moral man who pays his debts, tithes, and gives to charity. And to this illustrious resumé of good deeds, he adds another—that he left his own country. Yet he has retained the thinking of his native land. He thinks his own goodness will save him, not Christ. How can he, then, think he has forsaken all for Christ?

Our own righteous acts will never carry the weight necessary to take us through the Celestial Gate. How sad it is for those who assert, "I know my Lord's will," yet are so far out of his will. If only they would listen to the words of the truly wise. How good are you at gathering wisdom from the wise?

❦

Scripture: Proverbs 2:1-5; 19:20; 22:17; Luke 18:9-14

Prayer: Dear Lord, help me to listen to those who are older than I in the faith. Help me to appreciate their wisdom. I know I have much to learn from them. Amen.

DAY 263

"But you didn't come in at the Wicket-gate that is at the beginning of this Way. You came in here through this crooked lane. I fear that, in spite of how you may see yourself, when the day of reckoning comes, you will be counted as a thief and robber and will not gain entrance into the City."

"Gentlemen, you are absolute strangers to me. I don't know you. Please be content to follow the doctrine of your country, and I will be content to follow the doctrine of mine. I wish you well. But as for the Wicket-gate you mention, all the world knows that it is a long way from our country. I don't think a single person in our whole region even knows the way to it. Nor do they need to worry about whether they do or not, since we have, as you can see, a fine, pleasant, green lane that comes down from our country into the Way."

While Christian and Hopeful began their pilgrimages at the legitimate starting place, Ignorance, for his own misguided reasons, missed it. He still needs to humble himself and decide in his heart to relinquish his own opinions and accept God's instruction. Yet he recoils at the suggestion that the King could count someone so good as he to be less than perfectly acceptable. Bristling, he tells the two pilgrims that they are strangers, both to him and to his country. Since they are incapable of understanding local customs, he sees no reason to hearken to what he judges as ill-advised counsel. He will, regardless, allow for their right to travel according to their country's dictates and expects the same of them. Of course, no one from Conceit knows the way to the humble little Wicket-gate. The mere thought causes them revulsion. Because they all think alike, they convince themselves that they cannot all be wrong. Observing their lovely green lane, they consider it perfect sense that their way is as good as anyone else's. Thus Ignorance thinks that no one in his parts knows the way to the Wicket-gate, nor need they, since the area provides a more convenient way.

Where ignorance of the cross exists, in all likelihood either open hostility or at least nonchalance toward it is manifested. As we observe the modern church landscape, we should ask how much religiosity is culture and how much is truly Christian. Even within the church, "Sometimes there is a way that seems to be right, but in the end it is the way to death" (Proverbs 16:25 NRSV). Can you think of ways you could better protect yourself and your church from unscriptural substitutes for true godliness?

Scripture: Proverbs 12:15; 14:8; 19:20; Psalm 119:35

Prayer: Dear Lord, I do not want to partake of the cultural ignorance so prevalent in much of today's church life. Please deliver your people from "churchianity" so that we may truly know and walk with you. Amen.

D·A·Y 264

When Christian saw that the man relied on the wisdom of his own conceit, he whispered to Hopeful, "'Do you see a man wise in his own eyes? There is more hope for a fool than for him' [Proverbs 26:12]. 'Even as he walks along the road, the fool lacks sense and shows everyone how stupid he is'" [Ecclesiastes 10:3]. Then he asked, "What do you think? Shall we talk further with him or go ahead of him for a while and leave him to think about what he has already heard? We could stop and wait for him later and see if, by correcting him a little at a time, we can do him any good."

Then Hopeful said,

"Let Ignorance for a little while muse
On what's been said, and let him not refuse
To embrace good counsel lest he remain
Still ignorant of what's the greatest gain.
God says of them who discernment have waived,
Though He's their Maker, they will not be saved."

Hopeful added, "I don't think it will be good for us to say too much to him all at once. If it is all right with you, let us pass him for now and talk with him another time if he is open to it." So they both went on ahead of Ignorance.

When Ignorance refused the call to enter the path through the Wicket-gate, he failed a first test of genuineness. His is not the ignorance of one who never heard of his need but of a willfully ignorant person who refuses to acknowledge his own sin and need for the Savior. He stubbornly believes in his country's goodness. It is his country, and he has never troubled himself over its name—nor is he ready to now.

Someone has said, "We are all ignoramuses by nature." We are, then, natives of Conceit and intrinsically prone to its sins. Yet we can renounce it. Even so, how many professed believers there must be like Ignorance. Despite due warnings, they persist in traveling their own way, relying upon their own wisdom, and refusing God's instruction. The pilgrims recognize that at this point they may as well argue with the devil as convince Ignorance of his error. So they back off.

Those expecting salvation by their own efforts and not by Christ's redeeming grace are ignorant of the first principles of salvation. We should find ways to convey the seriousness of their error. We should also know when to back off and leave them in God's hands. Do you know any lost in ignorance whom you can help?

Scripture: Acts 18:24-26; 28:23; Proverbs 25:12; Mark 10:15

Prayer: Lord Jesus, help me to reach out to those who are ignorant of your truth. Help me also to leave the results of my witness to you. Amen.

D·A·Y 265

They had not gone far when they entered a very dark lane, where they saw a man whom seven demons had bound with seven strong cords. The demons were carrying him back to the door on the side of the Hill that the pilgrims had been shown earlier. Trembling, Christian attempted to see if he knew him, and it looked like it might be Turn-away, who lived in the town of Apostasy. He couldn't see his face clearly, however, because he was hanging his head like a captured thief. But after they had gone by, Hopeful saw a sign on his back with these words, "Self-indulgent professor and damnable apostate."*

*Originally *wanton*, a term now indicating immoral or cruel. The obsolete meaning, however, indicates one who frolics or roves in an unrestrained excessive manner.

This man is quite different from the last. While Ignorance was a "good" man who carefully lived a "good" disciplined life, Turn-away recklessly ran every which way. Turn-away would look upon Ignorance with disdain, saying the young man understood nothing of God's grace. Yet Turn-Away, with his Christian liberty, loses all restraint as he distorts God's grace into license to sin. He lives to please his flesh, utterly forsaking Christ. A traitor at heart to the laws of the pilgrimage, he ultimately dooms himself. How boldly and defiantly he heaped contempt upon the cross of Christ. Yet now with his pretentious mask torn away, he hangs his head in shameful regret. "Self-indulgent professors" often turn out to be "damnable apostates."

This is not the first time the pilgrims have brushed with apostasy. Christian trembled at the agony of the Man in the Iron Cage. He watched his companion Pliable return to the City of Destruction. Apollyon feverishly tried to get him to go back, too. Both pilgrims heard once-faithful Demas beckoning to them from out of the Way. Now this one who openly "turned away" from the faith he professed finds himself hopelessly bound by demons. What a strange turn for one who enjoyed such "liberty!"

When one who professes Christ becomes lax, and Christ's lordship is not firmly established, his former demonic lord resumes residence and "brings along seven other spirits more evil than itself." Turn-away, champion of freedom, was never as locked up in sin as now.

What a difference we see between this apostate and our pilgrims. They at times wandered; yet they never turned their backs on Christ. We, too, may stumble at times, but, by God's grace, we can keep our hearts directed toward God's Way. Beware of the sinful habits and lack of discipline that could lead you away from Christ.

Scripture: Matthew 12:43-45; Proverbs 5:22-23; 1 Corinthians 15:2

Prayer: Dear Lord, while some profess faith, I know I possess it. I pray that when I begin to wander, my heart will quickly run home to you. Amen.

D·A·Y
266

Then Christian said to his companion, "Now I remember what someone told me about a thing that happened to a good man in these parts. The name of the man was Little-faith, but he was a good man and lived in the town of Sincere. As I recall, the story goes like this: At the entrance of this passage, there comes down from Broadway Gate a lane called Dead-man's Lane. They call it this because of the murders that commonly take place there. This man, Little-faith, was going on a pilgrimage as we are, and he happened to sit down there and sleep."

After the disheartening failures of Ignorance and Turn-away, the pilgrims no doubt feel shaken. Christian, searching for encouragement, suddenly remembers a pilgrim named Little-faith. This man's story will serve as a blessed reminder that those whose pilgrimages seem to fall apart may yet recover. A sharp contrast can be drawn between apostate Turn-away and this misfortunate pilgrim called Little-faith.

When under trial, persecution, or in narcissistic regions, many who seemed faithful begin to return into the broad way to destruction. Traveling from the King's Way to the Broadway through Dead-man's Lane is exceedingly dangerous. That's where Satan murders human souls. Yet here comes a sincere pilgrim named Little-faith. While his faith is legitimate, he is not without his faults. His first apparent shortcoming is that he is a sleepy man. Of course, all pilgrims must sleep, but this sleep refers to careless slumber. Apparently, he became so drowsy that he wandered up the lane until sleepiness completely overcame him. Unaware of his danger, he fell asleep right there in Dead-man's Lane!

A pilgrim has no business being in such an unsafe place where so many murders are committed. Little-faith had come from the town of Sincere, but sincerity, while an obvious virtue, is not adequate by itself. Many sincere people are sincerely deceived. Cults are brimming over with people who are sincere but who lack discernment and truth. In Hosea 4:6 God tells us, "My people are destroyed from lack of knowledge." Note that it does not say "a lack of sincerity," although knowledge without sincerity is also deficient. Those who are sincere must also become discerning and knowledgeable, else they may end up like Little-faith, asleep on Dead-man's Lane!

We should apply ourselves to attaining wisdom and discernment by prayer, meditation on God's Word, fellowship, and reliance upon the Holy Spirit. We must keep ever alert to the persistent dangers that dog every stage of our pilgrimage. What things in your life most cause you spiritual sleepiness? How can you better foster spiritual alertness?

Scripture: Proverbs 6:4-5; Psalm 132:4; Mark 14:38

Prayer: Dear Lord, help me to keep alert so that I will not inadvertently amble up forbidden paths. I want to stay true to my pilgrimage. Amen.

D·A·Y
267

"Now at that time, three big bruisers were coming down the lane from Broadway Gate. Their names were Faint-heart, Mistrust, and Guilt—three brothers. They saw Little-faith, who had just awakened and was getting ready to resume his journey, and they came racing up to him. Approaching him with threatening language, they told him to stand up. At this, Little-faith turned as white as a sheet, and he had no strength either to run or fight. Then Faint-heart said to him, 'Give us your wallet.' But being reluctant to turn over his money, he moved too slowly. Mistrust ran up to him and, thrusting his hand into Little-faith's pocket, pulled out his wallet and grabbed his money.

"Little-faith cried out, 'Thieves! Thieves!' With that, Guilt struck him on the head with a large club that he held in his hand. Little-faith fell flat on the ground, where he lay bleeding profusely and looking as though he might bleed to death."

What persistent danger we find in sleepiness! Christian met Simple, Sloth, and Presumption mindlessly sleeping. Then he himself slept at the arbor on Hill Difficulty. He slept again with Hopeful on Doubting Castle's grounds. As we saw, the toll for such negligence can be immense. We will never be safe when we sleep spiritually.

Little-faith awakens from his foolish snooze to find himself in a veritable death-trap. Realizing his serious sin, he is too alarmed to recover immediately and implement the Gospel's provision—namely, grace through faith. While all true believers are preserved from eternal ruin, those weak in faith are particularly vulnerable to fears that can make them succumb to all kinds of unbelief. So Little-faith, feeling terrified and powerless, freezes before the three villains.

We met Mistrust before, fleeing back with Timorous from the lions at the Palace Beautiful. Now this coward-turned-bully has joined his brothers to form a gang that robs weak pilgrims. Faint-heart and Mistrust so victimize Little-faith that he doubts God's promises of forgiveness. As a result, he quickly acquiesces and forfeits all his money. Fortunately, he has not denied his conscience. But his conscience, unaffected as yet by God's grace, afflicts him viciously. Guilt clobbers him until he despairs of life.

In Little-faith we see the inner conflicts that rise from unbelief and disobedience. If we allow ourselves to slumber spiritually, we set ourselves up for trouble. Still we should have faith to believe that when we do sin, Christ has ample grace to forgive and restore us. Have you at some time found yourself in a similar circumstance? How did you fight off your thieves?

Scripture: 1 John 2:1; Romans 8:1, 34; Hebrews 10:19-22

Prayer: Dear Lord, thank you for your forgiving love. When I confess and repent of sin, please aid me in fighting off the demonic thieves that intend to lay waste to my faith. Amen.

D·A·Y 268

"All this time the thieves just stood there, but then they heard someone coming up the road. They feared that it might be Great-grace from the City of Good-confidence, so they took off running and left Little-faith there to fend for himself. Somehow he got up and managed to go on his way. This was the story I heard."

"But did they take from him everything he owned?" asked Hopeful.

"No, he had his Jewels hidden, so he was able to keep them. But I was told that he was very upset over his loss because the thieves had gotten most of his spending money. He had a little bit of money left, but not enough to bring him to his journey's end. No, if I am not misinformed, just to keep himself alive, he was forced to beg as he journeyed along. For he refused to sell his Jewels, and, in spite of begging and doing what he could to scrape by, he went hungry most of the rest of the way."

O, ye of little faith." This seemed to be one of our Lord's most-used names for his disciples, but he never rejected them. Instead, he patiently worked to strengthen their faith. Although most eventually became great champions of faith, not all of us will be so blessed. Isn't it gratifying to know that God honors even a little faith?

So many Little-faiths travel the pilgrim's Way. They may not sleep in Dead-man's Lane, yet they haltingly jitter and joggle their way along with such weak faith that bullies continually harass them. Rather than robustly believing in Christ, they conduct their pilgrimage as impoverished beggars. Still they are precious to the Lord. Bewailing their sins and failures, their tender consciences are so unlike those of the callous, indifferent, and self-sufficient.

Little-faith's spending money—nearly all his present confidence, comfort, and liberty from hoping in Christ—was stolen. Yet while the thieves took the present evidences of his salvation, he somehow retained his jewels. These jewels—the Spirit's graces that united his soul to Christ—were his most cherished possession.

How like Little-faith we often are. Like the poor man living in a tent on his land, not knowing that beneath him is oil to make him a billionaire, we have been blessed in Christ "with *every* spiritual blessing in the heavenly places" (Ephesians 1:3 NRSV). But we often live like spiritual paupers. We need to be awakened to who we are and what we have in Christ, so that we will not be vulnerable, like Little-faith, to the spiritual bullies of Faint-heart, Mistrust, and Guilt. Have you in some way been deprived of your "spending money"? How about claiming it back right now?

Scripture: Hebrews 10:36-39;
Colossians 1:22-23; 2 Thessalonians 2:16-17

Prayer: Dear Jesus, I want to walk in faith and victory. Help me never to doubt your promises. If spiritual bandits assault me, help me to grow strong by claiming your provision. Amen.

D·A·Y
269

"But isn't it a marvel that they didn't get his certificate for admittance at the Celestial Gate?" asked Hopeful.

"Yes, it is a marvel; they didn't miss it because of any cunning on his part. They so unnerved him at their coming that he had neither power nor skill to hide anything. It was the providence of God more than his own endeavor that saved the certificate."

"It must be of great comfort to him that they didn't get this Jewel from him," said Hopeful.

"It might have been of great comfort to him if he had used it as he should have, but those who told me the story said that he made little use of it all the rest of the way because of the dismay he felt over the loss of his money. He even forgot it for the better part of the rest of the journey. Besides this, whenever he thought of it and began to be comforted, fresh thoughts of his loss would come to his mind, and he would once again be overwhelmed."

Little-faith still has his jewels, including his certificate for entering the Celestial Gate. This fact owes completely to the Lord's own merciful intervention. By God's grace, the robbers could only steal present spiritual richness. Yes, it was nearly all his spending money, but so what? This was mere pocket change to what still remains. He has his soul! He has his title to heaven! His jewels are safe in God's keeping! What comfort this should bring to Little-faith.

Yet not knowing how to use his jewels for his welfare, he feels little comfort. He should use his eternal possessions to comfort and encourage his heart. He should lay hold of his salvation with all his might. Instead, because of his weak faith, whenever he begins to regain hope for a victorious walk, he immediately falls afresh under the harassments of woeful thoughts of his losses. Clearly, the relatively minor graces and emotions he remembers and now misses figure much too prominently in his mind. Yes, they were valuable, but he so magnifies their worth that he forgets the priceless jewel of his salvation. Careful, Little-faith! Where is your treasure? You are in danger of placing it on the earth!

We should gently try to build up the faith of those who are weak. With Satan's uncanny ability to manipulate feelings, these ones generally suffer much battering and bruising that the strong cannot relate to. Yet while some march toward heaven waving banners, and others dolefully force every step, both will find hearty welcomes at the Gate. Take a moment to thank God for the spiritual riches that are yours in Christ. Then pray for your weaker Christian brothers and sisters.

Scripture: Isaiah 42:3; Romans 14:1; Ephesians 3:16-17

Prayer: Dear Lord, I pray your blessing upon the weak members of our Christian family. I ask that you strengthen us all and help us to encourage each other along. Amen.

DAY 270

"Oh, the poor man! This must have caused him great grief."

"Grief? Yes, grief indeed! This would have been the case for any of us had we been so cruelly robbed and wounded in a strange place. Poor soul, it is a wonder that he didn't die with grief. I was told that he spent most of his remaining time on the Way mourning and complaining bitterly, telling all those he met where the robbery happened, how it occurred, who had done it, what was lost, how he was wounded, and how he had barely escaped with his life."

Little-faith is a man of infinitely sorrowful spirit. He moves in an atmosphere of gloom, and heaviness cleaves like a millstone tied around his soul. While he does press on to the upward call, a continual rush of bitter remembrance drags his perspective downward.

His trials, far from working toward refining his character, only make him worse off because he does not take them the right way. He forgets his responsibility for his circumstances and perpetually speaks of his victimization. He made the careless error of turning into and falling asleep in the wrong path. It is too bad he cannot simply confess his mistake to God, receive grace, and trust God to bring some good from it. How can he ever find victory if continues on in a never-ending state of self-pity and mourning?

Some people can suffer in silence, but others suffer and let everyone know it. Little-faith makes everyone else around him bear his trouble with him. He is a classic high-maintenance negative thinker who wearies and discourages those around him. He supports his pilgrimage by begging for scraps of faith and hope that other pilgrims offer him. His oh-the-pain-of-it-all attitude makes him a pain to all. Yet Christian feels great compassion for this "poor soul" who constantly relives his defeats and counts his losses. He wonders who would fare better under similar circumstances.

While many of us can relate to Little-faith's weakness, none of us need endure a lifetime of such misery. If we consider the positive—we were beaten and robbed but still have our relationship with Christ and are sealed with the Holy Spirit—we will soon realize what awesome treasure we still possess. And let us trust in the God who has promised, "I will repay you for the years the locusts have eaten" (Joel 2:25). Decide to make your best effort to turn your laments into praises and help others to do the same.

Scripture: John 14:1; Romans 8:35-39; Philippians 1:19

Prayer: Dear Lord, when I feel down and out, help me once again to catch sight of reality—that your grace is sufficient to cover my every sin and failure. Help me to rebuild my faith again by your promises. Amen.

D·A·Y 271

"It's a wonder," said Hopeful, "that he didn't out of necessity end up selling or pawning some of his Jewels to help relieve his misery."

"You're talking like one who isn't seeing clearly," Christian responded. "For what price should he have pawned them? Or to whom should he have sold them? His Jewels were not highly valued anywhere in the country where he was robbed. Also, he didn't want the relief that such a transaction would bring. Had his Jewels been missing at the Gate of the Celestial City, he knew that he would have been excluded from an inheritance there. That would have been worse for him than the confrontation of ten thousand thieves."

Little-faith's life is now miserable and his faith pitiful as he moves along on his sad and beggarly pilgrimage. He had never been a truly victorious pilgrim, however, even before his mishap. While sincere, he was too sleepy to read his Bible diligently, fervently pray, or exercise spiritual gifts. Thus after his personal catastrophe, he had little to fall back on and so seemingly lost what he did have. Under a cloud of perpetual gloom, he constantly pointed backward at how unfairly life had treated him instead of looking expectantly toward restoration and healing. Depending on others to help him, he became self-preoccupied and bitter. He carried on this way till his joyless journey's end.

Since the man's misery was so great, Hopeful suggests that he might understandably sell his jewels for relief. This suggestion sounds crazy to Christian. The jewels are all Little-faith has of value, his entire hope for eternity. How, then, could he sell them when to do so would forever doom him? Being weak and cowardly is one thing; letting go of eternal life is quite another. While Little-faith never gives up mourning and lamenting that his money is gone, lacking these minor graces that make the spiritual life enjoyable still does not make up the difference between eternal life and death.

God wants us to live an abundant life here on earth. But even if we lack the abundance and joy we seek, we must never sell the "jewels" of faith in Christ. Have you ever felt tempted to sell Christ out for an easier way? Be assured—there is no easier way. The way that seems "right and easy" leads to eternal death, and it will bring sorrow and trouble before the grave. Hold on to your faith in God—no matter how dismal your condition appears.

Scripture: Colossians 2:6-7; Hebrews 3:14; 4:14-16; 10:35

Prayer: Lord Jesus, thank you for the glorious hope you have given me. I resolve to hold on to the treasures of my salvation unflinchingly. Amen.

D·A·Y 272

"Why do you speak so sharply, brother?" asked Hopeful. "Esau sold his birthright for a serving of stew, and that birthright was his greatest Jewel. If he did it, why not Little-faith also?"

"Esau did indeed sell his birthright as do many others," said Christian, "but, like that wicked man, they exclude themselves from the chief blessing. However, you must recognize the difference between Esau and Little-faith and their situations. Esau's birthright was earthly, whereas Little-faith's Jewels were not; Esau's belly was his god, but Little-faith's belly was not so; Esau's desire lay in his fleshly cravings, but Little-faith's did not. Besides, Esau could see no further than fulfilling his lusts. He said, 'When a man is dying of starvation, what good is his birthright?' But Little-faith, though he had only a small amount of faith, by that small amount was not only kept from such indulgences but could see and prize his Jewels more than selling them like Esau did his birthright.

"You cannot read anywhere that Esau had so much as a little bit of faith. So where the flesh alone holds sway—as it will in the person who has no faith to resist with—it is no wonder if he sells his birthright and his very soul to the Devil of Hell. He is like a jackass that, because of its nature, cannot be turned away. When his mind is set upon lust, he will go for it, whatever the cost."

The pilgrims learned at the By-way to Hell that it was a place for hypocrites who, like Esau, sell their birthrights. Now they begin arguing about Esau, Jacob's twin brother. The birthright, a special honor given the firstborn son, belonged to him. With the birthright came a double portion of the family inheritance and the promise of one day leading the clan. In trading his birthright, Esau disregarded it; in trading it for a pot of lentil soup, he "despised" it.

Christian sees no connection between Esau and Little-faith. Esau impulsively traded the lasting advantages of his birthright for the immediate pleasure of a single meal. He never stopped for a moment to consider the long-term consequences of his action. Little-faith, on the other hand, sold nothing. He was robbed and plundered against his will. Esau, having no faith at all, let his lusts drive him. Little-faith's little bit of faith, however, was enough to keep him from forfeiting his jewels. He never fell away from Christ by preferring his flesh to his inheritance.

Like Christian, we should try to see the good in our weaker brothers instead of judging them too harshly. Can you think of any "Little-faiths" whom you have been ready to impatiently write off? Will you seek ways to love and encourage them?

Scripture: Genesis 25:29-34; Romans 9:13; 1 Corinthians 13:4-7

Prayer: Dear Lord, thank you for those who, while weak in faith, keep plodding along without selling out their faith. Please give them special grace and encouragement. Amen.

D·A·Y
273

"But Little-faith was different from that. His mind was on the things of God, and his means of support came from what was spiritual and above. Therefore, there would have been no reason for him to sell his Jewels simply to fill his mind with worthless things.

"Will a man pay a dollar to fill his stomach with hay? Or can you persuade the turtledove to live on dead flesh like the crow? For carnal lusts, faithless ones might be driven to pawn, mortgage, or sell what they have—along with their very lives to boot. But those who have faith, saving faith, though only a little of it, cannot do so. So here, my brother, is your mistake."

"I admit it," said Hopeful, "but your strong reaction almost made me angry."

"Why would you get angry? I only said you were acting like a man who wasn't seeing clearly. But please forgive me, and let's forget about this and return to the subject we have been discussing."

❧

Many who profess faith in Christ, upon meeting various afflictions or temptations, give up their faith to indulge in this present world. Yet it seems to Christian that anyone thinking a true believer would do such a thing lacks sound judgment. For between Little-faith and Esau there is a vast difference—the difference between the converted and the unconverted.

Esau represents those who, while living under the same roof with the converted, never truly repent of their sins and choose to follow Christ. Esau's sudden decision to forfeit his "jewels" only exposed his unconverted heart. Little-faith, on the other hand, truly belongs to Christ. While Esau sold his birthright for an earthly meal, Little-faith continually hungered and thirsted after God's righteousness. He kept looking for spiritual help from God, not from earthly resources. While he had trouble claiming heaven's resources for his earthly pilgrimage, he knew they were there for him and would eventually get him through the Celestial Gate. He had no desire whatever to forsake Christ.

As true followers of Christ, may we never trade in our spiritual treasures for the things of this world. The sinful nature cries for gratification, and those without true faith have no means by which to resist it. But we who have faith have been given a new nature in Christ. The Holy Spirit gives us the ability to say no to sin. Commit yourself now to refuse ever giving up any of your spiritual inheritance for worldly advantage.

❧

Scripture: Hebrews 12:16; Isaiah 55:2; Titus 2:11-12

Prayer: Heavenly Father, I would not trade a single spiritual jewel of your kingdom for all the world. The thought revolts me; for you satisfy my heart with hope. Thank you for the glorious privilege of walking in your Way. Amen.

DAY 274

"But, Christian, I am persuaded in my heart that those three thieves were nothing but cowards. Why else would they run at the sound of someone coming up the road? Why didn't Little-faith muster up greater courage? I think he should have at least tried to fight them, and if he couldn't win, then yield."

"Many have said that these three are cowards," answered Christian, "but few have found it to be the case in their own time of trial. As for a great heart, Little-faith had none. And, my brother, I think that if you had been the man, you perhaps would have had a short skirmish but then yielded. In addition, it is one thing to think we have courage when things are easy but quite another to have it when we are suddenly afflicted. You might have second thoughts if you were suddenly in that man's shoes."

Considering the three thieves cowards is easy for one like Hopeful. Try convincing Little-faith! They seemed like ravenous lions to him. Yet Hopeful feels little compassion. He thinks the weak pilgrim could have done better. Hopeful forgets his own weaknesses and uses himself as a yardstick. He feels sure he would have shown up the three robbers for the cowards they really are.

Yet in judging Little-faith's weakness, Hopeful reveals his own. How quickly he has forgotten his own failure now that God has forgiven and restored him to victory. He thinks Little-faith's trials are of trifling difficulty. Yet how can you know the strength of an attack unless you are its object? Standing back as a spectator and evaluating someone else's trial is easy. This air of superiority over a weak pilgrim who stumbles when sorely pressed annoys Christian. To him, even if Little-faith makes a sorry pilgrim, Hopeful's judgmentalism seems unfair. For he knows his own vulnerabilities and remembers his own faithless and even suicidal departure.

One like Little-faith is bound to be unpopular and his battles lonely. No one came to his help in his time of need—not even Great-grace. It touches Christian's heart that this poor man had to fend for himself, unaided and without sympathy, in his hour of need. Christian champions the weak brother, and such a plea is needed. To most people, this world's Little-faiths are immensely annoying and wearying individuals. Yet since weak believers keep trying and continue moving forward, however weak their fashion, we should offer them encouragement and mercy, not judgment. Do you have delusions about your own spiritual prowess as compared with others? Ask the Lord to grant you a more humble view of his grace in your life.

Scripture: Romans 15:1-2; 1 Corinthians 4:7; 10:12

Prayer: My Savior, help me to remember again how weak and vulnerable I really am. I know that any progress in my life's pilgrimage is due to your grace. Grant me a more compassionate heart to those weaker in faith than I. Amen.

D·A·Y
275

"And consider also that these are journeyman thieves. They serve under the King of the Bottomless Pit, who, if need be, will himself come to their aid with a voice like that of a roaring lion. I myself have been confronted as Little-faith was, and I have found it to be a terrible thing. These three villains set upon me once, and when I began to resist like a Christian, they called their master, and he immediately came. As the saying goes, I would have given my life for a penny, but, thank God, according to His will, I was clothed with the armor of assurance. Although I was so equipped, I still found it difficult to stand firm. No one knows what it's like to go through such combat except the one who is in the battle himself."

Because of his own sense of vulnerability, Christian feels great compassion for Little-faith. He admits that he, too, once encountered these assailants and knows firsthand their ruthless power. He probably refers to his struggles within the Valley of the Shadow of Death that he will never forget. The "armor of assurance" spared his soul. Even with this armor, he barely withstood the assault. Yet those safely out of the line of fire—the armchair critics—think they know how best everyone else should fight their battles.

Hopeful is correct on one count—these three are cowards who most effectively bully the weak of heart. They do not generally try to plunder the strong. Lest we think they are weak, however, we should know they are no mere apprentices at their craft. They are journeymen thieves who from ample experience know just how and when best to strike. If they get overwhelmed, they readily call for their master, Satan. He quickly comes with a fiercely intimidating show of strength. Most of us know that in times when faintness of heart, mistrust, and guilt assail us, many more temptations come along to help them out. These demonic bandits, with the resources of hell to back them up, are no small opponents.

If all self-righteousness and self-confidence were removed from our faith, how many of us would still feel we could stand better than Little-faith? If all were removed from our hearts but what is pure, sincere, and holy, how strong would we feel? If all "wood, hay and stubble" got burned from off our foundation, how much "gold, silver, and precious stones" would truly remain? These thoughts should restore our humility. Ask the Lord to reveal any blind spots and areas of false confidence in your life.

Scripture: 1 Corinthians 3:11-13; Isaiah 35:3-4; Colossians 3:12

Prayer: Dear Lord, help me to approach my strengths and others' shortcomings with sincere humility. I know I have many blind spots that keep me from rendering accurate assessments. I fall upon your grace, and extend that grace to others. Amen.

D·A·Y 276

"But they ran, you see," said Hopeful. "They fled as soon as they thought the one called Great-grace was coming."

"That is true; both they and their master have often fled when Great-grace has appeared, and no wonder, since he is the King's Champion. But I trust you will allow for some difference between Little-faith and the King's Champion. Not all the King's subjects are champions, nor are they able when tried to do such feats of war as Great-grace. Is it fitting to think that a toddler should handle Goliath as David did? Or that a wren should have the strength of an ox? Some are strong, some are weak; some have great faith, some have little. This man was one of the weak, and so he went to pieces."

"I wish Great-grace had appeared to them," said Hopeful.

"If he had, he might have had his hands full," said Christian. "For I have to tell you that though Great-grace is very highly skilled at using his weapons and has done well against them as long as he keeps them at the tip of his Sword, his victory is never assured. For if Faint-heart, Mistrust, or Guilt can get by his sword, they can throw him down. And once a man is down, what can he do? If you look closely at Great-grace's face, you can see numerous scars that prove what I say. Yes, once I heard that he said in combat, 'We despaired even of life'" [2 Corinthians 1:8].

Everybody loves champions, and Great-grace is the King's champion. Yet we can see from his name that his greatness derives not from his own strength but from the grace given him by God. Still this fact escapes Hopeful. Approaching Little-faith's failure much like one who is young and judgmental, he can't get over Little-faith's speedy surrender to the three cowards. He thinks if he had been in Little-faith's place, the outcome would be different. He wonders why, if Great-grace could send them fleeing, Little-faith could not.

Christian explains that you can't measure the strength given one against that given another. Little-faith is not Great-grace, nor should others expect him to be. God will judge us by what we do with what we have. Great-grace, himself, has no easy time winning battles against these demonic bullies. While they quickly fled the scene of their crime with Little-faith, Great-grace has battle scars proving that, although he can skillfully fight, so can they.

Would you be one of Christ's champions? Remember, no matter how strong in faith you would become, it will take God's grace. Champions in God's service are those who have learned to rely on grace. We should pray for more grace both for ourselves and especially for those weak in faith.

Scripture: Romans 12:3; 1 Corinthians 15:10; Acts 4:33

Prayer: Lord Jesus, thank you for your champions of faith. May you raise up many more in our day who know they stand by your grace alone. Amen.

D·A·Y

277

"And how these same criminals and their friends made David groan, mourn, and roar! Yes, and Heman and Hezekiah, who were champions of the faith in their day, were forced to rally when they were assaulted by them as well. In spite of their stand, they were not without bruises. Once Peter thought he would see what he could do, but even though some say he is the prince of the apostles, when they were through with him he was afraid of a weak girl."

In a battle between ancient kingdoms, instead of both armies fighting it out, each king often selected a champion to battle each other. Great-grace, one of the King's most valiant champions, has his scars to prove that battles against the three demons and their friends are not always easy, even for him.

Now Christian cites others of the King's champions who received scars while contending with these devils. David, full of courage, faced and felled the gigantic Philistine champion, Goliath of Gath. In this battle David proved himself one of the King's great champions. Yet later in a time of weakness he fled from King Saul into Philistine territory to Gath, of all places. Not only was he hated there for destroying their champion, but he happened to be carrying Goliath's sword with him. He so feared for his life as he stood before King Achish of Gath that he feigned complete insanity. (See 1 Samuel 21:11-13.)

Heman the Ezrahite wrote Psalm 88 during a time of misery. The enemy nearly made him give up. He says he cried day and night to the Lord because his life drew "near the grave" (vv. 1, 3). He complained to the Lord, "You have put me in the lowest pit, in the darkest depths" (v. 6). He asked, "Why, O Lord, do you reject me and hide your face from me?" (v. 14).

After the prophet Isaiah came to God's champion, Hezekiah, prophesying to put his house in order because he was going to die, Hezekiah got hit hard by these robbers. He wept bitterly. (See 2 Kings 20:1-3.)

Peter, who thought himself a champion, boldly asserted to Christ, "Even if I have to die with you, I will never disown you" (Matthew 26:35). Yet later that same evening, Peter became so gripped with fear that a couple of powerless girls terrified him. He denied even knowing his Master. (See Matthew 26:69-72.)

If when trials beset you, you tend to think you are alone and singled out for trouble, remember you have company. You stand in a long line of pilgrims stretching down through the ages whom the Lord has told, "Be strong; take courage; I am with you."

Scripture: Deuteronomy 31:6; Joshua 1:9; Luke 12:32

Prayer: Dear Father, as I experience various trials, I see how I stand in the best of company. As you faithfully carried them through, you will do so for me. Amen.

D·A·Y
278

"Besides, their helper comes at their whistle. He is never out of hearing range, and whenever they are hard-pressed, he comes to help them immediately, if possible. Of him it is said, 'When he rises up, the mighty are terrified; they retreat before his thrashing. The sword that reaches him has no effect, nor does the spear or the arrow or the javelin. Iron he treats like straw and bronze like rotten wood. Arrows do not make him flee; slingstones are like chaff to him. A club seems to him but a piece of straw; he laughs at the rattling of the lance' [Job 41:25-29]. What can one do in a case like this?

"It is true, if one could have Job's horse, along with the skill and courage to ride him, he could do notable things. For 'he paws fiercely, rejoicing in his strength, and charges into the fray. He laughs at fear, afraid of nothing; he does not shy away from the sword. The quiver rattles against his side, along with the flashing spear and lance. In frenzied excitement he heats up the ground; he cannot stand still when the trumpet sounds. At the blast of the trumpet he snorts, "Aha!" He catches the scent of battle from afar, the shout of commanders and the battle cry'" [Job 39:21-25].

Satan is called "the great dragon" in Scripture. Now Christian cites Job's description of Leviathan to remind Hopeful that the devil's assaults can be more terrible than anything in all creation. Although some have considered Leviathan a mere whale or crocodile, he may quite possibly have been a literal dragon. This now-extinct dinosaur-like animal may have had, much like the bombardier beetle, some explosion-producing mechanism that enabled him to be a real fire-breathing dragon!

Those who have never battled a dragon might be inclined to reduce the "helper" of demons to more pint-sized proportions. They think that with their faith and armor they could put a quick end to him. Full of zeal and confidence, they little recognize their own heart's frailty. They boast in ways that the experienced pilgrim knows better than to do. The latter speaks humbly of the past and unassumingly of the future while these revel in their imaginary crusades. Christian, however, will never forget his own battle with Apollyon. Since he barely survived his clash with this dragon, he feels no smug confidence about meeting another one.

Despite all this, Christian thinks that with the war horse of Job's description, along with skill and courage, one could do mighty things. Even in the midst of clashing armies, the horse remains full of resolute confidence in his rider. May we have such confidence in God! In the face of frightening enemy threats, can you trust God for victory?

Scripture: Isaiah 27:1; Psalm 91:13; Jude 20

Prayer: Dear Lord, help me to have faith to engage the enemy victoriously. At the same time, give me more appreciation for those wounded on life's battlefield. Amen.

D·A·Y
279

"But for those of us who walk on the ground, let us never desire to meet with an enemy, nor boast as if we could do better than another when we hear of their failings. Let us not flatter ourselves with thoughts of our own boldness, prowess, or power, for those who do this are often the ones who fall hardest under trial. Take Peter, for example, whom I mentioned before. His foolish mind convinced him that he would do better and stand more faithfully for his Master than all the others. In spite of his worthless boasting, these villains soundly defeated him."

❦

The war horse may fly across the plain into battle so confidently that he seems to eat up the ground. The rest of us, however, "who walk on the ground," must tread more cautiously.

Resenting the very idea that he could deny Christ, Peter vehemently declared to the Lord, "Though all become deserters because of you, I will never desert you" (Matthew 26:33 NRSV). He was so idealistic in his assumption that he could willingly embrace death for his Lord. He looked at the other disciples and saw their weaknesses and supposed they might fall away. But not Peter! No, never! Despite his certainty, several awful hours later he was torn from his delusional pedestal, landing with a tremendous thud. All his boasting proved utterly "worthless."

Just like Peter, those who overconfidently boast before the battle about what they will do for Christ and how they will gladly suffer for him generally fall the hardest. Despite their best intentions—for they abhor the thought of denying their beloved Lord—they painfully come to see their pathetic weakness. Peter's bold pronouncements made him even more vulnerable. When Faint-heart and Mistrust were finished mauling him, Guilt came with his club and nearly crushed his soul. Peter was left so shocked and dazed that he could scarcely figure out what had hit him. How sadly mistaken he had been; how wretchedly ashamed he felt! He would never have recovered but for the loving grace of his compassionate risen Lord.

If we think ourselves steadfast, if we trust our strength, knowledge, or gifts, we should beware. God's Word says that, rather than judging others, we should carefully watch our own walk. We should ever remember we possess nothing and can do nothing of ourselves that pertains to eternal life. We owe our entire being and our very preservation to God and his mercy. We have no graces or gifts that we have not received from him. Have you come to the end of yourself? Can you cast yourself completely upon Christ's grace?

❦

Scripture: Galatians 6:1-5; Romans 12:16; Matthew 18:1-4

Prayer: Blessed Lord, give me eyes to see that anything good in me comes from you and belongs to you. Thank you for graciously helping me stand against self-defeating pride and presumption. Amen.

D·A·Y
280

"When we hear of such robberies taking place on the King's Highway, I believe we should do two things. First, we must go out fully equipped, and this includes taking a shield with us. Without a shield, how can we hope to stand against one such as Leviathan? If we have no shield, he thinks nothing of us. Therefore, as one highly skilled in warfare has said, 'In addition to all this, take up the shield of faith, with which you can extinguish all the flaming arrows of the evil one'" [Ephesians 6:16].

❦

Christian offers some practical advice. First, never go out lacking any part of the armor—the belt of truth, breastplate of righteousness, shoes of the Gospel of peace, shield of faith, helmet of salvation, and all kinds of prayer. He especially gives prominence to the shield, without which a pilgrim has little hope of standing against the enemy.

If the King's champions need the shield of faith for defending themselves, how much more must we. By faith we lay hold of Christ, the power of his blood, the benefits of his redemption. In this way we rely upon abundant unseen provisions from him. We have a sure defense for every assault. By faith we protect ourselves from all the fiery darts in enemy arsenals. We not only repel our enemies with this shield, but we conquer them as well.

When we hold up the shield of faith, it protects every other piece of armor. It safeguards truth, righteousness, peace, and salvation against all kinds of satanic temptations. It alone quenches every fiery dart the enemy hurls. These assaults come as "darts" because they often hit as a sudden and thick barrage that can pierce us with much grief. They are "fiery" because the evil one intends them to inflame our passions and incite our minds and hearts to lust, anger, discouragement, and the like. In this way, he sets many a soul ablaze with hell's fire. Yet it matters not how numerous these fiery darts may be—the shield of faith is designed to fend off every one of them.

Faint-heart, Mistrust, and Guilt would all try to bring this shield down. They want to weaken our belief in our cause, in our Captain, in our armor, in our ability to use our armor effectively. Our cause, however, is just, our Captain true, our armor powerful, our victory assured. As we believe these things by applying God's Word and Christ's grace to our struggle, we hold up our shield and keep the advantage. However, if we begin to doubt, we give our enemies an unwarranted edge. What are some ways you can become more practiced in using your shield?

❦

Scripture: 1 Corinthians 15:57; 1 John 5:4; Isaiah 12:2

Prayer: Faithful Lord, please train me to use the shield of faith effectively so that every fiery dart from the enemy will fall powerless against it. Amen.

D·A·Y 281

"Second, I believe that it is good also to desire a convoy of the King's forces to accompany us for our protection. Indeed, we should petition the King Himself to go with us. This caused David to rejoice in the Valley of the Shadow of Death, and Moses would rather have died than to have gone one step without his God. Oh, my brother, if He will go with me, 'I will not fear the tens of thousands drawn up against me on every side' [Psalm 3:6]. But without Him, even the proudest warriors fall into the ranks of the slain."

After Christian's first practical advice, never to leave one's shield behind when going out on the King's Highway, he offers a second. He says he believes they should always desire a convoy—an escort of protective forces—to travel with them. Better yet, they should petition the King himself to go with them.

Why did David walk in complete peace in the same valley that so terrified Christian? Just listen as he prays: "Even though I walk through the valley of the shadow of death, I will fear no evil, for *you are with me*" (Psalm 23:4, italics mine). He feels *no* fear? How can this be? At this time in David's life, he felt certain of God's presence with him. Therefore, he didn't fear Satan or any of his hordes. Neither did he fear wolves, lions, evil men, or evil things. Who or what, after all, was greater than his God?

Moses also knew this secret. God appointed him to lead Israel out of Egypt's bondage, through the wilderness, and into the Promised Land. Moses, however, petitioned the Lord to convey him and the people safely through to their journey's end. He told the Lord that if God's presence did not go with them, he wanted to stay put.

Christian recognizes also that if the Lord's presence goes with him, he will have no reason to fear anyone, not even thousands of the enemy. Without God's very presence, however, even the greatest champions will fall slain.

Our Lord is sure to give us a convoy when we ask. But we should be careful neither to run ahead of nor behind him. He wants to walk with us; he is on our side. Do you tend to barge out on your own before first seeking God's presence? Try making a habit of waiting upon him first. Then you will have confidence even in the worst-seeming disasters because you will know he is with you.

Scripture: Exodus 33:11-17; Psalm 27:1-3; Judges 5:21

Prayer: Dear Lord, I need you. I am weak and inadequate and ask that your presence convey me safely through my pilgrimage. I love you and do not want to go one step without you. Amen.

D·A·Y
282

"As for me, I already have some experience in this warfare, and through the abundant grace of Him who is greatest, I am still very much alive, as you see. But I cannot boast of any strength on my part. As a matter of fact, I would be very greatly relieved if I never had to experience any such attacks again. I fear, however, that we have not yet gone beyond all danger. But as the lion and the bear have not yet devoured me, I trust that God will also deliver us from the next 'uncircumcised Philistines,' those enemies of God that seek our destruction." Then Christian sang,

"Poor Little-faith! Have you been among thieves?
Were you robbed? Remember, if you believe,
You'll get more faith; then a victor you'll be
Over ten thousand, and not a mere three."

Christian's faith is greater than Little Faith's and smaller than Great-grace's. Either way, God's grace has proved abundantly sufficient for his pilgrimage. He considers himself no champion; he dislikes warfare intensely; he even wishes never to fight another battle as long as he lives. Yet he knows enemies continue lurking along the Highway. Still, as with David who conquered Goliath, he trusts in God to enable him to overcome whatever enemies come his way.

For Little-faith Christian has a word: "God has not abandoned you!" Matthew, quoting Isaiah, said of Christ, "He will not break a bruised reed or quench a smoldering wick until he brings justice to victory" (Matthew 12:20 NRSV). Yes, Little-faith's enemies have bruised and wounded him. However, Christ stands compassionately ready to bind up his broken heart, heal his wounds, and restore to him comfort and joy in the Holy Spirit. Great hope remains for those who sincerely cry, "I do believe; help me overcome my unbelief!" (Mark 9:24).

Those who want God to work out his salvation in their lives must also be willing to work it out for themselves "with fear and trembling." Little-faith's recovery will come in due proportion to his applying the measure of faith God has given him. Do you desire a more solid, robust faith? Faith grows greater by the continual exercise of it; therefore, you should intentionally exercise it daily. If you make this your practice, then, soon to God's glory, your enemies will fall before you, whether by threes or by thousands. As C. H. Spurgeon said, "Little faith will bring your souls to Heaven, but great faith will bring Heaven to your souls."

Scripture: 1 Samuel 17:22-37; Luke 17:6; Psalm 18:29

Prayer: Gracious Savior, thank you for your patient love and grace that gently restores my soul after suffering defeat. Help me to grow in grace and faith so that every giant will fall before me. Amen.

DAY 283

So they traveled on, with Ignorance following along behind them, until they came to a place where another way joined the Way that they were on. Both ways seemed to lie straight ahead in the direction they were supposed to go. They were confused, unsure which of the two to take, so they stopped there, wondering what to do.

As they were thinking, a man wearing a white robe approached them and asked why they were standing there. They told him that they were going to the Celestial City but were confused about which of the ways to take. "Follow me," said the man. "I am going there." Impressed by his appearance, they followed him in the way that joined the Way they had come on. That way gradually turned, and by degrees it turned them away from the City.

After the distance they have come, wouldn't you think a deceiver could no longer sway the pilgrims? But this deception takes no looking over a wall into a parallel path. They see what looks just like the real path, straight and true. Not only that, but this impressive holy-looking man attests to its legitimacy and calls them to follow him to the Celestial City. Surely one in such saintly garb couldn't have ill motives, could he? Martin Luther wrote, "For the devil will not be ugly and black in his ministers, but fair and white. And to the end he may appear to be such a one, he setteth forth and decketh all his words and works with the colour of truth, and with the name of God."[27]

As we progress in our spiritual pilgrimage, temptations become increasingly subtle. Satan, a cunning strategist, realizes that we know better than to fall for traps that have become obvious, so he alters them with fresh appeal. We should also be keenly aware that in the last days, deceptions will multiply and intensify. Christ clearly warned that false prophets will come in his own name. Today they say things such as, "Follow me; I am the reincarnated Christ, the Christ-essence, the Illumined Master." These may say they represent Christ, but they are fake Christs, not the Christ of holy Scripture.

How, then, might the pilgrims have protected themselves? They should have paused to study, pray, and await the Holy Spirit's guidance. When there is a question about which way is God's Way, don't be presumptuous. Remember that your enemy is cunning and has more patience than you do and carefully leads his victims astray "by degrees." To avoid his designs, you should inquire of God at every step. Is there presently a concern for which you need to inquire of God?

Scripture: Matthew 24:4-5, 10-11, 23-27; 2 Corinthians 11:4; 2 Peter 2:1-2

Prayer: Dear Lord, I know I can presume nothing in this life. I must adamantly stick to your Word and your Way. Help me to tread extremely cautiously. Amen.

DAY 284

In a short time their faces were turned in the opposite direction, but they continued to follow him. Before they realized what was happening, the man led them into a net. They got so tangled up in it that they didn't know what to do. At that, the white robe fell off the man's back, and they saw the error of their way. They lay there crying for some time because they didn't know how to free themselves.

Eventually Christian said to Hopeful, "Now I can see that I am in error. Didn't the Shepherds warn us to beware of the flatterers, those deceivers who give false hope and deceitful encouragement? They are able to persuasively entice the careless into following their ways. As the saying of the wise man goes, we have found that 'whoever flatters his neighbor is spreading a net for his feet'" [Proverbs 29:5].

Can true believers be deceived? Although some think not, the Bible strongly suggests otherwise. Christ warned his disciples, "Beware that no one leads you astray" (Matthew 24:4 NRSV). Paul said to the Ephesians, "Let no one deceive you with empty words" (Ephesians 5:6 NRSV). He exhorted the Thessalonians, "Let no one deceive you in any way" (2 Thessalonians 2:3 NRSV). John told believers in general, "Little children, let no one deceive you" (1 John 3:7 NRSV).

Christian and Faithful have fallen to deception. The theological net Satan laid has so entangled them that they cannot find their way out. Yet the way seemed so true; its deviations were so subtle. Oh, how smooth, how slippery, how deceitful was this "flatterer." Because he had no horns or pitchfork—for "every devil has not a cloven hoof,"[28]—they naively took for granted that he was leading them aright. Now look at them—they cannot even remember the truth!

How did the pilgrims fall so easily into deception? The answer lies both within the flatterer's nature and within their own. Flattery strokes egos, and the men were especially vulnerable at this time. After their own mountaintop experience, they met someone ignorant, saw someone apostate, and discussed at length someone with little faith. Evidently the combined effect left them susceptible to this seducer's well-timed praises. Considering the Shepherds' forewarning, they should have known better.

But how about us? What is our response to end-time flatterers around us? When they try enticing us with a deeper, more enlightened spirituality through self-realization, self-actualization, contact with our own inner divine nature, consciousness of our ultimate self, how will we respond? Beware! Today's "sorcerized narcissism" is from the same one who flattered both himself in heaven and Eve in the Garden.

Scripture: Psalm 140:5; Matthew 7:15; Micah 6:8

Prayer: Lord of truth, I don't want to give heed to the seducing, self-glorifying spirits of this age. Help me to stay very close to the simple truth of your Gospel. Help me to see you more clearly in your Word. Amen.

D·A·Y 285

Then Hopeful said, "The Shepherds also gave us instructions so that we wouldn't have trouble keeping to the Way. But we were careless and forgot to read them and therefore haven't kept ourselves from the destroyer's path. David was wiser than we are, for he said, 'By the word of Your lips, I have kept away from the paths of the destroyer'" [Psalm 17:4].

So they lay there helpless in the net, crying over their captivity.

How demoralizing for those of us who had hoped that our pilgrim Christian might be the quintessential paragon of victorious Christianity. But Christian represents ordinary pilgrims of average achievement. Sometimes he shows himself wise and other times immensely foolish. This present blunder is not his first. He has exhibited vulnerability to strangers from the beginning of his pilgrimage when he listened to Worldly-wiseman. Now this flattering stranger says one smooth, commending word, and, intoxicated with self-glory, Christian immediately runs into a net. And not just him but Hopeful, too.

Those who disregard their godly shepherd's instructions and follow one who "tickles their ears" and reinforces them in an unscriptural manner may become tragically deceived. Hopeful remembers too late the reliable instructions given him. Both pilgrims forgot the Scriptures, the rule and standard for their faith and conduct. They forgot the faithful teaching of their appointed shepherds. Puffed up with some imagined attainment, they ignored their own weakness and need for the kind of support that would have kept them in the right Way. They overlooked danger, forgot truth, and neglected duty.

The human heart is always readily accessible to flattery in all its various forms. We so easily fall to self-congratulatory thoughts that soothe us into an unwarrantably high view of ourselves. Someone flatters us and we go with it. Feeling soothed and secure, our guard comes down. Then in the face of a difficult decision as to which way to go, we carelessly consult our own leaning and follow our own preference. We should have sought God's will and glory.

The church must guard against those dressed in white as much as those dressed in black. For Satan, like the mythological Proteus, assumes any form to best suit his purpose. We should also be very careful of our own hearts, for within each of us resides the arch-flatterer—our own proud and sinful nature. Will you commit yourself to put down flattery when you notice it beckoning you?

Scripture: Psalms 17:5; 119:116-17, 133; Daniel 11:32

Prayer: Dear Lord, again I humble myself. How easily I run ahead of your will thinking I know what is best. Please help me to remember godly instruction that I may avoid deception. Amen.

DAY 286

At last they noticed a Shining One coming toward them with a whip in his hand. When he came to where they were, he asked them where they came from and how they got there. They answered that they were poor pilgrims on their way to Zion, but they had been led out of their way by a man clothed in white who told them to follow him because he was going there also.

Then the Shining One with the whip said, "He is Flatterer, a false apostle who has transformed himself into an angel of light." He then tore the net and let them out, saying to them, "Follow me so that I may lead you back to the Way."

Christian has not seen a shining one since he first got saved. On that joyous occasion, they came with a gift of peace, garments of salvation, and a mark on his forehead. But this is another day, and today's shining one carries no gifts. He carries only a whip. At least it is not a sword! Still what a shameful occasion this is. After their experience on the Delectable Mountains, they were so full of knowledge, faith, hope, and assurance. They felt so superior to Ignorance; Hopeful showed such condescension toward Little-faith. Ignorance and Little-faith would have had their revenge if they could see these two proud old men now!

A false apostle undid these two supposedly mature pilgrims by flattery. He may have commended their wisdom, suggesting that they knew the enemy's schemes too well to be deceived. When their situation called for earnest prayer and a diligent search of the Scriptures, they seem to have presumptuously relied on their own spiritual prowess. They thought they had become such distinguished men of discernment that they were now on the fast track to the City. Indeed, a haughty spirit goes before a fall.

Yet in such a thankless, disheartening world, susceptibility to ego-gratification is predicated upon true need. Believers do need to bless one another. Those struggling to do their best can use some appreciation and encouragement. A little word of praise to those who labor among us can lift them up when they feel discouraged. We can thank God for the encouragers among us who draw out our best when we feel small and useless. These are blessed friends. But flatterers are different. With white robes cloaking their sinful hearts, they have a design in mind to their own end. Showering us with insincere compliments, they set us up for a fall as we gain false confidence in ourselves and in them. Can you learn to give and receive encouragement that builds up and to refuse flattery that puffs up?

Scripture: 1 John 4:1; 1 Thessalonians 2:5-8; Job 32:21-22

Prayer: Dear Lord, help me to guard my heart against vain flatteries. Help me likewise to be a sincere encourager and to flatter no one. Amen.

So he led them back to the Way, which they had left to follow the Flatterer. Then he asked them, "Where did you sleep last night?"

"With the Shepherds on the Delectable Mountains," they answered.

He then asked them if the Shepherds had given them a sheet of directions to direct them on the Way.

"Yes," they answered.

"But didn't you pull it out and read it when you were confused about which way to go?"

"No."

"Why not?"

"We forgot."

"Didn't the Shepherds warn you to beware of the flatterers?"

"Yes, but we didn't imagine that this fine-speaking man was one."

Everyone says he or she is traveling heavenward—fools, deceivers, and pilgrims alike. Some paths are so close to the true one that avoiding them takes extreme caution. C. S. Lewis said, "The safest road to hell is the gradual one—the gentle slope, soft underfoot, without sudden turnings, without milestones, without signposts." Satan lulls us into false security through his flattering agents.

Many ministers, starting in the truth, fall to flattery. Believing corrupt flatteries, either from within or from without, they embrace falsehoods, deceiving and being deceived. Before the white-robed flattering angel Moroni seduced Joseph Smith into founding Mormonism, he went to Christian churches. Charles Taze Russell founded Jehovah Witnesses but began as a Bible teacher. Sun Myung Moon, raised a Presbyterian, founded the Unification Church. Jim Jones pastored a Christian church of thousands, which ultimately became his People's Temple. David Koresh of the Branch Davidians was a former Seventh-Day Adventist. Marshall Applewhite, a former seminarian and Presbyterian preacher's kid, founded the Heaven's Gate cult.

Satan looks like an angel of light and his ministers like purveyors of truth. These apostate deceivers soothe with flattery those who have deep ego needs. These teachers lead troubled consciences into false peace. They mislead the simple and unwary, landing them into demonic nets. Satan has lures for all kinds of people. Believers can be vulnerable to exciting new teachings, fantastic dreams, or thrilling manifestations. Can you think of a more important word to be uttered in today's self-gratifying, self-preferring, self-absorbed church than the Shepherds' admonition to "beware of the flatterer"?

Scripture: 2 Corinthians 11:13-14; Jeremiah 5:31; Romans 16:18

Prayer: Merciful Lord, please have mercy on your people. We are so proudly independent and prone to deception. Help us to love your truth and honor the instructions of godly pastors and leaders. Amen.

D·A·Y 288

Then I saw in my dream that he commanded them to lie down, which they did, and he gave them a whipping to teach them the right way to walk. He said, "Those whom I love I rebuke and discipline. So be earnest, and repent" [Revelation 3:19]. This done, he sent them on their way advising them to pay careful attention to the other directions given by the Shepherds. So they thanked him for all his kindness and went carefully along the right Way, singing:

"Now come here, you who walk along the way,
See how the pilgrims fare who go astray:
Taking lightly good counsel, they forget
And are soon caught in an entangling net;
It's true they were rescued, but still you see,
They're whipped to boot: let this your caution be."

The pilgrims have come a great distance, but with spiritual growth comes corresponding dangers. When mature believers notice the rich grace blossoming in their souls, they can't help but feel good about it. God wants us to have satisfaction when we have done well. Possessing humility doesn't mean ignorance of our own spiritual growth. Unfortunately, we are so vulnerable to pride that although God might praise us, often he cannot. We must wait until the next life when, free of sin, we can respond to his "Well done" with pure unadulterated joy.

How easily the pilgrims wandered from healthy self-respect to sinful self-adulation. Fortunately, the Lord graciously sent his angel to rescue them and pluck their feet out of the net. Nevertheless, after releasing them, he severely humbled them with painful correction. Knowing the reasons for their scourging, they bore their discipline patiently. Afterwards they were even thankful for the "kindness" shown them. For this was not vindictive punishment, as Christ had already borne their punishment. This was their loving Father's discipline for their own good. Their gratitude in itself shows maturity.

The Lord knows how to discipline us. He can afflict our conscience, let our circumstances bring us misery, allow us to feel the Holy Spirit quenched and grieving, send his Word or his ministers to afflict us. However we experience it, he does it in love to correct and train us in righteousness. Rather than being alarmed, we should be grateful he didn't leave us in the net. Do you appreciate his loving discipline?

Scripture: Psalm 32:3-5; Proverbs 3:11-12; 15:31-33; Hebrews 12:5-13

Prayer: Heavenly Father, when I wander from your perfect Way, please train my heart to correct itself. If, however, I need your discipline, by all means, I welcome it as a gift of your love. Amen.

D·A·Y
289

Now after awhile they could see someone far in the distance coming toward them. Christian said, "There is a man with his back toward Zion, and he is coming to meet us."

"I see him," said Hopeful. "Let's be careful now; he may be a flatterer also." So he drew nearer and nearer until at last he came to them. His name was Atheist, and he asked them where they were going.

"We are going to the Mount Zion." At that, Atheist began to laugh uncontrollably. "Why are you laughing?" asked Christian.

"Ha! Ignorant people like you make me laugh. You take upon yourselves such a tedious journey only to end in all likelihood with nothing but your travels for all your pains."

"Why, sir," asked Christian, "don't you think we'll be received?"

"Received! There is not such a place as you dream of in all this world!"

"But there is in the world to come."

A whole parade of infidels to the King's Way has confronted the pilgrims in their lifetime. Some have flagrantly opposed the King's Way. Obstinate scoffed, Worldly-wiseman mocked, Vanity's witnesses scorned. For, "In the last time there will be scoffers . . ." (Jude 18 NRSV). Now this vociferous, blaspheming atheist with his soul-deep flaw sneeringly dismisses everything they believe. With his back to Zion, he insults their intelligence by laughingly calling them ignorant in the face of his hardheaded pragmatism. This could easily rouse their pride and elicit a self-defensive reaction—a defeat in itself. His aim is to provoke them to outrage, thus giving himself one more reason to reject the Gospel's claims.

To Atheist, the pilgrimage is one tedious, boring, asinine pursuit. Yet he is alone and empty in the silent void of a godless, purposeless universe. Just listen to atheist astronomer Carl Sagan: "The significance of our lives and our fragile planet is determined only by our own wisdom and courage. We are the custodians of life's meaning. We long for a Parent to care for us, to forgive our errors, to save us from our childish mistakes. But knowledge is preferable to ignorance. Better by far to embrace the hard truth than a reassuring fable."[29] How tragic for Carl Sagan that he apparently continued in unbelief to the day of his death. What will his "own wisdom and courage" do for him now? We do not need to defend ourselves in the face of godless scoffers and atheists. God will vindicate us. For in the end, all people will acknowledge God. When fools mock you, do you find yourself responding defensively, or do you give a confident yet gentle response?

Scripture: 2 Corinthians 4:3-4; Obadiah 3-4; Proverbs 3:34-35; Isaiah 47:10

Prayer: Lord Jesus, today's culture abounds with the philosophies of godless atheists. Help me to rise above their bold jibes at my faith. Thank you that I know your truth, and it has set me free. Amen.

D·A·Y
290

"When I was at home in my own country, I heard about your belief, and afterward I decided to pursue it. I have been seeking this City for twenty years but can find no more of it than I did the first day I set out."

"We have both heard and believe that there is such a place to be found," responded Christian.

"If I hadn't believed when I was at home, I wouldn't have come this far to seek it. But finding nothing—and I would have if it were there—I'm going back again and will seek to refresh myself with the things I had formerly cast away for those vain hopes."

Unlike agnostics with their "perhaps," Atheist lives in certainty that the Celestial City doesn't exist. After a twenty-year investigation, he has supposedly found *nothing*! Something was wrong with this man's pursuit. For the heavens themselves declare God's glory. The fact is, rarely can an atheist be found who is genuinely searching for truth. Most are willful hypocrites. We can safely say that pure atheism is a matter of the will. The atheist pits his mind and will deliberately against all the evidences of the universe and stands with the Russian cosmonaut who from space declared, "God isn't here!" Yes, fools say this in their hearts because their hearts first say it to them. Jesus said that even if they saw someone rise from the dead, they would not believe (Luke 16:31).

Atheists think that humanity created God (rather than the other way around). Best-selling author Karen Armstrong set out to prove that God is "a product of humankind's creative imagination." In her *A History of God,*[30] she makes belief in God a mind-trip, consisting of mystical subjective experiences rather than objective fact. To her, a religious pilgrimage will "not be an ascent to a reality outside ourselves . . . but a descent into the deepest recesses of the mind."

None are more likely to become avowed atheists than those who for years falsely professed the Gospel. Having never experienced its true effects, they turn to despising it, calling it stupid and fanatical. Thus God permits Satan to blind their eyes for refusing his truth. So Atheist with his dead faith and worldly heart plans to make up for his wasted years now that atheism has liberated him from the stifling confines of belief in God. He can now vigorously oppose what he considers ignorance and superstition. Thinking himself free, he is really a blind slave both to himself and to this world's god. When these types smugly think themselves enlightened while judging you as blind, remember that it's the other way around. Rejoice that God is alive and has shined his light of revelation into your heart.

Scripture: Proverbs 14:6-7; Habakkuk 2:4; Psalms 19:1-4; 33:8-9

Prayer: Blessed Jesus, thank you for your liberation. Far from stifling me, you give me the joy and freedom of walking in relationship with my Creator. Amen.

D·A·Y

291

Then Christian said to Hopeful, "Do you think what this man is saying is true?"

"Be careful," replied Hopeful, "for he is one of the flatterers. Remember what it has cost us already for listening to this type of fellow. What! No Mount Zion? Didn't we see the Gate of the City from the Delectable Mountains? Aren't we now to walk by faith? Let's go on, lest the man with the whip overtakes us again! You should have been the one to teach me this lesson, but I will whisper it in your ears: 'Stop listening to teaching that contradicts what you know is right.' My brother, I say, stop listening to him, and let us believe and thus secure the salvation of our souls."

"My brother," said Christian, "I didn't ask the question because I doubted the truth of our belief, but to test you and to draw out the fruit of integrity from your heart. As for this man, I know that the god of this world has blinded him. Let us both go on, secure in the fact that we believe the truth, knowing that 'no lie comes from the truth'" [1 John 2:21].

Then Hopeful said, "Now I rejoice in my hope of seeing the glory of God." So they turned away from the man, and he went his way, laughing at them.

Until Christian explains himself, Hopeful thinks he might be in trouble again. Both, however, jealously guard their faith against Atheist's claims. While the man never saw his brain, he believes it's in his head because he experiences the effects of it. Yet he rejects what he considers is never-never land because he has not seen it.

Of course the City exists. The pilgrims saw its gates from the Delectable Mountains! Atheist's contemptuous sneers may turn away those of unsound heart, but the pilgrims, along with John, can proclaim, "We have seen it with our own eyes!" (See 1 John 1:1.)

If only Atheist had sincerely searched in faith, he would have climbed the Delectable Mountains and seen visions of the City, too. Some things cannot be seen but on the high mountains of God's revelation-truth, and if someone refuses to climb above the level of his own common sense, he is in no position to assert anything.

Many today claim to be atheists—22.5 million in the United States alone. They build their beliefs upon the supposition that God doesn't exist. Whether these people simply scoff or fiercely oppose God's Way, true believers will hold fast and never leave it. Have dark temptations to doubt God hit at you? Look at God's creation and look back on former experiences of his loving care. Read his Word again. Never doubt in the darkness what God has shown you in his light.

Scripture: 2 Corinthians 4:6; Luke 10:21-23; Psalm 73:27-28

Prayer: Precious Lord, I know you have poured your love and light into me. Thank you for the glimpses I've seen of your eternal kingdom. Help unbelievers to see your light, too. Amen.

D·A·Y 292

I saw then in my dream that they went on till they came into a certain country where the air naturally tended to cause drowsiness in those unaccustomed to it. Hopeful's mind began to grow dull, and he became very sleepy. He then said to Christian, "I'm getting so drowsy that I can hardly keep my eyes open. Let's lie down here and take a short nap."

"No way!" said Christian. "If we sleep here, we may never wake up."

"Why not, my brother? Sleep is sweet to one who is exhausted. We may be refreshed if we take a nap."

"Don't you remember that one of the Shepherds warned us to beware of the Enchanted Ground? He meant that we should beware of sleeping there, 'So then, let us not be like others, who are asleep but let us be alert and self-controlled'" [1 Thessalonians 5:6].

An intoxicating soul-deadening spiritual virus hangs heavily in the atmosphere at the Enchanted Ground. Hopeful finds himself immediately susceptible to its spell. Fortunately, his brother reminds him of the shepherds' warning. Yet many pilgrims succumb here by taking a sweet but deadly rest before the time of rest has come. Yes, it is deadly! Unwarranted resting may quickly pass on to a fatal slumber of perpetual sensual ease. Such weariness is no mere natural weariness, but there is an enchantment about it. It is a worldly spirit that comes late in the pilgrimage and assumes various forms.

While the sins of the young openly betray them, the disintegration of one's spiritual life in later years is more subtle. Some get so enchanted with the next passage of their life that, after years of dedicated service, they settle into worldly alliances. They slip off the Lord's yoke, hand over their duty to others, and live to please themselves. This shift in devotion happens right at a time when the lessons of their experience should make them the most useful. Perhaps, like others, with their retirement from secular employment, they add an unwarranted early retirement from their spiritual duty. They think they have earned the right to become full-time vagabonds and loafers to the neglect of the church that Christ died to build and the lost whom he died to save. Few will run off the cliff into pure degeneracy, yet the dangers of this time of life are extreme.

During times of persecution and storm, we could not sleep if we tried, but these are pleasant times when the battle seems over with no seeming danger or opposition. Hearts can fall asleep from too much prosperity. Life is easy; we feel good, righteous, self-satisfied. Even those who have fought through every former trial and temptation often lose their vigilance in these enchanting circumstances. How alert are you?

Scripture: Hebrews 6:11-12; 2 Peter 1:5-11; Matthew 24:42

Prayer: My Lord, help me to stay alert to your will in every season of my life. I want to faithfully persevere till the end. Amen.

D·A·Y 293

"I admit my fault," said Hopeful. "If I had been here alone, I would have run the risk of death by falling asleep. I see that what the wise man said is true, 'Two are better than one' [Ecclesiastes 4:9]. Thus far your company has been a gift of mercy to me; 'you shall surely have a good reward for your effort.'"

"You have blessed me too," said Christian, "but to keep the drowsiness of this place from overcoming us, let's keep talking about those things that edify our spirits."

"Indeed, I agree with all my heart," Hopeful replied.

"Where shall we begin?" asked Christian.

"Where God began with us. But you start the discussion, if you will."

Then Christian said, "First, I will sing you this song:

When the saints grow sleepy, let them come here
And see how two pilgrims' words remain clear.
Yes, let them learn from these and become wise,
So to keep open their dull, slumbering eyes.
The fellowship of saints, if managed well
Keeps them awake, in spite of all Hell."

For some, drowsiness may not be a matter of mere sleepiness but of spiritual coldness. A story is told of a physician named Dr. Solander, who, on a boat in a certain frigid region, advised the men on deck that they would feel an overpowering desire to fall asleep. He warned that if they did, nothing on earth could awaken them. Yet he was one of the first to surrender to the irresistible urge to sleep. Fortunately, the other men forced him to stay awake.

Thank God for friends who keep us awake! Those who say they can worship God just fine without fellowship miss God's provision for desperate times.

Concerning cold weather, those who exercise physically are apt not to feel its effects. So it is with those who exercise their spiritual lives. The sleepiness of the Enchanted Ground does not come upon the vigorous but upon those who are lax. The sleep of death often begins with one short nap. We must, therefore, crucify our flesh. The creeping desire for spiritual sleep is a gradual yet powerful temptation. No situation requires more watchfulness than this. Therefore, get up, rouse each other, cry out to God earnestly. Ask him to save you from powerful worldly enchantments and to fill you with his life and vitality. Then walk on.

Scripture: Hebrews 10:32; Luke 21:34-36; Mark 13:35-37; 1 Timothy 4:13-16

Prayer: Dear Lord, thank you for Christian friends. Help us to keep one another from spiritual sleepiness. I want to keep my walk energetic and unhindered. Amen.

DAY 294

"I will ask you a question," Christian said. "How did you first decide to begin this pilgrimage?"

"Do you mean, how did I first come to care about my soul's welfare?" asked Hopeful.

"Yes, that's what I mean."

"For a long time I continued to delight in those things that are seen, which were sold at our fair—things that I now believe would have drawn me into Hell and destruction if I had continued with them."

"And what were those things?" asked Christian.

"All the treasures and riches of the world. Oh, I also found great pleasure in riotous behavior, wild parties, drinking, swearing, lying, immorality, Sabbath-breaking, and other things that contribute to the soul's destruction."

Nothing so interests pilgrims as reflecting upon their own experiences in the Lord. Christian and Hopeful begin now to share their personal testimonies and their beliefs. This will encourage them and stimulate them intellectually and spiritually. In this way, they can endure and overcome the area's bewitching spell. Christian asks Hopeful to share first. Hopeful shakes his sleepiness off and begins the personal story of his conversion to Christ.

Until the time when Christian and Faithful entered Vanity, Hopeful had lived like everyone else in Vanity. He was a shallow person, living wholly for what he could see. His primary passion was for earthly riches. He also loved drinking and partying and was no stranger to immorality. He had no regard for God's commandments, and he had obviously never thought deeply about his life. Growing up in Vanity, he had rested all his hopes and dreams on what Vanity had to offer. He now sees that his love for the riches and pleasures of Vanity had contributed to his soul's sickness and was drawing him to hell.

Reminding ourselves of how far God has brought us from our former sins can renew our fervent resolve to follow Christ. Reflect on this awhile—you were bereft of any knowledge of God, had no faith in him, possessed no love for him, experienced no fellowship with him, lacked any knowledge of his Gospel or his promises, knew nothing of his love. You were without hope, desperately lost, and blind to your true spiritual condition. But now you have been saved! Remembering these things should be enough to remove all the dull sleep from your eyes.

Scripture: Ephesians 1:7-8; 2:12-13; Colossians 1:21-22

Prayer: My Savior, thank you for my testimony—the story of your seeking and saving this lost one. Help me to find opportunities to share it with others, and remind me to ask them to share their testimonies with me. I know this will be renewing to us all. Amen.

"But I heard from you and also from beloved Faithful, who died in Vanity Fair for his faith and righteous living, that the consequence of the things I was doing is death. I heard that because of these things, the wrath of God is coming on those who are disobedient. Then I considered these and other things pertaining to God."

"And did you at once fall under the power of this conviction?"

"No, I wasn't immediately willing to admit the evil of sin or to acknowledge the damnation resulting from it. At first, when my mind began to be shaken by the Word, I tried to shut my eyes to its light."

Hopeful had witnessed the death of Faithful at the hands of Vanity's murderers. He had seen that following Christ can result in death. Yet ironically, he was awakened by Christian's and Faithful's witness to see that there is another kind of death—spiritual death—which would be the inevitable consequence of his sinful life. The Holy Spirit showed him that it was Vanity that was doomed, not Faithful, its martyr. Hopeful sensed authenticity and life in Faithful and suddenly became convicted of the masks he and everyone else in Vanity were wearing to cover their spiritual deadness. The enemy, who had purposed to destroy the truth, overshot his goal in killing Faithful. Hopeful saw the truth and got saved. Death's secret was betrayed—"that through death he (Christ) might destroy him who has the power of death, that is, the devil" (Hebrews 2:14 RSV).

Christian and Faithful had spoken and lived the truth. Because they had resisted the pressure to conform to the town's prevailing culture, Hopeful was now a believer. Through their bold and consistent proclamation, the curious onlooker for the first time heard the truth about sin, judgment, and salvation. At first Hopeful had resisted the Holy Spirit's conviction, unwilling to give up the vain hope and false security upon which his life had for so long rested. But God drove a wedge into his heart, and, try as he may, he just could not close his eyes to the truth. An encounter with truth changes everything, and Hopeful would never again be the same. He had but two options—to follow the truth or to live a lie.

Isn't it amazing to think that God can use our simple testimonies to alter a soul's eternal destiny? Never get discouraged with witnessing just because you see no immediate fruit. Although people may resist, seeds have been planted, and they may yet open their hearts to Christ.

Scripture: 2 Corinthians 4:13; Ephesians 6:19; Acts 14:3; 20:24

Prayer: Faithful Lord, it takes faith, obedience, courage, and love to proclaim your truth in the face of indifference or hostility. Please increase these in my life. Amen.

D·A·Y
296

"But what was the cause of your continuing to hold on to the sin when God's blessed Spirit was first beginning to work on you?" asked Christian.

"The causes were as follows: First, I was ignorant of the fact that God was acting upon me. Second, sin was still very desirable to my flesh, and I didn't want to part with it. Third, I didn't know how to break off relationships with my old friends; their companionship and the things we enjoyed together were very important to me. And fourth, the times I was under heavy conviction were so disturbing and frightening to me that I couldn't bear the thought of them, even for a moment."

Hopeful explains why, to begin with, he resisted the truth and tried to close his eyes to it. He had no idea that the source of his confusion was "God's blessed Spirit." How could he know that the miserable attack on his conscience was coming from the God who loves him?

He was also a sinner who loved his sin. The pilgrims challenged him to a completely new orientation toward God and away from sin, and he did not want to face it. He sensed that adjusting to God's values and ways would be costly. He knew that joining the pilgrimage would mean the loss of his cherished friendships, along with the sinful things they had so enjoyed doing together. How could he risk this? How could he suffer their contempt? The thought of a new perspective, a new philosophy of life terrified him, so he refused to engage in a thoughtful, painful assessment of his condition. He pushed aside the mounting evidence against him. He could not bear to think these things through. When the Holy Spirit shone a spotlight of conviction into his sinful heart, the sin nature recoiled in rebellion and dread. Hopeful tried to drown the powerful impressions and persuasions of truth, but his conscience was stricken, and he had to make a choice.

We are an impatient society; we want fast food, fast cars, instant rice, instant replays. Even in the church we get impatient and want instant conversions. Yet according to some surveys most people who make professions of faith do so after a long-term conversion process, not a sudden encounter. We need to allow those like Hopeful an opportunity to wrestle their way through to a well-understood and sincere commitment to Christ. Quick fixes and forced conversions seldom stand the test of time. How patient are you with those with whom you share your faith?

Scripture: Proverbs 1:20-22; Isaiah 30:18; Ephesians 4:2

Prayer: Dear Lord, help me to be willing to work with people and not grow impatient with those who struggle with salvation. I want to be a good witness to them from start to finish. Amen.

D·A·Y 297

"But then," said Christian, "it seems that at times you were freed from the turmoil."

"Yes, this is true, but it would again return to my mind, and then I would be as bad—no, even worse—than I had been before."

"Why, Hopeful, what was it that brought your sins to mind again?"

"Many things, such as if I met a believer in the street, or if I heard anything read from the Bible, or if my head began to ache, or if I was told that a neighbor was sick, or if I heard the bell toll for someone dead, or if I thought of dying myself, or if I heard of the sudden death of someone else—but especially when I thought of myself soon facing the judgment."

"Were there any times when you could easily dispel the feelings of guilt that came over you in these ways?"

"No, none at all. For they got an ever tighter grip on my conscience, and if I even thought of continuing in sin, it would mean double torment for me."

When Faithful and Christian presented the Gospel in Vanity, Hopeful heard more than he wanted to. Perhaps if their sole message had been, "Smile, God loves you and has a great plan for your life," he could have enjoyed peace. Then he could have rejected their message as it fell flat at Faithful's martyrdom. He could have responded, "Is this God's wonderful plan? Who needs it?" The pilgrims' testimony, however, made clear the call to and the cost of true discipleship. Their witness was so broad and deep that Hopeful became convinced of his guilt. He felt like David who cried, "My sin is ever before me" (Psalm 51:3 NRSV).

Jesus said of the Holy Spirit that "when he comes, he will convict the world of guilt in regard to sin and righteousness and judgment" (John 16:8). The Spirit continually drove his message home to Hopeful's heart. Every time his experience of conviction eased, something would happen to reawaken it—meeting a believer, hearing the Bible, hearing of someone sick, thinking of his or someone else's death. The thing, however, that really tied his stomach in knots was the terrifying prospect of facing God in judgment. This truth weighed so heavily that he could no longer enjoy his sin.

The last person an unrepentant sinner wants to meet on the other side of the grave is God. There will be no "Smile, God loves you" on Judgment Day. In our witness, we dare not hide the reality of God's judgment. The Holy Spirit often uses this very truth to awaken sinners to their need for Christ. Will you pray that the sinners you know will feel more of his convicting power in our day?

Scripture: Ecclesiastes 11:9; Acts 17:31; Ezekiel 33:10-11

Prayer: Holy Spirit, please increase your work today. Do a mighty work in calling sinners to repentance. Light a fire within my heart, too, that I might do my part in the task. Amen.

DAY 298

"Well, what did you do then?" asked Christian.

"I thought I must make every effort to change my ways or else I would surely be damned."

"And did you try to change?"

"Yes, and I fled not only from my sins but from my sinful friends as well. I began to perform religious duties such as praying, reading, weeping for sin, and telling my neighbors the truth. I did these things and many others that are too numerous to relate."

"Did you feel good about yourself then?"

"Yes, for a while, but finally my burden came tumbling down upon me again, despite all my efforts to reform."

Realizing how he had plowed iniquity and sowed vanity, Hopeful now feared a bitter harvest of death. He wanted to change. He had lost all interest in laboring for sin's wages. For every time he sinned, his awakened conscience hissed back at him with scathing rebukes. Thinking the thing he most needed saving from was his tormenting guilty conscience, he decided to reform himself, hoping to appease his stricken conscience and alleviate his fear of being damned. Thinking he had succeeded in pacifying his afflicted conscience, he was relieved to consider himself a "good man."

A Barna survey found that Hopeful was not alone in his approach. Most of the Methodists and Presbyterians polled and 88 percent of the Catholics agreed with the statement: "If people are generally good or do enough good things for others during their lives, they will earn a place in heaven." Even 27 percent of the Baptists subscribed to the salvation-by-works philosophy.[31]

But Hopeful's peace was fleeting. His righteous efforts began to go the way of most diets and New Year's resolutions—unraveling in failure. Though his effort at reformation was admirable, he learned the hard way that sin's burden is so heavy, sin's power so binding, and sin's extent so utterly pervasive that no person, however sincerely motivated, can be made righteous by his own efforts at self-reformation.

The only remedy for sin is the cross of Christ. As God's Spirit uses our witness, let us always be ready to bring our friends to the healing and cleansing blood of his cross. Do you have friends who are trying to make themselves "good" but need to recognize their need for the Savior? Tell them the truth about how to be saved.

Scripture: Job 25:4-6; Psalms 38:3-6; 143:1-2; Romans 5:8

Prayer: Dear Lord, Christendom is full of people trying to work their way to heaven. Please open their eyes to your truth. Amen.

"What renewed the conviction, seeing that you now thought you were reformed?" asked Christian.

"Oh, several things brought it upon me, especially such sayings as these: 'All of us have become like one who is unclean, and all our righteous acts are like filthy rags; we all shrivel up like a leaf, and like the wind our sins sweep us away' [Isaiah 64:6]. 'Know that a man is not justified by observing the law, but by faith in Jesus Christ' [Galatians 2:16]. 'So you also, when you have done everything you were told to do, should say, "We are unworthy servants; we have only done our duty"' [Luke 17:10]. I heard many other sayings like this also. From these I began to reason with myself along this line: 'If all my righteous acts are like filthy rags, and if obeying the law can justify no one, and if, when we have done everything we can, we are still unworthy, then it is foolishness to think that I can ever see Heaven by trying to be good.'"

❦

As hard as Hopeful tried to be a good man, he could not make himself right with God. Not only did his conscience buffet him, but the Word of God sorely afflicted him. He put himself in its line of fire, and it found its mark, piercing, penetrating, and scorching with burning conviction to his soul's depths. It kept working within him a fearful expectation of God's indignation toward his sin. As fire purifies gold and separates the dross, refining the metal to show what it really is, so the truth exposed all of Hopeful's efforts as worthless dross. He could find no gold in himself. All he found was his impurity, the insufficiency of his own righteousness, and his inability to do anything to rescue himself.

The Scriptures about his personal uncleanness were especially distressing. One who was covered with the spiritually incurable disease of sin was trying to shake hands with a holy God like one who was pure and clean. The righteousness in which he dressed himself—his best righteousness—was like filthy, vile, polluted rags. How could he think them fitting for standing before the King? With such an inappropriate, nauseating appearance, he would surely "shrivel up like a leaf" before God and blow away.

Hopeful tried his hardest, and it became obvious that his hardest wasn't good enough. With him, not one of us on earth—no matter how great our seeming goodness—can claim to be good enough for salvation. Let God's Word speak this truth deeply into your soul lest in any way you take unwarranted credit for your salvation.

❦

Scripture: Isaiah 55:11; Job 15:14-16; John 6:63

Prayer: Dear Lord, if I should begin striving for your approval by trying to be good enough, please bring me back to a healthy faith. I want to be good simply to bless you, not to earn favor. Amen.

D·A·Y 300

"Then I thought, 'If someone once charged thousands of dollars worth of merchandise at a clothing store, and since then has paid all his other bills, still, if this old debt remains on the ledger, the store may sue him, and he may even go to prison until the debt is paid.'"

"Well," asked Christian, "and how did this apply to your condition?"

"Why, I thought to myself, 'Because of my sins, I have accumulated a lot of debt on God's ledger, and even if I now reform, it will not pay off the balance. Therefore, I will still go under despite all the good changes I have brought about in my life.' So I asked myself, 'How then shall I find freedom from the prospect of damnation that my former sins have caused me?'"

Hopeful came to see God as like a storeowner with whom he had a running account. The money he owed was for his sins. His vain attempts at reforming himself disclosed two facts. First, even if he reformed his life and paid off his current debt, the debts incurred by former sins would still be left unpaid. Second, he had accumulated too much debt to pay off the balance. He could barely keep up with the interest owed, let alone pay off the principal. So, despite his best efforts, he would default on his debt and come to eternal punishment.

Religious people the world over try hard to pay their debt to God. In China the devout climb 7,000 steps up the sacred mountain Taishan to its summit where the spectacular Temple of the Azure Cloud sits. Upon arrival, they offer sacrifices that they believe will pay their debt. Despite their great dedication, their effort is futile, for these devotees are no closer to God than when they mounted the first step.

Martin Luther testified, "I kept the rules of penance so strictly that I may say that if ever a monk got to heaven by his sheer monkery, it was I. Had I kept on any longer, I should have killed myself with vigils, prayers, readings, and other works." His effort was as futile as that of a group of swimmers racing across the Pacific from California to Hawaii. Some may be exceptional swimmers, but could any reach Hawaii? Luther, a good "swimmer," could never span the distance to heaven.

If someone gave you the task of paying off the entire national debt, would you dig in and hope that one day you might just accomplish that? Of course, you know better. Even more impossible is the likelihood that you or anyone could ever pay off the debt of sin.

Scripture: Ezra 9:5-6; Job 40:3-5; Matthew 6:12; 18:23-27

Prayer: Blessed Savior, thank you for revealing to Martin Luther the truth that he could not earn his way into your favor. So many of us could use a similar revelation. Please show us the truth. Amen.

D·A·Y

301

"That was good thinking, but please go on," said Christian.

"Another thing that troubled me was that, if I looked carefully at even the best of what I was accomplishing during my efforts at reform, I could still see sin—new sin—mixing in and tainting the good within me. I was, therefore, forced to conclude that despite my former self-conceit and pride in my accomplishments, I could now recognize that I was presently committing enough sin in one duty to send me to Hell, even if I had been previously faultless."

❦

Hopeful's debt troubles are even worse than already mentioned. If he could somehow manage to entirely pay off all his staggering debts, he could still never get clear because—he just can't help it—he is addicted to sin! He accumulates fresh debt by continually charging more sins to his account. This negates all his efforts to repay his debt. Every good deed he does just compounds his trouble. He was committing enough sin in one duty to send him to hell. Therefore, Hopeful sees that even a reformed life continues to accumulate impossible debt.

W. Fullerton explains his dilemma this way: "One Sunday morning I made up my mind to be a Christian and never doubted that I knew what to do. I thought I must leave off this evil thing and that wicked habit and do only things that are good. I must read my Bible more, pray more, repent, and weep if possible. So I began. On Sunday I prospered, on Monday and Tuesday I almost succeeded, but on Wednesday and Thursday I made some serious slips. Finally on Friday I gave up in disgust. I began the same process again the next Sunday. In my self-confidence I thought I knew now where I had gone wrong, so I increased my devotions, prayed more, and was careful to restrain my evil habits. Still I did not find peace."

So it goes for those of us who believe there is no end to the power of initiative, who think they can simply analyze and solve their problem by reshaping their priorities and redoubling their efforts, who hope to be some reformer extraordinaire. Hopeful quickly learned he was no super-achiever. His earnest commitment to reform got him no further than those who passively sit back and simply hope they might be good enough.

Coming to the end of our own effort is really the dawn of light for our souls. Those who realize their helplessness are the ones on the road to true recovery. Are you completely convinced of your absolute helplessness to please God by your own efforts?

❦

Scripture: Ecclesiastes 7:20; Isaiah 59:12; Job 40:6-14

Prayer: Merciful Savior, thank you for showing me how desperately I fall short. I readily admit my weakness and inadequacy before you. Amen.

DAY 302

"And what did you do then?" asked Christian.

"Do! I didn't know what to do. I poured out my heart to Faithful because we were well acquainted. He told me that if I could not obtain the righteousness of a man who had never sinned, then neither my own righteousness nor all the righteousness this world possesses could save me."

"And did you think he was telling you the truth?" asked Christian.

"If he had told me this when I was pleased with myself and my reforms, I would have called him a fool for worrying about such a thing. But since I could now see my own malady and the sin that would latch onto my best efforts, I was forced to accept his opinion."

"But when he first told you this, did you think that a person existed of whom it could justly be said that he had never committed sin?"

"I must confess that at first these words sounded strange, indeed, but upon further discussion with him, I became convinced of their truth."

Hopeful went to see Faithful. How wonderful that he knew a loving Christian to whom he could turn. He didn't realize it, but the Holy Spirit had been preparing him for the Gospel. He now saw the worthless quality of any goodness to which he might attain. Still he came to agree that nothing but righteousness—perfect righteousness—would suffice to pay off his immense debt of sin. Oh, where in the world could such righteousness be found? Certainly not within himself or within anyone else he could think of. So there he sat facing Faithful, his body rigid, his heart pounding, his conscience stricken, his eyes pleading. How could he "obtain the righteousness of a man who had never sinned"?

As Hopeful stared into Faithful's eyes, he saw a disarmingly poised and confident man. His face glowed, and he seemed somehow grounded in a truth beyond anything this sinner could comprehend. On top of that, he cared. Faithful exuded genuine love and compassion. This is the essence of "friendship evangelism." Establish a beachhead with unbelievers by living authentically and building meaningful relationships with them.

When Hopeful was ready, he felt comfortable enough to come and share his personal concerns with Faithful. In turn, Faithful took the time to listen, to relate, to encourage, and to share the truth with him. Although his words sounded strange to Hopeful, they rang true. Do you know of unbelievers who would feel comfortable turning to you in their hour of decision? Perhaps it is time to make some new friends.

Scripture: 2 Corinthians 2:15-16; 1 Corinthians 9:19-22; Luke 5:29-32; 7:34

Prayer: Compassionate Lord, you were a friend of sinners. Help me to be more like you. I want to be one who is known for always having an open door in my heart for those who need you. Amen.

"Did you ask him who such a Man could be and how you could hope to be justified by Him?"

"Yes, and he told me it was the Lord Jesus, who sits at the right hand of the Most High. 'So,' he said, 'you must be justified by Him, and this through trusting in what He did in the days of His flesh by hanging and suffering on the tree.' Then I asked him how that one Man's righteousness could be so effective as to justify another person before God. He told me that this one Man was the Mighty God, and that He lived the life He lived and died the death He died not for Himself, but for me. Then he added that the inestimable value of what He had done would be credited to me if I put my trust in Him."

Could a perfectly righteous man exist by whom Hopeful could be justified? Faithful answers, "Yes," pointing him to Jesus Christ. Along with Faithful, countless voices throughout history resoundingly chime in, "Yes! The Lord Jesus Christ is he!"

Hopeful wonders how this can be. How can Christ be so entirely different from the rest of us that he alone can justify us before God? The Bible clearly reveals Jesus Christ as the God-man. Fully human, he was born of a woman, lived in human frailty, and died an agonizing death. Yet fully God, he was conceived by the Holy Spirit, lived a sinless life, rose from the dead, and ascended into heaven where he sits at the right hand of God the Father. Lest there be any confusion, not only is he the Son of God, but he is God the Son—the second Person of the triune God. With all the divine attributes of the almighty God, he is eternal, omnipresent, omniscient, omnipotent, and holy; he is the King of kings and the Lord of lords. Very shortly he will return in glory to judge the living and the dead. His kingdom will never end.

During his earthly ministry, Christ claimed the authority to forgive the debt of sin—something only God could do. Christ, the incarnate God, is both Priest, pronouncing forgiveness, and Lamb slain for the sins of all the world. Because he is wholly God and also perfectly righteous man, his blood, shed on Calvary's cross, has power to deliver us from sin. He has taken his blood as our atonement to the throne of almighty God. His intercession has been accepted, and we are forgiven and made righteous through faith in him.

How awesome it is to realize who Christ is and what he has done for us. Have you pondered his attributes lately and thanked him for who he is? Have you thanked him recently for what he has done?

Scripture: Romans 10:2-4; Titus 3:5; Acts 4:12

Prayer: Lord of life, you are so wonderful! I put my trust completely in you. Thank you for covering me with your righteousness. Amen.

D·A·Y
304

"What did you do then?"

"I had objections that were a hindrance to my believing; I thought He was not willing to save me."

"And what did Faithful say to you?"

"He told me to go to Him and see. I answered that this would be presumptuous of me, but he said that wasn't true since I had been invited to come. Then he gave me a Book that Jesus had authored to encourage me to come more readily. He told me that every word in the Book, down to the minutest details, stood firmer than Heaven and earth."

Coming to belief in Christ is seldom a simple process. Inquirers have doubts, questions, and objections that believers should know how to answer. Hopeful feels unworthy and wonders how Christ could want to save him. Faithful knows how to witness. Rather than pointing to himself, he points to Christ. He tells Hopeful to "*go to Him and see,*" for he has extended a blanket invitation, saying, "Come to me, all you who are weary and burdened, and I will give you rest" (Matthew 11:28).

Rather than seeking to persuade and convert Hopeful with his own wisdom and eloquence, Faithful points him to the Scriptures that stand "firmer than heaven." Reading the Scriptures will help an honest inquirer to more readily trust Christ. Concerning them, Paul told Timothy, they "are able to make you wise for salvation through faith in Christ Jesus" (2 Timothy 3:15).

Unfortunately, today the need for intelligent witnesses like Faithful is acute, as a proliferation of false teachers continually undermine the truth of Christ. Their antichrist teachings literally blanket our land.[32] To answer objections and refute lies, we should know God's Word well. Studying the writings of those who defend God's Word against deceitful criticisms can also be of immense benefit.[33]

Beware those leaders and teachers who would point to themselves or who would bid the spiritually desperate to "Follow me!" Only Christ is worthy of disciples. May we follow the example of John the Baptist who said, "*He* must become greater; *I* must become less" (John 3:30, *italics* mine). And let us also beware of those who would exalt their own teachings above the Scriptures. The life by which all lives will be judged is Jesus Christ. And the truth by which all words will be evaluated is the infallible Word of God. Let us not be ashamed to be people of "the Book." Do you desire to see the lost come to salvation? Are you prepared to take them to God's Word? Ask the Lord how you can better equip yourself.

Scripture: 2 Corinthians 4:2; Colossians 4:6; Psalm 37:30-31

Prayer: Lord of truth, I want to have a firmer handle on your truth. Make me a student of your Word that I may be able to dispel darkness and lies by bearing your light and truth. Amen.

"So I asked him what I would have to do when I went to Him. He said that I must fall on my knees and ask the Father, with all my heart and soul, to reveal Him to me. Then I asked Him further how I should entreat Him. He said, 'Go, and you will find Him sitting on a mercy seat; He sits there all year long to give pardon and forgiveness to those who come to Him.'"

When Jesus asked his disciples who people said he was, they replied that people thought he was John the Baptist or a prophet. He then asked, "But who do *you* say that I am?" Peter emphatically proclaimed, as have countless multitudes of believers after him, that he was God's Son, the Messiah. Jesus responded by telling Peter that this had come to him by a revelation from the heavenly Father. Faithful urged Hopeful to plead for just such a revelation, for humans can only come to know God through a revelation.

Faithful next explains that Hopeful will find Christ seated upon a "mercy seat." In the Old Covenant, the ark of the covenant symbolized God's covenant with his people. This rectangular wooden box sat within the Holy of Holies in the tabernacle. Its lid, the mercy seat, consisted of pure gold. It represented the throne of God in the camp of Israel, and once a year—on the Day of Atonement—the High Priest sprinkled it with blood to absolve the people of their sins and reconcile them to God.

Christ, our great High Priest and Mediator of the New Covenant, sits upon the mercy seat. It might also be said that he is our mercy seat in that God shows himself merciful to his people through him. The Hebrew word for the mercy seat signifies a covering. As it covered the ark, Christ covers his people. He covers our sins, and he covers and clothes us with his righteousness. By sprinkling his own blood upon the mercy seat, he made God's throne a place of mercy, not judgment, for his people. We have peace with God, and a way is opened into the holy presence of God. He bestows eternal life upon us.

That the mercy seat was made of pure gold indicates Christ's excellency, his pure obedience, and perfect atonement. He in every way fulfills the Old Covenant, answering its every requirement.

It is essential to remember that God is only merciful through Christ. Outside Christ we are all objects of his wrath. Do you need a fresh revelation of God's love in Christ for you? Visit Christ on his mercy seat. He is there for you.

Scripture: Matthew 11:25; 16:13-17; Hebrews 9:5, 11-15

Prayer: My Savior, without a revelation of your truth, I couldn't have come to believe in you. Without your grace and mercy, I couldn't have been reconciled to you. Thank you for showing me your mercy. Amen.

DAY 306

"I told him that I didn't know what to say when I approached Him, and he told me to say something to this effect: 'God, have mercy on me, a sinner and help me to know and believe in Jesus Christ. For I see that if Christ had not been righteous, and if I don't have faith in that righteousness, then I am utterly without hope and have been cast away. Lord, I have heard that You are a merciful God and have ordained that Your Son Jesus Christ should be the Savior of the world. Moreover, I have heard that You are willing to bestow Him upon such a miserable sinner as I am. Yes, I am a sinner indeed. Lord, take this opportunity and glorify your grace by saving my soul through Your Son, Jesus Christ. Amen.'"

"And did you do as you were told?"

"Yes, over and over and over again."

"And did the Father reveal His Son to you?"

"No, not the first time, nor the second, third, fourth, fifth, or sixth time either."

"Well, what did you do then?"

"What did I do? Why, I didn't know what to do."

Prayer plays a key role in the Christian life from its inception till its end. Those who come to Christ generally pray some form of a "sinner's prayer." He accepts all without exception, for "everyone who calls on the name of the Lord will be saved" (Romans 10:13) . Yet the prayer must issue from a sincere heart. In Christ's parable of the Pharisee and the tax collector, the Pharisee trusted his own goodness while the tax collector humbly cried for God's mercy. The second man properly approached God. Previously, Hopeful was like the Pharisee, but now, stripped of any inflated sense of his own worthiness, he prays sincerely.

So Faithful offers Hopeful an excellent prayer for approaching God. It humbly acknowledges personal sin, appeals to God's mercy, affirms Christ as the only hope of salvation, and professes God's willingness to impart salvation. It then requests salvation and states a desire to see God glorified through this work of grace. Hopeful prays this wonderful prayer. Yet this doesn't seem to resolve his conflict. Not only did he pray the prayer once, but he prayed it continually, yet without relief.

Sometimes, no matter how perfectly stated, a pat little prayer doesn't immediately settle the struggles in a person's heart. Moving from Satan's kingdom to Christ's kingdom is no small thing. We shouldn't be surprised or suspicious when some do not immediately experience peace. Did you feel upheaval and conflict as you came to Christ? If so, how were you helped?

Scripture: Luke 18:9-14; Psalms 40:12-13; 102:17-20

Prayer: Dear Lord, it seems we too often think we have done our duty by getting an inquirer to pray. Help us to understand how to minister to a person's spiritual needs following that prayer. Amen.

"Did you have any thoughts of giving up praying?"

"Yes, at least a hundred times over."

"Why didn't you?"

"I believed that what had been told me was the truth: That without Christ's righteousness all the world could not save me. So I reasoned with myself, 'If I give up, I will die, and I dare not die except at the throne of grace.' Then the words came to me, 'Though it linger, wait for it; it will certainly come and will not delay'" [Habakkuk 2:3].

Hopeful was left struggling in confusion. He had prayed as instructed, but seemingly to no avail, and he had considered giving up "at least a hundred times over." The poor man needed to learn to trust God's promises. It seems that while he had acknowledged his sin and surrendered to Christ, he lacked the faith to believe that God would answer his prayer. Perhaps the *Four Spiritual Laws* diagram of the train best illustrates Hopeful's dilemma. The engine—Fact—pulls the train; the coal car—Faith—provides the fuel; the caboose—Feeling—trails behind. When we come to Christ, faith must activate the truth in our hearts. We cannot rely upon feelings to push the train from behind.

Hopeful was frustrated, but he knew better than to give up. As Peter held on to Christ crying, "Lord, to whom can we go? You have the words of eternal life" (John 6:68 NRSV), so Hopeful realized he had no other place to run for salvation. No other person under heaven could help him now. He knew that trusting in his own righteousness could not justify him before God. Tears of repentance could not wash his sins away. More education, more effort, more good deeds—none of these could bring God's approval.

Where else could Hopeful go? Nowhere! For Jesus Christ is the only Savior. He is the only High Priest, the only Mediator between God and humanity. His blood is the only fountain of redemption for cleansing corrupt souls. He is the only Bread of Life for the starving, the only burden bearer for the weary and heavy laden. He is the only city of refuge to which guilty souls can flee, the only fortress within which they can hide, the only foundation upon which they can be established.

Hopeful saw no recourse but to linger at Christ's throne of grace. Then suddenly he heard a word to simply "wait." Oh soul, when you anxiously yearn for Christ and his reply seems to tarry, do not give in to running helter-skelter for alternative solutions. Wait for him.

Scripture: John 6:65-69; 14:6; Psalms 73:25; 130:5-6

Prayer: Blessed Lord, you alone possess life and truth. I look to you; I wait for you. Thank you for your salvation. Amen.

308

"So I continued to pray until the Father showed me His Son."

"How was He revealed to you?"

"I didn't see Him with my human eyes, but with the eyes of my understanding. This is how it happened: One day I was very sad; sadder, I think, than at any other time in my life. This sadness was the result of a new awareness of the enormity and ugliness of my sins. I then expected nothing but Hell and the eternal damnation of my soul. But suddenly I thought I saw the Lord Jesus looking down from Heaven at me and saying, 'Believe in the Lord Jesus, and you will be saved'" [Acts 16:31].

Hopeful had outgrown the belief that he could win his salvation by simply cleaning up his act. He now knew that he didn't deserve salvation, nor would he ever. Yet the recognition that he deserved to be lost haunted him. He believed *about* Jesus but hadn't yet begun to believe *in* him. He kept praying the sinner's prayer and crying out, "God be merciful to me a sinner," until he was worn out by it.

Realizing his sinful condition was an important first step for Hopeful, as it is for us all. We are all sinners, but Satan can make us feel that, because we are sinners, we are unworthy of forgiveness. Hopeful felt unworthy. He saw that he was conceived and born in sin; that he followed his sin nature and became a habitual, blatant, vile sinner deserving of God's wrath; that he had sinned against a holy God, insulting him, defying him, despising him; that his debt was so staggering that he could never pay it back. To believe differently would be to distort the truth. Yet contrary to how Hopeful felt, he was not beyond redemption.

While Hopeful had become aware of God's justice, he had to understand God's mercy. Forgiveness involves both justice and mercy. While Christ's sacrifice on the cross satisfies God's justice, and no pardon exists apart from it, his cross also perfectly demonstrates God's mercy. Those who call upon the name of the Lord Jesus Christ will find him rich in grace and plenteous in mercy.

As Hopeful kept his vigil, suddenly through spiritual eyes, he saw a vision of Christ encouraging him simply to believe in him for salvation. Christ is always with those who cleave to him despite the clouds that hide him from our eyes. Have feelings of unworthiness in any way blocked your ability to receive God's provision? If you would see a breakthrough, renounce those feelings and reach out to God in faith. He loves you!

Scripture: Exodus 34:5-7; Ephesians 1:18; John 1:12

Prayer: Gracious Lord, I pray against a spirit of unworthiness in your people. Help us to realize that through your atoning sacrifice, we can confidently receive your grace. Amen.

D·A·Y
309

"I replied, 'But, Lord, I am a great—a very great—sinner.' He answered, 'My grace is sufficient for you' [2 Corinthians 12:9]. Then I asked, 'But, Lord, what does it mean to believe?' He replied, 'He who comes to Me will never go hungry, and he who believes in Me will never be thirsty' [John 6:35]. Then I concluded that believing in Christ and coming to Him were one and the same, and that the one who comes to Him, whose heart and affections pursue Christ and His salvation, is indeed one who believes in Christ."

Assailed with tormenting anxiety, Hopeful couldn't bring himself to believe that Christ would actually forgive him. He thought the Lord must not realize the extent of his sinfulness, and that when he found out, he would surely change his mind. Christ, however, responds, "My grace *IS* sufficient for you"—not will be, may be, or might be. His grace is not a mere possibility; it is a reality.

Hopeful wondered what it really meant to believe in Christ. The Greek New Testament word *pisteuo,* meaning "to believe," indicates not only being persuaded about something but to place confidence in it, committing your trust to it. Saving faith, therefore, means entrusting your soul's welfare to Christ. A bare historical faith will not suffice. You can easily assent to gospel facts but not trust Christ to accomplish them. You can believe all the right things—that he is God's Son, the Savior, that he suffered, died, rose, ascended, etc. Yet this head belief must be translated into heart belief. This means trusting in him, relying upon him, committing your soul to him alone, not merely giving credence to him. It means believing that he is not only able to save, but is also willing and actually does save. It means expecting his imputed righteousness, forgiveness, and eternal life for your life. Anything other than this "believing" falls short of saving faith.

Salvation occurred objectively for Hopeful upon the cross. Yet salvation occurs subjectively as a person believes the Gospel—the good news. Hopeful had to receive this Gospel as good news for him personally. Until he could understand and receive this truth by faith, he could experience no peace of heart.

Suddenly daybreak came! The confusion cleared, and the torment gave way as Hopeful realized that "believing" in Christ and "coming" to him were one and the same. He had sincerely come to Christ and thus believed in him also. Now he is ready to receive salvation by faith. Believing in Christ is the key to every victory in the Christian pilgrimage. We cannot merely possess faith; it must possess us. How pervasive is your belief in Christ?

Scripture: Mark 1:15; John 6:40, 47; Galatians 3:22

Prayer: Dear Lord, I want to believe in you with all my heart, mind, and soul. Please make me a more faith-filled and trusting Christian. Amen.

D·A·Y 310

"At this realization tears filled my eyes, and I further asked, 'But, Lord, may such a great sinner as I truly be accepted and saved by You?' And I heard Him say, 'Whoever comes to Me I will never drive away' [John 6:37]. Then I asked, 'But, Lord, in my coming to You, how must I regard You so that my faith will rest properly on You?' He said, 'Christ Jesus came into the world to save sinners' [1 Timothy 1:15]. 'Christ is the end of the law so that there may be righteousness for everyone who believes' [Romans 10:4]. 'He was delivered over to death for our sins and was raised to life for our justification' [Romans 4:25]. He 'loves us and has freed us from our sins by His blood' [Revelation 1:5]. He is the 'one mediator between God and men' [1 Timothy 2:5]. And 'He always lives to intercede for them' [Hebrews 7:25].

"From all these words I gathered that I must look for righteousness in His person alone and for satisfaction of the penalty for my sins through His blood alone. I saw that what He had done in obedience to His Father's law, by submitting to the penalty therein, was not for Himself but for all who will gratefully accept it for salvation."

People can get into serious spiritual trouble by relying on visions to point the way. Those with "new revelations" sometimes start cults by overemphasizing some vision or dream. Hopeful's encounter, however, was a revelation that comes by scriptural truth, appealing to his spiritual understanding. Every text of Scripture was applied in its true meaning.

While Hopeful's story is uniquely his own, its substance corresponds with that of other believers. He was deeply humbled, sinking under discouragement. Yet he suddenly came to understand Christ's love for him, God's glorious salvation, his free invitation, and his great and wonderful promises. He understood the nature of justifying faith, that righteousness is only found in Christ, that his blood alone satisfies the penalty for sin. He saw that Christ's salvation is not simply one enlightened approach. Christ does not serve as a prophet who merely points out the way of salvation. He *is* the way to salvation—the only way. In him is life, grace, peace with God, membership in his body, eternal hope.

Hopeful also saw that what Christ did "was not for Himself." The Son of God who sits at the Father's right hand didn't come as we would anticipate a prince to come. Instead of enjoying pleasure and ease, he came to serve, to give his life as a ransom, to bring glory to his Father, to seek and to save, to suffer and to die—for you, me, and all the world. What a revelation! Praise him; praise him again!

Scripture: Mark 10:45; John 3:15-16; 5:24; 20:31

Prayer: Dear Lord, how sweetly your truth comes to distressed hearts wandering in the hopeless void of this world. Thank you for your promises that convince us of your sacrificial love. Amen.

D·A·Y
311

"By this time my heart was full of joy, my eyes were filled with tears, and my emotions were overflowing with love for the Name, the people, and the ways of Jesus Christ."

"This was indeed a revelation to your soul. But tell me, what effect did this have on your spirit?"

"It became clear to me that the world and all its standards of righteousness stand condemned. I saw that God the Father, although He is just, can legally absolve and justify any sinner who humbly comes to Him. I was greatly ashamed of the vileness of my former life, and I felt a strong sense of shame for all my ignorance. I had been so blind that I had never before considered the glorious beauty of Jesus Christ."

Hopeful's heart overflowed with the joy and wonder of a brand-new babe in Christ. He marveled at the Lord's love and salvation for him. He no longer needed to cry, "Lord, be merciful to me a sinner." How beautiful the Lord had suddenly become to him. What can compare with beholding his face, feeling the warmth of his smile, the sweetness of his breath, the joy of his presence, the tenderness of his touch? He is altogether lovely, full of grace and mercy.

Although he still felt shame for his former life, Christ's love overwhelmed Hopeful until he overflowed with love. He loved the Lord's name. Whereas he might previously have used it in vain, he now adored it. No name is so universal, so powerful, influential, and excellent as the name of the Lord Jesus Christ. One day as every knee bows before him, every tongue will confess his glorious name.

Hopeful loved the Lord's people, too. His friend Faithful had more character, courage, and beauty than all those in Vanity combined. He greatly esteemed Christian, too. Now these three were brothers in Christ, born again, adopted by grace into the same spiritual family with the same heavenly Father. They shared this common ancestry with all pilgrims, chosen from every kindred, tongue, people, and nation, enjoying together a common Lord, Spirit, faith, and baptism.

Finally, Hopeful loved Christ's ways. How could he not? He was only beginning to understand the Lord's ways, but what had thus far been revealed was almost too wonderful to fathom. Christ purchased him when he was worthless, as one who purchases a precious jewel. Suddenly he was a beloved son rather than a wretched sinner. Isn't Christ beautiful? Isn't he wonderful? We should rejoice in his love until our eyes well up with tears. Have you rejoiced in your salvation lately? How can you better express love for his name, his people, and his ways?

Scripture: Isaiah 12:3; Habakkuk 3:18-19; 1 Peter 1:8, 23

Prayer: Dear Lord, thank you for the first love of a newborn babe in Christ. Please help me to rekindle my first love also. You are so worthy! I rejoice in your salvation. Amen.

DAY 312

"I suddenly had a compelling love for the holy life and longed to do something for the praise and honor and glory of the Lord Jesus. Yes, I now felt that if I had a thousand gallons of blood in my body, I could have spilled it all for the sake of Jesus, my Lord."

Hopeful, at this point, legitimately becomes "Hopeful." What enrapturing hope he holds of one day awakening as pure as Christ when he sees him face to face! What extraordinary hope he possesses of entering the City Gate and having the right to eat of the Tree of Life! What glorious hope he enjoys of walking with Christ in white in his eternal Celestial City! What magnificent hope he savors of casting a golden crown at Christ's feet! What joyous hope he cherishes of one day sitting down at the marriage supper of the Lamb! What astounding hope he savors of hearing his Lord one day say to him, "Well done!" Ah, yes, what an excellent, fantastic hope!

Hopeful responded to the revelation, not only by loving Christ's name, his people, and his ways, but by loving the holy life. True converts always respond with a gratitude that translates into action. Hopeful wanted to walk blamelessly for Christ. He intensely longed to praise, honor, and glorify him. Oh, how he wanted to do some great exploit to prove his love for his wonderful Lord. Jealous of Faithful's martyrdom, he, too, would have gladly died for Christ, even a thousand times over.

Yet Christ did not choose for Hopeful to be martyred. He had another plan. Instead, Hopeful's way to the Celestial Gate would be a long and trying one by way of a pilgrimage. While he wanted to do some great thing, Christ gave him the opportunity to do many little things of surpassing worth. The process of sanctification is a precious work of the Spirit for instilling Christ's righteousness in his people. It is hardly automatic.

Hope of one day seeing Christ and of partaking of the Tree of Life should keep us repentant and prayerful. Hope of walking with Christ in white should keep us washing our garments in his blood. Hope of casting a crown at his feet should keep us guarding our crowns against theft or loss. Hope of being invited to the heavenly supper should make us willing to forgo material and sensual gratification. Hope of hearing him say, "Well done!" should motivate us to serve him faithfully until our journey's end. Think about ways you can better cultivate a more hopeful disposition.

Scripture: Romans 5:5; 15:13; 1 Peter 1:13; Hebrews 6:18

Prayer: Dear Lord, thank you for the rich hope that is now mine. Help me increasingly to understand what it is to walk in hope because "hope does not disappoint." Amen.

D·A·Y
313

Then I saw in my dream that Hopeful glanced back and saw Ignorance still following but at a good distance behind. "Look," he said to Christian, "Ignorance is dragging his feet and lagging far behind."

"Yes, I see him. He doesn't care for our company."

"But I don't think it would have hurt him to have kept pace with us."

"I don't think so either, but I'm sure he thinks otherwise."

"I can agree with that, but let's wait for him."

So they waited, and when Ignorance was within earshot, Christian called to him, "Come on, man! Why do you linger so far behind?"

❧

Those like Obstinate, Worldly-wiseman, or Atheist despise mature believers and want nothing to do with them. Folks like Ignorance, however, frequent churches because they want people to see them as religious. Yet when pressed concerning their faith's legitimacy, they get offended and distance themselves rather than accept instruction. Thus when the pilgrims had earlier challenged Ignorance's faith, he chose to walk alone. Now, after thinking over their earlier words with him, he may be more receptive to their correction.

While it is tempting to ignore people like Ignorance, we should be careful about ceasing all communication with them. If we try to maintain an open door, an open heart might follow. We can't always see how God might ultimately use our witness, so if we keep tossing our seeds out even on the stubborn soil, some might eventually take root. We should walk as wisely and inoffensively as possible, trying not to provoke, injure, or persecute these people. Instead, we should try to gain their respect and perhaps build a bridge for them to cross. Too often we lay stumbling blocks in the way.

But we should approach those walking in falsehood with wisdom and discernment. We must know how to join the gentleness of a dove to the wisdom of a serpent. Sincere yet unseasoned believers can easily let the ignorant steer them out of the way of truth. Even late in the pilgrimage, many people and circumstances confront us that we have not yet experienced. Staying surrendered to the Holy Spirit's guidance is vital.

How about reviving your concern for someone with whom you've lost patience?

❧

Scripture: Titus 2:7-8; 2 Corinthians 8:21; 2 Timothy 4:2

Prayer: Dear Lord, when I get irritated and impatient with those who seemingly refuse to hear the truth, help me to recall your patience with me. Please grant me more loving patience with them. Amen.

D·A·Y 314

And Ignorance called out, "I take more pleasure in walking alone than with others—unless I enjoy their company."

Then Christian said to Hopeful in a low voice, "Didn't I tell you that he doesn't care for our company? But let's wait for him anyway."

When Ignorance approached them, Christian said, "Join us, and let's talk away the time in this lonely place."

While most young pilgrims would love mentoring from the two older pilgrims, Ignorance still prefers to keep to himself. Despite their seasoned wisdom and rich experience, they have made Ignorance uncomfortable by meddling with his beliefs. Hearing the truth from them was not only painful but offensive as well. Nevertheless, despite his rebuff, the two care about him and decide to try to work with him some more.

In our current "tolerant" society, the pilgrims would seem unjustified in attacking Ignorance's beliefs. The polite thing to do would be simply to let him live out the truth as he sees it. Yet with an eternal destiny at stake, this wouldn't be the truly loving approach. How can you simply allow someone to slide into hell without a good rescue effort? One problem with trying to reason with Ignorance, however, is that he shows no desire for help. He resents being held accountable to the truth.

Accountability—why is it so difficult for us? Our flesh hates the thought of it. It hates honest rebuke and admonishment. It hates humbling itself and confessing its sin. It hates the thought of looking weak in other people's eyes. We don't really want true discipling because we don't want anyone to watch our life closely or speak into or shape it. Yet when we resist accountability, we may do so at our peril.

Christian and Hopeful have had an endearing accountability relationship. It has been of immense help and encouragement to both men. But unlike the wise, Ignorance is a loner. Charles Colson says, "Christians need to hold one another accountable. Though I know intellectually how vulnerable I am to pride and power, I am the last one to know when I succumb to their seduction. That's why . . . we must depend on trusted brothers and sisters who love us enough to tell us the truth." Accountability means letting people get close enough to ask hard questions. We need to give other Christians permission not only to love us but also to challenge and admonish us to spiritual wholeness. How can you make yourself more accountable to others?

Scripture: 1 John 4:6; Proverbs 27:6; James 5:20

Prayer: Dear Lord, I pray for good accountability structures for my friendships. Help me to humbly accept the interference of others in my life. Amen.

D·A·Y
315

"How are you doing now? How is your relationship with God?"

Ignorance replied, "Well, I hope, for I am always engaging in positive mental activities to encourage myself as I walk."

"What kind of mental activities?" asked Christian.

"Oh, I think about God and Heaven."

"That is good, but are you aware that demons and those who will suffer damnation do this also?"

"But I think about them and desire them."

"I am sure you are aware that many desire them who will never be accepted there. For 'the sluggard craves and gets nothing'" [Proverbs 13:4].

Desiring heavenly blessing is no guarantee of true saving grace working in a heart. If people remain ignorant, neglecting the proper way of attaining salvation, or if sloth or procrastination interferes, they may want it but fall short of it. Becoming convinced that without grace you are lost may motivate you for self-centered reasons to seek salvation. Yet if you remain unwilling to allow God to change your life, how can you ever truly possess his grace? Hungering and thirsting for God and his righteousness, knowing that nothing the world can offer will satisfy your longing, desiring to conform to Christ's image, renouncing all that interferes with this pursuit—this is true grace at work in a heart. Because Ignorance encourages himself by thinking positively, he "hopes" his relationship with God is acceptable. His hope however, is not a true Christian hope. True hope is not translated "I wish," "I want," or "I aspire to." Godly hope is grounded in fact. Because Christ died and rose again, because we receive his free gift, we are born again to a certain hope.

Therapists can detect fear of failure within us that robs us of our confidence. They can tell us to cast aside our self-doubt, to focus on our goal, to think positively about it, to be enthusiastic, to be persistent. Yet all the positive thinking in the world is not enough to bridge the gulf between an unregenerate sinner and a holy God. A "positive-thinking" approach to God, if devoid of true repentance and humble submission to Christ's lordship, can't assure acceptance by him. Positive attitudes are more desirable and attractive than negative ones, but attitudes in themselves have no necessary correlation with truth. We can have continual positive thoughts but be positively wrong. We must build our hope upon what Christ has accomplished. What is your hope built more upon—your efforts or Christ's?

Scripture: Deuteronomy 29:19; 1 Peter 1:3; Hebrews 6:19-20

Prayer: Father, thank you for a hope based not upon wishful thinking but upon reality. I thank you I can be positive because of my hope, not hopeful because I am positive. Amen.

D·A·Y 316

"But not only do I think of them; I have left everything for them."

"Can you really say that?" asked Christian. "For leaving everything behind is a very difficult matter—yes, a harder matter than most of us are even aware. But why do you believe you have left all for God and His Kingdom?"

Ignorance deems his commitment worthy because he has left everything to follow Christ. Yet he lacks true faith. He didn't come in at the Wicket-gate but came by way of a crooked lane coming out of his own country. To receive Christ's salvation, however, you must believe in his death and resurrection, turn away from your sins, and ask him to be the Lord and Savior of your life. This means you have to renounce and turn away from everything in your life that is contrary to what he wants. You give up your sinful self-centeredness and turn toward God.

Ignorance, however, has not renounced his country, Conceit. While he may have left it geographically and given up some material benefits, he retains its ways and thinking, and its proud, self-sufficient attitudes. This is reflected in his notion that his own goodness and self-effort will save him, not Christ. He is guilty of a distortion of true faith, some type of Christian humanism, where self-determination takes precedence over Christ's lordship. He was the one to decide that his crooked lane could replace the Wicket-gate. Instead of carrying a true cross of self-denial, Ignorance is a self-made man with a self-made religion. He has not even heard Christ calling, "Follow me."

So Christian questions whether Ignorance has really left all for Christ. Unless he has allowed Christ to direct his life, Ignorance doesn't really understand nor has he submitted to Christ's lordship. How can he then claim to be a pilgrim? He hasn't accurately counted the cost of true discipleship.

We so blithely, so easily say, "*Lord* Jesus." Have we given up all to follow him as his first disciples did? Or are we just fooling ourselves? We should be like Jonathan Edwards who said, "I claim no right to myself—no right to this understanding, this will, these affections that are in me; neither do I have any right to this body or its members—no right to this tongue, to these hands, feet, ears, or eyes. I have given myself clear away and not retained anything of my own. I have been to God this morning and told Him I have given myself wholly to Him. I have given every power, so that for the future I claim no right to myself in any respect. I have expressly promised Him, for by His grace I will not fail." How can you better submit to Christ's lordship?

Scripture: Romans 12:1; Luke 14:33; Philippians 3:8

Prayer: Oh Lord, I find it so easy to confess your lordship while not surrendering to it. Help me to truly follow you. Amen.

D·A·Y
317

"I know it in my own heart."

"Did you know that the wise man says, 'He who trusts in his own heart is a fool'?" [Proverbs 28:26].

"That is spoken of an evil heart; but mine is a good one."

"But how can you prove that it is good?"

"It comforts me with hopes of Heaven."

"But that may be through its deceitfulness; for a person's heart may minister comfort to him in hopes of something for which he doesn't yet have grounds for hope."

People are corrupt. Left to ourselves, our thinking is futile, consciences are seared, understanding darkened, affections vile, and hearts desperately wicked. What fool, then, remains ignorant of his own heart's plague? Yet Ignorance self-confidently trusts his heart, thinking it "is a good one." This is why his name is Ignorance. Ignorant of his own sinful condition, he searches his heart by the lantern of self-love, letting deceitful feelings "comfort" and guide him.

Peter thought his heart good. Yet the heart he so trusted deceived him, and he denied the Lord. The proud hearts of the scribes and Pharisees told them they were more righteous than others. Yet they weren't justified in God's sight. Saul of Tarsus thought himself righteous. Only a deceitful heart could make him think himself blameless as to the law's righteousness while persecuting Christ's church.

Oh, what fools we are to trust in the wisdom and counsel of our own hearts, to lean upon our own understanding, to be wise in our own eyes (see Proverbs 3:5-6). How foolish it is to trust in our own strength, our own righteousness, our own hearts. The deceitful heart can fool us concerning our knowledge, convincing us that we are intelligent, discerning, and wise when we are really blind and ignorant. It can fool us concerning religion, making us believe we are righteous and heaven-bound when our outward demeanor belies a sinful nature that proves us more deserving of hell. Who are we to give a pittance to God and think ourselves generous, to be miserly and think ourselves frugal, to judge the failings of others and think ourselves faithful, to greedily accumulate more things and think ourselves blessed? Only a deceitful heart assigns virtue to vice, calls good evil and evil good.

There is indeed "comfort" in Christ, but it is the comfort of truth, and before finding it, many discomforting questions must be settled in our hearts. Open your heart wide to the Holy Spirit's scrutiny.

Scripture: Jeremiah 17:9-10; Psalm 26:2; 2 Corinthians 1:3

Prayer: Holy Spirit, show me the pockets of resistance to Christ's lordship in my heart. Letting my heart lead me back to myself, rather than to Christ, is so easy. Please work in me a pure heart. Amen.

D·A·Y 318

"But my heart and life both agree; thus, there are good grounds for me to hope."

"Who told you that your heart and life agree?"

"My heart tells me so."

"Ask your heart if I am a thief. Does your heart tell you so? Unless the Word of God bears witness in the matter, no other testimony will be of any value."

"But isn't it a good heart that will have good thoughts? And isn't it a good life that is lived according to God's commandments?"

"Yes, a good heart has good thoughts, and a good life is lived according to God's commandments. But it is, indeed, one thing to possess these things and quite another to merely think so."

Ignorance believes his confidence is entirely justifiable. He looks at his heart and life and sees total consistency. Both tell him the same thing—that he is a very good man. Thus he feels assurance for his hope. But how can one say, "My heart is good because my life shows it, and my life is good because my heart tells me so"? This circular reasoning is no basis for formulating an accurate assessment. Our outward behavior might make us appear righteous, and our heart might agree. Nevertheless, this subjective analysis is too unreliable. Will a thief tell on a thief? Neither will these two collaborators—my heart and life.

So many, when asked why they think God should let them into heaven, listen to their hearts and reply, "Because I have been a good person." If only they would consult God's Word! It shines like a beacon of truth into our souls. Only by the light of God's Word can we see our personal corruption, the disobedience and waywardness of our hearts, the imperfection of our own efforts and good deeds, and our need for a better righteousness than our own to justify us before God. Without God's Word, we blindly grope around in the darkness of our own understanding. His Word gives us knowledge of God, his grace, mercy, and justice. It directs us to Christ and his salvation. The Word of God tells us how to conduct our pilgrimage. In our earthly state of imperfection as we move through this present darkness, we need God's Word to be our standard of faith and practice. By it, we know how to walk. It directs us how to live upright and sober lives, how to discern true and false doctrines, how to keep to the Way of truth and avoid pits and snares. What a gift God has given us in his holy Word! Do you have a passion for God's Word? Are you spending daily quality time in meditating upon its truth?

Scripture: Psalm 119:9, 105; John 17:17; 2 Timothy 3:16-17

Prayer: Dear Lord, when I am tempted to let my own subjective feelings and experiences lead me, please remind me to grab hold of your Word and consult it for guidance. Amen.

"Please tell me what you determine to be good thoughts and a life lived according to God's commandments," said Ignorance.

"There are many kinds of good thoughts—some concerning ourselves, some of God, some of Christ, and some of many other things."

"What are good thoughts concerning ourselves?"

"Those that agree with the Word of God," said Christian.

"When do our own thoughts of ourselves agree with the Word of God?" asked Ignorance.

"When we pass the same judgment upon ourselves that the Word of God passes. Let me explain myself. The Word of God says of a person in his natural condition, 'There is no one righteous, not even one' [Romans 3:10], 'that every inclination of the thoughts of his heart was only evil all the time' [Genesis 6:5], and that his 'bent is always toward evil from his earliest youth' [Genesis 8:21]. Now then, when we agree with these conclusions concerning ourselves, our thoughts are good because they agree with the Word of God."

"I will never believe that my heart is that bad," said Ignorance.

"Then," replied Christian, "you don't really have one truly good thought concerning yourself."

❦

Ignorance insists his heart is good because his life is good, and his life is good because his heart says so. Christian challenges his logic citing the difference between truly having a good heart and life and merely thinking you do. Ignorance "knows" in his heart he possesses them, so he asks Christian to prove him wrong.

Christian begins by explaining that truly good thoughts about yourself come by reading God's Word and accepting its judgment. When our thoughts about our condition agree with the condition the Word of God assigns to us, then our thoughts are true and good.

Ignorance can agree with this in theory, but he makes it clear that he will keep his misguided feelings as the star witness to his goodness. He thinks God's Word is clearly wrong about him and refuses to yield to its testimony. It may seem to us that Christian is overly negative, because God's Word has much to say about God's love as well as his judgment. But Christian is concerned that Ignorance, with his unwillingness to see and deal with his sin nature, is deceived about his true spiritual condition. Those who operate solely out of their natural minds cannot accept God's truth. Those born of God's Spirit, however, agree with God's Word. When it points at you, do you most often argue with or agree with its judgment?

❦

Scripture: 1 Corinthians 2:14; Romans 8:7-8; Matthew 13:15-16

Prayer: Lord, I submit my heart to your scrutiny. Let your truth cut deeply that you may heal and perfect me. I trust your judgment. Amen.

DAY 320

"But let me go on," said Christian. "As the Word passes judgment on our hearts, it also passes judgment on our ways. When the thoughts of our hearts and the way we live both agree with the Word of God's assessment of them, then both are good, because they are in agreement with it."

"Spell out what you mean."

"Why, the Word of God says man's ways are crooked—not good, but perverse. It says they have not known the good Way and therefore are naturally out of it. Now when a man views his ways from this perspective with wisdom and humility, then he has good thoughts concerning his ways because his thoughts now agree with the perspective of the Word of God."

Christian and Ignorance continue their discussion of good thoughts concerning ourselves. Christian explains that whereas good thoughts concerning ourselves are ones in agreement with what God's Word says about our hearts, they must also agree with what God's Word says about our ways. Ignorance thought it was enough for his heart and lifestyle to agree, but Christian makes it clear that both must be in agreement with God's Word. When these agree, then we can have good thoughts concerning ourselves.

Ignorance says, "Spell out what you mean," because he just doesn't get it. To him, it seems logical that if God's Word says bad things about his heart or life, it can't be considered good. To him, good thoughts about your life are positive and not negative. Christian, however, speaks the truth of God's Word. We may think our life is good, but God in his Word judges our ways crooked. Because we are ignorant of his law and Christ's Gospel, we swerve away from it. By nature we are children of wrath, out of God's Way, disagreeably disposed to the divine Word's rule over us. Intoxicated with ourselves, we are more like a stuporous drunk who sees his walk with distorted vision. We indignantly assert we are walking a straight line, that our lives are good, as we stagger a serpentine course, this way and that.

God's Word, however, acts as a spiritual sobriety test. The Holy Spirit, the Spirit of truth, gave it to us to enable us to escape walking anymore by the foolish, darkened influence of our own hearts. We must place it above our own feelings and intellect and submit to its judgment. While ignorant, self-flattering people prefer their own subjective brand of guidance, we can trust God's Word to tell us the truth and nothing but the truth, so help us, God. Commit yourself right now to allowing the truth of God's Word to impact your life even when it makes you feel uncomfortable.

Scripture: Isaiah 59:8; Romans 3:10-18; 1 Peter 1:24-25

Prayer: Dear Lord, I admit that I often want to go my way, thinking it's best. Yet you know what is best for me. Help me to keep my life in conformity with your Word. Amen.

D·A·Y
321

"What are good thoughts concerning God?" asked Ignorance.

"As I have said concerning thoughts about ourselves, so it is with our thoughts about God. We must agree with what the Word says about Him. We must think of His being and His attributes only in the light of the Word. I cannot discuss this in depth at this time, but I will speak about Him as regards us. We have a right view of God when we believe that He knows us better than we know ourselves and that He can see sinfulness in us when we see none in ourselves. We also have a right view of Him when we believe that He knows our inmost thoughts and that our heart, with all its hidden depths, can hide nothing from His eyes. Also, we have a right view of Him when we believe that all our own righteousness stinks in His nostrils and that because of this, He cannot tolerate seeing us stand before Him with any self-assurance, even if we present ourselves in our finest form."

How do you see God? Don't we each have our own subjective images? Some see him as a harsh frowning judge ready to strike them down at the slightest sin. Others see him as a kind and jolly old Santa who winks at their sins. We form subjective images like these because we cannot see God physically. To find out what he is really like, we must balance all our images with the objective revelation he has given us in his Word. In it we learn of Christ, "the image of the invisible God" (Colossians 1:15), "the exact imprint of God's very being" (Hebrews 1:3 NRSV). He shows us exactly what God is like.

However Ignorance imagines God, he is inaccurate since he has not delved into God's Word and accepted his testimony. Christian, nevertheless, points out some key points that impact the man's current faulty image. Specifically, right thoughts about God include recognizing that he knows us better than we know ourselves. He knows everyone's thoughts, even their inmost ones.

Furthermore, since God knows our hearts, he reads our thoughts and imaginations before they even register on our consciousness. "You perceive my thoughts from afar" (Psalm 139:2). We can put on our best face and fool ourselves, but we cannot fool him. He sees the sin in our hearts and abhors our misguided, proud self-effort and vain confidence. These are accurate views of God—they agree with his revelation of himself in his Word.

Again, how do you see God? You will honor him in accordance with how you see him.

Scripture: Hebrews 4:12-13; Job 9:2-4; Proverbs 15:3

Prayer: Lord God, I don't want an inaccurate perception of you so I look to your Word. By it I see what an awesome and glorious God you are and how I can never please you apart from Christ. Amen.

D·A·Y 322

"Do you think that I am such a fool as to think that God can see no farther than I can or that I could come to God through trusting in my own best effort?" asked Ignorance.

"Why? How do you view this matter?"

"Well, in short, I think I must believe in Christ for justification."

"For what reason? How can you think you must believe in Christ when you are unable to see your need of Him? You don't see either your original sin or your existing malady. Your opinion of yourself and of your efforts plainly exposes you as one who has not yet seen his need of Christ's personal righteousness to justify him before God. How can you then say, 'I believe in Christ'?"

"I believe," replied Ignorance, "that Christ died for sinners and that I will be justified before God from the curse through His gracious acceptance of my obedience to His law. Or, if that is not enough, Christ will make my religious duties acceptable to His Father by virtue of His merits, and so I will be justified."

❧

Ignorance says, "I must believe in Christ for justification," and "I believe that Christ died for sinners." On the surface, he might seem well-informed and his faith accurate enough. He sounds well versed in theology; however, he merely pastes the right words on his own faulty interpretations. Although he denies it, his faith still rests on himself. He thinks that his good works—"my obedience to His law"—will win him salvation.

Instead of thanking Christ for his merciful provision for his sins, Ignorance still wants to hold out for some credit. To him, Christ only makes his works acceptable to God; Ignorance does the rest. In this way, he stands beside Christ like a coredeemer, partnering with him to complete his salvation. This is entirely unacceptable because we have no merit in salvation. Christ alone won our salvation. He alone gets the glory, and he will not share it with another.

Giving Christ all the glory, however, is simply too far for Ignorance's sinful pride to bow. This shows the difference between a heart renewed by God's Spirit and an unrenewed heart that secretly opposes God's truth as an enemy. Rather than humbling itself, learning of Christ, and counting his truth precious, proud and sinful human nature concocts an image of Christ to please itself. Because it finds no system of truth to please it within God's Word, its view of God is distorted; its view of his Word is defective; and its view of itself is perilously wrong. Right now give Christ all the glory for your salvation.

❧

Scripture: John 6:28-29; Ephesians 2:8-9; Romans 3:20-28

Prayer: Dear Lord, thank you that you did it all on Calvary's cross. I gratefully give you all praise and glory for my salvation, recognizing I can do nothing to add to it. Amen.

D·A·Y
323

"Please, let me give a response to this confession of your faith," said Christian. "First, you believe with an imaginary faith; for this faith is nowhere described in the Word. Second, you believe with a false faith; it takes away justification from the personal righteousness of Christ and applies it to your own. Third, this kind of faith doesn't allow Christ to be the justifier of your person, but rather the justifier of your actions; it renders your person justified by your actions. This is false. Last, therefore, this faith is deceitful. It will lead you to wrath on the judgment day of the Almighty God. For true justifying faith puts the soul, which because of the law has become perceptive of its lost condition, fleeing to Christ's righteousness for refuge. And His righteousness is not an act of grace that makes your obedience acceptable to God. No, it is His personal obedience to God's law, in doing and suffering for us what the law required of us. True faith accepts this righteousness, and under its skirt the soul is hidden and is presented as spotless before God. The soul, therefore, is accepted and thereby acquitted of all guilt and condemnation."

Ignorance's faith is *imaginary*, constructed by fantasy instead of by God's Word. One's faith can only be as good as its object, and trusting in one's own goodness is not supported by Scripture. A faith placed completely in Christ is true saving faith because God's Word testifies to it.

His faith is *false*. The more those with true faith grow spiritually, the more they realize they must cast their entire selves upon Christ's redeeming love. Ignorance believes, however, that Christ justifies actions but is unnecessary for saving the person. Yet Christ will be Savior of our whole life or Savior of none of it.

His faith is *deceitful*. Many, like Ignorance, profess Christ and yet make him only half Savior, relying instead upon their own righteousness to justify them. How then do they still claim to adhere to the fundamental doctrine of justification by faith?

At the Diet of Worms in 1521, Martin Luther refused to recant his beliefs concerning justification by faith alone and was outlawed by the Roman Catholic Church. Joachin II, elector of Brandenburg, sending his ambassadors to these disputations, told them, "Bring back with you the little word *sola* or else dare not to come back." We, too, need to tightly guard a *sola* faith based on Christ alone. None but he can justify us before God—not ourselves, pastor, priest, saint, angel, Mary, or church; no ritual, sacrament, ordinance, or act of piety suffices—only Christ. How can you better maintain a *sola* faith?

Scripture: 1 Timothy 2:5-6; Hebrews 7:25; John 5:39-40

Prayer: Lord Jesus, I always want to remain true to you, trusting in your work alone. Help me to keep my faith grounded in your Word, and please show me if I should ever shift off its firm foundation. Amen.

D·A·Y 324

"Come on!" exclaimed Ignorance. "Would you have us trust only in what Christ in His own person has done, without us? This ill-founded notion would loosen the reins of our lust and allow us to live however we wanted. For it wouldn't matter how we live, if Christ's personal righteousness may justify us when we believe."

"Ignorance is your name, and it fits you perfectly," said Christian. "Even your answer demonstrates what I say. You are ignorant of what justifying righteousness is; you are just as ignorant of how to secure your soul by faith from the terrible wrath of God. Yes, you are also ignorant of the true effects of saving faith in Christ's righteousness, those effects being a bowing and surrendering of the heart to God in Christ, a love for His Name, His Word, His ways, and His people—and not as you ignorantly imagine."

Although there are hundreds of religions, one enormous difference makes Christianity stand apart from them all. Ignorance, representing most every religion, anticipates salvation by things he does to save himself; Christian faith, on the other hand, teaches that salvation is accomplished by what Another has done.

Ignorance cannot fathom Christian faith. He cannot tolerate getting something for nothing, and this is much worse—it is *everything* for nothing! He seizes upon the clear danger he sees in the doctrine of free grace using an old argument: If faith alone saves us, without good works, then nothing will keep us from continuing to sin. After all, those who trust only in what Christ has done will quickly grow careless about their conduct.

Christian, at this point, loses patience with Ignorance, for the man's ignorant mind prevents a reasonable discussion. Christian jabs at him in a final effort to shake him out of his blind self-confidence so he can see the truth.

If only Ignorance understood the Scriptures! Then he would realize that true believers are dead to sin and alive to righteousness. It is not that they do no work at all, but they do not work from motives of obtaining salvation by doing works. For they know they lack their own righteousness. Rather, love motivates true believers to obey God's commandments. Awakened to his love, their new nature within them makes them want to obey God. Nothing more effectually keeps us faithful than God's love expressed in Christ. He died that we might live, not to ourselves, but to him. Think about your motives for living for Christ. Does love motivate you or a striving for acceptance?

Scripture: Romans 4:5; 2 Corinthians 5:14-15; Ephesians 2:10

Prayer: Dear Lord, thank you for taking my place on the cross to ransom my soul from hell. I want to serve you with all my heart because I love you and am eternally grateful. Amen.

Then Hopeful said to Christian, "Ask him if he has ever had Christ revealed to him from Heaven."

"What!" exclaimed Ignorance. "You believe in revelations? I believe that what both of you, and all the others like you, have to say about this matter is nothing but the fruit of insanity in your brains!"

"Why, man!" declared Hopeful. "Christ is so hidden in God from the perceptions of the natural man that He cannot be known, and salvation in Him cannot be attained by any unless God the Father gives a revelation of Him to them."

"That is your faith, not mine," countered Ignorance. "Just because I don't have as many whimsical doctrines turning my head as you doesn't mean that my faith isn't as good as yours."

"Allow me to say one more thing," said Christian. "You shouldn't show such disregard for this matter. For I will boldly affirm, just as my good friend has done, that no one can know Jesus Christ except through a revelation of Him by the Father."

A revelation? Surely no thinking person could take revelations seriously! To Ignorance, the wise are ones who confine their views to those reached rationally, logically, analytically. Any experience that rises above the commonsense level must be unsound. Ignorance fails to realize, however, that while common sense is valuable at its own level, when improperly used, it can serve the devil.

While spiritual experiences should always be tested by the Scriptures, the days of supernatural Holy Spirit activity are not past. Acknowledging that God speaks today primarily through his written Word, we should nevertheless be open to God's desire and ability to speak to his people through visions, prophecies, revelations, and numerous other ways. Remember that Saul's conversion came initially not from gospel preaching but through a dramatic spiritual encounter—"But when God . . . was pleased to *reveal* his Son to me" (Galatians 1:15-16 NRSV, italics mine). And we should not forget Paul's impetus and confirmation to evangelize the Gentile world with Barnabas came presumably as a word of prophecy at a worship and prayer meeting—"Set apart for me Barnabas and Saul for the work to which I have called them" (Acts 13:2). While his Word tests the validity of our spiritual experience, spiritual experience in Christ activates and deepens our understanding of his Word.

Pride, unbelief, and carnal reasoning so close sinners' minds against Christ's redemption that nothing short of God's revelation can remove this veil. Thank God for his initial revelation to you and expect more as you read his Word.

Scripture: Matthew 11:25-27; Ephesians 1:16-17; Proverbs 29:18

Prayer: Dear Lord, thank you for revealing yourself to me. I always want to be open to receive further revelations of you. I want to know you more fully. Amen.

D·A·Y
326

"And another requirement for knowing Christ is faith fashioned by 'the exceeding greatness of His power' [Ephesians 1:19 KJV]. By such faith the person whose heart is right can lay hold of Christ. And I perceive, poor Ignorance, that you are still ignorant of the working of such faith. Be awakened then; see your own wretchedness, and flee to the Lord Jesus. By His righteousness, which is the righteousness of God—for He, Himself is God—you will be delivered from all guilt and condemnation."

To know Christ, one must first receive a revelation of him. Then one must respond to that revelation with faith—specifically, faith "that is fashioned by" Christ's power. Yet Ignorance disregards the power of Christ's Gospel. Thinking he can somehow meet God's standard by his own efforts, he dismisses his own personal insufficiency and Christ's all-sufficiency.

Just think of Christ's power! He is mightier than kings, emperors, generals, cherubim, seraphim—every earthly or demonic power. By his powerful wrath, he dethrones Satan and eternally damns sinners. By his powerful grace, he removes the dividing wall of hostility and eternally saves his people. His is an exceedingly great power, an explosive, dynamic power. As he lay entombed, stone-cold and lifeless for three days, suddenly, like a depth charge dropped into hell's heartland, his resurrection power annihilated death's grip. Triumphantly rising to sit at the Father's right hand of power, he promises to return with unrivaled power and glory. On that day, he will powerfully resurrect us from physical death.

Oh, his liberating, transforming power! It rescues us from our crushing burden of sin; it converts, regenerates, and gives us new life. It changes stony hearts to ones of flesh, dethrones self, puts off the old nature, and forms Christ in us. It augments his grace in our hearts, stamps his image upon our souls, enlightens our understanding, subdues our stubborn wills, removes our affection from worldly things, purifies our consciences. It enables us to resist temptations victoriously, to serve him faithfully, to endure persecution and even death unflinchingly.

Ignorance specifically fails to apprehend the power of God's grace. Christ's blood is exceedingly powerful. His work on the cross is so sufficient that Ignorance can add nothing to its efficacy. If only Ignorance believed this! Then he could lay hold of Christ's saving power by faith. To experience the mighty power of his divine grace, we must come to him in faith. Those like Ignorance fail to fully believe in Christ's power. What do you need? Affirm your belief that Christ's power is more than adequate for you.

Scripture: Ephesians 1:19-23; 3:20; 2 Corinthians 4:7

Prayer: Lord, give me a robust faith that comes from knowing your divine power. Thank you for your all-sufficient power available to me. Amen.

D·A·Y
327

"You go so fast that I can't keep up with you," Ignorance responded. "You go on ahead, for I must stay behind for a while."

Then Christian and Hopeful said,

> *"Well, Ignorance, will you foolish remain,*
> *Slighting good counsel, given once and again?*
> *If you still refuse it, you'll surely know*
> *Before long the evil of your doing so.*
> *Remember in time, man—bow, do not fear;*
> *Good counsel well taken, saves, therefore hear.*
> *But if you still slight it, you'll surely be*
> *The loser, Ignorance, most assuredly."*

❧

Every pilgrimage affords opportunity for deception. As Paul predicted, we see epidemic deception in these end times as people are "deceiving and being deceived" (2 Timothy 3:13). Rejecting the truth to go his own way, Ignorance willfully deceives himself. His willful ignorance blinds him to the truth. Those like him who, in the light of truth, simply choose deception are among the most baffling.

At one time or another most of us discover we were just fooling ourselves concerning some issue we didn't want to face. Still, we eventually own up to our fault. Those who keep refusing, however, can become chronically self-deceived. They use anything they can to maneuver around the truth about themselves—denial, cover-ups, rationalizations, justifications, excuses, evasions of responsibility, and even blaming others. With such skillfully woven deceptions, they often believe their own lies. And God is prevented from applying his grace to heal them because, not only do their hearts lie to themselves and to others, but they lie to God. Ultimately, they become so entangled in a deceitful web of their own making that they may never find their way back to the truth.

None of us yet perfectly walks in the light. We all have blind spots and need to ask God to show us these places before they become more serious deceptions. We need to ask our brothers and sisters to hold us accountable to the truth in our lives. David Burrell says, "The Christian moral life cannot be an individual achievement, but requires a community of friends we call the church to challenge our endemic drift toward self-deception."[35] When so challenged, we should decide to respond quickly so that we can enjoy a pure and honest walk with God. Ask him to show you any areas of self-deception in your life.

❧

Scripture: James 1:22; Psalm 51:6; 2 John 4; 3 John 4

Prayer: Father of light and truth, may I reflect your nature amid this world's darkness and lies. Help me be receptive when convicted of sin. Amen.

D·A·Y
328

After this, Christian said to Hopeful, "Well, come on, brother, it looks as if we will once again be walking by ourselves."

So I saw in my dream that they went on a ways ahead, and Ignorance came walking lamely behind them. Then Christian said to his companion, "I am deeply grieved for this poor man; it will certainly not go well for him when he reaches the end."

"It's tragic," replied Hopeful. "In our town there is an abundance of people in this condition. There are whole families, yes, whole streets, including pilgrims, too. And if there are so many like this in our region, how many do you think there are in the area where he was born?"

Christian added, "Indeed, the Word says, 'He has blinded their eyes and deadened their hearts, so they can neither see with their eyes, nor understand with their hearts'" [John 12:40].

Ignorance is not alone in his self-deception. It seems to the two pilgrims that the world is full of people just like him. Why can they not see their desperate condition? Why do they feel so content with their perspective? The verse of Scripture Christian quotes only seems to raise more questions.

The Lord doesn't directly blind people or harden them. He merely gives them up to their own blindness and hardness of heart, withholding the healing grace that would enlighten them and change their hearts if they but wanted it. When we stubbornly refuse God, he leaves us to our ignorance. The truth so evident to others may stare us in the face. It may plainly pound upon our heart's door. Yet we remain unresponsive. We cannot blame the Lord for this condition. We are to blame, for we choose it. Just as warm sunshine beating upon soft mud makes it grow harder until it becomes dry and brittle, God's light causes a hard heart to grow harder. By contrast, like butter melting in the warm sun—the same sun—a revelation of God makes a tender heart melt under his love.

The Lord, therefore, shines upon us all with his light and truth. For "his eternal power and divine nature, invisible though they are, have been understood and seen through the things he has made" (Romans 1:20 NRSV). As Hopeful says, it is tragic that so many people intentionally shut their eyes and hearts, fearing God's revelation, his light, his conviction. They don't want to turn from their evil ways, repent, and receive forgiveness for their sins, healing, and eternal life.

Consider your heart. Is it like hardening mud, or is it like softening butter? Be sure to allow the Spirit's conviction to soften, not harden, your heart.

Scripture: Romans 1:18-22; Acts 13:46-48; John 10:26-27

Prayer: Dear Lord, thank you for your light and truth. I want my eyes always open and my heart receptive to the revelation of your will. Amen.

D·A·Y
329

"Now that we are by ourselves, Hopeful, what do you think of such people? Do you think that at any time they feel the conviction of sin and fear that they are in a dangerous condition?"

"No, you answer your question since you are the older one."

"Then I will say that I think sometimes they may. But they, being naturally ignorant, don't understand that such convictions are for their good. Therefore, they desperately try to stifle and hide them and presumptuously continue to soothe their egos in the best way they know how."

"I believe as you do," said Hopeful. "I also believe that fear can be very beneficial in prompting them to begin their pilgrimage on the right foot."

"Without a doubt, if it is godly fear, for the Word says, 'The fear of the Lord is the beginning of wisdom'" [Proverbs 9:10].

Are those like Ignorance as confident and contented as they seem? The answer is that everyone feels some conviction upon hearing God's testimony concerning sin's wages. Some may come under fearful conviction, but ignorant of the spiritual value of this work of God, they quickly cast it off. A fear of exposure replaces godly fear of divine retribution. Seeking to justify themselves, "to soothe their egos," they quickly lay hold of any false assurance that satisfies them.

While Adam and Eve were innocent in the Garden of Eden, they were never ignorant. A godly fear kept them from taking the forbidden fruit until the day of temptation when the desire to soothe and satisfy their egos overrode their fear of God. They quickly forgot that their fear was "for their good." In suppressing it, they rejected God's command, sinned against his love, charted their own course, and quickly strayed from God. Consequently, they were forced to experience a fear never before known or imagined. Terrified, they hid from God and hid from the truth. Adam blamed Eve, and Eve blamed the serpent, but how could they hope to fool God? They ended up driven from their perfect garden paradise.

The fear of the Lord remains the beginning of wisdom. Yet how blessed we are to live under a dispensation of grace. Rather than fearfully hiding our sin, through Christ we can now confess it and be restored to full fellowship with God. Ignorant people don't understand this. They persist in their self-preserving, ego-soothing ways. They actually think they can hide their sin from God. If you have any secret sins, expose them to Christ now. Let him take them.

Scripture: Genesis 3:1-13; Proverbs 28:13; 1 John 1:8-10

Prayer: Holy Spirit, I never want to soothe my own ego by hiding my sin. I want rather to be open to your conviction. Let my solace come from openly walking with Christ in the light of his grace. Amen.

D·A·Y
330

"Will you elaborate on what you believe is the right kind of fear, Christian?"

"Well, I believe godly fear is recognized by three things: First, by what causes it—the type of conviction of sin that leads to salvation. Next, you can see that it drives the soul to grasp and cling tightly to Christ for salvation. And finally, it brings to birth and maintains within the soul a deep reverence for God, His Word and His ways, keeping the heart tender and making it afraid to turn from these things. That person will turn neither to the right nor to the left. He won't want to do anything that might bring dishonor to God, interrupt his peace with God, grieve the Spirit of God, or give an enemy reason to speak scornfully of God or His Kingdom."

Christian is no coward, but he has a strong regard for the role fear should play in a pilgrim's walk. Fear has two senses. One relates to danger and the other to reverence. Christian's interpretation includes both. First, he describes this fear by its cause—conviction of sin. This involves not only fear of punishment but alarm at the hideous nature of sin. Next, he describes the fear of God by its effect—salvation. This godly fear leads to embracing Christ, birthing a deep reverence that draws souls into seeking God, his Word, and his ways with tender hearts.

A reverential fear of God quickly becomes a believer's primary motivation. Unlike the cowering fear of slaves, it is the respectful fear children have of their father. As obedient children, we do not stand in fear of judgment and wrath, distrusting his grace and love, but we stand in awe and admiration of him. We wonder at his loftiness and holiness. This is consistent with strong faith and bold confidence, with joyful devotion and reverential affection. This fear, born of God's gracious love, produces a sanctifying work of grace in the heart. As the soul continues to grow in this grace, discovering more of God's pardoning love and goodness, this reverential fear also deepens.

This godly fear expresses itself in an appreciation and respect for God's honor, a strong regard for the value of peace with him, a sensitivity to the Holy Spirit's witness and leading, a loyalty so strong that it jealously guards God's reputation and does nothing to turn public opinion against him. Our God is a Person so wonderful, so loving, so magnanimously generous and forgiving that we should reverentially avoid anything that would bring reproach to his name. Do you "fear" God enough in your life? Think of some ways you can more fully reverence him.

Scripture: Jeremiah 9:24; 10:6-7; Revelation 14:6-7; 19:5

Prayer: Dear Lord, I stand in awe of you. I give you praise and glory! May my life always express a proper fearful regard for you. Amen.

"Well said," Hopeful responded. "I believe that you have spoken the truth. Do you think that we are almost out of the Enchanted Ground?"

"Why? Are you getting tired of this discussion?" asked Christian.

"No, definitely not, but I would like to know where we are."

"I don't believe we have more than two miles farther to travel on this ground, but let's return to our subject. Those who are ignorant don't realize that such convictions, which are intended to instill fear in them, are for their own good. Therefore, they seek to stifle those feelings."

Christian never seems to tire of discussing spiritual truth—not even here on the Enchanted Ground! Hopeful, while denying it, probably finds this heavy discussion a somewhat taxing mental exercise in this sleepy region. Christian, however, remembers the danger and continues with his mission to keep himself and his brother awake.

Way back at the beginning of Christian's pilgrimage, before he came to the cross of Christ, he felt a compelling fear that motivated him, despite mishaps, to continue seeking God. When he came to the Interpreter's House, he was shown many profitable things. When the Interpreter asked if he had paid close attention to these things, he replied, "Yes, and they fill me with both hope and fear." This reverent fear was as profitable to him as the hope he received. It enabled him to reverence Christ's authority, obey his commands, and shun ungodly ignorant ways. After this, he quickly arrived at the cross and received salvation. Ignorance, on the other hand, stifles and hides the fear that God intends to put in him. Instead, he comforts himself with false hope. Completely bypassing the cross of Christ, he experiences no saving change in his life.

It is godly fear that leads to repentance, to faith in Christ. It moves us toward watchful obedience and enables us to "realize the full assurance of hope to the very end" (Hebrews 6:11 NRSV). We should never attempt to stifle it. Of course, fears may become unreasonable and excessive, the effect of unbelief. This should be taken into account. Yet if we tend to avoid all caution and fear, we can easily fall to self-deception. Without godly fear, we will scarcely take the scriptural admonition seriously: "Therefore, brothers and sisters, be all the more eager to confirm your call and election, for if you do this, you will never stumble" (2 Peter 1:10 NRSV). Think about hope and fear. How do you see God using them both in your life?

Scripture: Luke 12:4-5; Hebrews 12:28-29; Psalms 2:11; 89:7

Prayer: Dear Lord, thank you for both the hope and the fear you have instilled in my heart. Let them continually balance each other that I may walk a straight path toward my eternal destination. Amen.

DAY 332

"How do you think they seek to stifle them?" asked Hopeful.

"One way is by thinking that the Devil brought about such fears, but the truth is that they are from God. In thinking this, they consequently begin resisting the fear as if it were a threat to their very existence.

"A second way is to think that these fears will spoil their faith when, in fact, these unfortunate people possess no true faith anyway. So they harden their hearts against the fear.

"A third way is to presume that they should project an image of courage; so they harden their hearts, repress the fear, and choose to become presumptuously confident.

"A fourth way is that when they notice that such fears tend to erode confidence in their sense of personal righteousness, they determine to resist them with all their might."

"I know something of this myself," said Hopeful. "Before I understood these things, I was just like this."

Many of those who ignorantly choose to stifle the fears that might lead them to repent are actually quite conventional in their attitudes and behavior. Ignorance had initially told Christian he was following the doctrine of his country of Conceit. All in that country hold a common worldview that they believe is correct. Because they presumptuously think God orders their affairs, they feel no reason to fear. Fear seems an unsettling and destabilizing force, a demonic messenger to resist at all costs.

Those who are ignorant see fear as an affront to their faith. Their faith, however, is nothing but an adherence to their conventional wisdom. Indeed, godly fear militates against this false security. So in an effort to preserve their status quo, they defend their hearts against its intrusion.

Rather than looking good because they are good, the ignorant feel good when they look good. If they can project a courageous image, they feel courageous and faith-filled. When godly fear begins to shake them, they feel they must protect their image from shattering. They reject the fear in favor of a foolish self-confidence. They can look in the mirror and still see their same confident image. Yet their confidence is a house of cards that they must protect with all their might.

Even while rejecting the clear teachings of Scripture and wandering down paths of their own making, these ignorant citizens of conventionality think theirs is the proper way of thinking and living. We shouldn't be afraid to lovingly yet incisively pull them out of the self-righteous denial of their true condition. Do you know such people? Ask the Holy Spirit how best to present the truth to them.

Scripture: Proverbs 1:7; 30:12; Job 24:13; John 3:20-21; 8:47

Prayer: Dear Lord, I pray for those who stifle the fear that would lead them to salvation. Please forgive their self-imposed ignorance. Tear down their defenses that they may respond to your love. Amen.

"Why don't we leave our neighbor Ignorance by himself for now," suggested Christian. "Let's discuss another beneficial question."

"Yes, that's a great idea, but you go ahead and choose the topic of discussion again."

"Well," Christian began, "about ten years ago, there was a man named Mr. Temporary living in your region. He was a very impulsive sort of man. Did you know him?"

"Yes, I certainly did," answered Hopeful. "He lived in the town of Graceless, about two miles from Honesty. I believe he lived next door to a Mr. Turn-back."

"That's him! Actually he lived under the same roof with Mr. Turn-back. I believe that he once experienced an awakening in his life where he suddenly had some insight into his sins and the wages that they would bring him."

"Yes, I believe that's true," said Hopeful. "My house wasn't over three miles from his, and he would often come to me in tears. I really felt for the man and even had some hope for him. But, as we all may see, 'not everyone who cries, "Lord, Lord," will enter the Kingdom of Heaven'" [Matthew 7:21].

"He once told me that he had resolved to go on a pilgrimage," said Christian. "But then he suddenly got acquainted with one called Save-self; after that he treated me like a stranger."

Temporary knows gospel doctrine but not its life-changing power. He once impulsively responded to godly fear, but not for long. For he lived in Graceless. But graceless people fall short of honesty in their profession of faith. While seeming sincere, they fail to sever worldly ties and soon turn back to the world.

Oh, they do feel godly fear, but rather than humbly responding, they hold to their self-confidence. How many pastors, counseling tearful penitents, envision wonderful conversions, only to be disappointed as the persons fall into deeper sin? Thomas Scott says, "Such convictions resemble the blossoms of the fruit tree, which must precede the ripe fruit, but do not always produce it: so that we cannot say, 'The more blossoms there are, the greater abundance will there be of fruit'; though we may be assured that there can be no fruit, if there be no blossoms."[36]

After Temporary's initial profession, he met Save-self, who convinced Temporary that they could save themselves by doing good deeds and reforming their own character. Alas, for all the self-centered religions today! Resisting their message when they so gratify the flesh is not easy. We should cautiously guard our hearts against their seductions. Renounce any urges to fall to this temptation.

Scripture: Proverbs 1:29-33; Isaiah 1:4; Psalm 57:7

Prayer: Dear Lord, you never turn away from me. May my heart never turn from you. I want to cleave to you in love forever. Amen.

D·A·Y
334

"Since we are talking about him, why don't we try to figure out why he and others suddenly backslide?" offered Hopeful.

"It may be of some profit, but you go ahead and begin."

"Well," said Hopeful, "in my judgment there are four reasons for it. First, though the conscience of such a person is awakened, their minds remain unchanged. Therefore, when the strength of the guilty feelings wears off, that which drove them to be religious ceases. So quite naturally they return to their former ways again. This is like a dog that is sick from what he has eaten. As long as the sickness persists, he will keep vomiting it up. He doesn't do this on purpose but because his stomach is upset. But as soon as the sickness is over and his stomach is soothed, because his desires are not at all alienated from his vomit, he turns around and licks it right back up. So what is written is true, 'A dog returns to its vomit' [2 Peter 2:22].

"Therefore, I think that they are eager for Heaven only out of a sudden sense of and fear of the torments of Hell. But when this sense of Hell and fear of damnation is gone, their desire for Heaven and eternal happiness dies also. At that point they simply return to their former course."

❦

Backsliding is an Old Testament term primarily used by the prophets Jeremiah and Hosea to describe the tragic spiritual state of the Jewish nation that had turned away from following God. Yet it also applies to those who have simply stopped growing and progressing in the faith. Failing to go forward in one's pilgrimage is backsliding.

Why do people seem to run well for a time, then stand still, and finally turn back? Christian already posed one significant reason—that of companionship. Mr. Temporary's friendship with Mr. Save-self gave him the impetus for making his wrong choice. Relationships are a matter of life and death, and many desertions can be traced to this relational inroad of deception.

Hopeful believes that the backslider's repentance was emotional and not sincere. Mr. Temporary anguished enough over his sin to visit Hopeful in Vanity about it. Yet fearing hell and feeling stirred by heaven on an emotional level wasn't enough to radically change his thinking and his will.

Times of testing inevitably arise during which our heart's true beliefs are revealed. Unless godly fear has thrust us into a genuine reliance upon God's grace, we may find our faith like that of Messrs. Temporary and Turn-back. Are there areas of backsliding in your life? Turn back to God in these areas. What things can keep you progressing in your pilgrimage? From now on, do these.

❦

Scripture: 2 Peter 2:19-23; Mark 4:16-17; Job 17:9

Prayer: Lord, coming to you brought a radical change of mind and heart. May I become even more unflinchingly committed to my pilgrimage. Amen.

D·A·Y
335

"Another reason is this: They have an oppressive fear that is overpowering to them—I am speaking of the fear that they have of men, for the 'fear of man will prove to be a snare' [Proverbs 29:25]. So, although they seem to be on fire for the Kingdom of Heaven as long as the flames of Hell are lapping around their ears, when the terror subsides, they begin to have second thoughts. Namely, they think that it is good to be wise and not run the risk of losing so much for who knows what. If not fearing they will lose all, then they at least fear they will bring themselves into unavoidable and unnecessary conflict. So they once again fall back into step with the world."

Hopeful sees the second reason for backsliding as the "fear of man." Temporary's proneness to the wrong fear matches Ignorance's deficiency in the right fear. Diametrically opposed to a godly fear that comes by God's grace, this fear of man is a human fear that distrusts God and brings bondage. It centers on how others will react if one should become a dedicated follower of Christ. People who fall to it may fear losing favor, friendship, honor, applause, or position. They may fear reproach and reviling. They may even fear death itself.

For a while those like Mr. Temporary may fear God's wrath, but as soon as those feelings subside, their unconverted minds and hearts convince them against making a radical departure from the world. For they fear raising eyebrows and causing public outrage more than they fear God.

This ungodly fear can catch sincere believers off guard, too. Rationalizing that they are merely being discreet, preachers can avoid certain biblical truths, and God's people can hide their light so as not to offend others. When we shy away from publicly displaying our faith, we should look for this undermining fear. Fear of man led many Jews not to profess Jesus as their Messiah though they believed in him. It moved Abraham to deny his wife before Abimelech. It caused Peter to deny Christ three times.

How must it look to God when he sees us so fearful of others' opinions? To avoid backsliding, we must trust God and fight off this ungodly fear. General George Patton said, "No matter what you do, people will be shooting at you. If you are afraid of being shot at, you are whipped before you start." When was the last time you courageously professed Christ before others? Think of steps you can take to take a more forthright stand for Christ among your friends and associates.

Scripture: John 12:42-43; Matthew 26:69-74; Psalm 118:6; Isaiah 51:12

Prayer: Lord Jesus, acknowledging you as my Sovereign Lord, I reject the fear of man. I ask for more of your Spirit's power to enable me to boldly shine your light before others. Amen.

DAY 336

"A third reason is that the scorn that so often accompanies a sincere religious experience is a stumbling block to them. They remain proud and haughty while true religion remains low and contemptible in their eyes. So when they have lost their sense of Hell and the wrath to come, they again return to their former course."

The bold-faced character Shame scornfully attacked Faithful before he had made an unwavering resolve to follow Christ. Shame made Faithful ashamed of having a tender conscience, calling it "unmanly." A true man, after all, is the "Marlboro Man," unabashedly proud, rugged, a man's man, or so the tobacco companies would have us believe. Shame scorned him for many additional reasons—for trying to speak and act righteously rather than acting like a real man; for losing his adventurous liberty; for becoming a laughingstock; for robbing himself of friendship with this world's rich, powerful, and wise and instead allying himself with failures, outcasts, and weaklings. Shame scorned him for losing everything he had gained in this world, for giving in to ignorance and naiveté by forsaking science, for breaking emotionally under a convicting sermon, for asking people for their forgiveness. Shame's relentless insults caused Faithful great consternation. Yet all his circumstances were a work of God's grace to deliver Faithful from fallen worldly values and prepare him for his entrance into the Celestial City. Fortunately, Faithful saw the light and forcefully commanded his enemy to leave him.

While Satan would use the scorn of worldly people to intimidate us, God uses it to strengthen us and work humility within our character. If we retain our pride and become defensive before their insults, letting feelings of shame and embarrassment about our faith seize our hearts, we could find ourselves quickly backsliding.

Instead of letting people's scorn drive us away from God, we should allow it to drive us closer to him and to his people. In his arms of love and in fellowship with his church, we will find strength, courage, and hope to face scornful rebukes victoriously. Our armor may even seem Teflon-coated. Insults will simply slide off us. Remember how David boldly praised God for his glory no matter what people thought. His relationship with God was so wonderful to him that hiding it was unthinkable. How excited are you about your faith—excited enough to bear insults without feeling ashamed? Renew your commitment to candidly follow Christ, and take steps to strengthen that commitment.

Scripture: Psalm 40:10; 1 Peter 4:16; Luke 9:26

Prayer: Dear Lord, thank you for lovingly bearing painful insults for my sake as you hung on the cross for me. I intend to bear your name courageously and never backslide. Amen.

D·A·Y 337

"Fourth, I believe that facing their guilt and contemplating the terrors to come are unbearable to them. They don't want to face their misery before the time comes. If they would heed the warning that has been given them, they would flee to where the righteous flee and find safety. But because they shun these thoughts of guilt and terror, once their realization has been effectively suppressed, they gladly harden their hearts and choose ways that will harden them more and more."

Have you ever engaged in "contemplating the terrors to come?" After David sinned, he did. He cried to God, "Do not cast me from your presence or take your Holy Spirit from me" (Psalm 51:11). Paul contemplated the terrors of becoming an apostate preacher as he confessed, "but I pommel my body and subdue it, lest after preaching to others I myself should be disqualified" (1 Corinthians 9:27 RSV). Even Christ, contemplating his upcoming terrors, perspired drops of blood in Gethsemane as he cried, "Father, if you are willing, take this cup from me" (Luke 22:42).

Backsliders, on the other hand, avoid discomforting thoughts of guilt, fear, or impending terrors. Accustomed to thoughts of love, peace, and comfort, they choose the present easy way rather than worrying about future troubles. They achieve this end run around the truth by hardening their hearts.

Found among the private papers of a Bishop Andrews were his contemplations of terror: "Lord, as Thou art loving, give me tears, give me floods of tears, and give me all that this day, before it be too late. For then will be the incorruptible Judge, the horrible judgment seat, the answer without excuse, the inevitable charge, the shameful punishment, the endless Gehenna, the pitiless angels, the yawning hell, the roaring stream of fire, the unquenchable flame, the dark prison, the rayless darkness, the bed of live coals, the unwearied worm, the indissoluble chains, the bottomless chaos, the impassable wall, the inconsolable cry. And none to stand by me; none to plead for me; none to snatch me out."

No Temporary or Turn-back ever seriously allowed these terrors to penetrate their hearts. If they had, they would have embraced Christ's saving grace, never turning from his salvation.

We should never hide from our spiritual condition. If we are in sin, we should fear. If we choose the easy way of denial, we rob ourselves of the grace to prepare us for what we face ahead. Are you trying to live a faithful Christian life? If so, you shouldn't be afraid of backsliding. If your commitment remains tentative, however, "contemplating the terrors to come" might be helpful.

Scripture: Isaiah 33:14-18; 2 Corinthians 13:5; Hebrews 4:1

Prayer: Dear Lord, if I should begin to backslide, I pray that I will contemplate the terrors of such foolish choices. Help me never to harden my heart. Amen.

D·A·Y 338

Then Christian said, "I think you are close to the mark, for the bottom line is that they need a change in their minds and in their wills. They are like the felon who stands before a judge. He will shake and tremble, repenting heartily. Underneath, however, there is the fear of punishment, not loathing for his offense. This soon becomes evident because, if you give the man his freedom, he will go right back to his criminal activities. If he had truly changed his mind, his actions would be quite different."

Christian agrees with Hopeful's reasons for why people backslide. He reiterates that he believes the bottom line is their lack of true repentance—a change of mind and will. The Greek word for repentance, *metanoeo,* literally means "to perceive afterwards." Yet it involves much more than mere mental reflection. In New Testament usage, the mind, the seat of moral reflection, looks back with abhorrence upon past sins and heartily changes direction. Thus both mind and will work together to effect a change for the better.

In society lawbreakers fear the day when the long arm of the law will catch up with them. Once caught, they may feel deep remorse before the judge. As prison inmates, they may think they will never again be so foolish. But are they just sorry they were caught? No one can know for sure until they are released. Then their freedom will test their repentance. Ex-convicts who truly repent look back with remorse at their former behavior and take a new direction by dedicating themselves to becoming law-abiding citizens. So many, however, soon exhibit a superficial repentance as their supposed reformation quickly falls apart.

Spiritual backsliders may similarly be very sorry for the prospect of God's punishment but lack genuine sorrow for their sins. As soon as they receive clemency or decide to cast off their fear, they use their freedom as an opportunity for the flesh. Their unconverted minds quickly return to their former way of thinking. Lacking any volitional purpose, their commitment unravels.

King Saul was a backslider who expressed sorrow for his sins but never truly repented. Ultimately, he lost everything. As God's people, we should allow his Spirit through his Word to convert and transform our thinking. When we begin to make sinful departures from his will, we need to deeply and sincerely repent. Can you think of sins that you have treated with mere lip-service repentance? Repent in the New Testament sense right now.

Scripture: 1 Samuel 15:11-28; Job 34:26-27; Psalm 18:21-23

Prayer: Dear Lord, when I sin, I pray that I will repent with all my mind and all my will. Right now I repent of everything that restrains my forward progress. Amen.

"And now," said Hopeful, "since we have discussed reasons for their backsliding, you tell me how it happens."

"I will try," said Christian. "I believe it happens by degrees. First they try as much as they can to pull their thoughts away from remembering God, death, and the coming judgment. Then they gradually cast off their personal obligations such as closet-prayer, curbing their lusts, being watchful, being sorry for sin, etc. Next they begin to shun the company of active and zealous Christians. Then they grow indifferent to their public obligations, such as attending church and other gatherings of believers. After this they start nit-picking and look for the faults in other Christians. They find a flaw in them and by that get an excuse to cast their faith behind their backs. Next they often begin to run with a carnal, hedonistic crowd. After this they give way to secret and profane discussions. And, incidentally, they are glad if they can find those with good reputations doing the same things. This enables them to use that person's example as an excuse to sin. Then they can easily begin to play with little sins openly.

"Finally, being hardened, they show themselves as they are. Once again they have launched themselves into the gulf of misery, and unless a miracle of grace prevents it, they will everlastingly perish in their own deceit."

Christian attempts to explain how backsliding happens. Naturally, not everyone who backslides does it the same way. Yet Christian's progression—or, should we say, regression—is as fine an analysis as one could find. The "slide" backwards "happens by degrees" and begins with early secret failures. People become backsliders long before "they show themselves as they are" publicly. Those who deny this fact are like a bald man awakening one morning to find his final hair gone and hollering, "Oh no, I am bald!" As soon as we begin backsliding, our danger should alarm us.

Our best defense against backsliding is to avoid ever taking the first step backwards. Julius Caesar, upon landing on Britain's shores, prevented his soldiers from backsliding from their duty. He took them to the edge of the Cliffs of Dover, and there they saw all the ships that had brought them across the channel engulfed in flames. They had no choice but to advance and conquer. As Christ's pilgrims, we need to burn our boats and our bridges behind us. If we do not, we could easily backslide and even perish. What "boats and bridges" still in the harbor might lure you into backsliding? Commit them to God and let him burn them from your heart.

Scripture: Hebrews 2:3; 10:39; Revelation 2:5; 3:2-3; Psalm 125:1

Prayer: Dear Lord, thank you for the ample warnings you give us in the Scriptures against backsliding. I resolve, by your grace, to keep moving forward in my pilgrimage to the end. Amen.

D·A·Y
340

Now I saw in my dream that by this time the pilgrims had gotten past the Enchanted Ground. They were now entering the Country of Beulah where the air is sweet and refreshing. Since their way lay directly through it, they enjoyed some peace and comfort there for a time. They enjoyed every day they spent in that place, seeing lovely flowers and hearing the continual singing of birds. In this Country the sun shines night and day; thus, it is beyond the Valley of the Shadow of Death. It is also out of the reach of Giant Despair; they could not so much as catch a glimpse of Doubting Castle.

❦

The pilgrims now trade the evil enchanting land for a blessed enrapturing one—Beulah. According to the prophet Isaiah, when God restores Israel to her land, she will no longer be called "Forsaken" or "Desolate." Instead, Israel and her God will again be united, and he will give her the name of Beulah, meaning "married." As the church, we are the bride of Christ with whom he renews his marriage contract. We look forward to a time of complete restoration climaxing when he comes and takes us with him to the wedding supper of the Lamb.

The Country of Beulah for Christian and Hopeful is a place of sweet peace and confidence. They, along with other well-tested believers, commonly come here toward the close of their lives. Oh, if only we could all stay in Beulah, experiencing similar triumphant joy. However, this is only one stage of the pilgrimage, and a very advanced one at that. Through their years of pilgrimage, the pilgrims have gradually progressed "from strength to strength, till each appears before God in Zion" (Psalm 84:7). Through much struggle and dying, their egos are crucified, their hearts live in an abiding state of sweet surrender, their hope is fixed and unshakable.

In Beulah, where "the sun shines night and day," Christian and Hopeful can hardly remember the dark and lonely separation they felt in such places as the Valley of the Shadow of Death and Doubting Castle. They find themselves released from badgering temptations and beleaguering doubts. For they are "married," fruitful, filled with the Lord's love. Here they enjoy fellowship with other saints, praying, praising, thanking the Lord without restraint. They enjoy the beauty of holiness, the consolations of the Holy Spirit's presence, the healing radiance of the Son of Righteousness, the precious light of continuing revelations upon their souls.

You should remember Beulah as you trudge along the pilgrim Way. Despite how you sometimes feel, your name is no longer Forsaken or Desolate. You are Married—married to Christ. Think about it!

❦

Scripture: Isaiah 54:4-5, 14; 62:4; Song of Solomon 2:10-13

Prayer: Dear Lord, I look forward to enjoying the Country of Beulah. Meanwhile, I ask for the grace to carry on patiently until I get there. Amen.

Quite the contrary, here they could see the City to which they were going. Because it was on the border of Heaven, the Shining Ones commonly walked in this Land. Also in this Land the covenant between the Bride and the Bridegroom was renewed. Yes, here as a bridegroom rejoices over his bride, so their God rejoices over them. Here they had no lack of grain or wine, for the place is filled with an abundance of all they had been seeking in their pilgrimage. They could hear voices from the City—loud voices proclaiming, "Say to the daughter of Zion, 'Surely, your salvation is coming! Behold, His reward is with Him!'" All the inhabitants of the Country called them "the Holy People, the Redeemed of the Lord" [Isaiah 62:11-12].

Beulah is so close to heaven that angels are seen frequenting it. Pilgrims readily discern their ministering care over them, the heirs of salvation. Above all, pilgrims are intensely aware of a joyful renewal of their covenant relationship with Christ. Expressions such as "knowing," "abiding in," "walking with," and "having fellowship with" take on new and profound meaning. They walk in habitual harmony, closest intimacy, and in consummate union with Christ. Besides loving them, the Lord rejoices over them as a bridegroom for his bride. Formerly they couldn't conceive of such affirmation. Now he sends them strong expressions of his passionate love—fresh tokens, pledges, gifts, and assurances—to show his delight.

The pilgrims clearly hear voices shouting God's promises from the City. Most of us in our good moments think we hear encouraging whispers upon our souls. Yet as we journey on in faith, we can be assured that God delights in us and will make us increasingly aware of that delight. Rejoice in your present relationship with Christ; rejoice, too, for the glorious discoveries yet ahead.

I am dwelling on the mountain where the golden sunlight gleams
O'er a land whose wondrous beauty far exceeds my fondest dreams;
Where the air is pure, ethereal, laden with the breath of flowers,
They are blooming by the fountain, 'Neath the amaranthine bowers.
I can see far down the mountain, where I wandered weary years,
Often hindered in my journey by the ghosts of doubts and fears
Broken vows and disappointments thickly sprinkled all the way,
But Spirit led, unerring, to the land I hold today.

—Harriet Warner ReQua

Scripture: Isaiah 62:5-12; 65:19; Revelation 21:2; Zephaniah 3:17

Prayer: Lord, thank you for Beulah where the bride excitedly awaits her wedding day. My heart thrills at the privilege of being part of your bride. That you rejoice over me in anticipation makes my heart glad. Amen.

D·A·Y 342

Now as they walked over this Land, they did more rejoicing than they had in all the other places in their journey put together. As they drew near to the City, they had an even more wonderful view of it. It was constructed of pearls and other precious stones, and they could see a street paved with gold. The City's beauty and the radiance of the sunbeams coming from it were so glorious to behold that Christian became sick with intense longing. Hopeful also was stricken with the same affliction, and because of their pangs they lay there for some time crying out, "If you find my beloved one, tell him that I am sick with love" [Song of Solomon 5:8].

Just as Christ delights in and rejoices over his pilgrims, they delight and rejoice in him. Christian and Hopeful are not yet in heaven, but heaven is bursting in upon their souls. This blissful life in the Spirit almost completely extends beyond the enemy's reach. No former self-denial, no struggle, no suffering in their lives was worthy of comparing with this blessed state.

How wonderful no longer to struggle with a dull spiritual vision. Formerly, faint glimpses of eternity would occasionally come like sparse crocuses of hope poking through the surface of their weary souls. Now, as their earthly pilgrimage draws to a close and they draw nearer to the Celestial Gates, the old habit of hoping against hope is replaced with a well-established, nearly effortless joyful expectation. Awash in this unbounded hope, free of previous conflicts and contrary evils, the pilgrims can actually see the pearly gates and golden streets through radiant streams of heavenly Light.

Because of their high degree of sanctification, they enjoy an abiding close relationship with God. Their spiritual perception of him becomes so clear and their experience so dynamic that it could easily resemble that of Moses and Elijah walking and talking with Christ on the Mount of Transfiguration. Suddenly in fervent adoration, undying devotion, and unrestrained joy, they begin to swoon. A glorious lovesickness seizes their God-intoxicated souls. Lost in a sea of bliss, they can only think of their Bridegroom's loveliness. Their heaven-entranced souls can hardly wait to reach the City.

Because of Paul's heavenly visions, he, too, could hardly wait to depart for glory. But he knew he had a ministry to complete. He faithfully pressed on and fulfilled his calling. And what about you? At times you, too, might have a strong desire to depart and be with Christ. Yet you should keep doing what the Lord calls you to do until you complete your pilgrimage. Very shortly he will call you home.

Scripture: Revelation 21:18-23; 2 Corinthians 12:3-4; Philippians 1:21-25

Prayer: Dear Lord, I may experience ecstatic heavenly visions or slogging on through mundane landscapes. Either way you have a call on my life that I ask for grace to fulfill. Amen.

D·A·Y
343

After a time, however, their strength was renewed, and they were more able to bear their sickness, and so they continued on their way. As they came nearer and nearer to the City, they saw beautiful orchards, vineyards, and gardens with gates opening into the Highway. As they approached one such gate, a gardener was standing there. They asked, "Whose lovely vineyards and gardens are these?"

He replied, "They are the King's, planted here for His delight and also for the comfort of pilgrims." So the gardener invited them into the vineyards and told them to refresh themselves with the delicious produce. He also showed them the King's walks and arbors where He delighted to visit. They lingered here and fell asleep.

Now I saw in my dream that they talked more in their sleep at this time than they ever had in all their journey. Because I was in deep thought over this, the gardener spoke to me and said, "Why do you contemplate this matter? It is the nature of the fruit of the grapes of these vineyards to go down 'smooth and sweet, causing the lips of those who are asleep to speak'" [Song of Solomon 7:9].

Beulah's delights make the pilgrims so utterly weary of this world that they long to realize their blessed hope. Yet their pilgrimage is not quite complete. They still must reach the City. They master their lovesickness, their strength returns, and heaven's gentle breezes waft them on.

As the two aged pilgrims press forward, they have no faith, hope, or expectation for restored health for their feeble bodies or for any other earthly satisfaction. The City alone fills their vision and desire. They reach the King's orchards, vineyards, and gardens. As the Old Testament Law permitted pilgrims to eat from a neighbor's vineyard, a gardener-pastor invites them in to partake of the succulent fruit. They stroll through the vineyards, noting how they flourish, tasting the grapes, quenching their thirst, and satisfying their hunger.

Just like well-aged wine, free of impurities, the old, old gospel story remains unadulterated. It produces no bad wine, no error—only truth. Ah, such wine! Reserved for Christ's pilgrims, it is the sweetest and best. The wine of his Gospel, as faithfully dispensed, delights our spiritual senses. It goes down sweetly and so relaxes the pilgrims that they fall asleep. Yet it so cheers, refreshes, and strengthens their spirits that they sleep-talk, exalting and magnifying him who has done such great things for them. Wouldn't it be wonderful to be so continually filled with God's Spirit that you could spend the remainder of your earthly days in Beulah? Anticipate this blessing as you mature in your Christian life.

Scripture: Song of Solomon 7:10-12; Zechariah 9:16-17; Romans 15:13

Prayer: Dear Lord, let me drink of Beulah's wine! May my relationship with you increasingly mean more to me than life. Amen.

D·A·Y 344

When they woke up, I saw that they determined to go up to the City. Being of pure gold, the City was so extremely bright and glorious that they could not look directly at it except through a special instrument that veiled its brilliance. I saw that as they went on, two Shining Ones met them. They were dressed in clothing that shone like gold; their faces also shone like the light.

These two asked the pilgrims where they came from, and they answered. They also asked them where they had lodged, what difficulties and dangers they had experienced, and what comforts and pleasures they had met in the Way. The pilgrims answered all their questions.

❧

If the pilgrims' experience here in Beulah represents the rule, there must certainly be some deviations from it. Some who live lives of utmost faith and service for Christ fall to bitterness toward the close of their lives. Perhaps they must deal with physiological conditions that affect them mentally and emotionally. Who then can expect them to dance through Beulah with blinding visions of the City Gate?

Yet our pilgrims enjoy a very close, intense, joyful communion with God in their final hours. As the Son of Righteousness draws them nearer and nearer, the City looms larger and larger, and they receive brighter and clearer revelations. Finally illuminating floods of glory coming from the open gates so fill their vision that the blinding radiance nearly overpowers them. After all, our frail human nature can only bear so much divine glory. Because of the intensity, the pilgrims must go back to looking through a glass darkly, relying upon lowly, less brilliant methods of faith. They receive something, presumably akin to sunglasses, to look through. Similarly, the Lord hid Moses from his glory in the cleft of a rock.

Just below the Gate of Heaven, they enjoy a visitation with two angelic inhabitants of the City. As old age delights in reminiscing, the pilgrims gladly share with them their former adventures. If we know saintly elderly folk, they sometimes bear such a sweetness that we can almost sense an angelic visitation. As we look beyond their beloved yet often shriveled and timeworn forms, we witness an otherworldly radiance. They seem to hold some joyful secret that is lost on us who are busily engaged in our younger years. How wonderful that God gives his saints, while still on earth, a foretaste of heaven's glory! If you haven't already done so, get to know some of God's elderly saints. Let them tell you their stories. It will bless you both. Pray for their well-being, that they will enjoy spiritual peace and joy for the remainder of their earthly pilgrimage.

❧

Scripture: Proverbs 4:18; 2 Corinthians 3:18; Luke 2:29-30

Prayer: Lord, thank you for the lovely radiance of your elderly saints. May I one day bear such a glow upon my wrinkled brow. Amen.

Then they said, "You have only two more difficulties to meet with, and then you will be in the City."

Christian and Hopeful asked the Shining Ones to go along with them, and they told them they would. "But," they said, "you must obtain it by your own faith." So I saw in my dream that they went on together until they came to within sight of the Gate.

Then I saw a River that flowed between them and the Gate. There was no bridge for crossing over, and the River was very deep. The sight of the River astonished the pilgrims, but the Shining Ones said, "You must go through it or you cannot approach the Gate."

The pilgrims experienced such foretastes of celestial glory as they drew near the City Gates, that all fears and pains of dying seemed dispelled. A man named Dr. Payson wrote to his sister a few weeks before his passing: "Were I to adopt the figurative language of Bunyan, I might date this letter from the Land Beulah, of which I have been for some weeks a happy inhabitant. The Celestial City is full in my view. Its glories have been upon me, its breezes fan me, its odors are wafted to me, its sounds strike upon my ears, and its spirit is breathed into my heart. Nothing separates me from it but the river of death, which now appears but as an insignificant rill that may be crossed at a single step, whenever God shall give permission."[37]

Yet as Christian and Hopeful now directly face its shore, they are astonished at the river's size. They immediately forget Beulah's delights, and even the heavenly glory fades to the background. Still this is the first of two remaining difficulties through which they must come. They mounted up with wings as eagles in their youth; they ran and were not weary in their middle-aged years; now as feeble seniors, by God's grace they will walk and not faint through these final pilgrim steps. They beseech the guardian angels to go with them—they will. Nevertheless, the pilgrims must see this trial through by the strength of their own faith.

Even at the end, there are unknowns to face. Staring out at this river, the pilgrims need to recall all the things they know so well in their hearts. We, too, must not forget that even in death Christ is in our hearts, that he has removed death's stinger, that crossing the river of death is but a momentary hurdle before reaching the shores of eternal glory. Give God your fears of dying.

Because I could not stop for death,
death stopped for me.
—Emily Dickinson

Scripture: 2 Timothy 4:6; Job 19:26-27; 2 Corinthians 5:8

Prayer: Lord, when my time to depart comes, grant me faith to remember all your covenant promises, especially that you will never leave me. Amen.

D·A·Y 346

The pilgrims then began to ask whether there was any other way to the Gate. The Shining Ones answered, "Yes, but there have been only two, Enoch and Elijah, who have been permitted to walk that path since the foundation of the world; it will not happen again until the last trumpet shall sound."

Then the pilgrims, and especially Christian, began to lose hope and become despondent. They looked this way and that but could find no way to escape the River. They asked the Shining Ones if the River were of the same depth in every place. The men answered, "No, but we cannot help you in this case either because the waters are of greater or lesser depth, depending on your faith in the King of the place."

The pilgrims' physical bodies are dying, and until now the thought of death seemed sweet. Their abundant revelations seemed to swallow up every fear of dying and the mortal pain in the process. They believed they were ready to lay aside their mortality to join Christ and be clothed with immortal heavenly garments.

Now, however, they find the morbid prospect of folding up their earthly tents and leaving them behind dreadful. Instead of the bright dawn, they see gloom. Never having imagined this river of death would look so dark and foreboding, they want to escape it! Like the man who said, "Everybody has got to die, but I have always believed an exception would be made in my case," they look for an alternate route. Yet only two men have ever avoided this river—Enoch, who "was not, for God took him" (Genesis 5:24 RSV) and Elijah, who "went up to heaven in a whirlwind" (2 Kings 2:11). None of Christ's church will similarly be translated until we are all finally caught up "in the clouds to meet the Lord in the air" (1 Thessalonians 4:17).

Death is life's one certainty; the river runs dry for no one. The pilgrims, however, look for an option. If only they could find a bridge; if only the rapture were now! Yet as Jordan's waters flowed between Israel and the Promised Land waiting to be crossed by faith, so most must cross this river. You may wish to be found alive at Christ's appearing, and perhaps you will be. Nevertheless, you should prepare for either eventuality by focusing your energies on living a faith-filled life pleasing to God.

Nearer my Father's house where many mansions be;
Nearer today the great white throne, nearer the crystal sea.
But, lying dark between, winding down through the night
There rolls the deep and unknown stream that leads at last to light.

—Phoebe Cary

Scripture: Hebrews 11:5; Ecclesiastes 12:7; Psalm 55:4-5

Prayer: Eternal Father, death is a scary prospect, but I thank you that I can trust you for strength when my time comes. You are faithful even in death. Amen.

D·A·Y
347

Christian and Hopeful finally resolved to go into the water. Upon entering, however, Christian began to sink. Crying out to his good friend Hopeful, he said, "'The engulfing waters threaten me, the deep surrounds me' [Jonah 2:5]. 'The waves of death swirl about me; the torrents of destruction overwhelm me'" [2 Samuel 22:5].

Then Hopeful said to him, "Cheer up, my brother, I can feel the bottom, and it is firm."

Christian responded, "Oh! My friend, the sorrows of death have surrounded me; I shall not see the Land that flows with milk and honey." At that, a great darkness and horror fell upon Christian. It was so intense that he could not see a thing ahead of him. Also to a great degree he lost his senses, and he was able neither to remember nor to talk rationally about any of the blessings and encouragements that he had met with in the Way of his pilgrimage.

❧

I have loved you with an everlasting love; I have drawn you with loving-kindness" (Jeremiah 31:3). Throughout their earthly pilgrimage, God has lovingly "drawn" his pilgrims ever nearer to himself and his eternal glory. First they were born of his Spirit, and finally they face this river. Still they have conflicting emotions. As humans, they do not naturally welcome death. It casts a frightening shadow over them, hiding heaven's radiance. Every other enemy may be overcome, but what mortal can overcome this enemy?

Christian and Hopeful resign themselves to the fact that "it is appointed for mortals to die once" (Hebrews 9:27 NRSV). God carefully chose when to call them into his presence, and that time is now. Thus, resolving bravely to enter the river, they begin to go the way of all flesh. Yet who can control their own style of departure? Even believers die differently—some peacefully, some valiantly, and some in anguished distress. Hopeful, now as always, seems able to rebound in hope quickly; Christian, however, does not fare so well. Typically more prone to discouraging temptations, he quickly loses confidence. A fear of death worse than death itself seizes him as, upon entering the cold, dark waters, he finds no footing. Soon in a panic, he loses all mental stability, unable to remember any of his many prior blessings. He even doubts his salvation. How wonderful is God's grace, however, that these two bosom friends can depart together. Hopeful has ample hope to share with his distressed companion.

Despite death's ferocious nature, we know Christ has already conquered it. When our time comes, we may weaken with fear, but God will faithfully provide resources to bring us through. You may feel fear even now. Recommit your life and your departure to him, praising him for his unfailing care.

❧

Scripture: Psalm 89:48; Lamentations 3:54-57; 1 Corinthians 15:50, 53

Prayer: Lord, I have an appointment set in eternity that I must someday keep. It scares me, but you will grant me the grace then. Thank you. Amen.

D·A·Y 348

Every word Christian spoke engendered a terror of mind and heart that he would surely be lost in that River and never obtain entrance at the Gate. Here also, as those who stood watching perceived, he was troubled greatly by thoughts of the sins he had committed, both before and since he had become a pilgrim. It was also observed that visions of hobgoblins and evil spirits were afflicting him; he talked endlessly about them.

Hopeful, therefore, had quite a task keeping his brother's head above water. Sometimes he would be completely under the water, and then for a while he would rise again, half-dead. Hopeful also would try to encourage him, saying, "Brother, I see the Gate and men standing by it to receive us." But Christian would answer, "It is you; it is you they are waiting for; you have been hopeful ever since I met you."

"And so have you, Christian," Hopeful would answer.

How easily we sing, "Thy lovingkindness is better than life" (Psalm 63:3 KJV). Christian, too, previously felt such sentiments, but now he fights and thrashes to save his life. Like a child whose father says, "Bedtime!" he throws his whole being into staying up, even while knowing he has no choice. All he really needs to do is lie still and fall asleep in his Father's arms of love. In his panicky state, however, he cannot yield to God's purpose. Like a fish on a hook, he desperately wants his freedom. Yet freedom for Christian lies ahead, not behind.

Poor Christian. Despite death being Christ's servant, with heaven soon following, Christian fears otherwise. His fear has opened the door for the enemy. Demonic spirits seize upon him, inflicting him with the guilty memories of past sins that sometimes come back to haunt believers at the hour of death. How dangerous it is to trust feelings! Because Christian currently judges the validity of his faith by how he feels, he thinks God has most assuredly abandoned him.

While death is the final enemy, for believers it is a conquered enemy. Further, with the curse removed, we who are in Christ can actually go as far as to call death a friend and ally. It doesn't come to damage us and separate us from God's love. We can rest assured that death has become the entrance to life. When fears rise up in your soul concerning death, consider how it will forever put an end to your sin and suffering and provide you a passage into eternal blessedness with your wonderful Lord. Let the God of comfort fill you with peace and confidence.

Scripture: 1 Corinthians 15:26; Psalm 49:15; 2 Timothy 1:10

Prayer: Dear Lord, thank you for the hope that is mine. Yet death seems to wear two faces—one of glory and the other of terror. When you call for me, help me to only see glory. Amen.

"Ah, brother," Christian responded, "surely if I were righteous, He would now arise to help me; but because of my sins He has brought me into a snare and left me."

"But, my brother," said Hopeful, "you have completely forgotten the Text where it is said of the wicked, 'For there are no pangs in their death, but their strength is firm. They are not in trouble as other men, nor are they plagued like other men' [Psalm 73:4-5]. These troubles and distresses that you are going through in these waters are no sign that God has forsaken you. They are sent only to test you to see whether you will remember what you have received of His goodness until now and whether you will lean on Him in your time of distress."

Christian, totally driven by his feelings, continues with his morbid fears of drowning. To him, his distressed feelings mean that God has rejected him. His reeling mind tells him that if God were truly with him, he would not be sinking to rise no more. His sins must be the reason that the jaws of death have locked on him and refuse his release.

Oh, beloved Christian, if only you could now see how dear you are to God. If only you could recognize that God *is* rising to help you. He has not forsaken you in death. For you, death is a mere law, not a sign of punishment. Yes! Because Christ died for you, he delivered you from death as a punishment, freeing you from its cursed sting. It's for your good; it's precious in the Lord's eyes; he even delights in it. It's but the funeral of all your sins and sorrows, the resurrection of all your hopes and joys.

Despite his current state, God knows Christian's heart, that beneath this fearful emotional flurry, he is dying in faith, that Christian still loves him and longs to be united with him. Hopeful reminds Christian of God's Word, his source of assurance. Whereas the Word describes the wicked as often having peace at their death, one's emotional state at that time cannot determine righteousness or wickedness. Hopeful also reminds Christian that this is a mere test, his final test of faith. Hopeful knows Christ has sufficient grace to carry them through the river of death, out past the grave, to the other side.

Death comes knocking for the righteous and the wicked alike. Nevertheless, the righteous can go to their eternal rest knowing that, just as their birth ends with death, their death ends with birth. The wicked enjoy no such hope. Their death ends in an infinitely worse second death. What a difference! Praise God right now for your hope in Christ.

Scripture: Proverbs 14:32; Psalm 116:15; 1 John 4:18

Prayer: My Savior, thank you for understanding my human frailties. I really have nothing to fear when I cross the dark river. No matter how I may feel, I know you will never forsake me. Amen.

D·A·Y

350

Then I saw in my dream that Christian was thoughtful for a while. And Hopeful, adding another word of exhortation, said, "Be of good cheer, for Jesus Christ is making you whole."

Immediately Christian yelled with a loud voice, "Oh, I see Him again, and He tells me, 'When you pass through the waters, I will be with you; and when you pass through the Rivers, they will not sweep over you'" [Isaiah 43:2]. Then they both took courage, and after that the enemy was as still as stone until they had crossed over. Therefore, Christian was able to find ground to stand on, and so it followed that the rest of the River was shallow. Thus, they got over.

Suddenly Christian's terror gives way to hope as God's truth penetrates his weary soul. Far from forsaking him, God is drawing him across the river to wholeness. Ah, yes. This corruptible is giving way to incorruptible; this finite darkness is giving way to infinite light. Christian doesn't need to struggle his way into eternal peace; he simply needs to believe. His Father is staying very near him and wants him, just as in times past, to simply believe. As he rises from his soul's dark Gethsemane with renewed courage, he shouts his affirmation of God's promise. Death, Job's "king of terrors" (Job 18:14), is dethroned, Satan's last desperate assault defeated. Christian once again sees Christ as his loving and sovereign King.

What encouragement Hopeful feels, too. Even in death, he has helped his brother with seeming unruffled serenity. Yet he must have carried some of his own apprehensions or he wouldn't have needed to take courage also. It appears that this wonderful saint and friend so occupied himself with ministering to his brother's greater need that he forgot his own troubles. Now, with their final battle won, both pilgrims entrust their souls to God's will. As did Christ, they commit their spirits into God's hands. Thus both pilgrims, glorifying God in death as in life, cross the rest of the way in tranquillity.

We should devote special effort to praying for and encouraging our departing friends and loved ones. Most unbelievers are never so open to Christ as when they near death. As to believers, we need to remind them of their glorious hope. Christ promises them, "I will never leave you or forsake you" (Hebrews 13:5 NRSV). If you are willing, God can use you to minister great hope and comfort to the dying.

Sleep on, beloved, sleep, and take thy rest; Lay down thy head upon thy Savior's breast. We love thee well, but Jesus loves thee best—Goodnight! Goodnight! Goodnight![38]

—"*The Christian's Good-Night*," sung at Charles Spurgeon's funeral

Scripture: Jonah 2:2-7; Song of Solomon 8:7; Luke 23:46

Prayer: Dear Lord, help me to be the kind of friend who holds others' hands as they transition into glory. Also help me to live faithfully as if this day might be my last. Amen.

D·A·Y
351

Now upon the riverbank on the other side they saw the two Shining Ones again, waiting for them. When the pilgrims came up out of the water, the two greeted them, saying, "We are 'ministering spirits sent to serve those who will inherit salvation'" [Hebrews 1:14]. So they went along together toward the Gate.

Oh, happy day! Christian and Hopeful traveled the uncertain thoroughfare of death in what appeared a dark, endless night. But joy comes in the morning, and what a morning awaits them! Just as promised, just as hoped for, they left a dying world to enter the land of the living. The two angels greet them in the eternal daylight of death's far shore. It is the birthday of their eternity!

The angels explain that they are "ministering spirits" here to serve those inheriting salvation. They are spiritual messengers or envoys from God. The Bible refers to angels 273 times (108 times in the Old Testament and 165 times in the New). Although the topic of angels is a current cultural fad, confusion reigns concerning them. Multitudes who lack solid biblical knowledge are diving into a mystical renaissance where every supernatural experience and entity is regarded as good. Tragically, Satan's angels, the antithesis of God's angels, are deceitfully working overtime today pretending to be from God.

What do we know about God's angels? In brief, should they appear, they only speak the unadulterated gospel truth. The Bible says God created them to serve him; they worship and obey him; they execute his judgments and purposes; they are magnificent, mighty, wise, and holy. They announced Christ's conception, birth, resurrection, and second coming. They will come with Christ at his second coming. They delight in Christ's Gospel and rejoice over every repentant sinner.

As "ministering spirits," they keep very busy. They express God's mind and will to his people. They have charge over believers. Often they provide them with food, bring healing to their bodies, protect them from harm, direct them on journeys, and bring them comfort in their distress. They also strengthen them against temptation, deliver them from disasters, protect them from things harmful, and rout their physical and spiritual enemies. They are present at death and will accompany the saints' souls to glory.

Believers must not worship angels, but we can thank God for them! We worship Christ, the divine Lord of all creation. Can you think of times when God may have sent an angel to your aid?

Scripture: Psalm 91:11-12; Daniel 3:28; 6:22; Acts 5:19; 12:7, 11

Prayer: Father God, you provide for your people in so many wonderful ways. Thank you for your servants, the angels, who minister unbeknownst to us in myriads of ways. Amen.

D·A·Y 352

Now I would have you note that the City stood upon a mighty Hill. The pilgrims, however, went up the Hill with ease because they had these two Shining Ones leading them up by the arms. They also had left their mortal garments behind them in the River. For though those garments entered the River with them, the pilgrims came out without them. Therefore they moved forward with great agility and speed although the foundation upon which the City was built was higher than the clouds. So they went up through the regions of space, happily talking as they went, being much comforted that they had safely gotten past the River and had such glorious companions to help them.

❧

The pilgrims' flesh—their "mortal garments"—was finally laid to rest in the river. How else could they put on dazzling robes of immortality but by shedding their rotten rags of mortality? How else could they be fit for the immortal dwellings?

The angels had told of two remaining difficulties. The first was crossing the river. Now they must scale heaven's heights to enter the Celestial Gate. This "mighty hill" refers to some notion of a purgatory. Many who perceive our sinful imperfections cannot imagine our being fit for the other side. Trusting God's grace rather than works seems too great a stretch. They think that God in his justice must somehow be cruel to be kind, making us exert some gargantuan effort to make us worthy. Thus they would allow us no peace even after the grave.

Yet rather than a long and tortuous climb to a City nearly impossible to reach, the pilgrims find the last difficulty no problem at all. Without pain or effort, they speed up the hill carried upward by their "glorious companions." So it was with their brother Faithful, as angels gathered him to heaven to join other martyrs around God's throne. Similarly, Jesus said that when Lazarus died, God's angels carried him safely to Abraham's bosom. You, too, can expect the same treatment. Praise the Lord!

From death, eternal life sprang up.
The world recedes; it disappears;
Heav'n opens on my eyes; my ears
With sound seraphic ring:
Lend, lend your wings! I mount! I fly!
O Grave! Where is thy victory?
O Death! Where is thy sting?
—Alexander Pope, *The Dying Christian to His Soul*

❧

Scripture: 2 Corinthians 5:1-4; Isaiah 26:19; John 11:25-26

Prayer: Dear Lord, to think that your angels will one bright day carry me from the grave into your loving presence is almost too much to fathom. Thank you for my blessed hope! Amen.

D·A·Y
353

The Shining Ones described to them the glorious splendor of the place. They told them that its beauty and glory was inexpressible. They said, "You are coming to Mount Zion, to the Heavenly Jerusalem, the City of the living God and to thousands and thousands of angels in joyful assembly and to the spirits of righteous people made perfect [based on Hebrews 12:22-23]. You are now going to the paradise of God where you will see the Tree of Life and eat of its never-fading fruit. White robes will be given you upon your arrival, and every day you will walk and talk with the King—even throughout all the days of eternity. There you will never again see such things as sorrow, sickness, affliction, and death, 'for the old order of things has passed away' [Revelation 21:4]. You are now going to join Abraham, Isaac, Jacob, and the prophets—ones whom God took away from the evil to come and are now cradled in eternal rest and walking in eternal righteousness."

As they ascend the heights, the angels describe the magnificence of God's residence. Even to them, the celestial glory nearly defies description. Describing heaven is like trying to describe God, since heaven is where God is. No material description does it justice. Its unending beauty and splendor is beyond anything mortals have seen, either awake or dreaming. Martin Luther must have touched it as he wrote, "I would not give one moment of heaven for all the joy and riches of the world, even if it lasted for thousands and thousands of years."

In heaven Christian and Hopeful will be enthralled at every turn as they see the innumerable heavenly hosts along with multitudes of saints. With death's curse forever removed, they will eat of the Tree of Life. Early in Christian's pilgrimage, after battling Apollyon, this tree's leaves healed his wounds. Now, eating its fruit, he will gain infinitely more. Shining white robes—their immortal glorified bodies, pure and sinless—will be given them. Also every eternal day, they will live in their King's presence, gazing at his beauty and talking with him, completely conformed to his image. They will be free of all afflictions of death, sorrow, sickness, and poverty. For they will be released from the struggles and calamities of this life. They will forever forget every loss, demonic affliction, disappointment, temptation, and sin. They will join the great saints and prophets who are already enjoying eternal rest.

This present life assails us with such discomforting limitations. Yet we know that these are temporary. One day we will leave our every trouble behind. When you begin to faint on the way, ponder awhile the joys of heaven.

Scripture: Revelation 2:7; 14:13; Psalm 17:15

Prayer: Dear Lord, when I get bogged down with my problems, help me to remember the transitory nature of this life and the marvelous glory soon to come. Amen.

DAY 354

Hopeful and Christian then asked, "What will be required of us in this holy place?"

"You must receive consolation for all your toil and receive joy for all your sorrow. You must reap what you have sown—the fruit of all your prayers and tears and suffering for the King on the Way. In that place you must receive your treasures and wear crowns of gold."

News of the fantastic glories beyond the Celestial Gate astounds Hopeful and Christian. On their way to meet their awesome and holy King in his infinitely majestic and holy City, they again wonder about their suitability. Perhaps God will require some additional work so they can better fit in. "What will be required of us in this holy place?" they ask.

What an answer they get! According to God's eternally gracious nature, the requirements bear no relationship with doing, only with *receiving.* What must they receive? They must trade consolation for their toil. Christ says, "I know your deeds, your hard work and your perseverance" (Revelation 2:2). Thus he noted and didn't forget their lives spent in his service, lived according to his will. He remembers their every labor of love, every effort to glorify him. He knows they did it all for him—sharing his Gospel with sinners, serving his church, laying down their lives. Now these good deeds follow them. After all they sowed, the time of reaping has come. Christ will reward them, not as requirements or debts owed for eternal life, but as fruits of his own grace. So their toil is behind them, their eternal Sabbath upon them.

They must also exchange sorrow for joy. In this world, they have grieved over their daily afflictions. Temptations, sins, unbelief, infirmities, frailties, follies, and failures all pained them. They lamented under the chastening and refining fire of God. Their hearts wept when other believers dishonored the Gospel. They agonized as profane and wicked unbelievers outraged the Spirit of grace. They helplessly watched a lost and dying world reject God. Far from joyfully bearing insults and persecution, they often anguished under them.

As the pilgrims mourned, they will now rejoice; as they wept, they will now be jubilant. Oh, such luscious fruit they must enjoy from all their prayers, tears, and suffering. What joy they must receive as they accept heaven's treasures and their golden crowns. How can we begin to conceive of the joy to come? The joyful tidbits of this life will then be multiplied millions of times over. Rejoice in your blessed hope!

Scripture: 2 Timothy 4:7-8; Romans 8:17-18; John 16:20-22; Psalm 126:5

Prayer: Dear Lord, when I begin to weary of serving you, when life's troubles seem so crushing, help me to refresh myself with thoughts of the eternal comfort and joy awaiting me. Amen.

D·A·Y
355

"You will receive perpetual joy from beholding the Holy One, for there you shall see Him as He is. You will also serve Him there continually with praise, shouting, and thanksgiving. You so desired to serve Him in the world, but it was very difficult because of your human frailties. Your eyes will be delighted by seeing and your ears with hearing the Mighty One."

What else will be "required" of the pilgrims in heaven? No longer walking by faith, they will walk by sight; no longer looking through a glass darkly, they will see God face to face. Who can begin to describe his people's amazement as their veil is removed, their view made clear, their vision perfected, and they see him as he is? Seeing Christ will bring an intensity of joy that far surpasses anything of earth. He will appear unspeakably glorious, radiant, enrapturing, altogether lovely. In his loving presence, his people will forget all the problems and fears they ever experienced while in their mortal flesh. Every shadow will forever vanish in the light of his glorious countenance.

Who can begin to describe the joy of living in uninterrupted fellowship with the eternal King of Kings? Even after beholding him for endless spans of eternity, his saints and angels will still marvel at him. They will still wonder at his grace, his beauty, and his glory. None of his creatures will ever fully understand the depths of his being.

Their joy will be expressed in worship. Far from simply strumming boring harps on billowy clouds, they will join in thundering exuberance—"praise, shouting, and thanksgiving." Freed from former self-conscious inhibitions, resistance, and restraint, they will finally express their love with full intensity of heart, mind, soul, and strength.

What excitement they will feel in having their full potential for serving him unleashed. So many frustrating restraints bridled them as they served him on earth. Now with their natures perfected, they will fulfill purposes beyond their wildest imaginations.

Not only will they delight in seeing their glorious King, but his thundering voice, before which the earth shakes and melts, will forever enthrall them. As his sheep on earth, they heard and followed his still, small voice. How different it will be when they hear that awesome, glorious, powerful, "sound of many waters" filling heaven.

If you get discouraged that you cannot better see or hear him, remember to praise God that he loves you, is with you, and promises you amazing future revelations of himself in glory.

Scripture: 1 John 3:1-3; John 17:24; Matthew 5:8

Prayer: Awesome Lord, I long to see you face to face. Nevertheless, help me to worship you with more heartfelt enthusiasm now. You are as worthy now as later. Amen.

D·A·Y
356

"You will once again enjoy your friends and loved ones who have gone there before you. And not only that, you will have the joy of receiving everyone who follows you into that Holy place. You will be clothed with glory and majesty, and you will be suitably equipped to ride out with the King of Glory. When the trumpet sounds and He comes in the clouds upon the wings of the wind, you will come with Him."

One of the greatest thrills for Christian and Hopeful will be that of seeing righteous friends and loved ones who have preceded them. Hearts that became so knit together that death couldn't dissolve their love will again be reunited. When they passed on, these righteous souls immediately resurrected to a joyful union with Christ. With all their human maladies forever erased, they suddenly found themselves with perfect knowledge, holiness, joy, and peace. They have eagerly waited in heaven for the moment when they could gleefully exclaim to the arriving pilgrims, "Everything we believed, everything we hoped for is true—all true, exceedingly true!"

Oh, what unbridled joy, delight, dancing, shouting, jubilation, hugs, kisses, tears, and who knows what else will attend their happy reunion. And the joyful celebrations won't end there. How can they when the two new arrivals will then joyously greet every other new arrival? Then as if all this joy weren't enough, they will receive dazzling new glorified bodies to replace their old mortal garments that they left behind. Still recognizing each other, they will gaze with utter awe and amazement at each other's beauty.

But then the most spectacular event since history began will take place—its climax! The trumpet will sound, and Christ will return to close out his affairs on earth. He, along with his heavenly armies including the saints, will triumphantly come blazing through the clouds in sudden, dramatic, cataclysmic glory. As he brings an end to human history, believers who have remained on earth until his coming will suddenly be caught up in the air to join him. Then every knee will bow before him and every tongue confess to his face that he, indeed, is the sovereign Lord. His people will joyously bow in adoring submission. Vanquished unbelievers, on the other hand, will bewail their insane imprudence as they surrender in fearful dread to the almighty King of Kings.

While we as believers can securely rest in our blessed hope, we should pour ourselves into bringing lost souls to salvation. Do you believe that Jesus is coming soon? If so, what are you doing for the lost?

Scripture: 1 Corinthians 15:54-55; 1 Thessalonians 3:13; Jude 14-15

Prayer: Dear Lord, I pray for a worldwide awakening before your return so that more people can share in the same hope that so thrills my soul. Please use me in your end-time harvest. Amen.

D·A·Y 357

"And when He sits upon His throne of judgment, you will sit beside Him. Yes, and when He passes sentence upon all the evildoers, whether angels or men, you will also have a voice in that judgment because they were your enemies as well as His. And when, at the sound of the trumpet, He again returns to the City, you will return also, and you will be with Him forevermore."

So now see how the holy pilgrims ride!
Clouds are their chariots, angels their guide;
Who for this joy wouldn't all hazards run?
What provision there is when this world is done!

Christian and Hopeful now hear that they will sit beside their King when he judges the world. Far from mere speculation, the Bible affirms that the saints will sit in prominent positions of authority in his kingdom. In Daniel's vision, he saw the saints reigning from heaven. In John's revelation, he saw their many thrones. Paul asserted that believers will judge the world and angels. What an awesome thought for Hopeful and Christian that they will reign with Christ in glory! As joint-heirs with him, they will serve as kings and priests with him, the King of Glory, for all eternity!

Just think of their shock and bewilderment as unbelievers cringe before Christ and see those they formerly despised and persecuted sitting beside him. Imagine their consternation as they stare at those whom they deemed so unworthy of respect, so undeserving of being heard on earth. As these believers went to their irrelevant little worship services, sang their stupid little hymns, tried to live by Christ's outmoded standards, who could have envisioned this? Those they counted as losers now sit poised in utmost grandeur, possessing supreme honor, and exercising regal authority in the eternal kingdom.

How will the prisoners then feel as the saints even share in deciding their fate? How will Satan and his fallen angels feel when those whom they so maliciously accused day and night now accuse them? When the Judge calls his saints to the bench, he will count their testimony and opinion conclusive.

After Christ has forever dealt with all evil in the universe, casting it into the eternal lake of fire, he will return to his Holy City with us. There we will enjoy our eternal reward. Does the world beat you down, making you feel like a nobody? Be of good cheer. You are very important. One day you will reign with Christ in heaven.

Scripture: John 5:22-23, 27; Daniel 7:9-10, 13-14, 18, 27; 1 Corinthians 6:2-3

Prayer: Dear Lord, thank you that when I feel bad about myself, you do not. It amazes me when I think that one day, when my sinful pride is gone, you will exalt me. Amen.

D·A·Y 358

Now as they drew ever closer to the Gate, a throng of the heavenly host came out to meet them. The two Shining Ones addressed them and said, "These are the men who have loved our Lord when they were in the world and who have left all for His holy Name. He has sent us forth to receive them, and we have brought them this far on their desired journey so that they may go in and look with joy into the face of their Redeemer."

Then the heavenly host gave a great shout, saying, "Blessed are those who are invited to the wedding supper of the Lamb!" [Revelation 19:9].

At this same time, several of the King's Trumpeters came out to meet them. They were clothed in brilliant white raiment, and blowing their trumpets, they welcomed Christian and Hopeful from the world with ten thousand shouts and trumpet blasts; the Heavens resounded with their loud and melodious sounds.

Suddenly a throng of angels greets the arriving party. The two angels explain how Christian and Hopeful loved the Lord and left everything for him. At this, they all rejoice that two more souls will share in the "wedding supper of the Lamb." While the angels are excited to be honored guests, God's people will be the beloved bride. In Jewish custom, on the wedding day the bridegroom went to the bride's house for the ceremony; then the bride and groom, along with a great procession, returned to the groom's house for a feast often lasting a week. Christ will also take his bride to his home to celebrate. What a glorious privilege to be counted in that number!

Oh, how excellent is the divine Bridegroom who bears all the fullness of deity in himself. How astonishingly gracious he is, having first proven his love for his people by dying for them but then by taking them to himself in an eternal covenant of love. Just think—those once so filthy and beggarly have been so entirely redeemed that their former state cannot hinder their marriage. Their husband only sees their beauty!

The heavenly Father chose the bride for his Son, presenting her to him as he presented Eve to Adam before the Fall. He gave the Bride to Christ, betrothing her to him by his sweet grace. On the last day, when he brings the full number of his people home with him, the bride, altogether lovely, will be fully prepared. Then the public ceremony and wedding feast will take place.

"Blessed are those who are invited to the wedding supper of the Lamb!" Blessed, indeed! We can all joyfully anticipate this upcoming marriage. How are you making yourself ready for that day?

Scripture: Revelation 19:7-9; Matthew 8:11-12; 25:10; Luke 14:15

Prayer: Dear Lord, although I cannot begin to imagine what this heavenly celebration will be like, I joyfully look forward to and prepare myself for it. Amen.

D·A·Y
359

After this, the pilgrims were surrounded by a joyful procession. Some were in front of them, some behind, and some on either side, as if guarding them while they traversed the upper regions. As they walked along, the Trumpeters continually sounded their trumpets, filling the Heavens with their jubilant sounds. It would have seemed to any observer that all Heaven had come down to meet them. So they proceeded together, and Christian and Hopeful could see how exceedingly great was the joy of the crowds as they came to meet them and how welcome the two of them were in their fellowship. It seemed to the men as if they had already reached Heaven before they had come to it! They were overwhelmed with joy and lost in wonder at seeing the angels and listening to their heavenly music. They could see the City, and it seemed to them that they could also hear all the bells within it ringing to welcome them. But what gave them the greatest joy of all was the thought that they themselves could be so fully accepted as to be invited to make their own dwelling here with such companions—not just for a short time but forever and ever. Oh, how could tongue or pen ever express such rapturous joy!

Just as heaven rejoices at one sinner who repents and joins God's family, so it rejoices at each one's eventual homecoming. The rollicking angels treat Christian and Hopeful like arriving kings. They excitedly sound trumpets and jubilantly celebrate with much heavenly hoopla. The joyful throng surrounds them just to assure that the prince of the power of the air can do nothing to prevent their safe arrival at the Gate. Their time of joy has come, and no one will steal it from them. Hence, no recessional will ever follow this processional. Every former source of grief and affliction now belongs an eternity away in another world.

How can human language express this transport of delight? The reverberating heavenly music by itself would cause any mortal flesh to faint. The beatific sight of the alabaster domes and glistening spires of the City towering high in the heavens is singularly breathtaking. Hearing the distant tolling of its glorious bells already welcoming them to their eternal home is utterly amazing. What a blessed, wonderful, extravagant hope they have!

Still what most causes the men to nearly burst with joy is the thought that they can be welcomed so unreservedly into the company of God's celestial angels. As the Spirit of adoption breathes upon them, they wonder why God would so love them. Isn't it mind-boggling to think that God loves you thus and that his holy angels literally celebrate over you?

Scripture: Isaiah 35:10; Psalms 30:11-12; 73:24

Prayer: Dear Lord, I look forward to heaven, but it is hard to imagine heaven looking forward to me. Yet it does! Thank you, Lord. Amen.

D·A·Y
360

So they approached the Gate, and when they arrived at it, they saw written above it in gold letters, "BLESSED ARE THOSE WHO DO HIS COMMANDMENTS, THAT THEY MAY HAVE THE RIGHT TO THE TREE OF LIFE, AND MAY ENTER THROUGH THE GATES INTO THE CITY" [Revelation 22:14].

Then I saw in my dream that the Shining Ones told them to knock at the Gate. When they did, some who lived inside looked over from a vantage point above the Gate—Enoch, Moses, Elijah, and others. The Shining Ones said, "These pilgrims have come from the City of Destruction because of the love that they possess for the King of this place."

Then the pilgrims presented the certificates that had been given them at the beginning. The certificates were brought to the King, and upon reviewing them, he asked, "Where are the men?"

The messengers answered, "They are standing outside the Gate."

The King then gave a command to open the Gate, saying, "Open the Gates that the righteous nation may enter, the nation that keeps faith" [Isaiah 26:2].

❦

The happy crowd reaches the awesome City Gate and read the golden words above it. Far from legitimizing a works-based religion, saving faith is incumbent upon a heart-based obedience to God's commandment of love. That is, the Spirit has transformed the hearts of the truly saved to love him and their neighbors with all their hearts. These are the ones who will partake of the Tree of Life and enter the City. Christian and Hopeful are such ones. Fear of wrath may have originally driven them to seek salvation, but love for their King has kept them intent on finishing their pilgrimage.

As Christian and Hopeful knock on the Gate, they see saints whose faithful lives had so inspired them during their pilgrimage. They hand over the certificates—their titles to heaven—that they have for so long carried. The saints take these to the King. Upon reviewing them and finding them in order, he issues the command to open the Gate to the men immediately. He had promised that he had gone to prepare a suitable place for them, and now he invites them in to receive it.

Who can imagine the ecstasy, the indescribable delight, the wide-eyed, open-mouthed amazement we will feel when the heavenly Gate swings open to admit us! What must it be like to step up for admittance to a City reserved for angels and glorified saints, the King's own residence? Do these thoughts thrill your heart? Share your joy with someone today.

❦

Scripture: John 14:2; Hebrews 12:22-23; Psalm 16:8-11

Prayer: Eternal King, I eagerly await your opening of heaven's gate for me, not because of my goodness but because of yours. You are a wonderful, awesome, loving Savior and Lord. I love you! Amen.

DAY 361

Now I saw in my dream that these two men went in at the Gate, and as they entered they were suddenly and gloriously transfigured! The clothes they now wore shone like gold! Some who met them presented them with harps and crowns. They gave harps for praising the King and crowns for their own honor. Then I heard in my dream that all the bells in the City rang out again for joy, and I heard it said, "Enter the joy of the Lord" [Matthew 25:23]. I could also hear Christian and Hopeful, along with the multitudes, singing with loud voices, "To Him who sits on the throne and to the Lamb be praise and honor and glory and power forever and ever!" [Revelation 5:13].

The wonder-struck men, adopted into the King's family by his rich grace, enter the Celestial City. No longer strangers and pilgrims in an unsavory alien world, they have finally come home to receive a kingdom prepared for them since before the world began. Their King freely and joyfully bestows this inheritance upon them. Inside the Gate, the men see their King as he is in all his radiant splendor. They suddenly change into beings of vast beauty. Set apart for God, their natures become completely pure. Their stunning new glorified bodies bear no imperfection and will never wear out. Their righteous deeds, not done for merit but as reflections of their King's grace, now adorn the men like lustrous and pure heavenly garments.

Christian and Hopeful not only inherit Christ's kingdom, but they inherit him. All that he is, all that he has, he shares with them—his love, grace, mercy, wisdom, truth, faithfulness, power, perfection—all the riches of glory! Who in such a state could help being filled with rapturous eternal joy? Finally, just as their king had desired for them, their joy is now full and complete. Beautiful melodic strains continually fill the heavenly air. Someone gives the two their own harps to add their sounds to the heavenly concert. Then because they had never let anyone seize their crowns, the lovely crowns safely stored up for them are placed upon their heads to commend their faithfulness.

All the bells of heaven ring for joy. Heaven is a joyful place because its King is joyful. Christian and Hopeful join untold multitudes of worshipers who have come from every tribe and nation in exultantly praising their King with all their hearts. Their joy has only just begun!

Regardless of your circumstance, cultivate a rejoicing heart. It will help prepare you for life in your eternally joyful heavenly home.

Scripture: Revelation 7:9-10; Daniel 12:3; Matthew 13:43

Prayer: Dear Lord, when we've been there ten thousand years, bright shining as the sun; we've no less days to sing your praise than when we've first begun. Praise you, Lord! Amen.

D·A·Y
362

Now just as the Gates had opened to let the men in, I looked in after them, and I could see that the City shone like the sun. The streets were paved with gold, and on them walked many saints with crowns on their heads and palm branches in their hands. They were playing golden harps as they sang praises to God. I could also see that some had wings, and they addressed one another continually, saying, "Holy, holy, holy is the Lord Almighty" [Revelation 4:8]. I wished that I myself was among those whom I had seen, but after this, the Gates were once again closed.

❧

As Christian and Hopeful enter the Celestial Gates, the dreamer steals a glance inside. The soul-thrilling rapture he feels from one small peek nearly makes his heart stop. The bedazzling City shines like the sun. Yet its source is not some external luminary; it diffuses stunning streams of light from within itself. Its light source is the radiance of God's presence—his shekinah glory—emanating from his wondrously lucent throne. For "the glory of God is its light, and its lamp is the Lamb" (Revelation 21:23 NRSV). Basking in this light, the new arrivals will perpetually enjoy gazing at God face to face, beholding Christ's glory, marveling at the multitudes of saints and angels with their own reflected halos of light. With this illumination, they clearly see answers to the previously baffling mysteries they struggled to make sense of in earth's dim flicker.

Through the almost blinding radiance, the dreamer sees streets that look like polished gold. Because of the purity of their gold, no foul sin can ever be found in them, no mortal has ever touched them. Christian and Hopeful will dance forever in these golden streets with the likes of Abraham, Moses, David, Mary, and Paul.

Oh, to be admitted into such a splendid place! The King provides magnificently for those whom he receives into his City. With exultant hearts, they live in eternal mansions of light, love, joy, peace, and comfort. What must it be like to call this place of bright jasper walls and ethereal pearly gates your home? How must it feel to live in perpetual ecstasy, waving palm branches, singing, celebrating, and crying "Holy, holy, holy" with saints and angels? What must it be like to live in uninterrupted communion with the Father, Son, and Holy Spirit? Soon this will be your experience. Will you praise him right now? What a blessed hope! Hallelujah! "Even so, come, Lord Jesus" (Revelation 22:20 KJV). In the words of Sir Thomas More: "Joy, Joy forever!—my task is done— / The gates are pass'd, and Heaven is won!"

❧

Scripture: Revelation 7:15-17; 22:5; Isaiah 60:19-20; Psalm 23:6

Prayer: Dear Lord, what a blessed, wonderful, extravagant hope you have given me. I will give everything to keep this hope ablaze in my heart. Fill me with joyful anticipation. Amen.

D·A·Y
363

Now while I was still pondering all these things, I turned my head to look back, and I saw Ignorance approaching the far bank of the River. He soon crossed over with less than half the difficulty that the other two men had experienced. For it just so happened that a ferryman named Vain-hope was waiting at that spot. He quickly ferried Ignorance across in his boat. So Ignorance, like the others, ascended the Hill to reach the Gate. He came alone, however; no one met him with the least bit of encouragement. When he approached the Gate, he looked up at the writing above and then began to knock, assuming he would quickly be admitted.

The men on top of the roof looked down and asked, "Where have you come from and what do you want?"

He replied, "I ate and drank in the presence of the King, and He taught in my streets."

The dream doesn't end with Christian and Hopeful inside the Celestial Gate. Ignorance still follows, and his time of departure has come. The two pilgrims had experienced a traumatic crossing of the river. Ignorance, on the other hand, is too shallow in his thinking and self-confident in his nature to feel fear. To our bewilderment, many who reject salvation die peacefully. Satan, however, wants them to die with no fear. If Ignorance had felt alarm at his crossing, he might have repented of his ignorant self-sufficiency and called upon the Lord for salvation. So Satan sent Vain-hope to ferry Ignorance across unruffled.

How blind and irrationally foolish was Ignorance to drift presumptuously across the river of death with one called Vain-hope! Those similarly ignorant might observe his passing and think, "Surely he is safe or he wouldn't have died so peacefully." Still such peace is no evidence of salvation. It may only prove that he continued to the very end in his original state of undisturbed ignorance.

Who is this Vain-hope? No doubt, he is some well-intentioned yet similarly ignorant minister, priest, or friend who holds the dying man's hand, tenderly consoling him with comforting words. With Vain-hope at his bedside allaying his fears, hopes for any deathbed conversion became impossible.

Self-deceived, Ignorance comes alone and makes his way clear to the City Gate. Because of this and all his other former works, he feels certain his knock will bring immediate admittance. All the same, those who look to their own good deeds for assurance are sadly mistaken. Be sure to drive out all religious ignorance from your life. Only a continual trust in and reliance upon Christ's atoning work on the cross will secure a welcome into heaven.

Scripture: Luke 13:23-26; Isaiah 5:21; Proverbs 28:26

Prayer: Lord, how sad that so many refuse your gracious provision for their sins. I choose the hope you give me, not vain earthly hopes. Amen.

D·A·Y
364

Then they asked him for his certificate so that they might take it in and show it to the King. He fumbled in his clothing for one but found none.

Then they asked, "Don't you have one?"

Ignorance remained silent.

So they told the King, but He would not come down to see him. Instead, he commanded the two Shining Ones who had escorted Christian and Hopeful to the City to go out and take Ignorance and bind him hand and foot and have him carried away. So they seized him and carried him through the air to the door that I had seen in the side of the Hill, and there they cast him. Then I saw that there was a way to Hell, not only from the City of Destruction, but even from the Gate of Heaven itself.

At this I awoke . . . and I realized it had all been a dream.

After such ecstatic joy in heaven, the dream ends in a nightmare for Ignorance. Heaven is a place only for those prepared for it. Ignorance, however, has nothing to present at the Gate to prove himself a believer. Oh, wretched fool! If only he had listened! The poor man was never far from the kingdom of God. He even made it to the Gate. How many would get half that far? Still his mindless optimism has undone him. He made a deplorable omission by ignoring God's Word. God considers this a serious sin against him, deserving of the severest consequences.

"But he went on a pilgrimage!" some might protest. Yes, he professed faith of sorts but fashioned it his own way. He is like the woman who won the Boston Marathon one year. She came running down the homestretch in record time to claim her victory. News photos showed her ecstatic with upraised arm in triumph. Then another picture hit the press—one with her head down and tears streaming down her face. Officials had stripped her of her honors for running a fraudulent race. Evidently, instead of beginning at the official starting point, she had slipped into the pack somewhere from the sidelines.

Ignorance, too, claims himself a winner. The Great Judge of souls, however, declares him a loser. You cannot cheat your way into heaven. Since he bypassed the official starting place, his pilgrimage was never authorized. Now because of his tragic soul-damning choices, he will only know the agony of eternal doom. As John Dryden said, "For my salvation must its doom receive, not from what others, but what I believe."

Are you a winner? You need only begin your pilgrimage at the cross and, trusting God's grace through life's ups and downs, persevere in faith till your journey's end.

Scripture: Matthew 7:21-27; 13:24-30; Luke 13:27-29

Prayer: Oh, Lord, how great is your salvation. Please keep me true to your straight Way that I might be a victor when this life ends. Amen.

D·A·Y
365

Now reader, I have told my dream to thee;
See if you can interpret it to me
Or to yourself or your neighbor, but take heed
Of misrepresenting, for that, indeed,
Will bring you no good but, instead, abuse;
By misinterpreting, evil ensues.

Take heed also that you don't be extreme
In playing with the limits of my dream.
Don't let this allegory now conclude
By sending you laughing or causing a feud;
The childish or fools in this way can be,
But you the substance of my work must see.

Draw back the curtains, look within my veil;
Ponder my metaphors, and please do not fail;
There, if you seek them, are things you will find
That will be helpful to an honest mind.

So what if my dross you find there, be bold;
Throw it away, yet preserve all the gold.
What if my gold is wrapped up in ore?
Who tosses the apple because of the core?
But if you cast all away as just vain,
I do not know when I might dream again.

Now the dreamer awakens to share with us his concluding remarks. Having given his dream's content, he leaves it to us to interpret it for him. The delightful climax to Christian and Hopeful's story would have been a good place for him to rouse himself from his dream. Yet his dream concluded with Ignorance's tragic end, perhaps to remind himself—and us—that this dream, while gloriously hopeful, is also solemnly troubling and infinitely serious.

Now that the dream is over, the dreamer seems to express some apprehension. He fears we might treat his dream too lightly or reject the entire matter over some nonessential points. He requests that we continue pondering it so we can preserve its gold. He thinks that we, as believers, may take our own ignorance too lightly, that it is our duty to know much more than we do. Indeed, if we hope to move beyond judging by appearances, we must become thoroughly grounded in biblical truth. Only then can we make proper distinctions about what is wise and what is ignorant among those who profess Christ in our world.

Let us ever remember that we are here on this earth as pilgrims with a clear destination, not as aimless and wandering Gypsies. A successful pilgrimage requires diligence on our part. With heaven in our hearts, we must stay focused and alert, pressing toward the upward call, running to win our race. Will you commit yourself to doing as the dreamer requests? Will you continue to preserve the dream's rich stores of truth—the gold—in your heart? If so, yours will be a blessed and prosperous pilgrimage.

❦

*Scripture: 1 Corinthians 2:6-7; Revelation 22:12;
Jude 24-25; Psalm 72:19*

Prayer: Thank you, Lord, for this amazing story of the Christian pilgrimage. May I preserve all the gold in these pages and clutch its truths and riches close to my heart as I pass through this life and into the next, where at journey's end, I will see you face to face. Amen.

NOTES

[1] Karl Barth, *The Word of God and the Word of Man* (Harper and Row Publishers, Inc.)

[2] Elizabeth Barrett Browning, *Aurora Leigh,* bk VII, l.101.

[3] "Womanist" theologian Dolores Williams, quoted in *Good News*, Jan/Feb 1994.

[4] Charles Williams, *Taliessin Through Logres, The Region of the Summer Stars, Arthurian Torso* (Grand Rapids, Mich.: Eerdmans, 1974). Introduction and commentary by C. S. Lewis.

[5] Noah Webster, *An American Dictionary of the English Language* (Springfield, Mass.: G. & C. Merriam, 1878).

[6] Ibid.

[7] *Emerging Trends*, May 1993, pp. 2-3.

[8] "Newsbriefs," *Impact,* June 1991.

[9] Robert Louis Stevenson, quoted in R. E. White, *You Can Say That Again* (Grand Rapids, Mich.: Zondervan, 1991).

[10] According to Regent College missiology expert David Barrett, "InfoSearch," (Arlington, Tex.: The Computer Assistant).

[11] Elisabeth Elliot, *The Mark of a Man* (Tarrytown, N.Y.: Fleming H. Revell, 1981), pp. 85-6.

[12] Canto xv., st. 13.

[13] John Crowne, *The Ambitious Statesman,* act V, sc. 3.

[14] Mark Noll, *The Scandal of the Evangelical Mind*, quoted in *Christianity Today*, April 24, 1995.

[15] Leo Tolstoy, *Invaders*, quoted in John Kelman, *The Road: A Study of John Bunyan's Pilgrim's Progress* (London, England: Oliphant Anderson and Ferrier, 1911-1912).

[16] Richard Morin, *Washington Post Weekly,* December 7, 1992, p. 36.

[17] Musical and movie adaptation of George Bernard Shaw's *Pygmalion.*

[18] "Born-again makes little difference in behavior," *National & International Religion Report*, October 8, 1990, p. 8.

[19] Samuel Butler, *Hudibras,* canto II, 1.257.

[20] Martin Luther, *Table Talk.*

NOTES

[21] John Milton, *Paradise Lost*, bk. VI, 1.2.

[22] Charles Haddon Spurgeon, quoted in *The Berean Call*, July 1992.

[23] In "Preparing for the 21st Century," quoted in *Pulse*, May 21, 1993.

[24] Statistics reported in "U.S.A. Suicide: 1994 Official Final Statistics," compiled for the American Association of Suicidology by John L. McIntosh, Ph.D., Professor of Psychology, Indiana University South Bend; Eva Stimson, "Young Opinions on Violence," *Presbyterian Survey*, January 1992, pp. 22-25.

[25] Research done by David Larson, National Institute of Mental Health, reported by Christopher Hall in "Holy Health!" *Christianity Today*, November 23, 1992, pp. 18-22.

[26] Doug Erlandson, "Recovering the Art of Hospitality," *Moody*, vol. 95, no. 3, November 1995.

[27] Martin Luther, *Commentary on Galatians,* Galatians 1:6.

[28] Daniel Defoe, *History of the Devil*, pt. II, ch. 6.

[29] In *Pale Blue Dot* (New York: Random House, 1994), quoted in *Impact*, June 1995.

[30] Karen Armstrong, *A History of God* (New York: Ballantine, 1994).

[31] *National & International Religion Report,* August 23, 1993.

[32]For instance, in *The Gospel According to Jesus: A New Translation and Guide to His Essential Teachings for Believers and Unbelievers* (Harper Perennial Library, 1993), Stephen Mitchell, a Jewish devotee of Zen and Taoism, claims Jesus was simply a Jew teaching Judaism to Jews. In *The Gospel of Peace* (Japan Publications, Inc., 1992), Michio Kushi, a macrobiotics guru, presents Jesus from a Buddhist perspective claiming to have "the true key to Jesus' life and thought." The Jesus Seminar, a consortium of renegade theologians, reduces Jesus to a moral teacher rather than who he said he was.

[33] A good book to begin with is Josh McDowell's *Evidence That Demands a Verdict,* vol. 1 (Nashville: Nelson, 1993).

[34] David Burrell and Stanley Hauerwas, quoted in *First Things*, January 1994.

[35] Thomas Scott, D.D., *The Pilgrim's Progress with Illusrative Notes* (Philadelphia: J. B. Perry Publishers, 1852).

[36] Rev. George B. Cheever, *Lectures on the Pilgrim's Progress* (New York: E. Walker Publisher, 1847), p. 453.

[37] Written by Sarah Doudney.

SCRIPTURE INDEX

* Indicates passages within the text. All others are in the Scripture section at the bottom of each day's selection. Right-hand numbers refer to the Day, not the page.

SCRIPTURE INDEX

SCRIPTURE INDEX

SCRIPTURE INDEX

SCRIPTURE INDEX

SCRIPTURE INDEX

SCRIPTURE INDEX

Every book of the Bible is here represented.